THE
CIVIL WAR
SOURCEBOOK

A Traveler's Guide

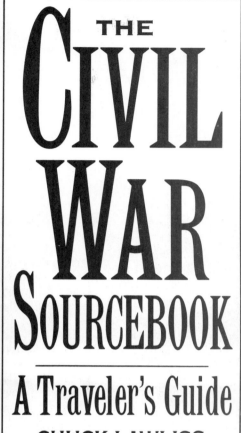

THE
CIVIL
WAR
SOURCEBOOK

A Traveler's Guide

CHUCK LAWLISS

HARMONY BOOKS
NEW YORK

Photograph credits appear on page 299.

Published by Harmony Books, 201 East 50th Street,
New York, New York 10022. Member of the Crown
Publishing Group.

HARMONY and colophon are trademarks of Crown
Publishers, Inc.

Manufactured in the United States of America

Library of Congress Cataloging-in-Publication Data
Lawliss, Chuck.
The Civil War sourcebook: a traveler's guide/
Chuck Lawliss.
Includes index.
1. United States—History—Civil War, 1861–1865—
Battlefields—Guidebooks. 2. Historic sites—United
States—Guidebooks. 3. United States—Description and
travel—1981—Guidebooks. 4. United States—History
—Civil War, 1861–1865—Collectibles. I. Title.
E641.L38   1991   90-19276
917.304′928—dc20   CIP
ISBN 0-517-57767-4
10 9 8 7 6 5 4 3 2 1
First Edition

Design by Lauren Dong

In memory of all the men in my family who answered
the call of their beloved Union

CONTENTS

PART III LEARNING ABOUT THE CIVIL WAR 248

INTRODUCTION

This book began a long time ago in the attic of a Victorian house in a picturesque Vermont town where a small boy in knickers used to play. One of the many treasures found there was a kepi, the distinctive forage cap worn by Union soldiers, with a brass insignia above the brim that read "6th Vermont." On the shelf next to it was a well-worn gadget, resembling a pocket knife, which slid apart and unfolded into a Union soldier's knife, fork, and spoon. I would put on the kepi, open the gadget, and pretend to be sitting with my comrades, eating by the campfire, swapping stories on the eve of a great battle. We were always brave, I remember, always victorious, and always emerged unscathed. The Civil War seized my imagination then and has never let go.

War stories were passed down in my family from generation to generation like heirlooms. By the time they reached me, they were the stuff of legends, more thrilling than the exploits of King Arthur or Robin Hood. My mother's grandfather and his brother fought at Gettysburg in the Vermont Brigade, Second Division, part of General John Sedgwick's Sixth Army Corps. My father's grandfather, a sergeant in a New York infantry regiment, had been captured in the Seven Days and imprisoned at Andersonville. The once-sturdy Welshman came home weighing ninety-four pounds, but recovered and lived vigorously for another fifty-five years.

More-distant relatives, nearly a dozen of them, also had answered Lincoln's call for volunteers. Like my great-grandfathers, they "saw the elephant," the Union

soldier's metaphor for being in combat, and they were forever changed.

I remember seeing a Civil War veteran on Decoration Day, as Memorial Day was once called. He was ninety-two, short and frail, with snow-white hair, parchment skin, and hands covered with liver spots. He seemed barely able to support the weight of his old uniform. I was mesmerized. Another elderly man once told me in vivid detail how his father ran across a field on their farm shouting, "They shot Lincoln, Billy! They shot Lincoln!"

I studied the war in grade school, but found it dull, all names and dates, and far too evenhanded. At nine I saw *Gone With the Wind,* and resented its Southern viewpoint. In my mind the war was all the South's fault, no two ways about that. Didn't my great-grandfathers fight to save the Union and free the slaves? Didn't the inscription on the monument say it was "The War of the Rebellion?" And didn't Confederates in civilian clothes ride down from Canada and rob the bank in St. Albans a few miles away from our home? Real soldiers didn't do things like that!

In the spring of my freshman year in college, I visited Gettysburg, expecting the past to come alive, but all I found was a confusing forest of monuments. My disappointment was acute, the fire of my passion banked. It flared up the following year, though, when I saw a dramatization of Stephen Vincent Benét's epic poem *John Brown's Body,* with Raymond Massey and Tyrone Power. I sat transfixed, transported back to my attic. My interest in the war never wavered again, although it became less emotional. The South is no longer my enemy, and I admire Robert E. Lee and Stonewall Jackson without equivocation.

Over the years I visited the national battlefields—some of them several times—and many minor battlefields. I went to war museums, specialized libraries, and the homes of many of the generals and statesmen of the period. But my early Civil War explorations were hit-or-miss. I made a lot of mistakes along the way, wasting time and money, and missing things I should have seen. My excursions weren't well planned. The information I needed was available, but I didn't know where to look for it, which is how this book came to be.

This guidebook contains the essential information you need to discover and relive the Civil War experience. Whether you are a novice or an experienced Civil War buff, your most basic questions are answered in detail.

To learn who was who in the war, turn to the capsule biographies of Union and Confederate leaders. Another section explains the organization of the Union and Confederate governments and armies. There's no need to be confused by references to A. P. Hill and D. H. Hill, both Confederate generals, or the South's Army of Tennessee and the North's Army of *the* Tennessee. To check which battle came first, Chancellorsville or the Wilderness, turn to the Chronology of the War. Every important wartime event is listed there.

Which battlefields are worth visiting? How does one get to them? What led up to a given battle, and what effect did it have on the war? What is the best way to tour the battlefield? How much time should you allow? Are reenactments and "living history" demonstrations held there? What are the public facilities? The battlefields are just the beginning. There are interesting sites near each one that played important parts in the war. To understand the Battle of Shiloh, for example, it is helpful to visit Corinth, Mississippi, from whence the Confederate army came to attack Grant. A visit to the town of Harpers Ferry, West Virginia, rewarding in itself, helps illuminate the Battle of Antietam. The town of Gettysburg is almost as historically significant as the battlefield itself.

There are many places where no battles were fought that are worth visiting: Richmond, New Orleans, Savannah, Montgomery. Visiting Fort Sumter without

exploring Charleston and the nearby plantations is to miss an opportunity to understand the antebellum South. No battle was fought in Biloxi, Mississippi, but it's worth a journey to Beauvoir, Jefferson Davis's home, where he spent the last twelve years of his life and wrote *The Rise and Fall of the Confederate Government.* And what buildings are more closely linked to the war than Ford's Theatre in Washington, where President Lincoln was shot, and the Peterson house across the street, where he died?

Sprinkled throughout are descriptions of hotels, inns, and bed-and-breakfast accommodations, as well as restaurants. Many are historic sites themselves; others capture the spirit of the war years. At Antietam you can stay on the battlefield in a farmhouse that was General Longstreet's headquarters; in Vicksburg, an inn is housed in the mansion where Grant stayed after he captured the city. In Charleston, there's even a restaurant that offers a discount to guests who arrive dressed in Confederate costumes.

Did one of your ancestors serve in the Civil War? You'll learn how to trace his service record in the government archives. Not sure whether an ancestor served or not? You'll find out how to make sure. A Civil War ancestor may make you eligible for one or more of the many Civil War organizations, although there are some where your interest alone will be sufficient to qualify you for membership.

A source guide to war museums, specialized libraries, and Civil War periodicals is included, as is an annotated reading list that highlights the best books about the Civil War. Another section lists audio recordings, videotapes, and movies about the war.

There is a section for those who collect Civil War antiques and reproductions. Some of the most popular items are listed with their approximate costs. There's a list of top dealers, and you'll find information on collectibles and reproductions, prints and paintings, models, and even where to order a tailor-made general's uniform, a saber to go with it, and an authentic tent to serve as your field headquarters.

The final section discusses the reenacting of Civil War battles and people who reenact them; it tells you how to become one, what equipment you'll need, and where to get it. All in all, this is a book with hundreds and hundreds of things to start you dreaming, even if you aren't a small boy in an attic.

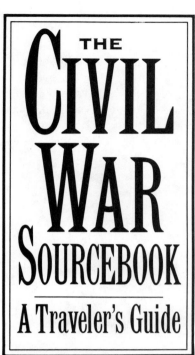

THE CIVIL WAR SOURCEBOOK

A Traveler's Guide

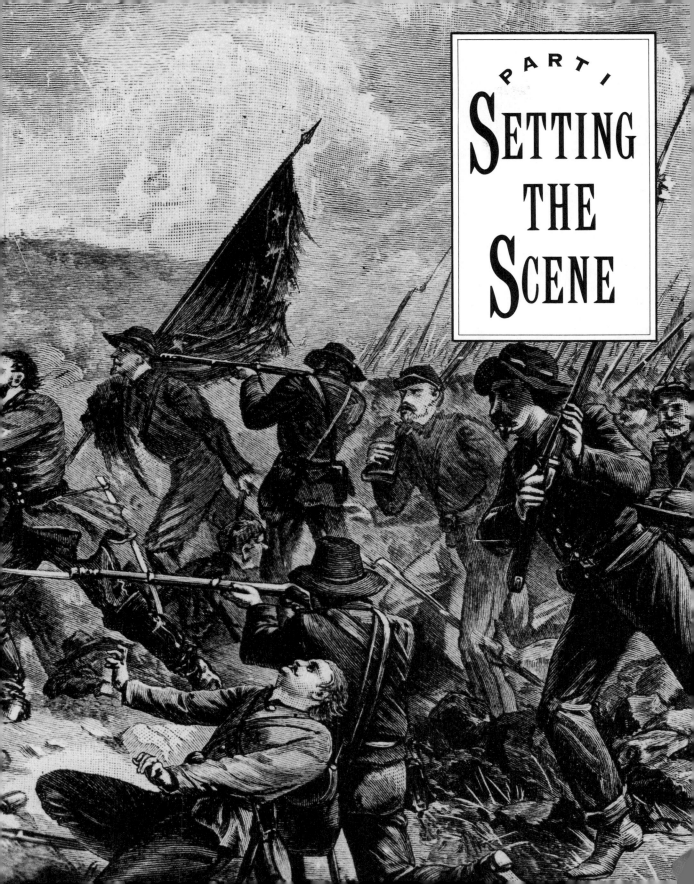

PART I
SETTING THE SCENE

A color guard proudly poses with the battle-torn flag of the 8th Pennsylvania Reserves. Troops followed these flags into battle, rallied to them, and defended them to the death. A regiment was disgraced if it lost its flag, and the honor of carrying the flag was not without peril. At Gettysburg, the 24th Michigan flag was riddled by 23 bullets, and nine color-bearers were killed as the regiment withdrew, fighting, from McPherson's Woods.

— 1 —

CHRONOLOGY OF THE WAR

1860

NOVEMBER 6   Abraham Lincoln is elected President of the United States.

DECEMBER 3   President Buchanan tells Congress that the South has no legal right to secede, but that the government has no power to prevent it.

20   South Carolina secedes from the Union.

1861

JANUARY 9   Mississippi secedes.
10   Florida secedes.
11   Alabama secedes.
19   Georgia secedes.
26   Louisiana secedes.

FEBRUARY 1   Texas secedes.
4   A convention at Montgomery, Alabama, forms a provisional government for seceded states and adopts a constitution similar to the U.S. Constitution, except that slavery is recognized and protected.
9   Jefferson Davis is named provisional President of the Confederacy; Alexander H. Stephens of Georgia is named provisional Vice-President.

18   Davis and Stephens are inaugurated.

MARCH 4   Lincoln is inaugurated, declares that secession will not be tolerated; the nation cannot be separated, but there will be no violence unless it is forced on the Union.
11   The Constitution of the Confederacy is unanimously adopted.

APRIL 11   South Carolina asks Major Anderson to surrender Fort Sumter.
12   The bombardment of Fort Sumter begins.
13   Fort Sumter surrenders.
15   Lincoln declares that an insurrection exists, calls for 75,000 volunteers for three months to put it down.
17   Virginia secedes over the objections of its western counties.
20   Robert E. Lee, offered command of Union forces, resigns to serve Virginia and the South.

MAY 6   Confederate Congress declares that a state of war exists with the United States. Arkansas secedes.
13   Queen Victoria declares Britain neutral, but recognizes the Confederacy as a belligerent.

Preceding spread: The artist portrays General Pickett at Gettysburg, hat raised on sword, leading the famous charge that bears his name. In truth, he observed the charge from a nearby farm. Nearly half—3,000 men—of Pickett's division became casualties, including two brigadier generals, six colonels, and all fifteen regimental commanders. For the rest of his life, Pickett grieved for the men he lost in the charge and blamed Lee for the disaster.

20   The Kentucky legislature declares that state neutral. North Carolina secedes.

21   Richmond, Virginia, is designated capital of the Confederacy.

JUNE 8   Tennessee secedes.

11   Western Virginia moves to secede from Virginia to form a new Union state.

JULY 4   Congress approves Lincoln's war measures.

21   Union forces are defeated at Bull Run in the first major battle of the war.

27   McClellan replaces McDowell, defeated at Bull Run, commander of the Union army in Virginia.

AUGUST 10   Union troops are defeated at Wilson's Creek, Missouri.

SEPTEMBER 6   Grant occupies Paducah, Kentucky, at the mouth of the Tennessee River.

20   Besieged Union troops surrender Lexington, Missouri.

OCTOBER 31   The "Rebel Legislature" votes Missouri out of the Union.

NOVEMBER 1   McClellan is appointed general-in-chief of Union armies, succeeding the ailing Winfield Scott.

6   Davis is elected as actual President of the Confederacy.

8   Confederate commissioners Mason and Slidell are taken from British ship *Trent* by the Union navy.

18   Pro-South leaders in Kentucky adopt secession.

DECEMBER 26   Fearing war with Britain, the United States releases Mason and Slidell.

1862

JANUARY 13   Edwin M. Stanton is appointed the Union Secretary of War, replacing Simon Cameron.

27   Lincoln orders McClellan to move into action, but McClellan ignores the order.

FEBRUARY 6   Grant takes Fort Henry.

7   Burnside captures Roanoke Island, off North Carolina.

16   Grant captures Fort Donelson after a four-day siege, taking 15,000 prisoners and gaining fame for demanding "unconditional surrender." The drive to split the South begins.

25   Don Carlos Buell occupies Nashville.

MARCH 6–8   The Union army defeats the Confederates at the Battle of Pea Ridge, Arkansas.

9   The Union ship *Monitor* fights a five-hour draw with the Confederate *Virginia* (formerly the *Merrimac*) in the first battle of ironclad warships.

11   McClellan is relieved of overall command, but continues as commander of the Army of the Potomac; Lincoln agrees to his Peninsula strategy.

14   Pope takes New Madrid, Missouri.

23   Jackson is defeated at Kernstown, Virginia.

28   The Confederates, defeated at Glorietta Pass, abandon New Mexico.

APRIL 5   Lincoln holds back McDowell's corps from the Peninsula to defend Washington from Jackson.

6–7   Grant survives an early onslaught to win the Battle of Shiloh.

7–8   Pope captures Island Number 10 on the Mississippi.

11   Federal troops capture Fort Pulaski at Savannah, Georgia. Federals capture Huntsville, Alabama.

24   Farragut smashes a weak Confederate fleet in a naval battle below New Orleans.

25   Federal troops occupy New Orleans.

MAY 3   Gen. Joseph E. Johnston evacuates

Yorktown and retreats toward Richmond.

8   Jackson wins at McDowell, Virginia, beginning the Shenandoah campaign.

11   Confederate forces evacuate the Norfolk naval base, destroying the ironclad *Virginia* to prevent its capture.

23   Jackson defeats Federal forces at Front Royal.

24–25   Jackson hits Banks at Middleton, then Winchester, Virginia.

29–30   Beauregard evacuates Corinth and moves his army to Tupelo before slowly advancing on Halleck, who has taken command from Grant.

31   Johnston's counterattack before Richmond at Seven Pines is blunted. Johnston is wounded, and Lee takes over the army.

JUNE 4   Confederate forces evacuate Fort Pillow.

6   Union troops capture Memphis, Tennessee.

8   Jackson defeats Frémont at Cross Keys.

9   Jackson defeats Shields at Port Republic, ending the first Valley campaign.

12–15   Jeb Stuart's cavalry rides around McClellan's army in a daring raid.

17   Bragg replaces the ailing Beauregard in the West.

25   The Seven Days campaign before Richmond begins.

26   Lee crosses the Chickahominy River to turn McClellan's right flank, cutting him off from his York River base; other forces hit Porter at Mechanicsville. Jackson joins Lee before Richmond. Lincoln sends for Pope to command a new Army of Virginia. Farragut's fleet prepares to run past Vicksburg to help Grant capture that strategic fortification.

27   Lee hits Porter at Gaines' Mill, and McClellan retreats south to the James River.

Bugles blare as a Union horse artillery battery starts to move out. The nature of the war placed a high premium on mobility: Battles were won or lost on the ability of units to get into action quickly. In the 1862 Shenandoah Valley Campaign, Stonewall Jackson's army of 16,000 tied up 63,000 Union troops and earned the sobriquet "foot cavalry" by marching 600 miles in five weeks, winning four battles along the way.

29   Jackson is late at Savage's Station, and robs Lee of victory.

30   McClellan holds off Lee at White Oak Swamp, retreats to Malvern Hill.

JULY 1   Lee assaults Malvern Hill, suffering heavy casualties. Federal Income Tax Act approved. Lincoln calls for 300,000 volunteers for three years' service.

2   McClellan abandons the siege of Richmond, ending the Seven Days campaign.

9   Lincoln visits McClellan at Harrison's Landing, where he expresses disappointment.

11   Halleck is made general-in-chief of all Union armies.

13   Forrest takes Murfreesboro, south of Nashville.

17   Grant is given command in the West.

4–28   Morgan raids Kentucky and Tennessee.

AUGUST 9   Jackson, back in the Shenandoah Valley, defeats Banks at Cedar Mountain.

11   Quantrill captures Independence, Missouri.

16   The Army of the Potomac evacuates the Peninsula; Lee moves north.

27–28   Bragg invades Tennessee and Kentucky, driving for Ohio River.

29–30   Lee and Jackson defeat Pope at Second Manassas.

SEPTEMBER 1   Lee tries to cut off Pope's retreat, but is stopped at Chantilly. Lincoln orders McClellan to defend Washington.

4–7   Lee crosses the Potomac into Maryland to invade the North.

14   McClellan attacks D. H. Hill at South Mountain.

15   Jackson captures Harpers Ferry.

17   The Battle of Antietam, the bloodiest single day of the war.

18   Lee retreats to Virginia without opposition.

19   Rosecrans defeats Price and Van Dorn at Iuka, Mississippi.

22   Lincoln issues a preliminary Emancipation Proclamation, freeing slaves in rebellious states only.

OCTOBER 3–4   Rosecrans wins the Battle of Corinth.

8   Buell defeats Bragg at Perryville, ending the invasion of Kentucky; Bragg retreats to Murfreesboro, Tennessee.

9–12   Stuart, with 1,600 cavalry, raids into the North, reaching Chambersburg, Pennsylvania.

25   Grant takes over the Department of Tennessee, lays plans to besiege Vicksburg.

NOVEMBER 7   Burnside replaces McClellan, moves his army to Falmouth, across the Rappahannock River from Fredericksburg.

13   Moving toward Vicksburg, Federal troops occupy Holly Springs, Mississippi.

DECEMBER 11   Burnside crosses the Rappahannock to attack Fredericksburg.

13   Lee defeats Burnside at Marye's Heights, inflicting heavy casualties.

14   Burnside retreats across the Rappahannock and settles in for the winter.

20   Grant moves Sherman from Memphis to aid in the attack on Vicksburg.

26   Rosecrans's troops arrive at Murfreesboro.

29   Sherman makes futile and costly attack at Chickasaw Bayou, Mississippi.

30   *Monitor* sinks off Cape Hatteras.

31   The Battle of Murfreesboro begins.

1863

JANUARY 1   Lincoln signs the Emancipation Proclamation.

2   The Battle of Murfreesboro ends

inconclusively; Bragg retreats to winter at Tullahoma.

11   The Confederate raider *Alabama* sinks USS *Hatteras* off Galveston.

20–22   Burnside makes his "mud march," looking for a place to cross the Rappahannock, but fails.

26   Lincoln replaces Burnside with Hooker as commander of the Army of the Potomac.

FEBRUARY 14   The Union ship *Queen of the West* runs past Vicksburg and captures several Confederate vessels, but runs aground and is captured.

MARCH 3   Congress approves Federal Draft Act and resolves to prosecute the war vigorously until the "rebellion" is suppressed.

8   Mosby captures Union General Stoughton at Fairfax Courthouse.

13–22   Several attempts by Union forces to pass through the Yazoo River and get behind Vicksburg fail.

APRIL 2   Bread riots erupt in Richmond.

16   Porter's fleet passes below the guns of Vicksburg.

28–29   Hooker marches his troops into the Wilderness.

30   Grant begins to cross the Mississippi below Vicksburg.

MAY 1   Grant moves inland and captures Port Gibson.

2   The battle of Chancellorsville begins. Outnumbered, Lee splits his army and routs Hooker. Jackson mortally wounded by his own men.

4   Sedgwick begins a campaign to take Fredericksburg from weakened Confederate defenses. Federal troops withdraw to the Rappahannock from Fredericksburg, and join the Army of the Potomac.

9   Johnston takes over Confederate command in Mississippi, but Pemberton continues to defend Vicksburg.

10   Jackson dies at Guinea Station.

14   Moving inland, Grant captures Jackson, Mississippi.

16   Grant defeats Pemberton at Champion Hill.

19–22   Attacks on Vicksburg fail; the siege of Vicksburg begins.

JUNE 9   Moving north, Lee is followed by Union cavalry; Stuart stops the Federal Cavalry at Brandy Station.

20   West Virginia becomes a Union state.

23   Rosecrans starts to maneuver Bragg out of middle Tennessee.

16   Lee's army starts to cross the Potomac.

25   Early captures supplies in York, Pennsylvania. Lincoln replaces Hooker with Meade as commander of the Army of the Potomac.

JULY 3   The three-day Battle of Gettysburg ends in Confederate defeat.

4   Vicksburg falls; Pemberton surrenders 20,000 troops to Grant, who paroles them.

8   Port Hudson surrenders, opening the Mississippi to Federal ships and cutting the Confederacy in two.

13–14   Hundreds are killed in New York draft riots.

21–23   Confederate cavalry, covering Lee's retreat, fight rearguard actions at Manassas Gap and Chester Gap.

AUGUST 20   Rosecrans heads for Chattanooga to battle Bragg.

21   Quantrill's Raiders kill 140 civilians at Lawrence, Kansas.

SEPTEMBER 2   Burnside occupies Knoxville, Tennessee.

5   Minister Charles Francis Adams threatens war against Britain if shipbuilding for the Confederacy is not halted. British comply.

8   Bragg moves out of Chattanooga, but is reinforced by Longstreet's forces from Virginia.

19–20	At the Battle of Chickamauga, Bragg is victorious but doesn't follow up, and Rosecrans retreats to Chattanooga.
OCTOBER 14	Meade and Lee fight inconclusively at Bristoe Station.
16	Grant is named to command the Division of the Mississippi.
23	Grant arrives in Chattanooga.
NOVEMBER 19	Lincoln delivers his Gettysburg Address.
25	Grant captures Missionary Ridge and defeats Bragg in the Battle of Lookout Mountain.
DECEMBER 2	Bragg is relieved of command of the Army of Tennessee, becomes military adviser to Jefferson Davis.
16	Gen. Joseph E. Johnston takes over command of the Army of Tennessee.

1864

JANUARY 19	Arkansas adopts an antislavery constitution.
FEBRUARY 3	Sherman occupies Meridian, Mississippi.
14	Federals capture Meridian, Mississippi.
17	Confederate submarine *Hunley* sinks the USS *Housatonic* off Charleston.
MARCH 9	Grant is promoted to the newly revived rank of lieutenant general.
12	Henry Halleck is named chief of staff. Red River campaign commences.
APRIL 4	Sheridan takes over the cavalry of the Army of the Potomac.
12	Forrest captures Fort Pillow, above Memphis, with high Union casualties resulting in persistent rumors of post-surrender massacre of the black and white garrison.
MAY 4	Grant leads his army across the Rapidan River.

5–6	Lee and Grant fight the inconclusive Battle of the Wilderness. Instead of retreating, Grant moves toward Spotsylvania Court House.
7	Sherman moves toward Atlanta.
8–21	Repeated attacks are launched on an entrenched Lee at Spotsylvania. Grant says, "I propose to fight it out on this line if it takes all summer."
16	Beauregard stops Butler south of Richmond at the Battle of Drewry's Bluff.
13–29	Sherman drives south toward Atlanta; Johnston fights a delaying action.
JUNE 1–3	At the Battle of Cold Harbor, Grant's casualties number 7,000, horrifying Northern leaders.
7	Lincoln is nominated for a second term.
10	Forrest defeats Sturgis at the Battle of Brices Cross Roads, Mississippi.
16–18	Grant launches a surprise attack at Petersburg, Virginia, but command delays deny him victory, and the siege of Petersburg begins.
19	USS *Kearsarge* sinks the Confederate raider *Alabama* off the coast of France.
27	Sherman is defeated at the Battle of Kennesaw Mountain, but continues to drive toward Atlanta.
JULY 2	Marietta, Georgia, is evacuated.
6	Early crosses the Potomac and enters Frederick City.
8	Schofield crosses the Chattahoochee River, forces Johnston into last defenses before Atlanta.
9	Lew Wallace musters volunteers to protect Washington from Early, loses to Early at the Battle of Monocacy, but delays his advance until the capital is reinforced.
14	Forrest wins a battle near Tupelo, Mississippi.
17	Davis relieves Johnston, gives command to Hood.

At a council of war near Massaponax Church, Virginia, in 1864, Grant looks over Meade's shoulder at the map Meade is holding. After his success at Vicksburg, Grant was called to Washington and placed in command of all Union armies. He made his headquarters in the field with the Army of the Potomac, effectively taking over command from Meade, the victor at Gettysburg. Sherman replaced Grant as commander of the Army of the Tennessee.

20   Hood attacks Sherman at the battle of Peachtree Creek, but falls back. The siege of Atlanta begins.

27–29   Extensive cavalry raids are launched by Sheridan, north of the James River.

30   Petersburg Mine explodes and subsequent Union assault is a debacle.

AUGUST 5   Farragut, with a fleet of fourteen wooden ships and four ironclads, wins the Battle of Mobile Bay, reportedly shouting, "Damn the torpedoes! Full speed ahead!"

7   Sheridan is given command of Union troops in the Shenandoah Valley.

18–22   Sherman conducts a wheeling movement to strike at Jonesboro, southeast of Atlanta.

31   Democrats nominate General McClellan for President, claiming the war is a failure. Hood attacks Sherman at Jonesborough, but falls back once more.

SEPTEMBER 2   Hood abandons Atlanta to Sherman.

19   Sheridan defeats Early at the Third Battle of Winchester.

29–30   Grant pushes his lines west of Petersburg with the Battle of Peeble's Farm.

OCTOBER 19   Confederates attack Sheridan's cavalry at Cedar Creek while he is away; in his famous "twenty-mile ride," Sheridan returns to save the day. Confederates raid St. Albans, Vermont, from Canada.

22   Hood begins the Tennessee campaign.

NOVEMBER 8   Lincoln is reelected, with Andrew Johnson as his Vice-President.

16   Sherman leaves Atlanta to begin his "march to the sea."

25   Confederate attempt to burn New York City fails.

30   At the Battle of Franklin, six Confederate generals die as Hood's frontal attack on Thomas fails.

DECEMBER 13   Sherman captures Fort McAllister, near Savannah.

15–16   At the Battle of Nashville, Thomas routs Hood and captures the city. Hood's Army of Tennessee is nearly gone.

20   Hardee takes his troops out of Savannah.

22   Sherman wires Lincoln, "I beg to present you as a Christmas gift the city of Savannah."

1865

JANUARY 13   Hood resigns, and turns over command of his beaten Army of Tennessee to Beauregard at Tupelo the next day.

15   Fort Fisher, at Wilmington, North Carolina, falls to Union troops.

31   The Confederate Congress names Lee commander-in-chief of all the Southern armies. U.S. House passes, 119 to 56, Abolition of Slavery, the Thirteenth Amendment.

FEBRUARY 3   Lincoln and Seward confer with Confederate Vice-President Stephens at Hampton Roads.

17   Sherman captures and burns Columbia, South Carolina.

18   Charleston is occupied without a fight.

MARCH 4   Lincoln inaugurated for second term.

13   Confederate Congress authorizes recruitment of black soldiers.

18   The Confederate Congress adjourns for the last time.

22   Schofield takes Wilmington, North Carolina.

29   Appomattox Campaign begins.

APRIL 1   Sheridan overwhelms Pickett at Five Forks.

2   The assault on Petersburg begins; A. P. Hill is slain. The Confederates evacuate Richmond.

3   Lee pulls his army out of the defense of Petersburg and moves west. Richmond occupied by Federal troops.

4   Lincoln visits Richmond.

9   Lee surrenders to Grant at Appomattox Court House.

12   The Confederate government meets at Greensborough, North Carolina. Mobile surrenders.

14   Lincoln is shot by John Wilkes Booth at Ford's Theatre in Washington. Johnston asks Sherman for terms of surrender. The Stars and Stripes are raised over Fort Sumter, Charleston, South Carolina.

15   Lincoln dies and Johnson becomes President.

26   The Confederate government meets at Charlotte. Johnston surrenders to Sherman near Durham Station, North Carolina. Booth is shot dead in a blazing barn near Bowling Green, Virginia.

MAY 4   Lincoln is buried at Springfield, Illinois. General Taylor surrenders all remaining troops east of the Mississippi at Citronelle, north of Mobile.

10   Davis is captured by Federal troops near Irwinville, Georgia, and is taken to Fort Monroe, Virginia, to await trial. President Johnson proclaims the end of armed resistance.

13   The last shots of the war are fired in the Battle of Palmito Hill near Brownsville, Texas.

23–24   Grand review of Federal armies in Washington, D.C.

26   Kirby Smith surrenders the Trans-Mississippi.

29 Johnson proclaims amnesty for all citizens of the South who pledge allegiance to the United States, Confederate officers and a few others excepted.

JUNE 23 President Johnson declares Federal blockade of Southern states at an end.

30 Lincoln conspirators convicted.

JULY 7 Lincoln conspirators executed.

NOVEMBER 6 Confederate cruiser CSS *Shenandoah* surrenders to British officers at Liverpool.

DECEMBER 18 Thirteenth Amendment to the Constitution abolishing slavery declared "in effect."

Lincoln (standing, center) delivers his Second Inaugural Address, March 4, 1865, to a crowd of 30,000. Important victories at Vicksburg and Gettysburg helped ensure Lincoln's reelection. His assassin, John Wilkes Booth, can be seen standing on the balcony behind the President, and one of Booth's fellow conspirators, Lewis Hine (wearing the light, wide-brimmed hat) is in the crowd below Lincoln.

2

Organization, Armies, and Leaders

The United States of America

"MY PARAMOUNT OBJECT IN THIS STRUGGLE IS TO SAVE THE UNION. . . . IF I COULD SAVE THE UNION WITHOUT FREEING ANY SLAVE, I WOULD DO IT; AND IF I COULD SAVE IT BY FREEING ALL THE SLAVES, I WOULD DO IT; AND IF I COULD SAVE IT BY FREEING SOME AND LEAVING OTHERS ALONE, I WOULD ALSO DO THAT. . . ."

—Abraham Lincoln, *in a letter to Horace Greeley, 1862*

President and Commander-in-Chief

Abraham Lincoln,
March 4, 1861–April 15, 1865
Andrew Johnson,
April 15, 1865–March 4, 1869

Secretary of War

Simon Cameron,
March 4, 1861–January 14, 1862
Edwin M. Stanton,
January 13, 1862–March 28, 1868

General-in-Chief of the Armies

(Brevet) Lt. Gen. Winfield Scott,
June 1841–November 1, 1861
Maj. Gen. George B. McClellan,
November 1, 1861–March 11, 1862
(No general commander existed between March 11, 1862, and July 11, 1862.)
Maj. Gen. Henry Wager Halleck,
July 11, 1862–March 12, 1864 (Chief of Staff, March 12, 1864–April 19, 1865)
Lt. Gen. Ulysses S. Grant,
March 12, 1864–March 4, 1869
(promoted to the newly created grade of general of the army on July 25, 1866)

The seventy-five-year-old Winfield Scott was general-in-chief of the armies when war came, and effectively prepared the new forces for battle. He was replaced by the youthful George McClellan, and when McClellan was relieved of his overall command in March 1862, he still led the Army of the Potomac. The post was vacant for four months until the appointment of Henry Wager Halleck. After Ulysses S. Grant was made general-in-chief, Halleck continued as chief of staff and military adviser to the President, but was subordinate to Grant. Grant served as general-in-chief until he was inaugurated as President.

Abraham Lincoln

Jefferson Davis

THE CONFEDERATE STATES OF AMERICA

PRESIDENT AND COMMANDER-IN-CHIEF

Jefferson Davis,
February 18, 1861–May 10, 1865

SECRETARY OF WAR

LeRoy P. Walker, February 21, 1861
Judah P. Benjamin,
September 17, 1861–March 18, 1862
George W. Randolph,
March 22, 1862–November 17, 1862
Maj. Gen. Gustavus W. Smith,
November 17, 1862–November 20, 1862
(acting)
James A. Seddon,
November 21, 1862–February 4, 1865
Maj. Gen. John C. Breckinridge,
February 4, 1865 to end

GENERAL-IN-CHIEF

Gen. Robert E. Lee,
February 6, 1865–April 9, 1865
(post created by Confederate Congress
for Lee)

President Davis was commander-in-chief of the army and navy by virtue of the Confederate Constitution. He functioned as such, and there was no general-in-chief until a few months before the war's end, when Congress created the post of general-in-chief for Robert E. Lee. Davis did have military advisers. The Confederacy instituted the rank of general, conferring it upon Samuel Cooper, who served as both adjutant general and inspector general; Albert Sidney Johnston; Robert E. Lee; Joseph E. Johnston; and P. G. T. Beauregard. Lee served as military adviser to President Davis before assuming command of the Army of Northern Virginia. When relieved of command of the Army of Tennessee, Braxton Bragg served as military adviser to President Davis. Until he was superseded by Lee, Bragg was the acting commander-in-chief of the Confederate armies.

> "ALL WE ASK IS TO BE LET ALONE."
>
> —JEFFERSON DAVIS, *1861*

STARS AND BARS

The Confederate battle flag had thirteen stars, yet only eleven states officially seceded. The other two stars represented Kentucky and Missouri, whose governors were pro-South. The Confederate Congress voted both into the Confederacy, but neither state actually seceded.

13

UNION ARMIES

ARMY OF THE POTOMAC

Units of the Military District of the Potomac fought at First Bull Run on July 21, 1861, under the command of Maj. Gen. Irvin McDowell. After this defeat, the Army of the Potomac was created from the Military District forces on August 20, 1861, and placed under the command of Maj. Gen. George B. McClellan. During McClellan's command, the army was organized into a cohesive unit and taken to the Peninsula to attack Richmond. In the Seven Days battles near the Confederate capital, the Army of the Potomac was pushed back to the James River.

Despite this defeat, McClellan was made general-in-chief of the armies, a post he held until March 11, 1862. Maj. Gen. John Pope assumed the field command of the Army of Virginia until he was routed at Second Bull Run.

Taking total command again, McClellan reorganized his army and halted Lee's northern invasion at Antietam in the fall of 1862. For failing to follow up his victory at Antietam, McClellan was removed from command by President Lincoln and was replaced by Maj. Gen. Ambrose E. Burnside on November 7, 1862. An ineffectual general, Burnside led the army in the tragic charge at Fredericksburg.

The morale of the Army of the Potomac was low when Lincoln replaced Burnside with Maj. Gen. Joseph Hooker on January 26, 1863, and it sank lower after an overconfident Hooker led the army to defeat at Chancellorsville in the spring. Lee had crossed the Potomac on his second northern invasion when Hooker was replaced on June 25, 1863, by Maj. Gen. George Gordon Meade. In a matter of days, Meade was fighting Lee at Gettysburg.

Meade would continue in command of the army until the end of the war, although in a secondary role. When Lt. Gen. Ulysses S. Grant was named general-in-chief of the armies, he decided to make his headquarters with the Army of the Potomac, actually directing the advance to Richmond, the siege of Petersburg, and the final Appomattox campaign, issuing his orders through Meade.

The Army of the Potomac held McClellan in deep affection, disliked Burnside, felt that Hooker was incompetent, respected Meade, and was intensely proud of Grant. The army had suffered many defeats and physical losses, but learned from experience and grew in strength as the war went on. By the end of the war, the Army of the Potomac was the mightiest army on earth.

ARMY OF VIRGINIA

When McClellan took the Army of the Potomac to the Peninsula, various elements

> "IT IS CALLED THE ARMY OF THE POTOMAC BUT IT IS ONLY MCCLELLAN'S BODYGUARD. . . . IF MCCLELLAN IS NOT USING THE ARMY, I SHOULD LIKE TO BORROW IT FOR A WHILE."
>
> —ABRAHAM LINCOLN, *1862*

NORTH VS. SOUTH

On the eve of the war, there were more than 22 million people in the North; the South had 9 million, more than a third of them slaves. The North controlled 90 percent of the country's manufacturing capacity, two-thirds of its railroad mileage, and most of its deposits of iron, coal, copper, and precious metals. Control of the Atlantic Ocean gave the North access to the factories of Europe. Huge surpluses of food produced in the North could be sold to pay for quantities of munitions. The North's advantages seemed overwhelming.

The South, however, was not without advantages. The North would have to invade, and an invader needs a substantial superiority in numbers. The Confederacy was large. Northern supply lines would be long, and many troops would be needed to guard them. The long Confederate coastline was beyond the blockade capacity of the Union navy. The most important factor, however, was that the South would be fighting to protect its homeland, the North for the abstract idea of the Union. The South could win if the North lost its desire to pursue the war, but the North could win only if it destroyed the South's ability to fight.

around Washington were organized into the Federal Army of Virginia on June 26, 1862, to defend the capital. Maj. Gen. John Pope, a veteran of fighting in the West, was placed in command, and he tried to create a new army overnight. A vain man, Pope poorly led the Army of Virginia at Second Bull Run, and his troops fell back to Washington. On September 12, 1862, the short-lived Army of Virginia was merged into the Army of the Potomac.

ARMY OF THE TENNESSEE

After the Battle of Shiloh, General Grant's Army of West Tennessee was renamed the Army of the Tennessee on October 16, 1862, and went on to fight in the Vicksburg campaign, the battles around Chattanooga, the Atlanta campaign, and Sherman's march to the sea. When Grant took over the entire western command, Maj. Gen. William T. Sherman was put in command of the Army of the Tennessee, October 25, 1863. When Sherman assumed command in the west, he was replaced by Maj. Gen. James B. McPherson on March 26, 1864. Mc-Pherson was slain on July 22, 1864, and after a few days under Maj. Gen. John A. Logan, the army was commanded by Maj. Gen. Oliver Otis Howard, from July 27, 1864, until the end of the war.

Despite the number of commanding generals, the Army of the Tennessee was really Sherman's army. He forged it into an effective fighting force, capable of moving fast and fighting hard when it arrived, and he used it superbly in taking Atlanta and on the march to the sea. It never had even the limited military polish of the Army of the Potomac, but beneath its devil-may-care attitude was a rugged strength.

ARMY OF THE CUMBERLAND

When Maj. Gen. Don Carlos Buell took over command of the Department of the Ohio on November 15, 1861, his troops be-

BLACK SOLDIERS

During the last three years of the war, 178,895 blacks served in the Union army, 12 percent of the entire Union force. They were organized into 120 infantry regiments, 12 heavy artillery and 10 light artillery batteries, and 7 cavalry regiments. Most of them came from slaveholding states, Louisiana leading with 24,052. In the North, Pennsylvania contributed 8,612 blacks to the army; New York 4,125; and Massachusetts 3,996. Black soldiers participated in at least 39 major battles and 410 minor engagements. Losses in black units were high: 68,178, or more than one-third of the total enlistment. Of these, 2,751 were killed in action, the rest succumbing to wounds or disease. The Medal of Honor was awarded to 21 black soldiers.

Some 130,000 blacks fought for the Union during the war, helping transform the war from simply preserving the Union to one of overthrowing the old order. Frederick Douglass said, "Once let the black soldier gets upon his person the brass letters, U.S. . . . and a musket on his shoulder . . . there is no power on earth which can deny that he has earned the right to citizenship."

came known as the Army of the Ohio. After relieving Grant at Shiloh, Buell took Nashville, only to be outmarched in the Confederate invasion of Kentucky. However, Buell was successful at the Battle of Perryville in October 1862. Buell was replaced on October 30, 1862, by Maj. Gen. William S. Rosecrans, and the army was renamed the Army of the Cumberland. It fought at Murfreesboro and moved toward Chattanooga in the brilliant Tullahoma campaign.

UNION DUES

A Union private was paid $13 a month; a colonel, $95; and a brigadier general, $124. A musket cost $13.

THE HUMAN COST OF WAR

The First Maine Heavy Artillery sustained the greatest regimental loss of the war. In less than a year, more than half of its 2,202 men were hit. Assaulting Petersburg in June 1864, 604 of the regiment's troops were killed or wounded in less than twenty minutes. The greatest regimental loss in a single battle was suffered by the 16th North Carolina Infantry at Gettysburg. It went into battle with about 800 men, and by the end of the third day 708 were dead, wounded, or missing. In one company of 84, every officer and man was hit.

Rosecrans was defeated at Chickamauga in September 1863, and retreated into Chattanooga, where he was besieged. Maj. Gen. George H. Thomas, "the Rock of Chickamauga," replaced Rosecrans on October 29, 1863, and led the Army of the Cumberland to victory at Missionary Ridge.

Under Thomas, the Army of the Cumberland was a part of Sherman's forces until Atlanta fell, then returned to Nashville to defend against Hood's invasion of Tennessee. Thomas destroyed Hood's army in the battles of Franklin and Nashville late in 1864. Never as free and easy as the Army of the Tennessee, the Army of the Cumberland became an effective fighting force under Thomas and achieved a number of important victories.

SECONDARY UNION ARMIES

FEDERAL ARMY OF THE OHIO

When the Army of the Ohio became the Army of the Cumberland in the fall of 1862, a second Federal Army of the Ohio was formed from scattered units. It finally was assembled on March 25, 1863, under Burnside. After fighting at Knoxville, the army was commanded by Maj. Gen. John M. Schofield and took part in the Atlanta campaign. The Army of the Ohio fought well against Hood at Franklin, and again with the Army of the Cumberland at the Battle of Nashville.

FEDERAL ARMY OF THE MISSISSIPPI

Organized in February 1862, the Army of the Mississippi fought under Maj. Gen. Pope at Island Number 10. After Pope was sent east, the army was commanded by Maj. Gen. Rosecrans. The army was discontinued October 26, 1862, following the battles of Iuka and Corinth, and its units were then incorporated into the Army of the Tennessee.

ARMY OF SOUTHWEST MISSOURI

The Army of Southwest Missouri was created in December 1861, and operated for a year in the Trans-Mississippi area, fighting at Pea Ridge and in lesser battles, before being merged into a department.

ARMY OF THE JAMES

Troops from the Department of Virginia and the combined Department of Virginia and North Carolina became the Army of the James in April 1864. Under Maj. Gen. Benjamin F. Butler, the army fought in the fierce attacks on Petersburg that summer, becoming bottled up and nearly useless.

ARMY AND DEPARTMENT OF THE GULF

Federal forces operating in the Gulf states were consolidated in February 1862 into the Army and Department of the Gulf. The army's commanders included Butler and

Major Generals N. P. Banks, S. A. Hurlbut, and E. R. S. Canby. Its operations included the unsuccessful 1864 Red River expedition and fighting around Mobile late in the war.

ARMY OF GEORGIA

Despite its impressive title, the Army of Georgia consisted of two corps during the march from Atlanta to the sea and into the Carolinas. It was commanded by Maj. Gen. Henry W. Slocum and was part of Sherman's general command.

ARMY OF THE SHENANDOAH

During Early's invasion into the Shenandoah Valley, the Army of the Shenandoah was created in August 1864. Under the command of Maj. Gen. Philip H. Sheridan, the army, accompanied by troops from the Department of West Virginia, known as the Army of West Virginia, laid waste to the valley and brought the fighting there to a virtual end late in 1864. The Army of the Shenandoah was disbanded on February 28, 1865.

ARMY OF THE MOUNTAIN DEPARTMENT

In March 1862, the Army of the Mountain Department was organized under Maj. Gen. John C. Frémont. The army operated without success against Stonewall Jackson at McDowell and Cross Keys, and was discontinued in June 1862.

OTHER UNION UNITS

Besides the formal Federal armies, the Union was divided into a variety of divisions, departments, and districts, all of which had troops for garrison duty and for fighting in lesser battles. This organization was changed numerous times throughout the war.

CONFEDERATE ARMIES

There were many scattered Confederate forces called "armies" at the beginning of the war, but they quickly coalesced into two great forces: the Army of Northern Virginia and the Army of Tennessee. These early antecedents are mentioned simply to clarify the nomenclature used in early battles.

ARMY OF NORTHERN VIRGINIA

Gen. Robert E. Lee took command of the Confederate forces during the battles in front of Richmond on May 31, 1862, gave the Army of Northern Virginia its name, and commanded it until the end of the war. The force had been commanded by Gen. Joseph E. Johnston and called the Army of the Potomac at First Bull Run and during the early days of the Peninsula campaign. As the Army of Northern Virginia, it fought many battles: the Seven Days, Second Bull Run, Antietam, Fredericksburg, Chancellorsville, Gettysburg, the Wilderness, Spotsylvania, Cold Harbor, the siege of Petersburg, and the Appomattox campaign. The

STRENGTH IN NUMBERS

An infantry regiment consisted of ten companies, thirty officers, and 1,300 men. But when a new regiment reached the field, it often would have fewer than 800 men available for combat. Men who fell ill or who were serving as cooks, teamsters, orderlies, and clerks accounted for the reduced numbers. In many of the larger battles, the fighting strength of some regiments was less than 500.

THE TRUE ENEMY

Twice as many soldiers died from disease as from enemy bullets. Diarrhea and dysentery alone took the lives of 44,558 Union soldiers.

history of one of the most famous of American armies ended with its surrender on April 9, 1865.

This was Lee's army, and it fought entirely in the East except for one corps under Longstreet at the Battle of Chickamauga in the fall of 1863. The Army of Northern Virginia had a number of outstanding generals: Stonewall Jackson, Jeb Stuart, James Longstreet, A. P. Hill, Jubal Early, and Richard Ewell. Early in the war it gained such a reputation for brilliance in movement and fighting that a legend of invincibility rose around it, although it suffered defeats at Antietam and Gettysburg and in the Richmond campaign. The army shared the spirit and faith of its commander. When the Army of Northern Virginia surrendered, the war, for all practical purposes, was over.

ARMY OF TENNESSEE

The Army of Kentucky and the Army of the Mississippi were joined on November 20, 1862, to form the Army of Tennessee, the other principal Confederate army, under the command of Gen. Braxton Bragg. It fought at the Battle of Murfreesboro, in the Tullahoma campaign, and at Chickamauga and Chattanooga. The officers and men of the Army of Tennessee had little faith in Bragg; opportunities were lost at Chickamauga, and the army was pushed off the heights at Missionary Ridge. Gen. Joseph E. Johnston replaced Bragg on December 16, 1863, and overhauled the army. He made a skillful retreat before Atlanta, but President Davis grew impatient and replaced him with General Hood. Hood engaged Sherman with great losses in the battles of Peachtree Creek, Ezra Church, and Jonesboro, but failed to save Atlanta. Hood then led the army northward, striking Sherman's supply line and entering Tennessee, only to be defeated at Franklin and again at Nashville.

Johnston took over what was left of the Army of Tennessee, but it was too late to offer more than token resistance. Johnston surrendered to Sherman at Durham Station on April 26, 1865. Excellent officers had served under the various Army of Tennessee commanders: William J. Hardee, Leonidas Polk, Patrick R. Cleburne, B. F. Cheatham, A. P. Stewart, Joseph Wheeler, and the cavalry leader Nathan Bedford Forrest. But Bragg and Hood were mediocre commanders, and Johnston lacked the support of the Confederate government.

ARMY OF THE KANAWHA

Commanded by Brig. Gen. John B. Floyd, the Army of the Kanawha fought in the fall of 1861 in what was to become West Virginia.

ARMY OF EASTERN KENTUCKY

Operating in the eastern counties of Kentucky, the Army of Eastern Kentucky existed from late 1861 to early 1862.

ARMY OF NEW MEXICO

Formed in December 1861 under Brig. Gen. H. H. Sibley, the Army of New Mexico attempted to capture New Mexico and Arizona. After capturing Santa Fe, however, it was defeated at the Battle of Glorietta Pass and forced to retreat into Texas.

ARMY OF LOUISIANA AND ARMY OF PENSACOLA

Louisiana state troops were known briefly as the Army of Lousiana; troops near Pensacola were called the Army of Pensacola from October 1861 to March 1862.

ARMY OF THE SHENANDOAH

Early in the war, forces in the Shenandoah Valley commanded by Gen. Joseph E. John-

The coming of age of Lee's army is shown in field sketches by Confederate veteran A. C. Redwood. An 1862 recruit (right) reacts poorly to military discipline, his uniform fit only for the parade ground. The bearded 1865 veteran (above) is lean and hard from many months in the field. He carries the tools of his trade: rifle, cartridge box, bayonet, knapsack, canteen. A slouch hat shades his face, and tucked-in trousers keep out insects.

ston were known as the Army of the Shenandoah until they moved east to fight at First Bull Run.

ARMY OF THE PENINSULA

Forces on the peninsula east of Richmond were known as the Army of the Peninsula from November 1861 until April 1862, when they became part of the Army of Northern Virginia.

ARMY OF THE NORTHWEST

Consisting of forces in northwestern Virginia from June 1861 to February 1862, the Army of the Northwest was disbanded following the loss of much of the new state of West Virginia to the Federals.

ARMY OF MOBILE

Troops around Mobile constituted the Army of Mobile from January 1862 until late June of that year.

NUMBERS AND LOSSES

	UNION	CONFEDERACY
Population	22,400,000	9,103,000 [1]
In service, 1861–65	2,470,000	1,003,600
Total strength, July 1861	219,400	114,000
Peak strength, 1864–65	1,044,660	1,003,600
Total hit in battle	385,100	320,000
Total battle deaths	110,100	94,000
Killed in battle	67,100	54,000
Died of wounds	43,000	40,000
Wounded (not mortally) [2]	275,000	226,000
Captured [3]	211,400	462,000
Died in prison	30,200	26,000
Died of disease	224,000	60,000
Desertions [4]	199,000	—
Surrendered 1865	—	174,223

[1] Includes 3,760,00 in the seceded states.
[2] A number of these were returned to duty.
[3] An undetermined number were exchanged and returned to duty.
[4] Many deserters returned to duty. In the Union army, where a $300 bounty was paid for a three-year enlistment, many soldiers picked up their bounty in one regiment, then deserted to join another for an additional bounty.

NOTE: Confederate figures are based in part on estimates.

CENTRAL ARMY OF KENTUCKY AND ARMY OF THE MISSISSIPPI

The Central Army of Kentucky was organized in September 1861, but was merged with the Army of the Mississippi in March 1862.

ARMY OF EAST TENNESSEE AND ARMY OF KENTUCKY

Both of these forces were attached as a corps to the Army of Tennessee in November 1862.

ARMY OF MIDDLE TENNESSEE

Small forces near Murfreesboro, Tennessee, in October 1862, were known as the Army of Middle Tennessee.

ARMY OF THE WEST

This Trans-Mississippi force fought at Pea Ridge and crossed east of the river to fight at Corinth and Iuka before being merged with other Confederate forces under this name.

ARMY OF THE MISSOURI

Forces under Maj. Gen. Sterling Price operated under this name in Missouri in August 1864.

ARMY OF THE SOUTHWEST (ARMY OF THE TRANS-MISSISSIPPI)

This small force was active in Arkansas and Louisiana before being absorbed by other Confederate armies.

ARMY OF WEST TENNESSEE

This force, formed in September 1862, was joined with the Army of the West and other units to become known as the Army of Mississippi. It was commanded by Lt. Gen. John C. Pemberton, and was the force that surrendered at Vicksburg on July 4, 1863. (After Vicksburg, the term "Army of the Mississippi" was applied to troops under Lt. Gen. Leonidas Polk. This later incarnation was organized in midsummer 1863, but by May 1864 it had become part of the Army of Tennessee.)

ARMY OF THE MISSISSIPPI

Confusing though it seems, another army known as the Army of the Mississippi was formed in March 1862 under the command of Gen. P. G. T. Beauregard, and later commanded by Gen. Albert Sidney Johnston. For a while it was a major Confederate army, and fought at Shiloh on April 6–7, 1862. Upon the death of Johnston, Beauregard resumed command but was relieved on June 17, 1862. Shortly afterward, Gen. Braxton Bragg took over the army, and in November 1862 it became the Army of Tennessee.

POLITICAL PATRONAGE

During the war, ambitious men without military experience were made generals to reward loyal Republicans, to attract Democratic support, or to appease powerful groups. Some of these "political generals" were embarrassments. The heavy-handed conduct of Ben Butler of Massachusetts was criticized throughout the war. Dan Sickles of New York had a poor battle record. John McClernand, who recruited thousands of soldiers in the Mississippi Valley, was relieved by Grant for undermining him. Franz Sigel was a mediocre general, but rallied German-Americans to the Union cause. Confederate officers were chosen solely on merit, and the Southern army benefited from this policy.

UNION LEADERS

Charles Francis Adams, 1807–1886; born Boston, Mass. The son of President John Quincy Adams, Charles Francis Adams was educated abroad before graduating from Harvard in 1858. A congressman, he was appointed by Lincoln as Minister to Great Britain. Adams understood the British and proved a firm, skillful diplomat. He is given a large share of the credit for keeping Britain from recognizing the Confederacy as a separate nation, and for halting the construction of Confederate raiders in British shipyards.

Robert Anderson, 1805–1871; born Louisville, Ky. West Point class of 1825. A veteran of the Black Hawk and Mexican wars, Robert Anderson was a major in 1860 when he was given command of the forts in Charleston Harbor. When Fort Sumter was attacked, he refused several demands for surrender before finally giving up the battered fort. Later he served as a brigadier general in Kentucky until his health failed.

Nathaniel Prentiss Banks, 1816–1894; born Waltham, Mass. A self-taught man, Nathaniel Banks was an actor, editor, lawyer, and politician before the war. Elected to Congress in 1853 as a Democrat, he became a Free Soiler and was elected Speaker of the House in 1856. Commissioned a major general in 1861, he was badly defeated by Stonewall Jackson in the Shenandoah Valley campaign. He fought at Cedar Mountain and succeeded Butler as commander at New Orleans in 1862.

Mathew B. Brady, 1823–1896; born Warren County, N.Y. An artist before becoming interested in photography, Mathew Brady set up a successful daguerreotype studio with a branch in Washington. Granted permission at the beginning of the war to take photographs with the armies, he hired other photographers and they fol-

owed the war with wagonloads of clumsy equipment. Their 3,500 photographs represented the first time in history a war was ...nted photographically.

...s **Buell,** 1818–1898; born ... West Point class of ...minole and Mexi- ... a lieutenant ... a briga-

...le in ... of
... Abner
... general.
... he was a
... Sumter. He
...ond Bull Run
...tain, Antietam,
... a major general,
...ancellorsville and
... briefly commanded a
...eynolds was slain. He
... war in Washington.

...gow **Farragut,** 1801– ... Knoxville, Tenn. The most ...val figure of the war, David ...ned the navy at the age of ten ...ction on the *Essex* in the War of ... served briefly in the Mexican War ...mmander. He was made a captain in ... Island, California. When the war ...oke out, Farragut had been in the navy ...orty-nine years. He commanded the fleet at the capture of New Orleans and on the Mississippi during the Vicksburg campaign. As a rear admiral, he led the fleet to victory at Mobile Bay, shouting "Damn the torpe- does! Full speed ahead!" In 1864 the rank of vice-admiral was created for Farragut, as was the rank of full admiral, in July 1866.

Gustavus Vasa Fox, 1821–1883; born Saugus, Mass. Annapolis class of 1841. After the Mexican War, Gustavus Fox re- signed from the navy to enter business. He was consulted by the navy about assuming command of a relief expedition to Fort Sumter, and soon became chief clerk in the Navy Department. Navy Secretary Gideon Welles created the position of Assistant

1839–
...est Point
...last in his
...uster fought
...e was an aide
...stinguished him-
...battles, and was
...l in June 1863. He
...and in the later Vir-
...war's end he was a
...d major general, and

Salmon Portland Chase, 1808–1873; born Cornish, N.H. After graduating from Dartmouth, Salmon Chase practiced law in Cincinnati, taking part in antislavery activities and defending fugitive slaves. He was elected to the Senate in 1849. Later, as governor of Ohio, he became a Republican. Chase was a candidate for the Republican presidential nomination in 1856 and then in 1860, when he was defeated by Lincoln. Lincoln appointed him Secretary of the Treasury, and he served in that post from March 1861 to July 1864. He tried to resign several times, and Lincoln reluctantly let him go, appointing him Chief Justice of the Supreme Court in 1864.

served in the West at a lower rank until h[is] death at the Battle of the Little Bighorn in 1876. Custer was both damned as a "glory hunter" and praised for his courage and ability to command.

Abner Doubleday, 1819–1893; bor[n] Ballston Spa, N.Y. West Point class[of] 1842. Although remembered for his r[ole in] developing the game of baseball, Doubleday was an important Union A veteran of the Mexican War, captain at the defense of Fort commanded a brigade at Se and a division of South Mou[ntain] and Fredericksburg. As Doubleday fought at C Gettysburg, where he corps after General spent the rest of th

David Glas 1870; born nea successful na Farragut jo and saw 1812. H as a c 1855 Ma b

George A. Custer

George Armstrong Custer 1876; born New Ramley, Ohio. class of 1861. After graduating class at West Point, George at First Bull Run. In 1862 on McClellan's staff. He d self in several cavalry made a brigadier gene served at Gettysbur ginia campaigns. A twenty-five-year-o

Secretary of the Navy for Fox. A superb administrator, Fox effectively developed a high degree of wartime efficiency, making vital changes in personnel and management, and promoting such new vessels as the *Monitor*.

John Charles Frémont, 1813–1890; born Richmond, Va. In 1841, Frémont married Jessie Benton, the daughter of Missouri Senator Thomas Hart Benton, and became famous for his expeditions in the West. In 1845, Frémont entered California and helped defeat the Spanish there. Found guilty of charges that included mutiny, Frémont resigned from the Topographical Corps, but continued his explorations. Elected senator from California, he was the first Republican presidential candidate in 1856, losing to Buchanan. In 1861, Frémont was appointed a major general and sent to St. Louis. He issued an emancipation proclamation for Missouri, but the government did not support him and he was removed. He subsequently served without distinction in western Virginia and the Shenandoah Valley. Frémont was nominated for President by the Radical Republicans in 1864, but he withdrew and entered business.

John Gibbon, 1827–1896; born Holmesburg, Pa. West Point class of 1847. Although raised in North Carolina, John Gibbon remained loyal to the Union. Early in the war he showed a remarkable ability to mold volunteers into crack soldiers. He became a brigadier general in May 1862 and put in command of volunteers who would become the famous Iron Brigade. He fought at Second Bull Run, South Mountain, and Antietam, and commanded a division at Fredericksburg until he was wounded. He commanded a corps at Gettysburg and again was wounded. Back in action, Gibbon led a division in the Wilderness and at Spotsylvania. In the final campaigns of the war, he again commanded a corps.

Ulysses S. Grant

Ulysses Simpson Grant, 1822–1885; born Point Pleasant, Ohio. West Point class of 1843. After serving with distinction in the Mexican War, Ulysses S. Grant resigned from the army in California, apparently homesick and drinking too much. He went into business in St. Louis, went bankrupt, and joined his brothers in the family store in Galena, Illinois. When war came, he drilled local volunteers and petitioned repeatedly for a commission. He was named a colonel in June 1861. By August he was a brigadier general in command at Cairo, Illinois. Grant led the forces that captured Forts Henry and Donelson, becoming famous for demanding and receiving the "unconditional surrender" of Fort Donelson. He narrowly avoided defeat at Shiloh, and restored his reputation in his Vicksburg campaign. When Vicksburg surrendered, Grant was named commander in the West. After Grant defeated Bragg at Missionary Ridge, Lincoln placed him in command of all the Union armies. He led the Army of the

Potomac to victory in Virginia, but incurred tremendous troop losses in the Wilderness and at Spotsylvania, Cold Harbor, and the siege of Petersburg. Grant accepted Lee's surrender at Appomattox on April 9, 1865. He was involved in the controversy between President Johnson and Secretary of War Stanton, but emerged as the Republican presidential candidate in 1868. His two terms as President were riddled with scandal. He left office in 1877, toured the world, again failed in business, and wrote his *Personal Memoirs* to provide for his family, completing the book as he was dying of throat cancer.

Horace Greeley

Horace Greeley, 1811–1872; born Amherst, N.H. One of America's greatest editors and popular educators, Horace Greeley founded the *New York Tribune* in 1841 and built it into one of the country's most influential newspapers. He took a strong antislavery stand, and during the war he opposed compromise with the South. Greeley believed in letting what he called the "erring sisters" go. He opposed Lincoln's reelection in 1864 and later attempted to make peace with the South through private negotiations. After the war, Greeley broke with Grant and ran against him unsuccessfully in 1872 as the candidate of the Liberal Republicans and Democrats.

Benjamin Henry Grierson, 1826–1911; born Pittsburgh, Pa. A former school teacher and merchant, Benjamin Grierson commanded a cavalry brigade on a raid that made him famous. Leaving La Grange, Tennessee, in April 1863, his 1,700 men cut a swath through Mississippi, destroying railroads and public property, greatly aiding Grant's Vicksburg campaign. He was promoted to brigadier general, then major general, and later held important commands in the West.

Henry Wager Halleck, 1815–1872; born Westernville, N.Y. West Point class of 1839. Henry Halleck, known as a student of military science, left the army in 1854 to become a lawyer. When war came, he succeeded Frémont in command at St. Louis. Under Halleck's command, Grant captured Forts Henry and Donelson, and Pope was victorious at Island Number 10. Early in 1862, Halleck was put in command of the entire West, but proved overcautious. Lincoln respected his administrative abilities and appointed him general-in-chief. Again his overcautious nature led to charges of failing to follow up victories. In March 1864 he became chief of staff of the army, a post in which his administrative talents could best be used.

Winfield Scott Hancock, 1824–1886; born Montgomery Square, Pa. West Point class of 1844. An aggressive leader, Winfield Hancock served with distinction in Mexico, the Seminole War, and the West before being made a brigadier general of volunteers in 1861. He fought in the Peninsula campaign and at South Mountain and Antietam, led a division at Fredericksburg and Chancellorsville, then took over the Second Corps. His best command came at

Gettysburg, where he defended against Confederate attacks on the second and third days. After the war he led Western expeditions. Hancock was the Democratic presidential candidate in 1880, losing to Garfield.

Joseph Hooker, 1814–1879; born Hadley, Mass. West Point class of 1837. After fighting in the Mexican War, Joseph Hooker resigned to a farm in California. In May 1861, as a general of volunteers, he led a division in the Peninsula campaign. Promoted to major general and nicknamed "Fighting Joe," he fought at Second Bull Run, South Mountain, and Antietam. After Burnside's debacle at Fredericksburg, Lincoln put Hooker in command of the Army of the Potomac, cautioning him against rashness. Greatly optimistic at first, he lost his drive after being beaten severely at Chancellorsville. On June 25, 1863, Hooker was replaced by Meade. Hooker took two corps west and fought at Lookout Mountain and in the Atlanta campaign. Passed over for command after the death of McPherson, Hooker retired.

Joseph Hooker

Oliver O. Howard

Oliver Otis Howard, 1830–1909; born Leeds, Me. West Point class of 1854. At the start of the war, Oliver Howard commanded a Maine regiment. Rising to general, he fought at First Bull Run and lost an arm at Fair Oaks, but continued in service and fought at Second Bull Run, South Mountain, Antietam, Fredericksburg, Chancellorsville, and Gettysburg. Howard was criticized for being surprised by Jackson at Chancellorsville, and received censure for his actions on the first day of Gettysburg. Transferred to the West in 1863, he fought at Chattanooga and commanded a corps in the Atlanta campaign. After the war he worked on behalf of freed slaves, helping to found Howard University.

Andrew Johnson, 1808–1875; born Raleigh, N.C. A tailor in Greeneville, Tennessee, Andrew Johnson educated himself with the help of his wife and became successful, first in business, then in politics. He served in the Tennessee legislature and Congress, becoming governor in 1853 and U.S. senator in 1855. Johnson was a Democrat who held to a strict conservative interpretation of the Constitution. When the

"I CLAIM NOT TO HAVE CONTROLLED EVENTS, BUT CONFESS PLAINLY THAT EVENTS HAVE CONTROLLED ME."

—ABRAHAM LINCOLN, *1864*

war broke out he remained loyal to the Union, and in 1862 Lincoln appointed him military governor of Tennessee. Lincoln chose Johnson as a running mate in 1864 in recognition of the Democrats and the Southern unionists. After the death of Lincoln, on April 15, 1865, President Johnson was considered a tool of the Radical Republicans, but soon broke with them. Subsequent quarrels led to impeachment by the House of Representatives in February 1868. By a margin of one vote the Senate failed to convict him. Johnson's attempts to carry out Lincoln's plans for reconstruction failed, partly because of his inability to lead and partly because of the temper of the times.

Abraham Lincoln

Abraham Lincoln, 1809–1865; born Hodgenville, Ky. Born on the western frontier, Abraham Lincoln received little education. His family moved to Illinois in 1830, and he was soon on his own. Lincoln worked in a store, served briefly in the Black Hawk War, was postmaster, learned surveying, studied the law, and was elected to the state legislature, where he served four terms. He began the practice of law in Springfield, and in 1842 he married Mary Todd, daughter of a prominent Kentucky family. Running as a Whig, he was elected to Congress in 1846 and served one term. He then devoted himself to his law practice. Lincoln reentered politics in 1854, opposing the spread of slavery but not the institution itself. He joined the new Republican party and received 110 votes for Vice-President at the first Republican national convention. He ran unsuccessfully against Stephen A. Douglas for the Senate in 1858, and their famous debates added to his growing reputation. He was a dark-horse Republican candidate in 1860 and received the nomination largely because he was more moderate and had fewer enemies than his rivals. He won the four-way election with less than half of the total vote. Lincoln made no public pronouncements before his March 4, 1861, inauguration except to affirm his desire to maintain the Union. When Fort Sumter was bombarded, on April 12, 1861, he acted promptly. As the war progressed, he continually sought a general who could win, and after many tries he found his man in Grant. Lincoln's political skills were taxed severely during the war as he tried to keep various elements of opposition under control. The Union victory at Antietam gave him the opportunity to announce his Emancipation Proclamation, which placated antislavery elements in the North and prevented the recognition of the Confederacy by Britain and France. Renominated in 1864, he despaired of reelection, but a combination of victories around Atlanta, the soldier vote, and some shrewd politicking gave him the election over Democrat George B. McClellan. During the war he was attacked violently by both abolitionists and antiwar Democrats, but he managed the affairs of the nation to ensure victory. Shortly after Lee surrendered, Lincoln was shot by John Wilkes Booth and died the following day.

John Alexander Logan, 1826–1886; born Jackson County, Ill. A veteran of the Mexican War, John Logan was a lawyer and the holder of a number of local and state offices. He was elected to Congress as a Democrat in 1858. Accused of Southern sympathies, he actually was a strong Unionist and raised a regiment in Illinois. He fought at Belmont, Fort Donelson, and in the Vicksburg campaign, rising to major general. He commanded a corps at Atlanta and briefly commanded the Army of the Tennessee. Sherman, however, mistrusted his political activities and relieved him. After the war, Logan helped organize the Grand Army of the Republic.

Nathaniel Lyon, 1819–1861; born Ashford, Conn. West Point class of 1841. A veteran of the Seminole and Mexican wars, Nathaniel Lyon was a captain at the St. Louis Arsenal in 1861. He seized Camp Jackson from the pro-Confederates, then organized Union forces in Missouri, pushing state troops out of Jefferson City and Boonville. Lyon's forces fought the Confederates at Wilson's Creek, near Springfield. A possible Union victory was thwarted by the rout of Franz Sigel and by Lyon's death on the battlefield.

George Brinton McClellan, 1826–1885; born Philadelphia, Pa. West Point class of 1846. After service in Mexico, George McClellan was sent abroad to study military affairs during the Crimean War, and later designed a cavalry saddle that still bears his name. He resigned from the army in 1857 and held high positions with several railroads. At the outbreak of the war he

George B. McClellan

was made a major general in command of the Department of the Ohio. He met with success in West Virginia, and after the defeat at First Bull Run he was given command of the Division of the Potomac. Demonstrating great organizational ability, he set about assembling what was to become the Army of the Potomac. In November 1861 he succeeded Scott as general-in-chief. Lincoln demanded action from the army, but McClellan wouldn't act, protesting that he wasn't ready. In March 1862 he was relieved as general-in-chief, but left in command of the Army of the Potomac. McClellan persuaded Lincoln to let him take the army to the Virginia peninsula. Once

THE COST OF WAR

It cost the U.S. government approximately $2 million a day to conduct the war, an estimated total cost of more than $6 billion. From 1861 to 1865, the national debt rose from $2.80 to $75.00 per capita. The total cost of the war to the South has been estimated at $4 billion.

there, he began an extremely cautious advance on Richmond, continually overestimating the enemy strength. He held off an attack at Seven Pines, but Lee and Jackson forced him to retreat to the James River during the Seven Days. McClellan bitterly blamed Washington for his failure. After Second Bull Run, McClellan was given command of the entire Army of the Potomac. He followed Lee north and engaged him at Antietam, but failed to follow up on his victory, and was removed from command. He left the army and was the Democratic candidate for President in 1864, but lost to Lincoln.

Irwin J. McDowell

THE TIES THAT BIND

The Union and Confederate generals often knew each other personally. The officer corps was small before the war, fewer than 1,500, and many were West Point graduates. At First Manassas, P. G. T. Beauregard faced Irwin McDowell, both of the class of 1838. George B. McClellan and Thomas J. Jackson graduated in 1846. Ellen Marcy was courted by two West Pointers, rejecting A. P. Hill to marry George McClellan. Robert E. Lee was superintendent of West Point before the war. His last class was 1856; when war came, twenty-three of the class served in the Union army, and fourteen in the Confederate army.

Another bond was the Mexican War. P. G. T. Beauregard and George McClellan were on the staff of Gen. Winfield Scott. Capt. Robert E. Lee once commended Lt. Ulysses S. Grant in a dispatch. Grant was thanked for his role in capturing Mexico City by Lt. John Pemberton, whom he would face later at Vicksburg. James Longstreet and Winfield Scott Hancock, who fought at Churubusco together, opposed each other at Gettysburg. Col. Jefferson Davis commanded Mississippi volunteers at Buena Vista; George H. Thomas and Braxton Bragg were fellow artillery officers in the attack. At Monterey, Joseph Hooker and Albert Sidney Johnston were comrades in arms. Joseph E. Johnston and George Meade were engineer officers at the siege of Vera Cruz. The Civil War was brother against brother, and brother officer against brother officer.

John Alexander McClernand, 1812–1900; born Hardinsburg, Ky. A lawyer, John McClernand entered politics in Illinois as a Jackson Democrat and served ten years as a congressman. He left Congress to become a brigadier general and fought at Belmont, Fort Henry, and Fort Donelson. At Shiloh he strongly criticized Grant's leadership. In October 1862, Lincoln authorized McClernand to gather a force to attack Vicksburg. He tried unsuccessfully to replace Grant. Grant relieved him in June 1863 for issuing unauthorized orders. He returned in February 1864 to command a corps in the West, but resigned within the year.

Irvin McDowell, 1818–1885; born Columbus, Ohio. West Point class of 1838. A veteran of the Mexican War, Irvin McDowell was a staff officer until, as a brigadier general, he organized the army in front of Washington at the outbreak of the war. He was pressured to move the still-unprepared army toward Manassas Junction and suffered defeat. Replaced by McClellan, he continued to lead a division and fought at Second Bull Run in 1862. He was severely criticized for ineptitude in that battle, and never again held a major command.

James Birdseye McPherson, 1828–1864; born Sandusky, Ohio. West Point class of 1853. A first lieutenant when war came, he served as an aide to General Halleck, becoming a field officer after the Fort Donelson campaign. As a brigadier general, he reinforced Rosecrans at Corinth. Known as "the whiplash of the army," he rose in rank quickly, first leading a corps in the Vicksburg campaign, then being given the Army of the Tennessee in March 1864, when Sherman assumed command in the West. McPherson, considered one of the most capable generals in the Union army, distinguished himself at Kennesaw Mountain, but was killed on July 22, 1864, in the fighting near Atlanta.

George Gordon Meade, 1815–1872; born Cadiz, Spain. West Point class of 1835. The son of a U.S. naval agent, George Meade fought in the Seminole and Mexican wars and was a captain of engineers at the beginning of the war. He led a brigade in the Seven Days, and was badly wounded, but recovered to fight at Second Bull Run and Antietam. Promoted to major general in 1862, he commanded a corps at Fredericksburg and Chancellorsville.

George G. Meade

A PERFECT SPY

Gen. George B. McClellan hired Allan Pinkerton, founder of the famous Pinkerton detective agency, to direct his secret service. His duties included espionage behind Confederate lines and counterespionage behind Union lines. Pinkerton performed well in finding and arresting Confederate agents, but consistently overestimated the Confederate numbers at two or three times their actual strength. McClellan, overcautious by nature, trusted Pinkerton implicitly and, believing his army outnumbered, often refused to take the offensive.

Meade replaced Hooker as commander, and concentrated his forces to halt Lee's northern invasion. Victorious at Gettysburg, he was criticized for not counterattacking and pursuing Lee. He commanded the army in the Rapidan and Mine Run campaigns, although Grant accompanied the Army of the Potomac and directed operations. Surprisingly, the stubborn, somewhat unpopular Meade worked well with Grant, despite being overshadowed. He was made a major general in the regular army in August 1864, and commanded several army departments after the war.

Allan Pinkerton, 1819–1884; born Glasgow, Scotland. Allan Pinkerton emigrated to Chicago in 1842, and as a private citizen, discovered a group of counterfeiters, organized a posse, and captured them. He set up a private detective agency, solved several railroad express robberies, and gained a national reputation. An abolitionist, Pinkerton also operated an Underground Railroad station. He guarded Lincoln on his inaugural trip to Washington in 1861, stayed in the capital, and became friends with McClellan. Under the general's aegis, Pinkerton set up an intelligence and espionage service that operated behind Southern lines. When Lincoln relieved McClellan, Pinkerton resigned from the service and returned to his detective agency.

THE CIVIL WAR

The war is called the Civil War almost by default. Southerners called it the War for Southern Independence. In the North, particularly New England, it was the War of the Rebellion. The War Between the States, like the Civil War, is a scrupulously nonpartisan term, but never achieved common usage.

John Pope, 1822–1892; born Louisville, Ky. West Point class of 1842. An army engineer, John Pope was made a brigadier general of volunteers at the outbreak of war. He commanded the Army of the Mississippi, capturing New Madrid, Missouri, and Island Number 10. He was promoted and put in command of the scattered forces around Washington, which he formed into the Army of Virginia while McClellan was still on the Peninsula. Pope was overconfident in his first major battle, at Second Bull Run. He issued a flamboyant, ill-advised order, saying his headquarters were "in the saddle." Pope was defeated and retreated to Washington, where he was relieved, his army then being merged into the Army of the Potomac. Pope spent the rest of the war fighting Indians in the Northwest.

David Dixon Porter, 1813–1891; born Chester, Pa. The son of a naval officer, David Porter followed his father to sea. He became a midshipman at the age of sixteen, and saw action in the Mexican War. Porter led a mortar flotilla in the attack on New Orleans, capturing the forts below the city. He commanded the Mississippi River Squadron during the Vicksburg campaign, but had less success leading the naval arm in the Red River campaign. Porter organized the North Atlantic Blockading Squadron and helped to capture Fort Fisher, North Carolina. After the war he was superintendent at Annapolis, where he reorganized the academy.

Fitz-John Porter, 1822–1901; born Portsmouth, N.H. West Point class of 1845. When the war began, Porter, a veteran of the Mexican War, was a colonel of infantry. A general of volunteers in the Shenandoah Valley, he commanded a division, then a corps, serving with distinction at Mechanicsville and Gaines' Mill. Sent to aid Pope in the defense of Washington, he was ordered to attack Jackson at Second Bull Run, but his troops ran into Longstreet's arriving corps. Porter either failed to attack or was unable to do so, and was relieved of his command and charged with disobedience, disloyalty, and misconduct. He was found guilty and turned out of the army. He worked for years to clear himself, and was reinstated in 1882.

John Aaron Rawlins, 1831–1869; born Galena, Ill. John Rawlins was a prominent pro-Union Democrat when General Grant, his hometown friend, asked him to be his aide in 1862, and his career was linked to Grant's throughout the war. Rawlins reputedly exercised great influence over Grant. He was made brigadier and chief of staff of the army in March 1865. President Grant appointed him Secretary of War, but Rawlins died five months later. A man of strong moral fiber, Rawlins was often called "Grant's conscience."

William Starke Rosecrans, 1819–1898; born Delaware County, Ohio. West Point class of 1842. Resigning his commission in 1854, William Rosecrans became an engineer and businessman. Appointed a general when war came, he served with McClellan in West Virginia, defeating the Confederates at Rich Mountain. Transferred to Grant in Mississippi, he led a successful attack at Iuka, and defended Corinth. He succeeded Buell in Kentucky and fought at Murfreesboro, winning one of the bloodiest battles of the war. In the summer of 1863, he forced Bragg into Chattanooga. An attack hit his overextended lines at Chickamauga, crushing much of the

Union army. It was a personal defeat for Rosecrans, who had gone to pieces early in the battle. He was relieved of his command and resigned from the army.

John McAllister Schofield, 1831– 1906; born Chautauqua County, N.Y. West Point class of 1853. While stationed at a St. Louis army post, John Schofield taught physics in his spare time. He was a brigadier general of volunteers, and commanded the Army of the Frontier in Missouri. More promotions followed. As a major general he commanded the Department of the Missouri; in 1864 he commanded the Army of the Ohio, one of three armies under Sherman in the Atlanta campaign. Schofield held off Hood's advance on Nashville, defeating him in the Battle of Franklin, then fighting in the Battle of Nashville under Thomas. He rejoined Sherman in North Carolina

William S. Rosecrans

David D. Porter

near the end of the war. He was Secretary of War in 1868–69, and in 1888 was made commanding general of the army.

Winfield Scott, 1786–1866; born Petersburg, Va. A law student before joining the army, Winfield Scott overcame early difficulties and fought in the War of 1812 at the battles of Queenstown, Fort George, Chippewa, and Lundy's Lane. He led the army in the Black Hawk War and the Florida Indian uprising of 1835. In 1841, Scott was appointed general-in-chief of the army. During the Mexican War, he personally led the army from Vera Cruz to Mexico City. Nominated by the Whigs for President in 1852, he was defeated by Franklin Pierce. Scott was the first soldier after Washington to be awarded the rank of lieutenant general. He was sixty-five when war came, but despite his age and almost crippled condition, he supervised recruiting and training and built up the Union armies, ignoring the attempts of the Confederates to lure him to his native South. He was pushed out of office by the young McClellan, and retired in October 1861.

John Sedgwick, 1813–1864; born Cornwall Hollow, Conn. West Point class of 1837. A veteran of the Seminole War, the Canadian border disputes, and the Mexican War, John Sedgwick was serving on the frontier when the war broke out. Promoted to brigadier general, he commanded a division in the Peninsula, where he was wounded. He was wounded again at Antietam. Known to his men as "Uncle John," Sedgwick commanded the forces attacking Fredericksburg during the Battle of Chancellorsville. He served with distinction at Gettysburg. Leading his corps, he was killed on May 9, 1864, in the fighting at Spotsylvania.

William Henry Seward, 1801–1872; born Florida, N.Y. A graduate of Union College, Seward settled in Auburn, New York, to practice law. He entered politics as a Whig, and after several terms in the state legislature he ran unsuccessfully for governor. Eight years later he was elected to the U.S. Senate, where he became known for opposing all compromise on slavery. Seward was the leading candidate for the Republican nomination in 1860, but lost to Lincoln. After the election, Lincoln chose Seward as his Secretary of State. At first, Seward tried to be a sort of "prime minister" in the administration, but grew to like and respect Lincoln and worked well with him. Early in 1865 he was badly injured in a carriage accident. While convalescing, he was stabbed by one of the conspirators on the night of Lincoln's assassination. He recovered to serve in the Johnson administration, and negotiated the purchase of Alaska.

Philip Henry Sheridan, 1831–1888; born Albany, N.Y. West Point class of 1853. In 1861 Sheridan was a captain on the frontier. He became a colonel of cavalry in May 1862, and after the fighting at Boonville, Missouri, he was promoted to brigadier general. One of the few successful commanders at Perryville and Stone's River, Sheridan was promoted and commanded a corps at Chickamauga and Missionary Ridge, drawing praise from Grant. When Grant went east, he gave Sheridan command of the cavalry of the Army of the Potomac, which he turned into a hard, fighting force. In 1864 he took command of the Army of the Shenandoah, driving the Confederates from the valley while laying waste to the countryside. At Cedar Creek, the last major battle in the Shenandoah, Sheridan made his famous "twenty-mile ride," arriving at a critical moment to turn the tide of battle. An aggressive, hard-fighting soldier, "Little Phil" Sheridan then moved from Winchester to Petersburg, destroying the countryside en route. In April 1865 he turned the Confederate flank at Petersburg, and triumphed at Five Forks. He participated in the final Appomattox campaign, later fought in the West, and in 1883 succeeded Sherman as commander-in-chief of the army.

William T. Sherman

William Tecumseh Sherman, 1820–1891; born Lancaster, Ohio. West Point class of 1840. After service in the Mexican War, William "Cump" Sherman resigned from the army and quickly failed in the banking business. He became superintendent of a military college that is now Louisiana State University. He was offered high rank in the Confederacy, but refused and for a time was president of a St. Louis street railway. Sherman rejoined the army and, after fighting well at First Bull Run, was sent to command in Kentucky. There his heavy responsibilities and nervous disposition led to his being relieved for mental instability. He was restored to command and fought with Grant at Shiloh. Commanding a corps at Vicksburg, Sherman at first opposed Grant's strategy, though he later recognized its brilliance. In the relief of Chattanooga in 1863, Sherman again fought under Grant at Missionary Ridge, and when Grant was called to Washington, he became commander in the West. Sherman captured Atlanta, then led the "march to the sea" to Savannah, cutting a swath of destruction across Georgia. He turned north into the Carolinas, burning Columbia, and fighting one of the last battles of the war at Bentonville. On April 17, 1865, he accepted the surrender of Joseph E. Johnston. When Grant became President, Sherman was appointed a full general and general-in-chief of the army, serving until his retirement in 1883. He was urged to run for President, but refused.

Edwin McMasters Stanton, 1814–1869; born Steubenville, Ohio. Forced by financial problems to drop out of college, Edwin Stanton read the law and was admitted to the bar in 1836. His practice grew as he moved first to Pittsburgh, then to Washington. President Buchanan appointed Stanton his Attorney General in 1860. A Democrat and a strong supporter of the Union, Stanton distrusted Lincoln and supported General McClellan. Lincoln named

Edwin M. Stanton

Stanton Secretary of War in 1862, in which post Stanton overhauled the War Department. He broke with McClellan and helped Lincoln find competent commanders. Although he made many enemies, Stanton was able to take much of the pressure off Lincoln. Stanton's treatment of Sherman at the end of the war was extremely harsh, and during the Johnson administration he intrigued with the "Black Republicans." His clashes with Johnson led to the President's impeachment. Stanton resigned when Johnson was exonerated. President Grant named him to the Supreme Court, but he died before taking the bench.

George Henry Thomas, 1816–1870; born Southampton County, Va. West Point class of 1840. Despite his Southern background, George Thomas stayed with the Union and his family never forgave him. He had served in Florida, Mexico and the West and was a major when war came. As a colonel he led a brigade in the Shenandoah, and in Kentucky won the small but important

George H. Thomas

explained, Wallace lost his way at Shiloh and his forces took little part in the battle. He defended Cincinnati in the Confederate 1862 campaign in Kentucky, and was rewarded with command of a corps. He held off Early in the Battle of the Monocacy, possibly saving Washington from capture. After the war he was governor of New Mexico and minister to Turkey, but he is best known for his writing, particularly his novel *Ben Hur*.

Gouverneur Kemble Warren, 1830–1882; born Cold Spring, N.Y. West Point class of 1850. An army engineer in the West, Gouverneur Warren served in the Peninsula and other early actions of the war. After Second Bull Run and Antietam, he was made a brigadier general. He fought at Fredericksburg and served briefly as chief engineer of the Army of the Potomac. At Gettysburg, upon discovering that the vital position of Little Round Top was undefended, he rounded up troops and held the position. Commanding a corps, he fought in the 1864 Virginia campaign. At Five Forks in April 1865, Warren was accused of slowness by Sheridan and removed from his command. He fought to clear his name for the rest of his life. A hearing in 1879 exonerated him for Five Forks, but the judgment wasn't handed down until after his death.

battle of Mill Springs on January 19, 1862. He became a major general in Buell's army, taking part in the advance on Corinth and the Kentucky campaign. Thomas fought well under Rosecrans at Murfreesboro. His finest hour came at Chickamauga, when he held the vital Snodgrass Hill against the victorious Confederates, earning the sobriquet "Rock of Chickamauga." Grant made Thomas commander of the Army of the Cumberland, and he led that force to victory at Missionary Ridge. Thomas moved with Sherman toward Atlanta, bearing the brunt of the Southern attack at Peachtree Creek. After the fall of Atlanta, Thomas and his forces were sent to defend Nashville against Hood, and he routed and almost destroyed Hood's army on December 15–16, 1864.

Lewis Wallace, 1827–1905; born Brookville, Ind. "Lew" Wallace was a volunteer officer in the Mexican War, and then practiced law in Crawfordsville, Indiana. In the Civil War he was a popular officer, rising to major general after the siege of Fort Donelson. For reasons never satisfactorily

James Harrison Wilson, 1837–1925; born Shawneetown, Ill. West Point class of 1860. After service in Virginia and in the Vicksburg campaign, James Wilson was made brigadier general of volunteers. He commanded a division in Sheridan's corps in the Army of the Potomac, fighting in the many battles that led up to Petersburg. As a brevet major general, he commanded the cavalry of the Military Division on the Mississippi. He fought well against Forrest in the Battle of Nashville and led the advance into Alabama, capturing Selma in April 1865. Despite his youth, he was considered one of the outstanding commanders of horse troops. He resigned from the army in 1870 to enter business, but came back to fight in Puerto Rico in the Spanish-American War, and later in the Boxer Rebellion in China.

CONFEDERATE LEADERS

Edward Porter Alexander, 1835–1910; born Washington, Ga. West Point class of 1857. As a teacher at West Point, Edward Alexander helped develop the "wigwag" signal flag system. After resigning his commission, he became a captain of engineers in the Confederate army in 1961, then was chief of ordnance in the Army of Northern Virginia, commanding artillery at Fredericksburg, Chancellorsville, and Gettysburg. In February 1864 he was made brigadier general and chief of artillery in Longstreet's corps, and took part in the Virginia campaign against Grant. Alexander was with Lee in the retreat to Appomattox.

Richard Heron Anderson, 1821–1879; born Statesburg, S.C. West Point class of 1842. A veteran of the Mexican War and the frontier, Robert Anderson resigned from the U.S. Army and became the commander of a South Carolina regiment at Fort Sumter. As a general he led brigades in the Peninsula campaign. Anderson commanded a division with Longstreet at Second Bull Run, and was wounded at the "Bloody Lane" at Antietam. He also fought at Fredericksburg, Chancellorsville, and Gettysburg. After Longstreet was seriously wounded in the Battle of the Wilderness, Anderson took over, fighting well at Spotsylvania. He commanded divisions for the remainder of the war.

Turner Ashby, 1828–1862; born Fauquier County, Va. A farmer and businessman, Ashby organized a company of horsemen that was made part of the Confederate Cavalry. He commanded a regiment with Stonewall Jackson at the battle of Kernstown, fought at Winchester, and helped pursue Union troops toward Harpers Ferry. Promoted to brigadier general, he covered the retreat of Jackson in the Shenandoah Valley. One of the South's early heroes, Ashby was killed near Harrisonburg on June 6, 1862.

Pierre Gustave Toutant Beauregard, 1818–1893; born New Orleans, La. West Point class of 1838. A dashing figure, known as "the Great Creole" and "Napoleon in Gray," P. G. T. Beauregard, a distinguished veteran of the Mexican War, directed the attack on Fort Sumter. With Joseph E. Johnston, he commanded at First Bull Run and was rewarded with promotion to full general. Sent to the West, he took command at Shiloh after Albert Sidney Johnston was killed. Beauregard did not get along with President Davis and was relieved from his command because of politics and illness. He was in charge of the defense of the South Atlantic coast until he took

Pierre G. T. Beauregard

over the defense of Petersburg in 1864. He bottled up Butler at Bermuda Hundred, holding Petersburg against Grant until Lee's forces arrived.

Judah Philip Benjamin, 1811–1884; born St. Thomas, British West Indies. Reared in Charleston and educated at Yale, Benjamin was a successful lawyer, businessman, and politician in New Orleans. He served in the Senate as a Whig, but became a Democrat, advocating secession after the election of Lincoln. President Davis appointed Benjamin Attorney General. He later became Secretary of War and received undeserved blame for Confederate failures. Appointed Secretary of State, in 1862 he served until the end of the war, then fled to England, where he built a very successful law practice.

Braxton Bragg, 1817–1876; born Warrenton, N.C. West Point class of 1837. An outstanding artillery officer in the Mexican War, Bragg resigned from the army in 1856 and became a Louisiana planter. As a Confederate, he was a rigid disciplinarian, unpopular with his officers and men. He commanded a corps at Shiloh. Promoted to full general in April 1862, he commanded the Army of Tennessee, invading Kentucky after holding Chattanooga, only to be defeated at Perryville. He commanded at Murfreesboro and during the Tullahoma and Chattanooga campaigns, winning a major victory at Chickamauga, then losing at Missionary Ridge. He turned over his command to Joseph E. Johnston in December 1863, and became a military adviser to Jefferson Davis.

John Cabell Breckinridge, 1821–1875; born Lexington, Ky. The scion of a distinguished family, Breckinridge graduated from Centre College in 1839 and practiced law in Kentucky. After service in the Mexican War, he entered Democratic politics and was elected to Congress. Breckinridge was elected Vice-President with

Judah P. Benjamin

Buchanan in 1856. After the breakup of the Democratic Party, Breckinridge was the presidential candidate of the Southern Democrats in 1860. Elected to the Senate, he worked for a compromise to avoid war, although he opposed the coercion of states by the federal government. In October 1861 he resigned to serve in the Confederate army at Shiloh, Murfreesboro, Chicamauga, Missionary Ridge, the Shenandoah Valley, and Cold Harbor, rising to major general. Breckinridge was appointed Secretary of War on February 4, 1865. At the end of the war he escaped to Cuba, then went to Europe.

Franklin Buchanan, 1800–1874; born Baltimore, Md. A navy midshipman at fifteen, Franklin Buchanan helped found the Naval Academy at Annapolis in 1845 and became its first superintendent. He returned to active duty in the Mexican War and was with Commodore Perry on the expedition to Japan in 1853. At the outbreak of the war he resigned his commission and became a captain in the Confederate navy. He commanded the CSS *Virginia,* the ironclad constructed from the old USS *Merrimac,* and destroyed two Union vessels in

Hampton Roads on March 8, 1862. Buchanan was wounded in the engagement and turned over his command to Lt. Catesby Jones, who fought the Federal ironclad *Monitor* to a draw. Promoted to admiral, he commanded the Confederate squadron at Mobile Bay.

Simon Bolivar Buckner, 1823–1914; born Munfordville, Ky. West Point class of 1844. After service in the Mexican War, Buckner became a successful businessman. When war came, he refused commissions in both armies, but with the abandonment of Kentucky neutrality he joined the Confederate forces. He was third in command at Fort Donelson when Grant attacked, surrendering the fort when his superiors fled. After some months in prison, he was exchanged and took part in Bragg's invasion of Kentucky. He fought in East Tennessee, at Chickamauga, and in Louisiana, rising to lieutenant general. He was governor of Kentucky after the war.

Patrick Ronayne Cleburne, 1828–1864; born County Cork, Ireland. A veteran of the British army, Cleburne came to the United States in 1849 and settled in Helena, Arkansas, becoming first a drug-

Simon B. Buckner

WHAT'S IN A NAME

Many battles were given different names by the Union and the Confederate forces. The Union tended to name a battle after the nearest landmark, usually a river or stream (Bull Run); the Confederacy after the nearest town (Manassas). In the North, Sharpsburg was known as Antietam. Stone's River was known in the South as Murfreesboro; Opequon Creek was called Winchester. The South named one battle Shiloh from a church that was near where the Confederates attacked; to the Union it was Pittsburg Landing, because that was where Grant's troops were encamped.

gist, then a lawyer. He organized the Yell Rifles in 1860, and upon the secession of Arkansas he was made a captain. By early 1862, Cleburne was a brigadier general and served at Shiloh and Perryville. He was promoted to major general and distinguished himself at Murfreesboro and Chickamauga, and against Sherman at Missionary Ridge. He was with Johnston in the retreat to Atlanta, and with Hood in the Battle of Atlanta. He was killed at the Battle of Franklin. Cleburne urged that the slaves be freed and used in the army, an opinion that may have kept him from higher command. Loved and respected by his officers and men, Cleburne was called "the Stonewall Jackson of the West."

Samuel Cooper, 1798–1876; born Hackensack, N.J. West Point class of 1815. After staff duties in the Mexican War, Cooper was promoted to colonel and made adjutant general of the army. Although born in the North, Cooper married a Virginia woman and had many Southern friends. At the outbreak of war, he resigned and offered his services to his close friend Jefferson Davis. He was made a full general and appointed inspector general of the Confederate army. Despite outranking all the other Confederate officers by seniority, Cooper made no tangible impression on the conduct of the war.

Jefferson Finis Davis, 1808–1889; born Christian County, Ky. West Point class of 1828. A veteran of the Black Hawk War and service on the frontier, Jefferson resigned from the army when he married Sarah Knox Taylor, daughter of Zachary Taylor. His wife died in 1835, and he was in semi-seclusion for ten years as a slave-owning planter in Mississippi. He remarried in 1845 and was elected to the U.S. House of Representatives as a States Rights Democrat. After resigning in 1846, he served with distinction in the Mexican War. He was in the U.S. Senate from 1847 to 1851, then ran unsuccessfully for governor of Mississippi in 1851. From 1853 to 1857, Davis was Secretary of War under Franklin Pierce, then returned to the Senate. A gifted debater, Davis defended slavery and the right of a state to secede. Following the election of Lincoln, he announced Mississippi's withdrawal from the Union. He hoped to be given command of the Southern armies, but instead was elected President. Davis was criticized for interfering with his generals and appointing incompetents to government posts, yet he kept the Confederacy in the fight for four years. He personally never surrendered, and was captured near Irwinville, Georgia, on May 10, 1865. He was imprisoned at Fort Monroe for two years. After retiring in 1879 to Biloxi, Mississippi, he wrote his defense of the South and the Confederacy, *The Rise and Fall of the Confederate Government.*

Jefferson Davis

Jubal Anderson Early, 1816–1894; born Franklin County, Va. West Point class of 1837. After the Seminole War, Early resigned from the army and practiced law at Rocky Mount, Virginia, later serving in the state legislature. Early opposed secession, but entered the Confederate army and was a colonel at First Bull Run. Commanding a division in 1862 and a corps in 1864, he campaigned in the Shenandoah Valley, and his small force entered the suburbs of Washington. Driven off, Early retreated into Virginia, where he was defeated by Sheridan at Winchester and Fisher's Hill. Early attacked Sheridan at Cedar Creek, but Sheridan arrived in time to turn the tide of battle.

Richard Stoddert Ewell, 1817–1872; born Washington, D.C. West Point class of 1840. A Mexican War veteran, Richard Ewell resigned to become a brigadier general in the Confederate forces. He fought at First Bull Run and was promoted to major general. Commanding a division under Jackson, Ewell fought in the Shenandoah Valley and in the Seven Days campaign. During Second Bull Run he was wounded and lost a leg. Upon returning to duty, he commanded a corps and led Lee's advance into Pennsylvania. He was criticized for his failure on the Confederate left at Gettysburg. His corps was in some of the heaviest fighting at the Wilderness and at Spotsylvania. His last command was at Richmond, the remnant of his forces surrendering at Sayler's Creek.

Nathan Bedford Forrest, 1821–1877; born Bedford County, Tenn. The sole support of a large family, Nathan Forrest had little education, but became rich through land purchases and dealing in slaves in Memphis. He enlisted as a private and became an officer by equipping a mounted battalion at his own expense. As a lieutenant colonel he managed to escape from the surrounded Fort Donelson. He fought at Shiloh, and in 1862 began a series of daring cavalry raids that made him famous. Union forces tracked Forrest for the rest of the war, but every time they caught up with him they were defeated. A man of great courage and violent temper, his military ability bordered on genius. After the Nashville campaign, he was promoted to lieutenant general. Forrest is credited with the statement that the one who "gits there furstest with the mostest" is victorious.

John Brown Gordon, 1832–1904; born Upson County, Ga. Although he reached the rank of lieutenant general, John Gordon is best remembered for his service after the war. He attended the University of Georgia and later was a lawyer and a businessman. When war came, he had no military experience and served in lower command until he was named brigadier general in November 1863. He served in the Seven Days campaign and at Chancellorsville, Gettysburg, the Wilderness, and Spotsylvania, and commanded a corps in the Petersburg-Appomattox campaign. After the war he was governor of Georgia and a U.S. senator for three terms. He was commander of the United Confederate Vet-

Nathan B. Forrest

erans from its inception in 1890 until his death. Gordon was deeply involved in reconstruction, and was one of Georgia's most honored sons.

Wade Hampton, 1818–1902; born Charleston, S.C. From a distinguished family, Hampton was a natural leader, both in war and politics. He was a planter after college, serving in the state legislature and opposing secession in 1860. At his own expense he organized what was known as "Hampton's Legion" and led it at First Bull Run. He was made a brigadier general and commanded a brigade on the Peninsula. He took part in most of the movements of Jeb Stuart. After Stuart's death in 1864, Hampton commanded the cavalry corps of the Army of Northern Virginia.

William Joseph Hardee, 1815–1875; born Camden County, Ga. West Point class of 1838. After the Mexican War, Hardee wrote the influential manual *Rifle and Light Infantry Tactics,* known as "Hardee's Tactics." A lieutenant colonel when war came, he joined the Confederate army and by June 1861 was a brigadier general in Arkansas. He fought at Shiloh, Perryville, Murfreesboro, Missionary Ridge, and in the Atlanta campaign. As a lieutenant general he commanded forces against Sherman in South Carolina, Georgia, and Florida.

Ambrose P. Hill

Ambrose Powell Hill, 1825–1865; born Culpeper, Va. West Point class of 1847. A veteran of the Mexican War and the frontier, A. P. Hill joined the Confederate army as a colonel of infantry, and was a major general by May 1862. He commanded the left of the Confederate line in the opening of the Seven Days, and fought at Second Bull Run. One of Hill's brilliant actions was to bring his division into the fight at Antietam just in time to stem the Union advance. He fought at Fredericksburg and Chancellorsville, and from May 1863 he commanded a corps as a lieutenant general. He fought at Gettysburg, the Wilderness, and the siege of Petersburg. One of the South's most brilliant commanders, A. P. Hill was killed in the retreat from Petersburg on April 2, 1865.

Daniel Harvey Hill, 1821–1889; born York District, S.C. West Point class of 1842. After fighting in Mexico, Daniel Hill resigned to teach. He joined the Confederate army as a colonel, led a division during the Seven Days, and commanded at South Mountain. He defended Richmond in the spring of 1863, then was sent to the Army of Tennessee as a lieutenant general. Hill had difficulties with Bragg and President Davis, and his only later command was a small division at Bentonville. After the war he was a writer and educator.

John Bell Hood, 1831–1879; born Owingsville, Ky. West Point class of 1853. A veteran of the frontier, John Hood resigned in April 1861 to become a Confederate lieutenant. He was a brigadier general by March 1862, however, and took command of the Texas Brigade, leading it at Gaines' Mill, Second Bull Run, and Antietam. Hood led a division at Gettysburg, where he was wounded in the arm. He was wounded again at Chickamauga and lost his right leg. Hood commanded a corps under Johnston in the fighting before Atlanta, then replaced him when Johnston fell out of favor with President Davis. Hood was rash, and he lost the fight for Atlanta. Leading his army back into Tennessee, he was outmarched at Spring Hill, beaten at Franklin, and again at Nashville. His army was nearly destroyed.

John B. Hood

Thomas Jonathan Jackson, 1824–1863; born Clarksburg, Va. (now West Virginia). West Point class of 1846. After serving with distinction in Mexico, Thomas Jackson left the army in 1851 to teach at Virginia Military Institute. Although opposed to civil war, he was made a brigadier general in June 1861. At First Bull Run, where his troops stood firm, General Barnard Bee said, "There is Jackson, standing like a stone wall." The name stuck, and it was as "Stonewall" Jackson that he marched to fame. He made his reputation in the Shenandoah Valley in the summer of 1862, fighting, retreating, and advancing in one of the most brilliant campaigns in American military history. Jackson was secretive, somewhat eccentric, and at his

Joseph E. Johnston

Thomas "Stonewall" Jackson

best in independent command, where he could move freely and rapidly, striking hard when he chose to strike. This ability showed at Second Bull Run and at Antietam. Jackson's greatest triumph was Chancellorsville. Detached from Lee, he swung around the entire Union force to deliver the crushing blow. That night he was mistakenly shot by his own men and died of pneumonia eight days later, on May 10, 1863. It was an immeasurable loss to the Confederacy. Lee rightly said, "I know not how to replace him."

Joseph Eggleston Johnston, 1807–1891; born Prince Edward County, Va. West Point class of 1829. After eight years of service, Joseph Johnston resigned from the army to become a civil engineer. He rejoined at the start of the Mexican War, and by 1860 he was quartermaster general. As a Confederate, he was with Beauregard at First Bull Run. In August 1861 he was made a full general in command in northern Virginia. In the retreat up the Peninsula, he was wounded at Seven Pines in front of Richmond, and replaced by Lee. Johnston did not get along with President Davis, to the detriment of his career. Placed in nominal command in the West, he tried unsuccessfully to relieve General Pemberton at Vicksburg. He took command of the Army of Tennessee south of Chattanooga and began a masterful retreat toward Atlanta, trying to lure Sherman into a trap. Johnston was relieved for having failed to attack or halt Sherman. He resumed control of the doomed Army of Tennessee in February 1865, surrendering to Sherman on April 26.

Fitzhugh Lee, 1835–1905; born Fairfax County, Va. West Point class of 1856. A nephew of Robert E. Lee, Fitzhugh Lee saw duty in the West before resigning to join the Confederacy. He was a staff officer and a lieutenant colonel of cavalry before being promoted to brigadier general in July 1863. He led a number of cavalry raids, commanded at Kelly's Ford, and fought at Chancellorsville. Lee fought in the 1864 Virginia campaign, later serving with Early in the Shenandoah. Late in the war, he commanded the cavalry of the Army of Northern Virginia. He was governor of Virginia after the war, and commanded a corps in the Spanish-American War.

Robert Edward Lee, 1807–1870; born Westmoreland County, Va. West Point class of 1829. The son of Revolutionary War hero "Light Horse Harry" Lee, Robert E. Lee combined military life with the active social life of a Virginia gentleman. In 1831 he married Mary Ann Randolph Custis, great-granddaughter of Martha Washington, with whom he would have seven children. He had a distinguished record as a captain in the Mexican War, and later was superintendent of West Point. Stationed in Washington in 1859, he commanded the troops that captured John Brown during his raid on Harpers Ferry. Lee freed his slaves and disassociated himself from Southern extremists. He declined the command of the U.S. Army, and resigned his commission when Virginia seceded. At first he was a military adviser to President Davis. When Joseph E. Johnston was wounded on May 31, 1862, Lee took command of what would become the Army of Northern Virginia. He launched the Seven Days campaign, pushing McClellan back from Richmond. He moved rapidly to victory at Second Bull Run, then invaded Maryland, only to be halted at Antietam. He defeated Burnside at Fredericksburg, and Hooker at Chancellorsville. Once again he launched an invasion of the north and was beaten by Meade at Gettysburg. Lee fought Grant at the Wilderness, Spotsylvania, North Anna, and Cold Harbor in a desperate campaign for survival. Until the war was nearly over, both armies were in action around Petersburg. Although the appointment was opposed by Davis, Lee was made general-in-chief of all Confederate forces in February 1865, too late to affect the course of the war. Forced out of Petersburg in April, Lee retreated toward Appomattox in the hope of joining forces with Johnston. He surrendered at Appomattox. After the war he was president of Washington College in Lexington, Virginia (now Washington and Lee University). A splendid gentleman, a great general, an inspiration to his troops—like Lincoln, Lee became a legend.

Stephen Dill Lee, 1833–1908; born Charleston, S.C. West Point class of 1854. Coming to the Confederate army from service in the West, Stephen Lee saw action with artillery commands at Fort Sumter, the Peninsula campaign, Second Bull Run, and Antietam. He fought at Vicksburg, and in June 1864 he became the youngest Confederate lieutenant general. He fought at Tupelo and in the Atlanta and Nashville campaigns.

Robert E. Lee

James Longstreet

James Longstreet, 1821–1904; born Edgefield District, S.C. West Point class of 1842. A veteran of the Mexican War, Longstreet was a major in the paymaster's office when war came. Commissioned a brigadier general, he became a major general after First Bull Run. He fought throughout the Peninsula campaign and commanded half of the Army of Northern Virginia at Second Bull Run. After service at Antietam, he became a lieutenant general. Longstreet's corps was in the defense of Fredericksburg, and following the death of Jackson he was Lee's principal lieutenant. At Gettysburg he was charged with disagreeing with Lee's plans and delaying their execution. Sent to Georgia, he was with Bragg at Chickamauga, but failed to capture Knoxville in an independent campaign. Returning to Virginia, Longstreet was severely wounded in the Wilderness, but recovered and fought until the end of the war. Longstreet became a Republican and was active in politics, alienating many Southerners.

John Bankhead Magruder, 1810–1871; Port Royal, Va. When war came, Magruder entered the Confederate army as a colonel. After the battle of Big Bethel he was promoted to brigadier general. Defending Yorktown in the spring of 1862 with 12,000 men, Magruder fooled McClellan and his huge army. Magruder's performance in the Seven Days disappointed Lee, and he was sent to command in the District of Texas. In January 1863 he captured Galveston. A very social man with a quick temper, Magruder was known as "Prince John."

William Mahone, 1826–1895; born Southampton County, Va. An 1847 graduate of Virginia Military Institute, was an engineer in the railroad business. In the war he first commanded the Norfolk District as a colonel, then joined the Army of Northern Virginia, becoming a brigadier general. After capably defending the crater at Petersburg, he was promoted to major general. Following the war, he built a powerful Republican machine in Virginia and served as a U.S. senator.

Stephen Russell Mallory, 1813–1873; born Trinidad, British West Indies. Growing up in Key West, Florida, Stephen Mallory had only a modest education, but became a lawyer. He was first elected to the U.S. Senate in 1851, and in his second term became chairman of the Naval Affairs Committee. When Florida seceded, he resigned to become Secretary of the Navy of the Confederacy. There was no navy, so he set out to create one. He obtained vessels in England, procured commerce raiders, and developed ironclads, showing ingenuity and administrative ability in a difficult assignment. He was one of the very few Confederate leaders who didn't clash with President Davis.

John Hunt Morgan, 1825–1864; born Huntsville, Ala. After service in Mexico, John Morgan became a successful businessman. He joined the Confederate army as a scout, and soon was made a captain. In 1862 he began the series of famous raids that earned him the title "Morgan the Raider." As a reward for capturing a Federal force at Hartsville, Tennessee, he was promoted to brigadier general. In July 1863, Morgan crossed the Ohio and rampaged through southern Indiana, reaching beyond Cincinnati. His men exhausted, Morgan surrendered near New Lisbon, Ohio. He escaped from the Ohio Penitentiary at Columbus and made his way to Virginia, where he was given a command. On September 3, 1864, he was killed by Federal troops at Greenville, Tennessee.

John Singleton Mosby, 1833–1916; born Edgemont, Va. A lawyer, Mosby enlisted in the cavalry, and soon was a lieutenant operating as a scout. He was on Jeb Stuart's staff during the Peninsula campaign and at Second Bull Run and Antietam. In early 1863 he began independent operations with a few troops in Loudoun County, Virginia, and his raids against Federal outposts were successful. On March 9, 1863, he captured General Stoughton in bed at Fairfax Court House and was rewarded by promotion to captain. He later became a colonel, but refused command assignments and continued to lead his Partisan Rangers. Mosby became a Republican and practiced law after the war. An admirer of Grant, he held several government posts.

John Clifford Pemberton, 1814–1881; born Philadelphia, Pa. West Point class of 1837. A veteran of fighting in Florida, Mexico, and the West, John Pemberton was a career soldier married to a Virginia woman. Despite his Northern upbringing, he joined the Confederacy. As a major general he commanded in South Carolina, Georgia, and Florida. President Davis ordered Pemberton to hold Vicksburg at all costs. Later, Joseph E. Johnston told him to evacuate Vicksburg. Faced with conflicting orders and an intolerable military situation, Pemberton retreated into the city and was besieged by Grant. When defeat became inevitable, Pemberton surrendered on July 4, 1863. He resigned his general's commission and fought as a lieutenant colonel of artillery for the rest of the war.

George E. Pickett

George Edward Pickett, 1825–1875; born Richmond, Va. West Point class of 1846. Last in his class at West Point, George Pickett was sent to Mexico upon graduation. He resigned at the start of the war, and became a Confederate brigadier general in 1862. He was wounded during the Seven Days, but won notice for his daring. He commanded a division at Fredericksburg and in the Suffolk campaign. He became legend on July 3, 1863, when he led his division in a fearless attack on the center of the Union line, only to be repulsed in bloody defeat. Pickett's Charge ended the battle of Gettysburg. He later commanded the Department of Virginia and North Carolina. He bore the brunt of the main attack at Five Forks, near Richmond, in April 1865, and was relieved of his command for alleged dereliction of duty.

Leonidas Polk, 1806–1864; born Raleigh, N.C. West Point class of 1827. Resigning his commission to study theology, Leonidas Polk became a Protestant Episcopal priest, and in 1838 was made the Bishop of Louisiana. In 1860 he founded the University of the South at Sewanee, Tennessee. Polk accepted President Davis's offer of a major generalcy in June 1861. He fortified Columbus, Kentucky, and served under Johnston defending the Mississippi.

He was a corps commander at Belmont and Shiloh, in the invasion of Kentucky, at Perryville, and at Murfreesboro. He had difficulties with Bragg and was criticized for being slow in attacking at Chickamauga. Polk was killed in the battle of Pine Mountain, near Marietta, Georgia.

Sterling Price, 1809–1867; born Prince George County, Va. A lawyer, Sterling Price went to Missouri and entered politics. After several state legislative positions, he was elected to the U.S. Congress in 1844 but resigned to serve in the Mexican War, rising to brigadier general of volunteers. He was governor of Missouri from 1852 to 1856. Price leaned toward the Union at the start of the war, but became so incensed at the actions of local Unionists that he joined the Confederates. He served with the Missouri State Guard and fought at Wilson's Creek. Price captured Lexington, Missouri, and retreated into Arkansas, fighting at Pea Ridge. Promoted to major general, he fought at Iuka and Corinth, Mississippi, and defeated the Union troops headed for the Red River in 1864.

William Clarke Quantrill, 1837–1865; born Canal Dover, Ohio. A schoolteacher, Quantrill went to Kansas in 1857 and worked on wagon trains. He later lived near Lawrence, Kansas, where he was known as Charley Hart. An unsavory character, he was a gambler, a horse thief, and probably a murderer. At the start of the war he organized a group of guerrillas who robbed and pillaged in Missouri and Kansas. The North declared Quantrill and his gang outlaws in 1862. He and his men then joined the regular Confederate army, in which he became a captain. On August 21, 1862, Quantrill sacked Lawrence, Kansas, killing some 150 men and burning part of the town. Dissension broke up the gang in 1864, and Quantrill was fatally wounded in May 1865 by Federal troops in Taylorsville, Kentucky, while on a robbing and foraging expedition.

James Alexander Seddon, 1815–1880; born Fredericksburg, Va. A successful lawyer in Richmond, James Seddon served two terms as a congressman and was active in Virginia social life. When war came, he was elected to the Confederate Congress, then replaced George Randolph as Secretary of War in November 1862. Seddon had no military experience, but he was a skilled politician with administrative ability, and he wielded considerable influence. After several quarrels with the Confederate Congress, he resigned early in 1865.

Raphael Semmes, 1809–1877; born Charles County, Md. Appointed a midshipman in 1826, Raphael Semmes studied and practiced law in Maryland and Ohio on leave from the navy. He was a naval aide to the army during the Mexican War. A commander when war came, Semmes resigned to accept the same rank in the Confederate navy. He took command of the commerce raider CSS *Sumter* and harried Union commerce until his ship was blockaded in Gibraltar. He then went to England and took command of the *Alabama,* which had been built there for the Confederacy. He sank the USS *Hatteras* off Galveston in January 1863. The *Alabama* was at Cherbourg, France, when the USS *Kearsarge* appeared and destroyed her after a spirited fight. Semmes was promoted to rear admiral in February 1865, and commanded the James River Squadron. As a raider, Semmes captured a total of eighty-two Union merchant vessels valued at more than $6 million.

John Slidell, 1793–1871; born New York, N.Y. A Columbia graduate, John Slidell failed in business in New York before moving to New Orleans to practice law. An active Democrat, he was Commissioner to Mexico in 1845 and served in the Senate from 1853 to 1861. After the election of Lincoln, he resigned and was appointed Confederate Commissioner to France. Slidell and James M. Mason, Commissioner to England, were taken off the British steamer *Trent* by the Union navy and detained in Boston. They were released after the incident threatened to rupture relations between Britain and the United States. Slidell was unsuccessful in winning recognition of the Confederacy by Napoleon III but did arrange for loans and the construction of ships in French yards.

Edmund Kirby Smith, 1824–1893; born St. Augustine, Fla. West Point class of 1845. After service in Mexico and on the frontier, Kirby Smith resigned to join the Confederate army. He was a brigadier general when he was wounded at First Bull Run, and he was with Bragg in the 1862 invasion of Kentucky. Smith commanded the Trans-Mississippi Department, which became known as the "Kirby Smithdom." He turned back the Union's Red River campaign in April 1864. Smith surrendered the last major Confederate force on June 2, 1865. After the war he was chancellor of the University of Nashville.

Alexander Hamilton Stephens, 1812–1883; born Wilkes County, Ga. After graduating first in his class at the University of Georgia, Alexander Stephens taught school before beginning the practice of law. He served in the Georgia legislature and was elected to the U.S. Congress as a Whig in 1843. Known as "Little Aleck," Stephens was a slight, emaciated-looking man with feeble health. Although he had a shrill voice, he was a persuasive speaker. He upheld the right of a state to secede, opposed the centralization of government, and defended slavery as being best for the blacks.

AT WHAT PRICE?

More Union and Confederate soldiers perished in the Civil War than in all the nation's other wars put together, including Vietnam.

Having retired from Congress in 1859, he urged moderation in the 1860 secession crisis. Stephens was named Confederate Vice-President, but became disenchanted with President Davis and his appointments. In February 1865, Stephens led an official delegation that talked with Lincoln at Fortress Monroe, but could not negotiate an armistice. He was arrested at the end of the war and held prisoner until October 1865. Elected to the Senate in 1866, Stephens was not allowed to serve. He later did serve in the House of Representatives.

Alexander Peter Stewart, 1821–1908; born Rogersville, Tex. West Point class of 1842. Known as "Old Straight," Stewart resigned from the army in 1845 to teach mathematics and philosophy. He was a Whig and opposed secession, but joined the Confederate army as a major. He fought at Belmont and was a brigadier general at Shiloh. After fighting at Chattanooga and Chickamauga and in the Atlanta campaign, he was a lieutenant general commanding a corps. Stewart finished the war with the Army of Tennessee, and later was chancellor of the University of Mississippi.

James Ewell Brown Stuart, 1833–1864; born Patrick County, Va. West Point class of 1854. After serving with the cavalry in Texas and Kansas, J. E. B. Stuart, known as "Jeb," resigned to become a colonel of the First Virginia Cavalry. He was made a brigadier general after First Bull Run. In the Peninsula campaign, Stuart led his troops on a ride around McClellan's entire army. He was at Second Manassas and Antietam under Lee, who considered Stuart the eyes of his army. Stuart temporarily commanded Jackson's corps after the latter was killed at Chancellorsville. At the battle of Gettysburg, he left Lee and toured around Meade's army, not returning until the second day of the battle, and his absence affected Lee adversely. Stuart covered Lee's operation in the Wilderness. On May 9, 1864, Stuart fought Sheridan's cav-

James E. B. "Jeb" Stuart

alry at Yellow Tavern, north of Richmond. Two days later he was wounded and died the next day.

Richard Taylor, 1826–1879; born Louisville, Ky. The only son of Zachary Taylor, Richard Taylor graduated from Yale in 1845 and started a plantation in Louisiana. When war broke out, he became a colonel of infantry, serving under Jackson in the Shenandoah Valley and during the Seven Days. Promoted to general, Taylor commanded the district of West Louisiana, halting Banks's Red River campaign in April 1864. For this victory, Taylor was given command of the Department of East Louisiana, Mississippi and Alabama. On May 4, 1865, Taylor surrendered the last Confederate force east of the Mississippi.

Robert Augustus Toombs, 1810–1885; born Wilkes County, Ga. Toombs began the practice of law in 1830, and entered politics. He served in the state legislature and went to the U.S. Congress in 1844 as a Whig, where he was a leading defender of the South. Elected to the Senate, he became a Democrat. He believed the election of Lincoln made secession imperative. He left the Senate with the hope of becoming the President of the Confederacy. He was made Secretary of State, but quickly broke with Davis, and in July 1861 he commanded a Georgia brigade in Virginia. He was a "political" general, and often antagonized his superiors. Passed over for promotion after Antietam, he resigned.

Earl Van Dorn, 1820–1863; born Port Gibson, Miss. West Point class of 1842. After service in Florida, Mexico, and the West, Earl Van Dorn resigned the U.S. Army and became a colonel in the Confederate army. Serving in Texas, he was made a major general and later commanded the Trans-Mississippi. Defeated at Pea Ridge, he crossed the Mississippi River, only to be beaten at Corinth, Mississippi. In December 1862, Van Dorn led a brilliant raid on the Federal supply depot at Holly Springs, Mississippi. He was shot dead by a jealous husband in 1863.

Joseph Wheeler, 1836–1906; born Augusta, Ga. West Point class of 1859. Joseph Wheeler joined the Confederate army as a lieutenant, and soon became an infantry colonel. He fought at Shiloh, was given a brigade, then took over the cavalry of the Army of the Mississippi in July 1862. As a general, he led the western cavalry ably through the Kentucky campaign, Murfreesboro, Chickamauga, and Chattanooga. He led a number of raids around Atlanta, and attempted to oppose Sherman's march to the sea. "Fighting Joe" Wheeler was a twenty-eight-year-old hero at war's end, ranking with Stuart and Forrest as one of the great Southern cavalry leaders. He became a merchant, served in Congress, and was a major general of volunteers in the Spanish-American War, fighting in Cuba and the Philippines.

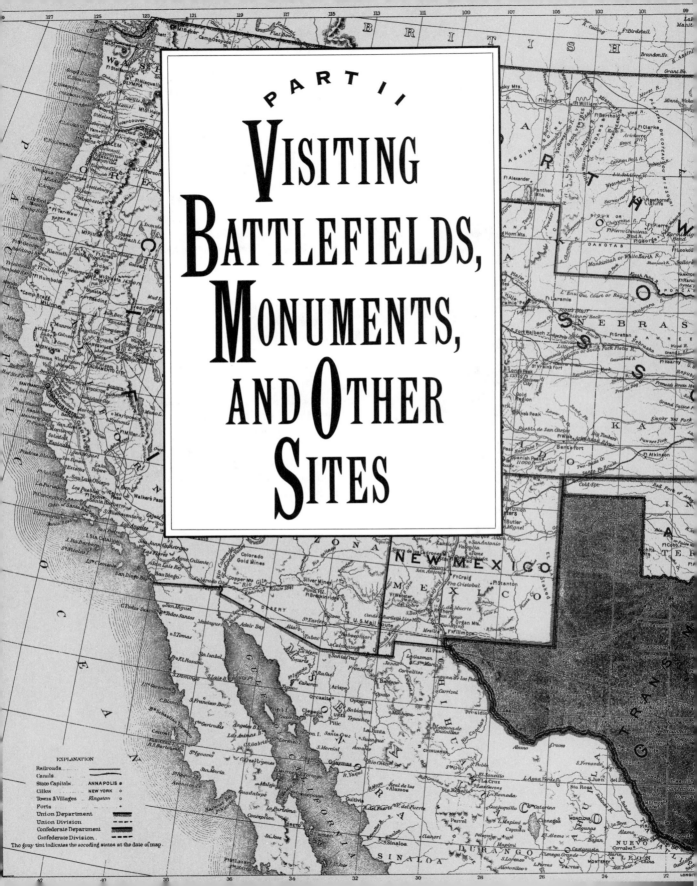

PART II

VISITING BATTLEFIELDS, MONUMENTS, AND OTHER SITES

MAP
OF THE
UNITED STATES
OF AMERICA
SHOWING THE
BOUNDARIES
OF THE
UNION and CONFEDERATE
GEOGRAPHICAL DIVISIONS
AND
DEPARTMENTS,
APRIL 9, 1865.

✳ On April 9, 1865, the Army of the Potomac (MEADE) and the
Army of Northern Virginia (LEE) were operating in the
vicinity of Appomattox Court-House, Virginia.

✵ SHERMAN'S Army was en route from Goldsborough toward
Raleigh N.C., confronted by the Army of Tennessee and
other forces under JOHNSTON.

Stonewall Jackson Monument, Manassas, Virginia

VISITING NATIONAL BATTLEFIELD PARKS

The national military parks, sites, monuments, and memorials relating to the Civil War described in this book are part of the National Park Service, which has the responsibility of preserving America's historic heritage. Visiting them will be more enjoyable and informative if you know some things about the Park Service and how it administers military parks and other historic properties.

All National Park Service properties charge entrance fees, although most are free to anyone under sixteen and over sixty-two. Call ahead to the park if fees are a concern. There are several special passes to those who qualify. An annual entrance permit—the Golden Eagle Pass—may be purchased for $25 at any Park Service property. Persons sixty-two and older are entitled to a free lifetime entrance permit, the Golden Age Passport. Persons who are eligible for federal benefits as a result of a physical disability may obtain the Golden Access Passport. Entrance fees are waived for holders of Golden Eagle Pass and the Golden Age and Golden Access Passports and for anyone accompanying the holder in a noncommercial vehicle. More information on these annual passports may be obtained from the National Park Service in Washington, D.C., phone (202) 343-4747.

Park Service properties usually are open daily, except Christmas, New Year's Day, and some exceptions noted in the individual descriptions. At the military parks there are visitor centers where park rangers are available to answer questions. Exhibits in each center describe the historical importance of the park. In the larger parks there are audiovisual presentations to indoctrinate visitors before touring. If time permits, you should see the presentations; they can help the parks come alive for you.

Free brochures available at the visitor center describe the park and the events that occurred there, and contain a detailed map. Some parks offer ranger-led tours; others have self-guided tours, which are shown on the map; still others offer a choice. At some parks visitors may rent tape players with recorded tour descriptions. The ranger at the visitor center information desk will tell you about the tour, how long it takes, whether it is strenuous, and if it is accessible by wheelchair. Brochures on the parks you plan to visit are available without charge by writing to: National Park Service, Office of Public Information, Department of Interior, Washington, DC 20240.

Living history demonstrations are presented at many of the military parks. The schedules of these demonstrations may be obtained by phoning the park. The park's telephone number is included in its description.

Other facilities at park visitor centers include parking, washrooms, drinking fountains, telephones, first aid, and gift shops offering books and other material relating to the park. All National Park Service visitor centers are accessible to wheelchairs.

Neither food facilities nor accommodations are available in any of the National Park Service properties described here. Almost all have picnic areas, though, and a picnic at a military park can be delightful. The locations of nearby restaurants and overnight accommodations are included in the individual descriptions.

There are a few rules for visitors to military parks. Alcoholic beverages are not permitted, nor is the use of metal detectors. Obey the speed limit on park roads, and park only in designated areas. Be particularly careful where park roads cross other public roads. If you picnic, clean up after yourselves. Don't climb on statues, fences, or battlements. Stay on the marked trails. Take only photographs, leave only footprints. And if in doubt, ask a ranger first.

~ 3 ~

THE WAR IN VIRGINIA

VIRGINIA

APPOMATTOX

APPOMATTOX COURT HOUSE NATIONAL HISTORICAL PARK

The end of the line for Robert E. Lee and the Army of Northern Virginia came on Palm Sunday 1865, in this sleepy little village, ninety-two miles west of Richmond. Although his surrender to Ulysses S. Grant did not end the war, it might as well have. Richmond had fallen; Jefferson Davis and his government were on the run; in North Carolina, Sherman was closing in on Johnston's army. The South despaired as spontaneous celebrations broke out in the North.

When Grant broke through the Confederate defenses at Petersburg and captured Richmond, Lee's scattered army numbered only 35,000. They rendezvoused at Amelia Courthouse, Lee's plan being to follow the railroad to Danville to link up with Johnston. A trainload of supplies for Lee hadn't arrived, so he allowed his troops to forage for food for a day. While they searched for food, Sheridan's cavalry cut the railroad. Lee marched wearily for Lynchburg, with Grant in hot pursuit.

At the Battle of Sayler's Creek, on April 6, Sheridan's corps cut off a quarter of Lee's army, capturing 7,000 men and a wagon train. The next day, Grant sent Lee a note asking him to surrender. Lee's reply was vague, and Grant felt that Lee meant to fight.

The next day, Lee clashed with Sheridan's cavalry near Appomattox Station. Breaking through, Lee was met by two corps of Union infantry. As they prepared for attack, a horseman galloped between the lines, waving a white flag and carrying a message from Lee to Grant. Lee decided, "There was nothing left for me to do but go and see General Grant, and I would rather die a thousand deaths."

On Sunday morning, April 9, 1865, Lee was waiting in the parlor of the Wilmer McLean House when Grant rode up. They quickly agreed on the terms of surrender. Confederate officers would retain their sidearms and baggage; officers and men could keep their horses; finally, in Grant's

ON THE HIGH SEAS

The *Shenandoah*, a Confederate cruiser, sailed completely around the world, raiding Union merchant ships and whalers. The ship was surrendered to British authorities at Liverpool in November 1865, seven months after Appomattox.

words, "each officer and man will be allowed to return to his home, not to be disturbed by the United States authorities. . . ."

Grant later wrote, "I felt . . . sad and depressed at the downfall of a foe who had fought so long and valiantly, and had suffered so much for a cause, though that cause was, I believe, one of the worst for which a people ever fought."

After the surrender, Union batteries began to fire salutes. Grant ordered them stopped. "The war is over," he said, "the rebels are our countrymen again, and the best sign of rejoicing after the victory will be to abstain from all demonstrations." Grant ordered three days of rations sent to feed Lee's half-starved troops.

A formal ceremony was held three days later, during which Lee's troops surrendered their arms and battle flags and received their paroles. As they marched by, a Union general ordered his men to present arms. The Confederates returned the salute, a soldier's farewell.

When war came to Appomattox County, it was a rural, agricultural area with a population of 9,000 people, more than half of whom were black. Appomattox Court House was the county seat, post office, and social center for the farmers and plantation owners in the area. The war changed the village forever. The county seat and post office moved a few miles away, to Appomattox Station, which prospered because it was on the railroad. In the late 1880s a group of Union veterans formed the Appomattox Land Company to sell lots and build houses, but nothing came of the venture. The courthouse burned down in 1892. The next year the McLean House was dismantled to be taken to Washington as a war museum, but the pile of bricks and lumber was never used. The village was falling apart.

In 1930, Congress voted to build a monument at the site of the old courthouse, but it was never built. In 1934 the National Park Service, inspired by the restoration of Colonial Williamsburg, suggested that the entire village be restored. Legislation was

"THE WAR IS OVER —THE REBELS ARE OUR COUNTRYMEN AGAIN."

—ULYSSES S. GRANT, *after Lee's surrender at Appomattox, April 9, 1865*

passed in 1935, and work began on acquiring the land and researching the record. Reconstruction began in earnest after World War II, and on April 6, 1954, the area was designated a National Historical Park. Now most of the village looks as it did in April 1865.

VISITING APPOMATTOX COURT HOUSE

The Appomattox Court House National Historical Park is situated on 1,326 acres, fourteen miles east of Lynchburg and three miles northeast of Appomattox on VA 24. The Visitor Center is in the old county courthouse building. On the second floor is a museum containing a small auditorium where a slide presentation is shown every half hour. Living-history presentations in the park show how the war affected the people of the village and how they lived from day to day. No vehicles are allowed in the village. A leisurely stroll around the village should take about two hours. Park rangers and guides in period dress are available to answer questions.

McLean House. In the Second Battle of Bull Run, troops overran the farm of Wilmer McLean. He moved to this quiet village to get away from the war, only to have it end in his parlor. This reconstruction of the original includes the house, the servants' quarters, and the kitchen.

Meeks' Store. Over the years, this 1852 building has been a store, a private residence, and the manse of the Presbyterian church. Francis Meeks was the postmaster and druggist.

Woodson Law Office. John Woodson bought this office in 1856 and practiced law here until his death, eight years later. It is a typical lawyer's office of the period.

Clover Hill Tavern. The brick tavern, built in 1819, is the oldest structure in the village, which was known as Clover Hill until it was chosen as the county seat. At one time it had two frame additions, one for the dining room and one for the bar. Behind the tavern are the kitchens, now a bookstore, and the servants' quarters, which now contain restrooms. Beside the tavern

McLean House, Appomattox National Historical Park, Virginia

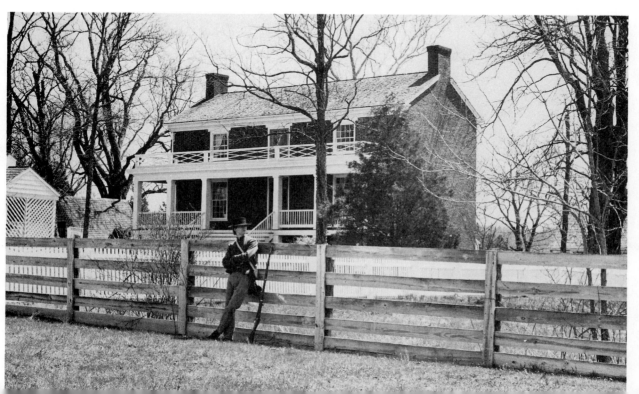

Robert E. Lee signs the instrument of surrender as Ulysses S. Grant looks on in the McLean House at Appomattox Court House, Virginia, April 9, 1865. (Many Union generals shown in this vintage print were not actually present.) Later Lee rode among his men, saying: "Go to your homes and resume your occupations. Obey the laws and become as good citizens as you were soldiers."

is the guest house where people stayed when the tavern was full. Presses were set up in the tavern to print the passes the Confederates needed to return to their homes. The presses broke down, however, and the job had to be completed in Lynchburg.

Courthouse. None of the surrender events took place here. The structure is a reconstruction of the original, which was built in 1846.

Jail. The jail was built about 1870 and served as the county jail and sheriff's office for the next twenty-two years.

Kelly House. From the porch of this house, the Kellys probably watched Lee's troops lay down their arms on April 12, 1865.

Mariah Wright House. Constructed in the mid-1820s, this is one of the older buildings in the village. The stone-and-brick chimneys, like that of the Kelly house, are typical of this region.

Surrender Triangle. On the fourth anniversary of the firing on Fort Sumter, 28,231 Confederates laid down their weapons and furled their battle flags. After the ceremony, Lee, who had not taken part, left for Richmond. Grant was already in Washington.

Isbell House. This house was built by two brothers, one of whom, Thomas S. Bocock, was speaker of the Confederate Congress. Not open to the public.

Peers House. George Peers, clerk of the court for Appomattox County for forty years, lived in this 1850s frame house. Not open to the public.

Outside the village are a few sites associated with the surrender. The site of *Lee's Headquarters* is northeast of the village, a five-minute walk from a small parking lot on VA 24. In the opposite direction from the village is the site of *Grant's Headquarters.* Nearby is the *State of North Carolina Monument* marking the farthest advance of its troops on the morning of the surrender. A

"SECESSION IS
NOTHING BUT
REVOLUTION. . . .
STILL A UNION
THAT CAN ONLY
BE MAINTAINED
BY SWORDS AND
BAYONETS, AND IN
WHICH STRIFE
AND CIVIL WAR
ARE TO TAKE
THE PLACE
OF BROTHERLY
LOVE AND
KINDNESS, HAS NO
CHARM FOR ME. IF
THE UNION IS
DISSOLVED, THE
GOVERNMENT
DISRUPTED, I
SHALL RETURN TO
MY NATIVE STATE
AND SHARE IN
THE MISERIES OF
MY PEOPLE. SAVE
IN HER DEFENSE,
I WILL DRAW MY
SWORD NO
MORE."

—ROBERT E. LEE,
*in a letter to his
son, January
1861*

small *Confederate Cemetery* just west of the village contains the graves of eighteen Southern and one Northern soldier killed on April 9. These sites can be reached by car or by hiking trails.

The park is open daily, except New Year's Day, Martin Luther King, Jr.'s Birthday, Washington's Birthday, Veterans Day, Thanksgiving, and Christmas. The park is accessible to the disabled, and wheelchairs are available on request. There are restaurants and two motels in the nearby village of Appomattox, although many visitors stay in Lynchburg. For further information, write to the Superintendent, Appomattox Court House National Historical Park, P.O. Box 218, Appomattox, VA 24552, or phone (804) 352-8782.

ARLINGTON HOUSE

THE ROBERT E. LEE MEMORIAL

No place on earth was more loved by Robert E. Lee than Arlington House, his mansion on a hill overlooking Washington across the Potomac. At Arlington House, Lee wrote, "my affections and attachments are more strongly placed than at any other place in the world."

Arlington House was built by George Washington Parke Custis, the grandson of Martha Washington by her first marriage, to Daniel Parke Custis. After his father died, young Custis was raised by his grandmother and her second husband, George Washington. Custis grew up to be an agricultural pioneer, a painter, a playwright, and an orator. Designed by George Hadfield, a young English architect who for a time was in charge of the construction of the U.S. Capitol, the Greek Revival mansion, begun in 1802 and completed fifteen years later, was the centerpiece of Custis's 1,100-acre estate.

In 1804, Custis married Mary Lee Fitz-

hugh. Their only child to survive infancy was Mary Anna Randolph Custis, born in 1808. Young Robert E. Lee, whose mother was a cousin of Mrs. Custis, was a frequent visitor. Two years after graduating from West Point, Lee married Mary Custis at Arlington House on June 30, 1831.

For thirty years, Arlington House was home to the Lees. They spent much of their married life traveling between here and various army posts, sharing Arlington House with Mary's parents. Six of the seven Lee children were born here. When Mr. Custis died in 1857, he left the Arlington estate to Mrs. Lee for her lifetime, afterward to the Lees' eldest son, George Washington Custis Lee. The estate needed repairs and reorganization, and Lee took a two-year leave of absence from the army to begin the necessary agricultural and financial improvements.

Back in the army, Lee was distressed when Virginia seceded from the Union on April 17, 1861. He supported the preservation of the Union and opposed slavery, but felt that his first loyalty was to his native state. He was at home at Arlington on April 20, 1861, when he made his decision to resign his army commission. Two days later he left for Richmond to take command of Virginia's military forces, and never returned to Arlington. When it seemed certain that Union troops would occupy Arlington, Mrs. Lee left after sending some of the family valuables to safety.

Arlington House became the headquarters for officers supervising the defenses of Washington. Later, a wartime law required that in areas occupied by Union troops, property owners had to appear in person to pay their taxes. Unable to comply, Mrs. Lee saw her estate confiscated in 1864. A 200-acre section of the estate was set aside as a military cemetery, the beginning of Arlington National Cemetery.

In 1882, G. W. C. Lee successfully sued the government for the return of his property. By then, thousands of graves covered the nearby hills and he accepted the government's offer of $150,000 for the property. For some years the superintendent of the cemetery and his staff used the mansion as offices and living quarters. Restoration of Arlington House began in 1925, and in 1933 it was transferred to the National Park Service. In 1955 it was designated as a memorial to Robert E. Lee.

VISITING ARLINGTON HOUSE

Arlington House is open from 9:30 A.M. to 6 P.M. April through September, and from 9:30 A.M. to 4:30 P.M. October through March. Park Service personnel are on duty to answer questions. The house can be reached from Washington and Alexandria at the Arlington stop on the Metro trains (Blue Line). Parking is available at the Arlington Cemetery Visitor Center. From there, it is a short walk to the house. Visitors also may take Tourmobile, a concession, from the parking lot to the house, from 8 A.M. to 7 P.M. April through September, 9:30 A.M. to 4:30 P.M. October through March. For further information, write to the Superintendent, George Washington Memorial Parkway, Turkey Run Park, McLean, VA 22101, or phone (703) 557-0613.

Visitors may tour Arlington House at their leisure, entering from the portico as guests did when the Lees lived here. The Park Service suggests the following highlights:

Center Hall. In 1824 the Marquis de Lafayette described the view across the Potomac to Washington from here as "the finest view in the world." The center hall was the scene of many happy homecomings and farewells for Lee. The ceiling lantern is a copy of the Mount Vernon lantern that Custis brought to the house with other furnishings. High on the walls at the west end of the hall are hunting scenes painted by Custis about 1818.

Family Parlor. Lieutenant Lee and Mary Custis were married here on June 30, 1831. It served as the family's main parlor from 1817 until the White Parlor was completed in 1855.

Family Dining Room. It was Lee's custom to gather roses in the garden each morning and place one beside the plate of each woman present at breakfast. Original pieces include china, silver, glassware, and the twin serving tables.

White Parlor. The Lees decorated this room in 1855. Left unfinished when the rest of the house was completed about 1817,

Robert E. Lee already was legendary when he posed for Mathew Brady at home after the war; in death he would become a mythological figure. As commander of the Army of Northern Virginia, Lee symbolized the militant Confederacy. As animosities faded, however, he became the embodiment of the lost cause and an aristocratic system of values, gone but mourned. In a particularly American way, he is beloved of all, North and South.

Arlington House

the White Parlor served as a storeroom for nearly forty years. Lee personally selected the marble mantels and purchased the Victorian parlor furniture.

Morning Room. Built as a parlor, it was furnished as a morning room by Mrs. Lee in 1855. Custis used it as his auxiliary painting studio.

Conservatory. This was also called the "camellia house" by both the Custises and the Lees. Once an open porch, it was later enclosed and used to protect Mrs. Lee's plants in winter.

Office and Studio. Through the doorway at the top of the steps on the left at the south end of the Conservatory is the room where Custis, and later Lee, managed the estate.

Colonel and Mrs. Lee's Chamber. Here, on the night of April 19, 1861, Lee faced the grim choice of honoring family ties in Virginia, dating back six generations, or of supporting the Union his family had helped to create. From a long night of solitude, Lee emerged with a letter of resignation, thus ending a thirty-two-year career of service to his country. Two days later he left Arlington, never to return. "I did only what my duty demanded," he said later. The door on the right leads to the dressing closet.

Bath. This bath and water closet were installed by Lee in the 1850s.

School and Sewing Room. Here clothing was made, and the children and servants received their education from Mrs. Custis and later from Mrs. Lee.

Mr. and Mrs. Custis's Chamber. This part of the north wing of the house was designed as one large banquet room, but was partitioned to serve as this chamber, as well as a sewing room, a guest chamber, and an inner hall. The wooden mantelpiece is the oldest in the house.

Winter Kitchen. The kitchen is equipped with a cookstove and utensils. A huge center chimney warmed the upstairs rooms. The area beyond the chimney was used as a laundry.

Wine Cellar. Wine and brandy made from fruit grown at Arlington and on other Custis farms were stored here. Exit through the cellar door.

Visitors may stop by the *Slave Quarters* located on the west circular drive. The *Museum,* just beyond the vegetable garden north of the mansion, contains memorabilia of the Custis and Lee families.

Arlington National Cemetery. The most famous national cemetery was established in 1864 on part of the Custis-Lee estate, and now more than 200,000 servicemen and servicewomen are interred here, including eighty-one Union generals, Confederate General Joseph Wheeler, and Robert Todd Lincoln. One monument stands over the mass grave of 2,111 Union dead. At Jackson Circle, near the rear of the cemetery, are the graves of 250 Confederate soldiers. In their midst is a large bronze monument by Sir Moses Ezekiel, who is buried nearby. The *Visitor Center* is located at the base of the hill at the south end of Arlington Memorial Bridge. Automobiles may enter by permit only. Tourmobiles with guides leave from the Visitor Center.

FREDERICKSBURG, CHANCELLORSVILLE, THE WILDERNESS, AND SPOTSYLVANIA COURT HOUSE

FREDERICKSBURG AND SPOTSYLVANIA COUNTY BATTLEFIELDS MEMORIAL NATIONAL MILITARY PARK

In 1861, Fredericksburg was a quiet town of 5,000 inhabitants, midway between Washington and Richmond, on a railroad and protected by the Rappahannock and Rapidan rivers. Its strategic location made it one of the main barriers to a Union invasion. Engulfed by the war, Fredericksburg would change hands seven times between 1861 and 1865.

Four great battles—the heaviest, most concentrated fighting ever seen on this continent—were fought in and around Fredericksburg between December 1862 and May 1863. The battles, in which casualties totaled more than 100,000, were all distinguished by the military genius of Robert E. Lee.

THE BATTLE OF FREDERICKSBURG, (DECEMBER 13, 1862).

When President Lincoln approved Gen. Ambrose Burnside's plan to drive to Richmond through Fredericksburg, he commented, "It will succeed if you move very rapidly; otherwise not." Burnside didn't move rapidly and met with disaster.

In mid-November 1862, Burnside's Army of the Potomac arrived on Stafford Heights, overlooking Fredericksburg, but it wasn't until December 11 that his troops started to cross the Rappahannock. By this time, however, Lee's Army of Northern Virginia was entrenched on the high ground west of the city.

On December 13, Burnside launched two attacks. Gen. George Meade struck on the left against Stonewall Jackson's corps at Prospect Hill, achieving temporary success until Confederate reserves drove him back to his original position.

The second attack was aimed at the heart of Lee's defenses on Marye's Heights directly beyond Fredericksburg. Union soldiers were slaughtered by artillery on the

Ambrose E. Burnside

Soldiers of the 6th Maine Infantry stand at attention after the second battle of Fredericksburg. Lucky to be alive, they took part in the Union attack across the stone wall at the foot of Marye's Heights. From daybreak until noon, attempt after attempt failed before a Confederate division was driven from its commanding position on Marye's Heights. The division was the rear of Lee's army then fighting at Chancellorsville.

Fredericksburg, Virginia, as it looked in February 1863 from across the Rappahannock River. The war left Fredericksburg worn and bleeding. Situated midway between Richmond and Washington, it repeatedly was an objective for both Union and Confederate armies, and it changed hands several times. When Burnside attempted to take the city in December 1862, he narrowly escaped having his army destroyed, suffering more than 12,600 casualties.

heights and infantry behind a stone wall. By the end of the day Lee had won his most one-sided victory of the war. A Northern correspondent attached to Burnside's army wrote: "It can hardly be in human nature for men to show more valor, or generals to manifest less judgment."

THE BATTLE OF CHANCELLORSVILLE, (APRIL 27–MAY 6, 1863).

President Lincoln replaced Burnside with Joseph Hooker after the debacle at Fredericksburg. Hooker divided his army of 134,000 into two attack groups, hoping to catch Lee's 60,000-man army in a pincer movement. On April 27, 1863, three Union corps crossed the Rappahannock and the Rapidan well beyond the Confederate left flank and marched toward Fredericksburg. At the same time, two corps began to cross below Fredericksburg.

Within three days, Hooker was at the Chancellorsville crossroads. Discovering this threat to his position, Lee rushed westward and attacked. Hooker lost his nerve and abandoned the initiative. He established a defensive line that was fatally weak on the right flank. Lee, though badly outnumbered, moved boldly, sending Stone-

wall Jackson's corps on a risky twelve-mile march around the Union army. Everything depended on Jackson's not being detected. After a long day's forced march, Jackson fell on the Union right, destroying it. Shortly after dark, Jackson was mortally wounded by shots from his own troops. Upon hearing the news of his death, Lee said, "I have lost my right arm."

While the battle raged at Chancellorsville, Gen. John Sedgwick's corps stormed Marye's Heights in Fredericksburg and drove off Jubal Early's defenders. Sedgwick then marched toward Chancellorsville, but Lee, leaving four divisions to watch Hooker, turned and held Sedgwick off at Salem Church, six miles from Chancellorsville. On May 4, Hooker withdrew across the river, soon to be relieved of his command by President Lincoln.

THE BATTLE OF THE WILDERNESS, (MAY 5–6, 1864).

The first of the classic encounters between Lee and Grant took place in the dense thickets and tangled undergrowth of the Wilderness. Grant wanted to force Lee out of his entrenchments. To do this, he planned to move quickly through the Wilderness, turn Lee's right flank, and bring him out of his lines to protect Richmond.

On May 4, 1864, Grant began crossing the Rapidan, but his supply trains fell behind, and he was unable to move out of the Wilderness before Lee could attack. For two days the armies sparred indecisively along the Orange Turnpike. On the Plank Road to the south, Union forces almost crushed A. P. Hill's troops on May 5.

In the Wilderness, soldiers rarely could see as far as a hundred yards. A Union private wrote that "it was a blind and bloody hunt to the death, in bewildering thickets, rather than a battle." Another soldier called it "simply bushwhacking on a grand scale." Heavy gunfire set the Wilderness undergrowth ablaze, burning to death countless soldiers who were too badly injured to crawl to safety.

Grant resumed the offensive the next day, breaking through Hill's position. Then Longstreet's corps arrived and crashed head-on into the advancing Union troops. The Confederates were advancing, but Longstreet was shot accidentally by his own soldiers and the momentum was lost.

When the battle ended, Grant had lost more than 17,500, Lee fewer than 8,000. It seemed like another Chancellorsville, but as the Union army moved out late the following night, Grant's troops realized that they were not retreating but heading south. When Grant rode by, they cheered.

THE BATTLE OF SPOTSYLVANIA COURT HOUSE (MAY 8–21, 1864).

On May 7, Grant and Lee raced for the vital intersection at Spotsylvania Court House that controlled the shortest route to Richmond. Lee arrived first, entrenched, and successfully withstood a series of small-scale Union attacks.

Spotsylvania actually was one sprawling, twelve-day battle, with continuous fighting somewhere along the opposing lines. On

---

UNION LOSSES

During May and June 1864, Union armies in Virginia lost 77,452 men—more men than Lee had in his entire army.

---

the morning of May 7, 1864, two Union corps charged from the woods opposite a vulnerable section of the Confederate line known as the Mule Shoe Salient. The initial assault, in a dense fog, overwhelmed the Confederates. As a second assault reached the Confederate line, Lee's reinforcements hit the oncoming Union troops.

For the next twenty hours the Mule Shoe Salient was the scene of the most intense hand-to-hand combat of the war; at least 12,000 men fell struggling for one square mile of ground. This desperate fighting at the "Bloody Angle" earned Lee enough time to build new earthworks, which he defended until Grant abandoned the field on May 21.

The armies had been fighting since Grant crossed the Rapidan nearly three weeks

After the Battle of Chancellorsville, medics tend wounded soldiers in the field. Medical care during the war was woefully inadequate. Few doctors knew why wounds became infected, and pus was thought to be a good sign. Neither medical instruments nor bandages were sterilized. In camp, diseases like typhoid, dysentery, and pneumonia were dreaded killers. Military hospitals were fearful places, as dangerous in their way as battlefields.

"IT IS WELL THAT WAR IS SO TERRIBLE, OR WE SHOULD GROW TOO FOND OF IT."

—ROBERT E. LEE, *to Gen. James Longstreet at the Battle of Fredericksburg, 1862*

before. Grant's losses averaged 2,000 a day; Lee's were considerably fewer, although Grant could sustain heavier losses. The burden on Lee was growing heavier: Jackson was gone, Longstreet severely wounded, A. P. Hill sick.

More bad news came on May 12. Gen. Philip Sheridan had moved on Richmond with a strong cavalry force. In a brief battle at Yellow Tavern, Lee's cavalry commander, Jeb Stuart, was slain. Lee said, "I can scarcely think of him without weeping."

VISITING THE BATTLEFIELDS

The Fredericksburg and Spotsylvania County Battlefields Memorial National Military Park is situated on 5,900 acres and includes parts of all four battlefields and the Fredericksburg National Cemetery, the house near Guinea Station where Stonewall Jackson died, Old Salem Church, and Chatham Manor. Miles of trenches and gun pits are accessible from the park roads.

One Visitor Center is in Fredericksburg, on U.S. 1, at the foot of Marye's Heights.

There is another at the Chancellorsville battlefield, ten miles west of Fredericksburg on VA 3. (Physically disabled visitors should start their visits at the Chancellorsville Visitor Center.) The centers are open daily except Christmas and New Year's Day, from 9 A.M. to 5 P.M., usually to 6 P.M. in the summer. Both centers have museums containing war artifacts, interpretive exhibits, and living-history demonstrations in the summer. There are picnic grounds at each battlefield, at Chatham, and at the Stonewall Jackson Memorial Shrine, but no food facilities in the park. Fredericksburg has a number of restaurants. A schedule of events is posted at the information desks in the centers. Allow two full days to properly visit the battlefields and explore Fredericksburg.

Note: Do not confuse the Fredericksburg Battlefield Visitor Center, maintained by the National Park Service, and the Fredericksburg Visitor Center (706 Caroline St.), which is operated by the city to provide information on other historical attractions and accommodations in and near the city.

A telegrapher sends a message from a Union field station somewhere in Virginia. Almost daily, Lincoln walked to the telegraph office in the War Department across from the White House. "I come here to escape my persecutors," he told the operators. There he received news of his armies and wrote out his replies to the queries and complaints of his generals.

Union soldiers at Marye's Heights in Fredericksburg, Virginia, survey the carnage caused by a siege gun's 32-pound shell that hit a Confederate caisson pulled by two horses. This was a battle of lost opportunities. Burnside lost his nerve and failed to commit vital reserves, a mistake that cost him victory. Lee might have been able to destroy the disorganized Union army, but waited too long to counterattack.

For further information, write to the Superintendent, Fredericksburg and Spotsylvania County Battlefields Memorial National Military Park, P.O. Box 679, Fredericksburg, VA 22404, or phone (703) 373-4461.

Watch your footing while on trails. Beware of biting insects, poison ivy, and snakes in the fields and woods. The self-guided auto tour involves turning onto and off heavily traveled roads.

Begin your tour at the *Fredericksburg Battlefield Visitor Center.* After viewing the audiovisual program and visiting the museum, take in some sites that are within walking distance of the center.

Marye's Heights and National Cemetery. This famous ridge was named for the French Huguenot Marye (pronounced "Marie") family, who settled in Fredericksburg and built an impressive mansion, Brompton, which still stands on the northern tip of the Heights. On December 13,

1862, Confederate cannon crowned the hill, pouring destruction on the Union lines advancing west from the town.

At that time, Fredericksburg was a third of the size it is now, and a great bare plain stretched from the base of these heights to beyond the point where the Union troops formed for their assaults near the edge of town. The scene can be visualized by walking to the crest of the hill within the *National Cemetery.* A large painting depicts the scene at the time of the battle, and a recorded message tells the dramatic story.

After the war, the government established a national cemetery here for the Union dead. Nearly 16,000 soldiers, most of them unknown, are buried here. The *Confederate Cemetery* is located about a mile to the east, in the midst of the Union positions on the plain.

At the far end of the parking lot behind the Visitor Center, a marked trail leads to the *Sunken Road and Stone Wall.* Facing

The historic Innis House on the Sunken Road, National Military Park, Fredericksburg, Virginia

steep trail leads to a commanding outlook at the top of the hill from which Lee and his generals directed the victorious Confederate defense. Lee Hill also served as an artillery position. Confederate guns helped blunt the Union offensives, occasionally dueling with Union artillery. During one of these exchanges, an incoming shell buried itself near Lee but failed to explode.

Continue along Lee Drive four miles to the *Federal Breakthrough*. While some of the Union forces suffered repeated bloody repulses in front of Fredericksburg to the north, one Union division managed a limited but temporary success here. General George Meade, later to command the Union army at Gettysburg, led the attack and found a large undefended gap in the Confederate lines. His troops rushed through the gap and penetrated to this spot. A South Carolina brigade under Brig. Gen. Maxcy Gregg was in reserve nearby, oblivious of Meade's breakthrough. Meade's forces struck, overrunning the brigade and mortally wounding Gregg. Confederate reserves arrived shortly afterward and drove Meade out of the woods and across the plain.

A few hundred yards along Lee Drive is *Prospect Hill*. On this cleared hilltop Stonewall Jackson located much of his artillery strength. Fourteen guns maintained a steady fire on the attackers. Scattered across the knoll are the remains of the fortifications that protected the guns. Through the trees to the left, beyond the railroad, is a large stone monument erected to mark the location of the fighting. The Richmond, Fredericksburg, and Potomac Railroad still runs across the battlefield just in front of Prospect Hill. In 1862 the track had been torn up by the warring armies, but the embankment served as a ready-made earthwork for Southern skirmishers.

Just south of Prospect Hill, a short path leads to where the railroad crosses a country road. *Hamilton's Crossing*, named for

the reconstructed stone wall and the steep slopes of Marye's Heights, you stand near the heart of the Confederate infantry position. The paved street running along the base of the heights was sunken in 1862 because of its heavy use as the main highway to Richmond. Stone retaining walls flanked the road on the town side and, in places, on the hill side as well. Lee found this an ideal military position. Confederate soldiers, jammed several ranks deep along 600 yards of the road, held off repeated Union assaults. Along the road are numerous signs and markers.

The restored *Innis House* still stands, as does a section of the original stone wall at the far end of the road. Here, too, is a large monument to Sergeant Richard Kirkland of the Second South Carolina Infantry. The day after the battle, Kirkland was so moved by the cries of the Union wounded that he went among them to give them water.

Return to your car and begin the self-guided auto tour. Turn right and proceed south on U.S. 1 a half-mile to Lee Drive, turn left, and proceed to *Lee Hill*. A short, one of the early residents of the vicinity, anchored the end of the main Confederate line. Cavalry and skirmishers guarded the swampy lowlands from here to the river.

In addition to the auto tour, there are other sites of interest on the battlefield, their locations indicated on the map.

Canal Ditch. Kenmore Avenue now follows the course of what in 1862 was a drainage ditch for the town's canal. The ditch posed an obstacle to the attacking Union soldiers, who could only cross on narrow bridges, such as the one on Hanover Street.

Upper Pontoon Site. At this point on December 11, Union soldiers landed clumsy pontoon boats, driving Confederate sharpshooters from the streets.

Chatham. This 18th-century Georgian mansion was the home of William Fitzhugh, one of the wealthiest landowners in Virginia. In 1862 it became a frontline headquarters for various Union generals. Gen. Edwin V. Sumner used it as a strategic and artillery center during the Battle of Fredericksburg. Two pontoon bridges spanned the river below the mansion. The house also served as a field hospital in which hundreds of wounded Union soldiers received treatment from regular medical personnel and volunteers like Clara Barton and Walt Whitman. Open 9 A.M. to 5 P.M. daily.

The Federal Line. The Bowling Green Road (also called the Richmond Stage Road) was the point from which several Union assaults toward Prospect Hill began. From routes 2 and 17, visitors look across the fields toward the Confederate ridges.

Pelham Marker. Here a youthful Confederate cannoneer fought a lone delaying action against heavy odds, while both armies looked on from the surrounding hills. Lee's report called him "the gallant Pelham."

Chancellorsville Visitor Center. After visiting the museum and seeing the twelve-minute audiovisual program, begin the self-guided battlefield tour by turning right on historic Bullock Road and proceeding to its dead-end intersection with Ely's Ford Road (route 610). This intersection marked the apex of the Union army's last line. Turn right for seven-tenths of a mile to *Chancellorsville Tavern Site.*

Only a few scattered remains are left of the large roadside inn built in 1815 by George Chancellor. For four decades it served the traffic from the west along both the Orange Turnpike and the Orange Plank Road. When Hooker brought his army across the river, he made this his headquarters. It was here that he lost his confidence and on May 1 ordered the abandonment of his good positions. Hooker was leaning against one of the porch pillars when a Confederate shell injured him painfully. On May 3, 1863, Confederates captured this vital crossroads, marking the end of the battle. As General Lee rode up, the soldiers staged a spontaneous demonstration.

Continue straight across VA 3 and along the Orange Plank Road (route 610) for a mile to the *Lee-Jackson Bivouac.* Among the pines at this junction, Lee and Jackson met for the last time on the night of May 1 to plan the Battle of Chancellorsville. They agreed to a bold maneuver that divided the Confederate forces, sending Jackson on a dangerous march almost entirely around the Union army. Early the next morning, Jackson rode down the road to the west. Lee would never see him again.

Proceed along the Furnace Road for a mile and a half to the *Catharine Furnace Remains,* the site of an early-19th-century iron furnace, abandoned before the war but reopened to manufacture Confederate munitions. During the fighting of May 1, an artillery duel raged around here. The next day, Jackson's march around the Union army swung past the furnace along this road. The furnace was destroyed by Union cavalry in 1864.

The *Jackson Trail* begins at the gravel road just beyond the furnace, and follows Jackson's route for ten miles to the place where he made his surprise attack on the Union right. The trail winds through the woods, and a series of signs and markers along the way explain the action. The trail then continues to the Visitor Center by way of VA 3.

To continue the auto tour, go back to Sickles Drive and follow the arrows to the left for a mile to *Hazel Grove*. The high ground in this clearing was the most important military position on the battlefield of Chancellorsville. The tangled woods did not leave room for the use of artillery, except along the roads and in infrequent open spaces. On the morning of May 3, Confederates took Hazel Grove from the retreating Union troops. Within minutes they had three dozen guns in the clearing firing on the Union lines. The fire was returned by Union artillery 1,200 yards away on another open ridge known as Fairview. ·

A short trail leads to Fairview, where a few guns are displayed. Fairview also can be reached by driving back to the intersection and turning left.

While the artillery duel raged, infantry fought a desperate battle in the thick woods surrounding these clearings. As the effects of the Confederate artillery were felt, the supporting infantry overran the Union positions.

OTHER SITES OF THE BATTLE OF CHANCELLORSVILLE

Hooker's Last Line. Forced to abandon the Chancellorsville crossroads on May 3, Hooker took up positions along a new line that had its apex here. From this point the Union army stretched off toward the river, across which it retreated three days later.

Maury Birthplace. Near the road lie the ruins of the brick house in which the pioneer oceanographer Matthew Fontaine Maury was born in 1806. During the battle, this high ground was so conspicuous that some of the troops on Jackson's march had to make a detour to avoid shelling from the Union guns at Hazel Grove.

Burton Farm. Jackson climbed to a wooded hilltop on this farm and surveyed the unaware Union troops, whom he attacked a few hours later. Until then, he had intended to direct his assault up the Orange Plank Road toward Wilderness Church. Instead, he moved on to the Orange Turnpike and formed his attack.

Start of Jackson's Attack. Here Jackson's corps spread into two-mile-long lines, then came roaring out of the woods and fell upon the stunned Union troops. As the Union line caved in, the Confederacy reached one of its highest points. Within a few hours the sun set, the attack became disorganized, and Jackson fell mortally wounded.

TOURING THE WILDERNESS BATTLEFIELD

To reach the *Wilderness Exhibit Shelter* from Fredericksburg, drive west on VA 3 for fifteen miles to the intersection with VA 20 at Wilderness. Turn left and drive 1.3 miles. From the Chancellorsville Visitor Center, drive west on VA 3 about four miles to the intersection with VA 20 and proceed as above.

The displays at the shelter give an understanding of the opposing armies and the fighting in the Wilderness. These dense woods were the scene of bitter and confused fighting. Units lost all semblance of order in the woods. Many times, troops accidentally shot their comrades, or became surrounded by the enemy without knowing it. Deadly ambushes were frequent. To add to the horror, the dry woods caught fire from the artillery muzzle flashes. The flames roared out of control as soldiers of both sides tried to drag the screaming wounded to safety. By dark the Wilderness was filled with blackened corpses.

Proceed along Hill-Ewell Drive, along which are trenches dug by Confederates after the fighting on May 6. Turn right at the intersection of Hill-Ewell Drive with VA 621, continuing for two-tenths of a mile to the turnoff at the *Widow Tapp Farm.* In this clearing on May 6, occurred one of the most dramatic incidents of the war. One Confederate corps had been roughly handled, and reinforcements were being rushed to the front. When they reached this crucial point, Lee rode ahead to lead them in a counterattack. Realizing the danger to their beloved commander, they shouted him back with the cry, "Lee to the rear! Lee to the rear!"

Retrace the route along the Plank Road for 1.1 miles to the *Brock Road–Plank Road Intersection.* Union infantry occupied this intersection at noon on May 5, holding it despite repeated Confederate assaults. The next day they launched an attack down the Plank Road and routed the Confederate Third Corps.

The Battle of the Wilderness ended in an apparent draw. On the night of May 7, Union troops began pulling out of their lines. Under past commanders, the Army of the Potomac always had withdrawn after an engagement with Lee. But the columns turned to the south and further fighting. When the soldiers caught sight of Grant, they cheered him for his decision not to retreat.

Driving down the Brock Road (route 613) 8.5 miles to the Spotsylvania Court House Battlefield, a visitor follows the route taken by many Union troops in the move for the strategic crossroads village of Spotsylvania Court House, en route to Richmond, passing the site of *Todd's Tavern,* where heavy infantry and cavalry action occurred during the march.

The Bloody Angle, National Military Park, Spotsylvania, Virginia

TOURING THE SPOTSYLVANIA BATTLEFIELD

Displays at the *Spotsylvania Exhibit Shelter* help visitors understand the complex maneuvers of the fourteen-day battle, the second in Grant's drive south. The beloved "Uncle John" Sedgwick, commander of the Union Sixth Corps, was killed near here by a sharpshooter on May 9. A monument to Sedgwick is near the park entrance.

From the intersection at the park entrance there is a view of the *Laurel Hill* area, where the battle opened. This engagement was fought on May 8, from the low ridgeline to a point about 600 yards south across the open fields. Dismounted Confederate cavalrymen fought a bitter holding action against thousands of Union troops. Confederate infantrymen raced across the fields and reached the battle line seconds before the Union troops did. Lee's troops also pushed toward Spotsylvania on roads farther west, arriving there first.

A seven-mile walking tour of the battlefield begins at the shelter. Descriptive folders are in a box at the trailhead.

Continue driving along Grant Drive for nearly a mile to a parking area on the left near the *Bloody Angle*. About 4:30 A.M. on May 12, Grant launched a massive assault on the tip of the Mule Shoe Salient, a mile-long protrusion from the Confederate line, capturing most of a Confederate division and twenty cannon. Savage fighting followed. Men bayoneted, clubbed, and fired at point-blank range at each other across the log fortifications. Several yards behind the Confederate line, a living oak tree twenty-two inches in diameter was cut down by the intense small-arms fire. At 3 A.M. on May 13, the Confederates, dazed but still defiant, retired to a new line constructed across the base of the salient.

A thirty-minute loop trail covers the *Bloody Angle Battlefield*. Descriptive folders are in a box at the top of the hill.

Turn onto Anderson Drive and go four-tenths of a mile to the intersection with Gordon Drive. Turn left and go a short distance to the gravel road on the left. Turn and proceed to the *McCoull House Site*. This house stood at the center of the Confederate salient and served as headquarters for Gen. Edward "Allegheny" Johnson. Heavy fighting occurred nearby during the Union assault on May 10. Two days later, when the Union troops had broken through at the tip of the salient, their massed attack was blunted here. In the confusion following the initial Union onslaught, Lee rode up to the McCoull House area to lead Confederate troops in a desperate counterattack. He met Gen. John B. Gordon's troops, who sent Lee to safety and threw themselves into the path of the assault.

Return to Gordon Drive, turn left, and drive a half-mile to the intersection with Burnside Drive. Turn left and drive to the *Apex of Salient ("East Angle")*. Union troops swarmed over the Confederate entrenchments here on May 12, maintaining control of these earthworks for the rest of the battle. Fighting continued at Spotsylvania until May 21, when Grant pulled away from the lines and started southward again. Union losses at Spotsylvania were about 18,000. Confederate losses are unknown.

OTHER SPOTSYLVANIA BATTLEFIELD SITES

Upton's Attack. On May 10, Colonel Emory Upton led twelve Union regiments down this dirt farm road to attack the northwest face of the Confederate salient. They broke the entrenched line and pushed almost to the McCoull House. The attack was unsupported, however, and in the face of a determined Confederate counterattack, Upton abandoned the trenches. Grant promoted the twenty-four-year-old Upton to brigadier general on the spot, "for gallant and meritorious services."

Landrum House Ruins. This house served as the headquarters for Union General Winfield S. Hancock, who directed the battle for the salient from here. Union artillery used the high ground around the house to support the attacks.

Harrison House Site. About one-third of a mile south of the junction of Anderson and Gordon drives is the site of the Harrison House. Lee made his headquarters near here on May 11 and 12. Lee's final line runs a short distance behind the house.

Lee's Final Line. Located at the base of the salient, about one-half mile to the rear of the first line, was the Confederate defense line erected on May 12. Gen. Martin L. Smith, who had constructed the defenses at Vicksburg, laid out these earthworks. On May 18, Union troops assaulted this line in the hope of duplicating their earlier successes, but were hurled back by thirty massed cannon.

Spotsylvania Court House. The present Court House complex is on the site of the original wartime structure, which suffered heavy damage in the fighting.

Spotsylvania Confederate Cemetery. Here lie the remains of some 570 Confederate soldiers killed in the fighting around Spotsylvania, moved here from temporary battlefield graves.

OTHER SITES IN THE AREA

The Stonewall Jackson Memorial Shrine. Following his accident on May 2, Jackson was removed to a field hospital near Wilderness Tavern, where his left arm was amputated. On May 4 he endured a twenty-seven-mile ambulance ride to T. C. Chandler's Fairfield Plantation at Guinea Station. Here, well behind Confederate lines, Jackson was placed in a small-frame office building. The general's wounds were

Stonewall Jackson Memorial Shrine, the building at Guinea Station, Virginia, where the Confederate general died after being wounded by his own men at the Battle of Chancellorsville.

complicated by pneumonia. He died here on May 10, after murmuring, "Let us cross over the river, and rest under the shade of the trees."

The shrine—the white clapboard building—is located twelve miles south of Fredericksburg on I-95 to Thornburg exit, then five miles east on VA 606, in Guinea. Open daily from mid-June to Labor Day; Friday to Tuesday from March to mid-June and Labor Day through October; Saturday to Monday the rest of the year.

Old Salem Church. Built in 1844 to provide the Baptists of upper Spotsylvania County with a more geographically convenient place of worship, this structure served during the Battle of Fredericksburg as a refugee center for scores of women and children who fled the city. Following the Battle of Salem Church, fought in and around the sanctuary during the Chancellorsville campaign, the building was used by Confederate surgeons to attend the wounded of both sides. Located one mile west of I-95 on VA 3.

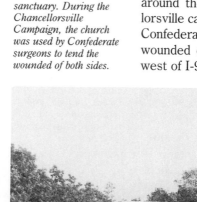

The Battle of Salem Church was fought in and around this sanctuary. During the Chancellorsville Campaign, the church was used by Confederate surgeons to tend the wounded of both sides.

VISITING FREDERICKSBURG

Fredericksburg was a historic town long before the Civil War began. Captain John Smith visited the area in 1603 and gave a glowing report of its potential for settlement. In 1727 the General Assembly of Virginia directed that fifty acres of "lease-land" be laid out and that the town be called Fredericksburg, after Frederick Louis, the Prince of Wales. George Washington went to school here, and this is where his mother, Mary Ball Washington, lived and died. One of the seeds of the American Revolution was planted here when a resolution declaring independence from England was passed on April 29, 1775. James Monroe practiced law on Charles Street. Guns for the Revolution were made in Fredericksburg workshops, and many buildings erected before 1776 still stand.

A walking tour of Fredericksburg from the Visitor Center at 706 Caroline St., includes several places of Civil War interest. At the *Presbyterian Church,* at the southwest corner of Princess Anne and George

streets, cannonballs fired in the 1862 bombardment are lodged in the front pillar. Pews were torn loose and made into coffins for soldiers. Clara Barton, founder of the American Red Cross, is said to have nursed the wounded in the church, and a plaque to her memory is in the churchyard.

On Washington Avenue between Amelia and William streets is the *Confederate Cemetery.* Here lie some 2,000 Confederate soldiers, only 330 of whom, including six generals, were identified.

At the corner of William and Charles streets, the *Old Slave Block* was used to auction slaves before the war.

One of the finest restorations in Virginia is *Kenmore,* 1201 Washington Ave., the former home of Col. Fielding Lewis, commissioner of Fredericksburg gunnery, who married George Washington's sister Betty. There is an admission charge, but tea and gingerbread are served free in the kitchen. (Open daily, except December 24, 25, 31, and January 1.)

Near Kenmore is the *Kenmore Inn of Fredericksburg* (1200 Princess Anne St., 22401; phone [703] 371-7600), an excellent place to stay or dine. This 18th-century inn has thirteen guest rooms, four with fireplaces and some with canopied beds. Outside of town on VA 3 is the *La Vista Plantation,* (Rte. 3, Box 1255, Fredericksburg 22401; phone [703] 898-8444), an 1838 Greek Revival manor home on ten acres, offering bed and breakfast.

An unusual and excellent place to dine nearby is the *Old Mudd Tavern,* one-quarter mile west of the Thornburg exit off I-95; phone (703) 582-5250. A collection of vintage Civil War photographs graces the walls, and the simple country fare is delicious. Entertainment is featured Fridays and Saturdays. In Fredericksburg, *La Petite Auberge,* 311 William St., phone (703) 371-2727, offers French café fare at attractive prices. Closed Sundays.

FIRST AND SECOND MANASSAS

MANASSAS (BULL RUN) NATIONAL BATTLEFIELD PARK

In the first major battle of the war, July 18, 1861, two great armies clashed on rolling land overlooking a small, meandering stream named Bull Run, some thirty miles south of Washington. With this battle, hopes that the war would be over quickly went up in smoke.

On July 16, Gen. Irvin McDowell's army of 35,000 marched out of Washington in an attempt to capture the Confederate capital of Richmond and end the war. The people of Washington thought it would be a festive occasion, and many congressmen were among those who tagged along with picnic baskets, expecting to see the Confederates run when the first shot was fired. McDowell's troops were green, most of them ninety-day volunteers summoned by President Lincoln after the fall of Fort Sumter the preceding April. They possessed few martial skills, and knew nothing of the horror of battle.

McDowell's first objective was Manassas, where the Orange & Alexandria Railroad met the Manassas Gap Railroad, which led west to the Shenandoah Valley. If McDowell captured Manassas, the best approach to Richmond would be under his control. The first day's march covered barely five miles; many of the young soldiers broke ranks to pick blackberries and fill canteens. On July 18 the Union army reached Centreville, five miles from Bull Run. Guarding the fords at Bull Run were 22,000 Confederate troops, led by P. G. T. Beauregard, McDowell's West Point classmate.

McDowell first attempted to move toward the Confederate right flank, but was stopped at Blackburn's Ford. McDowell spent two critical days organizing his troops and checking the Confederate left flank. Beauregard, meanwhile, called for rein-

forcements. Gen. Joseph E. Johnston brought 10,000 troops from the Shenandoah Valley, giving a Union force there the slip, transporting his troops on the Manassas Gap Railroad. They arrived at Manassas Junction on July 20 and 21, many marching directly from the trains into battle.

On the morning of July 21, McDowell sent most of his army around the Confederate left to the Sudley Springs Ford. To divert Beauregard, a diversionary attack was made at the Stone Bridge, where the Warrenton Turnpike crosses Bull Run. The success of McDowell's plan depended on speed and surprise, but his inexperienced troops weren't up to the task. They lost time stumbling along narrow roads at night.

At Stone Bridge, Col. Nathan Evans quickly determined that the Union attack was a diversion. Leaving a small Confederate force to hold the bridge, he rushed the rest of his troops to Matthews Hill in time to meet McDowell's lead forces. Evans halted the Union advance, but his force was too small to hold on for long.

Generals Barnard Bee and Francis Bar-

tow marched their brigades to reinforce Evans, but the Union force continued to advance. The Confederate troops fell back in disarray toward Henry House Hill. As Bee attempted to rally his troops, he spied Gen. Thomas Jackson and his newly arrived brigade. "Look," shouted Bee. "There stands Jackson like a stone wall! Rally behind the Virginians!" Minutes later Bee was shot dead, but his sobriquet for Jackson passed into legend. Then Generals Johnston and Beauregard arrived on Henry House Hill, where they helped rally the shattered brigades and redeployed fresh units into the line.

Stiff Confederate resistance formed around Jackson's brigade as the Union forces attacked again. Some Union artillery was pushed too far forward, and a counterattack by Jeb Stuart's cavalry captured the guns. The battle swayed back and forth over Henry House Hill. Victory hung on which side would be reinforced first. Gen. Kirby Smith arrived with the last of Johnston's brigades from Winchester and attacked on the Confederate left, but the force wasn't sufficient to carry the day. At this crucial moment, Col. Jubal Early's brigade arrived from the opposite end of the battlefield and hit the Union right on Chinn Ridge. For the first time in the war, the rebel yell was heard up and down the line.

McDowell's troops had had enough, and began to withdraw. Screened by veteran soldiers, the young ninety-day volunteers retired across Bull Run to find the road to Washington jammed with the carriages of the spectators who had ridden out from the capital. When a Confederate shell struck a Union wagon, the wreckage blocked the road, causing soldiers and spectators to panic. The withdrawal became a frantic flight. But the Confederates were too exhausted and disorganized to press the attack on the fleeing Union troops. By dawn on July 22, McDowell's army was back in Washington.

In a battle decided by reinforcements, it was ironic that so few of the troops present actually fought. Only 18,500 of the 35,000 Union troops and 18,000 of the 32,000 Confederates were engaged, and fewer still took part in the heaviest fighting. The Union suffered 2,900 casualties; the Confederates, 2,000. The Confederates captured a considerable amount of arms and supplies.

The Union and the Confederacy fought again at Manassas, but led by different commanders. After the 1861 defeat here, Gen. George B. McClellan replaced McDowell and reorganized the forces around Washington into the mighty Army of the Potomac. In March 1862 he struck out on a bold venture.

Leaving a strong force to protect the capital, McClellan took his army by sea to Fort Monroe, on the tip of the York-James Peninsula, a hundred miles southeast of Richmond. Early in April he advanced toward the Confederate capital. The Confederate troops headed south from Manassas to meet this new threat. By the end of May, McClellan's troops were within sight of Richmond.

Gen. Joseph Johnston's army struck the Union troops in the inconclusive Battle of Seven Pines. Johnston was wounded, and President Davis made an inspired choice for his replacement: Gen. Robert E. Lee, his military adviser. Seizing the offensive, Lee sent his Army of Northern Virginia across the Chickahominy. In a series of savage battles, McClellan was pushed back from the edge of Richmond to a position on the James River.

While Lee was attacking, the scattered Union troops in northern Virginia were organized into the Army of Virginia under the command of Gen. John Pope. Lee sent Stonewall Jackson's corps north to attack Pope, gambling that McClellan wouldn't attack again.

Jackson struck at part of Pope's army at Cedar Mountain on August 9, but the battle was indecisive. McClellan started to send his army north by sea to reinforce Pope. Learning of this, Lee marched with Gen. James Longstreet's corps to Jackson's aid.

An attempt to gain a tactical advantage over Pope was thwarted at the Rapidan River. Pope then took up a position north of the Rappahannock. Lee knew that his

John Pope

only chance of defeating Pope was to strike before McClellan's army arrived. He boldly sent Jackson's corps on a march of nearly sixty miles around Pope's right flank to strike from the rear.

Two days later, Jackson's troops captured Pope's supply depot at Manassas Junction, burned the supplies, and took up a position in the woods at Groveton, near the old Manassas battlefield.

Angered by the attack on his supply base, Pope abandoned the line at the Rappahannock and headed toward Manassas. Meanwhile, Lee and Longstreet were moving north to join up with Jackson. To bring Pope to battle, Jackson struck at a Union column as it marched past on the Warrenton Turnpike. This was known as the Battle of Brawner's Farm.

Pope was convinced that Jackson was isolated and could be destroyed before Lee and Longstreet arrived. He ordered his troops to converge on Groveton. On August 29 the Union troops found Jackson posted north of the turnpike along an unfin-

ished railroad grade. Pope attacked, but couldn't break Jackson's line. Longstreet's troops arrived during the afternoon and deployed on Jackson's right, unknown to Pope. The Confederates overlapped the exposed Union left. Lee urged Longstreet to attack, but he wouldn't, saying the time was not right.

Both sides stayed in place during the morning of August 30. Just before noon, Pope blundered badly. Believing the Confederates were retreating, he ordered his army to pursue. Lee, Longstreet, and Jackson had gone nowhere. Pope's "pursuit" was thrown back. Pope ordered another attack against Jackson's position at the unfinished railroad's "Deep Cut." The Confederates cut the attackers to ribbons.

Seeing the Union forces thrown back, Longstreet attacked Pope's left flank. The Army of Virginia was close to annihilation, but a valiant stand, first on Chinn Ridge, then on Henry Hill, bought sufficient time for Pope to withdraw his army that night across Bull Run toward Washington.

Many Union and Confederate infantry units adopted distinctive Zouave uniforms only to discover, like this wounded Union soldier, that they made attractive targets on the battlefield. The kepi cap, short blue jackets, baggy red pantaloons, and white leggings were first worn by French colonial troops who fought in the Crimean War. General McClellan, an official observer in that war, brought back glowing reports of the Zouaves' colorful ways.

Lee's brilliant campaign at Second Manassas set the stage for his invasion of the North that culminated at Antietam.

VISITING MANASSAS

Manassas (Bull Run) National Battlefield Park is located on 3,000 acres twenty-six miles southwest of Washington, D.C., near the intersection of I-66 and VA 234. The Visitor Center near the entrance to the park houses a museum and a bookstore. A twelve-minute slide presentation depicts the highlights of the two battles. The collection of artifacts and photographs in the museum helps the visitor to understand how the soldiers lived and fought. No food is sold in the park, but there is a forty-five-acre picnic ground two and one-half miles past the Visitor Center on VA 234. A bridle trail circles the park, but visitors must bring their own horses. With the exception of the trails in wet weather, full access is provided to the disabled.

Two major battles fought on the same ground would seem to present the visitor with a confusing set of images, but this is not so at Manassas National Battlefield Park. There are separate self-guided car and walking tours for each battle, and the National Park Service has clearly marked the points of interest. Some sites overlap, of course, particularly around Henry House Hill. Allow a full day to see everything at Manassas.

For further information, write to the Superintendent, Manassas National Battlefield Park, P.O. Box 1830, Manassas, VA 22110, or phone (703) 754-7107. The town of Manassas, four miles south on VA 234, has a variety of restaurants and motels.

FIRST MANASSAS BATTLEFIELD

A one-mile self-guided walking tour begins behind the Visitor Center at the rebuilt *Henry House,* and taped messages and interpretive signs lead visitors around Henry

A LACK OF UNIFORMITY

The First Battle of Manassas was marked by understandable confusion. Some Union troops wore gray; some Confederates wore blue. A New York City regiment dressed in Highland kilts. Zouave units on both sides wore the fez and baggy trousers patterned after those worn by the French army in North Africa. The original Confederate flag had three red and white stripes and a blue field with stars, and looked like the United States flag at a distance. Needless to say, firing on friendly troops occurred frequently.

THE CONFEDERATE FLAG.

Hill, the scene of the critical fighting at First Manassas. Nearby is a monument to the "Memory of the Patriots who fell at Bull Run, July 21, 1861," and the grave of Mrs. Judith Carter Henry, the only civilian killed in the first battle.

From the Henry House the trail heads north to the Confederate artillery positions overlooking Matthew Hill. These guns were vital during the early stage of the battle. The trail goes across the fields to the *Robinson House,* where Wade Hampton led his South Carolina troops into battle.

From the Robinson House the trail loops back along the *Confederate Line,* where Gen. Thomas Jackson "stood like a stone

The first flag of the Confederacy, red and white stripes with a blue field and white stars, resembled the U.S. flag and caused confusion on the battlefield. After the first Battle of Manassas (Bull Run), the flag was replaced by the Stars and Bars. The seven stars here represent the seven states that had seceded when the flag was adopted. The Stars and Bars had thirteen stars.

wall," continuing to the site of the capture of Capt. Griffin's *Union Cannon,* a turning point in the battle. The final stop overlooks *Chinn Ridge,* where a Confederate attack late in the afternoon crushed the Union right, beginning the rout of the Union army.

There are two walking trails for visitors with a particular interest in First Manassas: a 1.4-mile loop from the *Stone Bridge* and a .6-mile trail from Sudley. Information about these trails is available at the Visitor Center. The trails are not paved, and the ground is uneven and slippery in wet weather.

SECOND MANASSAS BATTLEFIELD

The Second Battle of Manassas raged over an area four times as large as that of the first battle. A twelve-mile, self-guided auto tour covers twelve sites that figured prominently in the second battle. Two heavily traveled highways divide the park. U.S. 29 follows the roadbed of the historic Warrenton Turnpike, which played a major part in both battles, and the Manassas-Sudley Road (VA 234) crosses the turnpike at the Stone House. Use caution in driving across or turning onto and off these highways. The sites on the tour include:

Battery Heights. Late in the afternoon of August 28, 1862, Stonewall Jackson ordered an attack on a Union column as it marched past on the Warrenton Turnpike. As the leading elements of Gen. Rufus King's division emerged from the woods to the west, Jackson's infantry advanced from the distant ridge into this open field. The Union troops swung to meet the attack, and for ninety minutes a battle raged. This was the opening struggle in Second Manassas. Nearly one-third of the 7,000 troops who fought here were casualties.

Stone House. Certain that he could destroy Jackson before Lee and Longstreet arrived, General Pope ordered his columns to converge here and attack. Pope made

his headquarters directly behind this house during the fighting on August 30. The Stone House served as a field hospital during First and Second Manassas.

Dogan Ridge. On August 29, Pope's army found Jackson's troops posted along an unfinished railroad grade about a half-mile west of here. Assault after assault, bloody but uncoordinated, was made on the Confederate position without success. Key Union artillery positions were on the low ridges surrounding Dogan Ridge.

Sudley. On August 29, Union troops made several bloody but unsuccessful attempts to break through the extreme left of Jackson's line, positioned on the knoll just west of here. As the battle raged, Longstreet's troops arrived and deployed on Jackson's right, overlapping the exposed Union left. Pope was unaware of their presence. Lee urged Longstreet to attack, but he wouldn't, saying the time was just not right.

Unfinished Railroad. The center of Jackson's line was near here. It ran from near the Sudley Church to a point southwest of here, a distance of a mile and a half. The unfinished railroad, the focal point of Jackson's position, is still visible running into the woods on both sides of the road.

Deep Cut. On August 30, Pope erroneously decided the Confederates were retreating and ordered his troops to pursue. The entrenched Confederates threw them back. Pope foolishly ordered another attack on Jackson's line. More than 5,000 men under Gen. Fitz-John Porter moved forward across the road into the field, hitting Jackson's line in the area around the Deep Cut. Porter's troops were savagely repulsed. A trail about one-third of a mile long begins at the road and traces the footsteps of Porter's attack.

Groveton. The small, white frame building just to the west is the only remaining structure of the wartime village of Groveton, one of only two Civil War houses still standing in the battlefield park. The Groveton Confederate Cemetery nearby is the last resting place of more than 260 soldiers, most of them unknown.

New York Monuments. After the repulse of Porter on August 30, the Union line was in disarray. Longstreet advanced and staggered the Union left. The Fifth and Tenth New York regiments made a gallant but futile stand on this ridge. In five minutes, 123 men of the Fifth New York were killed, the greatest loss of life in any single infantry regiment in any battle of the war.

Hazel Plain (Chinn House). All that remains of the Chinn House is the stone foundation. Late in the afternoon of August 30, Longstreet's troops converged on this ridge, passing by the house as they bore down on the Union line. The Union troops fought fiercely, buying time for Pope.

Chinn Ridge. Along this ridge the Union forces desperately fought to delay Longstreet's advance while Pope was setting up a second defensive line on Henry House Hill, just to the east. A nearby marker indicates where Fletcher Webster, Daniel Webster's eldest son, was slain while leading the 12th Massachusetts Infantry into battle.

Henry House Hill. A final stand against Longstreet's attack was made here by parts of McDowell's, Porter's, Sigel's, and Reno's corps. From a position in the bed of Sudley Road, they beat off Confederate attacks from Anderson's and Jones's division. When darkness came the Union army was beaten but still intact.

Stone Bridge. In the night the defeated Union army withdrew across this bridge over Bull Run toward Centreville and the safety of Washington.

Stone House, National Military Park, Manassas, Virginia

PETERSBURG

PETERSBURG NATIONAL BATTLEFIELD

Both Grant and Lee knew the importance of Petersburg. "The key to taking Richmond is Petersburg," said Grant. The supply center for Richmond, Petersburg was linked to the capital by four railroad lines and many roadways. If these were cut, Richmond would fall. Lee tried valiantly to stop Grant before he got to Petersburg, saying, "We must destroy this army of Grant's before he gets to the James River. If he gets there it will become a siege and then it will be a mere question of time."

Lee's worst fears were realized. Grant got to the James, and it became the longest siege in American history. Grant gradually but relentlessly encircled Petersburg and cut Lee's supply lines from the south. For the Confederates, it was ten months of desperately hanging on. Their only hope was that the North would tire of the war. But Petersburg finally fell, and Richmond came tumbling after. Lee surrendered a week later.

The campaign began in May 1864, when Grant's army of 122,000 crossed the Rapidan River near Fredericksburg and engaged Lee's army of 65,000 in a series of battles. For a month the armies would clash, march, then clash again. The first two major battles were the Wilderness and Spotsylvania Court House. After each encounter, Grant moved southward, closer to the Confederate capital.

At Cold Harbor, on the Chickahominy River near Richmond, Grant tried a frontal attack on the defenses and suffered appalling losses. Abandoning his plan to capture Richmond by direct assault, he moved south of the James, and on June 16–18 he attacked Petersburg. The three days cost Grant 10,000 casualties, but two of the railroads leading into the city were cut and several roads captured.

Grant struck out to the south and west against the Weldon Railroad in the brutal heat of August. After three days of fighting, his troops were astride the railroad near Globe Tavern. Lee lashed back at Ream's Station, five miles to the south, but Union troops continued to hold the railroad.

The noose around Petersburg tightened.

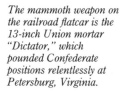

The mammoth weapon on the railroad flatcar is the 13-inch Union mortar "Dictator," which pounded Confederate positions relentlessly at Petersburg, Virginia.

By October, Grant's lines were three miles west of the Weldon Railroad. When winter came the armies settled down to everyday skirmishing, sniper fire, and mortar shelling. Early in February, Grant extended his lines westward to Hatcher's Run. Lee was forced to extend his already thin defenses. Meanwhile, supplies poured in to Grant over the newly completed U.S. Military Rail Roads from City Point.

By mid-March, Lee was desperate. Grant seemed certain to either get around his right flank or pierce the line somewhere along its forty miles that nearly encircled the city. Lee decided to try to breach the Union line at Fort Stedman, hold the gap, and cut Grant's railroad a few miles away. Confederate troops captured Fort Stedman, but were crushed by a Union counterattack.

Gen. Philip Sheridan, Grant's cavalry commander, struck at Five Forks on March 25, defeating Gen. George Pickett's troops, and seized the Southside Railroad. On April 2, Lee's right flank crumbled under a Union onslaught. Only a stout Con-

federate defense at Fort Gregg kept the battle out of the streets of Petersburg. On the night of April 2, Lee evacuated the city and marched west. The price of Petersburg was 70,000 Union and Confederate casualties.

VISITING THE BATTLEFIELD

The Petersburg National Battlefield comprises 1,530 acres and is made up of five major units. Begin at the Visitor Center in the main unit, east of the city of Petersburg, off VA 36. Other units are Grant's headquarters at City Point, extensive fortifications, battlefields, and the Poplar Grove National Cemetery.

The battlefield is open from 8 A.M. to dark, every day except Christmas and New Year's Day. At the Visitor Center, an hourly seventeen-minute map presentation describes the battles and the complexities of the siege. From mid-June to late August, demonstrations of Civil War soldiers' life and firing of mortar and cannon are presented. Visitor Center facilities are acces-

In a break from the fighting at Petersburg, Virginia, in 1864, Union soldiers relax by reading letters from home and playing cards. The siege, the longest sustained operation of the war, began in May 1864 and lasted until March 1865, covering an area of more than 170 square miles, with 35 miles of trenches. In September 1864, nearly 175 cannons fired a daily average of 7.8 tons of mortar into the Confederate defenses.

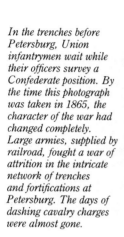

In the trenches before Petersburg, Union infantrymen wait while their officers survey a Confederate position. By the time this photograph was taken in 1865, the character of the war had changed completely. Large armies, supplied by railroad, fought a war of attrition in the intricate network of trenches and fortifications at Petersburg. The days of dashing cavalry charges were almost gone.

sible to the disabled. There are no food facilities in the park, but there are restaurants and a picnic area a half-mile west on VA 36 and in Petersburg. There are several motels on East Washington St. in Petersburg. There are bicycle and hiking trails. Information on special events is posted in the Visitor Center. For further information, write to the Superintendent, Petersburg National Battlefield, P.O. Box 549, Petersburg, VA 24134, or phone (804) 732-3531.

There are two self-guided auto tours: a four-mile *Battlefield Tour,* and a sixteen-mile *Siege Line Tour* to park areas south and west of the city. In addition, visitors should see *City Point.* Allow a full day to see everything.

The major sites on the battlefield tour include:

Battery 5. Reached by a walking trail from the Visitor Center, Battery 5 was on the original Confederate defense line, called the Dimmock Line. Nearby is the site where "the Dictator," a huge Union mortar, was located.

Battery 8. This battery was captured by black Union troops and renamed Fort Friend for the large Friend House located nearby. The fort was refaced, and served as a supporting artillery position for the duration of the siege.

Battery 9. Black troops of Hink's division captured this Confederate position during the first day of fighting. It is a ten-minute walk from here to the site of *Meade Station,* an important supply and hospital depot on the City Point & Army Line, the military railroad built during the siege. The winter quarters of the Union Ninth Corps were in the surrounding area.

Harrison Creek. Driven from their original line in the opening battle, Confederate forces fell back and dug in along this stream. Here they held for two days, finally withdrawing to a new line closer to Petersburg, which they held until the fall of the city. In March 1865 the main Confederate advance of Lee's last offensive, the Battle of Fort Stedman, was stopped along this stream.

Fort Stedman. This Union stronghold was the focus of Lee's attack on March 25, 1865, in his attempt to relieve heavy pressure west of the city. A loop trail from here leads to *Colquitt's Salient,* where the Confederate attacks originated. The trail also passes the *First Maine Monument,* commemorating the greatest regimental loss in a single action of the war.

Fort Haskell. Union artillery and very heavy infantry fire stopped the southward Confederate advance here during the Battle of Fort Stedman. Union troops who had been driven down the line of works were jammed so tightly into this fort that most could only load weapons and pass them forward to be fired.

Taylor Farm (site). All the original buildings of Taylor's Farm were destroyed at the start of the siege. Along this ridge, nearly two hundred pieces of artillery were concentrated and fired during the Battle of the Crater.

The Crater. Here a Union mine was exploded under a Confederate fort, but an infantry attack through the gap failed. A walking trail circles the crater.

A short drive northeast on VA 38 is the *City Point Unit* of the national battlefield. It is in the city of Hopewell, at the corner of Pecan Avenue and Cedar Lane, where the Appomattox River meets the James. Between June 1864 and April 1865, City Point was transformed from a sleepy village of fewer than a hundred inhabitants into a bustling supply center for the 100,000 Union troops on the siege lines in front of Petersburg. By the spring of 1865, when Lee was forced to abandon Petersburg, more than 280 new buildings of all descriptions, a half-mile of new wharves, and a vastly expanded railroad terminal had been built.

CITY POINT

Throughout the siege, Grant made his headquarters on the lawn of *Appomattox*

The engine President *chugs into the depot of the U.S. Military Railroads at City Point, Virginia, Grant's headquarters and the supply depot during the siege of Petersburg. Henry Haupt, in charge of military rail transportation, was an authority on railroad construction who bypassed military red tape to get his job done. By contrast, the South was perpetually hampered by the lack of railroads, and gaps in some lines made them useless.*

Black laborers pose on a wharf on the James River in Virginia. A flotilla of merchant ships transported the supplies Union forces needed for the siege of Petersburg. Grant's men wanted for nothing as they pounded away at Lee's starving, ill-equipped forces. The North's growing domination of the sea slowly strangled the South.

Manor, which now may be toured. Tents and cabins occupied nearly every available square foot of ground as the area became a nerve center for the Northern war effort. From here the Union telegraph system linked field commanders with Washington, enabling Grant to coordinate operations in all theaters of the war. President Lincoln visited City Point on two occasions, and was here for two of the last three weeks of his life.

SIEGE LINE TOUR

This tour begins when you exit the main battlefield and turn left onto Crater Road (U.S. 301). This is the original Jerusalem Plank Road of the war period, one of the main roadways leading into the city from the southeast. Although modern development has destroyed most of the trenches, some traces still can be found. As a rule, Union works were located to the left of the road, Confederate works to the right. The tour covers both state and county roads, so beware of fast-moving traffic.

The sites along the sixteen-mile tour include:

Fort Sedgwick (site). Union troops built this fort in July and August 1864 to control the Jerusalem Plank Road. Named for Gen. John Sedgwick, killed in the Battle of Spotsylvania, it was a key Union post along the eastern portion of the siege line. It was nicknamed "Fort Hell" because of heavy Confederate mortar and sniper fire. This was also the site of a major assault by the Union Ninth Corps against *Rives' Salient* and *Fort Mahone* on the Confederate line, April 2, 1865. A monument nearby honors Col. George Gowan, 48th Pennsylvania Volunteers, who was killed in this attack.

Fort Sedgwick was leveled in the late 1960s. It stood at the southeast corner of Crater Road and Morton Avenue. A nearby marker identifies the site of Rives' Salient, defended on June 9, 1864, by local militia in the first attack on Petersburg.

Fort Wadsworth. This was a key strategic point on the Petersburg front. Named for Gen. James S. Wadsworth, killed in the Battle of the Wilderness, the fort stands on the site of the Battle of the Weldon Railroad, August 1864, and was built to strengthen the Union hold on this sector. Interpretive markers in the fort discuss its significance in more detail. The *Hagood Monument* on the grounds memorializes the South Carolina soldiers who broke through the Union lines in this area on August 21, 1864.

What is now Halifax Road follows the original bed of the Petersburg & Weldon Railroad. The site of *Globe Tavern,* Gen. G. K. Warren's headquarters during part of the siege, is a half-mile on the left side of the road.

Poplar Grove Cemetery. This national cemetery was established in 1868 for Union soldiers who died during the Petersburg and Appomattox campaigns. Others are buried in the *City Point National Cemetery* in Hopewell. Of the 6,178 interments, 4,110 are unknown. Most of the Confederate soldiers who died during the siege are buried in *Blandford Cemetery* in Petersburg.

Fort Urmston and Conahey. These forts were built in October 1864 on ground captured by Union troops during the Battle of Peeble's Farm, September 29–30. They, like several other nearby forts, were named for Union officers killed in the battle. The interpretive marker at Fort Conahey describes its significance on the siege lines.

Fort Fisher. This was the largest earthen fortification on the Petersburg front. Union soldiers completed it in March 1865. Because the Confederate works were more than a mile to the north, there was little shelling along this part of the line. Fort Fisher never saw any fighting, but did play a part in the campaign. On April 2, 1865, a day after the Union victory at the Battle of Five Forks compelled Lee to abandon Petersburg, elements of the Sixth Corps assaulted the Confederate defenses between Forts Fisher and Welch. Nearby Fort Wheaton originally was the Confederate Fort Archer, a part of the Southern line captured during the Battle of Peeble's Farm. Access to Fort Welch, which, along with Fort Gregg, forms a continuation of the Union trench system, is across Church Road (VA 672) and can only be reached by foot trail.

Fort Gregg. This Confederate fort (not to be confused with the nearby Union fort of the same name) was built as an outpost guarding the western approach to Petersburg. On April 2, 1865, when Grant ordered his final assault on the Confederate lines, the 600 men defending Forts Gregg and Whitworth to the north held off the 24th Corps for two hours. This enabled Lee's army to withdraw safely from Petersburg that night.

Pennsylvania Monument. Located on the site of Confederate Fort Mahone, this

THE BATTLE OF THE CRATER

The plan sounded promising. Shortly after the siege began, members of the 48th Pennsylvania Infantry, many of whom were coalminers before the war, began digging a tunnel toward a Confederate fort at Pegram's (sometimes called Elliott's) Salient, southeast of Petersburg. They planned to explode four tons of gunpowder under the salient and send troops through the gap created by the explosion. If they succeeded, Petersburg might be captured without a long siege, shortening the war by many months.

The tunnel took a month to dig. It was 511 feet long, with lateral extensions at the end to hold the powder. When the explosion went off on the morning of July 30, it blew up a Confederate artillery battery and left a crater some 170 feet long, 60 feet wide, and 30 feet deep. But instead of going around the crater, many Union troops plunged directly into it, bogged down, and were unable to get out. Confederate counterattacks retook the position, inflicting more than 4,000 Union casualties.

monument was dedicated in 1909 and honors the service of the Union regiments in the Third Division, Ninth Army Corps. Fort Mahone, also known as Battery 29 and "Fort Damnation," fell to Union forces on April 2, 1865. The Union attack originated at Fort Sedgwick, only 600 yards away.

RICHMOND

RICHMOND NATIONAL BATTLEFIELD PARK

Richmond was the symbol of the Confederacy: the seat of its government, a manufacturing center, and the primary supply depot for troops operating on the South's northern frontier. The North decided early in the war that if Richmond could be captured, the South would lose its will to resist. Seven major drives were launched against Richmond, two bringing Union armies within sight of the city. The first of these, George B. McClellan's Peninsula campaign of 1862, was thwarted by Robert E. Lee. During the series of battles called the Seven Days, Lee sent the Union army reeling back toward Washington, 110 miles to the north. But in 1864, Grant's crushing

The last full measure of devotion was paid by this Confederate soldier in the defense of Richmond. During the fervor at the beginning of the war, few stopped to consider just how terrible the human cost might be. In the four years of conflict, more than 620,000 men lost their lives—360,000 Union soldiers and at least 260,000 Confederates.

overland campaign captured Richmond, and the Confederacy came tumbling down.

General McClellan took command of all Union forces after the debacle of First Manassas, and by early 1862 he had forged the "cowering regiments" into the disciplined 100,000-man Army of the Potomac. The army was transported by boat to Fort Monroe, Virginia, to advance on Richmond up the Peninsula, the neck of land between the James and the York rivers. To support McClellan, Gen. Irvin McDowell would attack overland from the north, and the navy would force its way up the James.

The Union naval attack was halted May 15 at Drewry's Bluff, but by May 24, McClellan was only six miles from Richmond. However, President Lincoln, increasingly alarmed by Stonewall Jackson's successes in the Shenandoah Valley, overruled McClellan and kept McDowell's army to protect Washington.

Believing that McClellan would stay north of the James, Gen. Joseph E. Johnston, the Confederate commander, decided to attack. His troops hit the Union army near Fair Oaks. McClellan, always cautious, became obsessed with the notion that his army was badly outnumbered. Even more important, Johnston was seriously injured in the battle, and President Davis replaced him with Gen. Robert E. Lee.

McClellan was in a dangerous position astride the Chickahominy River, and he stayed there too long. Lee attacked on June 26, rolling up the Union right at Mechanicsville, then suffering heavy losses against the strong Union positions at Beaver Dam Creek. In a week of almost continuous fighting, Lee attacked at Gaines' Mill, Savage's Station, Frayser's Farm (also called Glendale), and finally Malvern Hill, where a stiff Union resistance halted Confederate pursuit. The Union army avoided disaster by circling east of Richmond to the security of navy gunboats on the James at Harrison's Landing.

The Seven Days ended with 35,000 Union and Confederate casualties. One young Georgian soldier wrote home: "I have seen, heard and felt many things in the last week that I never want to see, hear nor feel again."

During the next two years, while the Army of the Potomac and the Army of Northern Virginia fought indecisively in other areas, a massive defensive system was built around Richmond. The first part of the system was an outer ring of defenses about ten miles from the city, stretching for more than sixty-five miles. Within that ring was an intermediate line about four miles from the city. At the city's outskirts were star forts.

When Gen. Ulysses S. Grant assumed command of all Union armies in the field, he attached himself to the Army of the Potomac, then commanded by Gen. George Meade, and launched an unyielding campaign against Richmond, beginning with a series of flanking movements to cut Lee off from the city. Although his force suffered heavy losses, Grant slipped by Lee at the Wilderness and Spotsylvania Court House. At Cold Harbor on June 3, 1864, Grant made a near-fatal error, launching a massive frontal attack against strongly entrenched Confederate lines. Some 7,000 Union soldiers fell in thirty minutes. A Confederate colonel noted that "the dead covered more than five acres of ground about as thickly as they could be laid."

For ten days, both armies suffered in the trenches under 100-degree heat, then Grant withdrew, crossed the James River, and drove toward Petersburg, an important rail center south of Richmond. Meanwhile, Richmond withstood all attacks, including a massive assault on its outer defenses north and south of Fort Harrison. Life in the trenches and forts around the city became routine. Troops spent much of the time finding enough to eat.

Grant's siege of Petersburg intensified during the winter of 1864–65, and Lee was forced to retreat westward on April 2. Shortly after dawn the following day, Jo-

One of the technological innovations used by the Union in the war was the observation balloon, such as this one being inflated during the Battle of Fair Oaks, Virginia, May 1862. Such balloons helped in tracking troop movements and artillery fire accuracy. The war also saw the introduction of repeating rifles, explosive shells, trenches, rifled cannon, the telegraph, railroads, ironclad warships, and the submarine.

When the Confederate line broke at Petersburg, Richmond panicked. Everyone who could, including the government, fled the city, and everything of military or industrial value was torched. When night came, mobs swarmed the streets and the flames spread. Southerners burned more of their own capital than the Yankees had burned of Atlanta. Union troops arrived the next morning and set about putting out the fires and restoring order.

seph Mayo, the mayor of Richmond, delivered a message to the commander of the Union forces entering the Confederate capital:

"The Army of the Confederate Government having abandoned the City of Richmond, I respectfully request that you will take possession of it with organized force, to preserve order and protect women and children and property."

After evacuating the city, the Confederate government ordered the burning of warehouses and supplies, and the fire did considerable damage to factories and houses in the business district. As the ashes of Richmond cooled, Lee surrendered to Grant at Appomattox Court House on April 9, 1865.

VISITING THE BATTLEFIELD PARK

The Richmond National Battlefield Park consists of ten units comprising a total of 770 acres. Start at the *Chimborazo Visitor Center,* 3215 East Broad St. It occupies the site of one of the Confederacy's largest hospitals, Chimborazo General. Considered a medical marvel, the hospital accommodated the influx of wounded arriving daily in Richmond, a total of nearly 76,000 during the war.

At the Visitor Center, exhibits and an audiovisual program depict the defense of Richmond. There also is a museum containing war artifacts and a small bookstore. Living-history programs are presented at the center and other locations in the park at various times of the year. It is open from 9 A.M. to 5 P.M. daily except Christmas and New Year's Day, and is accessible to the disabled. There is a picnic ground, but no food is sold. Restaurants are nearby on the highway. A schedule of events is posted in the Visitor Center. For further information, write to the Superintendent, Richmond National Battlefield Park, 3215 Broad St., Richmond, VA 23223, or phone (804) 226-1981.

A 100-mile, self-guided auto tour of the park takes a full day and covers sites associated with both the 1862 and the 1864 campaigns. Visitors may select their own route, visiting some or all of the sites. If time permits, the sites of the 1862 campaign should be visited one day, the 1864 sites on another day. Four of the sites have interesting walking trails totaling three and a half miles and well worth the time spent. Do not stray into the woods, where there are poisonous snakes, ticks, and poison ivy.

There is an unstaffed Visitor Center at Cold Harbor, sixteen miles northeast on VA 156, and another at Fort Harrison, ten miles southeast at the juncture of VA 5 and Battlefield Park Road. The Fort Harrison Visitor Center is open from June through August.

1862 CAMPAIGN SITES

Chickahominy Bluff. A part of the outer Confederate line defending Richmond, this bluff offers a fine view of Mechanicsville and the Chickahominy River Valley. Within sight of these earthworks, General Lee watched the beginning of the Seven Days battles.

Beaver Dam Creek. Part of the three-mile Union front that the Confederates unsuccessfully attacked on June 26 lies here, in the valley of Beaver Dam Creek at Ellerson's Mill. Few Confederates crossed the stream as Union artillery and infantry fire stopped Lee's attack all along the line. The earthwork beyond the creek contained a mill race that, said one Confederate officer, was "waist deep in blood." Raw courage and the crude tactical arts possessed by both sides were demonstrated here.

Watt House (Gaines' Mill Battle-field). Most of the fighting during the Battle of Gaines' Mill on June 27 took place a mile from the actual mill. Near the Watt House, a restored landmark of the battle, Gen. Fitz-John Porter established his head-

quarters during a crucial point in the fighting. Texas and Georgia troops broke the Union line within a few hundred yards of the house.

The short trail to *Breakthrough Point* leads to the remains of the shallow trenches defended by Union soldiers. The house, which is not open to the public, was built about 1835 and is a typical middle-class farmhouse of the period.

Malvern Hill. The last of the battles of the Seven Days was fought here, after which McClellan withdrew to his base at Harrison's Landing. The Union troops dug no defensive trenches and stood at bay in parade-ground, line-of-battle formation across the gently sloping fields as their massed artillery and infantry fire shattered the ranks of the attacking Confederates. The steep slopes of Malvern Hill on the Union left and the swampy bottoms on the right forced the Confederates to advance across open ground. One Confederate officer said, "It was not war—it was murder."

Drewry's Bluff. Union soldiers called this Confederate guardian of the James River "Fort Darling." On May 15, 1862, four Union gunboats, including the famous ironclad *U.S.S. Monitor,* and one revenue steamer, attacked the fort but were driven off. The unsuccessful attack prevented Richmond from being shelled early in the war, and the presence of the fort acted as a deterrent to other Union naval forays up the James. (In May–June 1864, the fort assisted in repulsing land attacks by Gen. Benjamin Butler's Army of the James.) The fort and the surrounding area served as the Confederate Naval Academy and Marine Corps Camp of Instruction throughout much of the war. Exhibits and markers along a trail give details of the fort's history:

Parking Area. Near here were the quarters for the men and their families stationed at the bluff, and the quarters of the chaplain.

"THE ART OF WAR IS SIMPLE ENOUGH. FIND OUT WHERE YOUR ENEMY IS. GET AT HIM AS SOON AS YOU CAN. STRIKE AT HIM AS HARD AS YOU CAN AND AS OFTEN AS YOU CAN, AND KEEP MOVING ON."

—ULYSSES S. GRANT

Site of Chapel. Near the entrance to the fort is the site of the chapel. A grave depression can be noticed next to the site.

Captain Tucker's Gun. The path ahead leads to Tucker's Battery. The land east of the fort was the site of Camp Beall.

Observation Platform. To the left, up the James, was Richmond, seven miles away. Norfolk is ninety miles downriver, the direction from which the Union gunboats came.

Eight-inch Columbiad. Also known as a Confederate Rodman, this cannon, when loaded with a 10-pound charge, shot a 64-pound shell up to two and a half miles. The barrel was made at Bellona Arsenal in 1862, and weighs 8,800 pounds. The cannon is mounted on a barbette carriage and positioned for action.

Well and Bombproof. Here the gun crew was protected from enemy fire while firing the cannon.

Powder Magazine. Now caved in, the magazine once provided protective storage for gunpowder and ammunition within the fort.

Subway. The subway, a fortified chute, protected men bringing in supplies from the fort's south side during a battle.

Only traces remain of other battlefields not part of the national park but important to an understanding of McClellan's 1862 campaign. They include *Fair Oaks, Seven Pines, Savage's Station, White Oak Swamp,* and *Frayser's Farm (or Glendale).* State historical markers and monuments explain the fighting at these sites.

1864 CAMPAIGN SITES

Cold Harbor. Midway between two shabby crossroads taverns—Old and New Cold Harbor—the Confederates on June 1–2 dug in to await Grant's attack. It came on June 3, a frontal assault on a narrow section of the Confederate line, and it cost Grant 7,000 casualties in thirty minutes. Grant's troops knew the odds they were facing, and pinned bits of paper bearing their names and those of their next of kin to the backs of their uniform jackets. This was the beginning of the identification plates, or "dog tags," later issued routinely to servicemen. The actions at Cold Harbor changed the war from one of maneuver to one of siege. Cold Harbor also influenced the strategy and tactics of future wars by demonstrating that well-selected, well-manned entrenchments, supported by artillery, were practically impregnable against frontal assaults. The well-preserved trenches along the one-and-a-quarter-mile tour road are fine examples of Civil War field fortifications. A self-guided tour includes the principal sites of the battlefield.

Confederate troops established themselves at Cold Harbor after Sheridan's attack on May 31, and re-formed here after repulsing the Union charge of June 1. The gap in the line between the divisions of Robert Hoke and Joseph Kershaw was approximately 300 yards to the south. Behind the Visitor Center are the fields on both sides of route 156 over which Gen. Horatio Wright's Sixth Corps attacked on June 3. Here also was the horseshoe in the Confederate line where some of the heaviest fighting took place. The battle line extended to the south across what is now route 156 for about a mile and a half.

Confederate Turnout. These breastworks were dug and manned by Gen. Thomas Clingman's brigade. On June 1, Hoke's and Kershaw's troops left these positions in an uncoordinated and unsuccessful attack. On June 3, this was the site of the attack by the flank of the 13th Corps and the right flank of the Sixth Corps. The ravine to the right split the ranks of the Sixth Corps and funneled them into fields of Confederate crossfire.

Union Turnout. Across the field, devoid of trees at that time, Union troops attacked the entrenched Confederates three times on June 3. The earthwork remains to the rear mark the high-water mark of the third and last attack. Unable to advance or retreat, the Union troops dug shallow trenches for cover. These later became the main Union battle line in the area.

Route 156. Known as Cold Harbor Road, this was the main road to Mechanicsville to the west and Seven Pines to the south. Cold Harbor Crossroads, to the west of here, was deemed strategically important if Grant was to attack Richmond.

National Cemetery. This small cemetery contains the remains of 2,000 Union soldiers, more than 1,300 of them unknown. The cemetery and five others in the Richmond area were created by Congress in 1866 to honor the Union war dead.

Garthright House. This house was behind the line of the Eighth New York Heavy Artillery during the battle. From June 3 through June 12, the house was used as a Union field hospital. During this time, the Garthrights lived in the basement. Portions of the restored house, which is not open to the public, date to the early 1700s.

Fort Harrison and Vicinity. After Cold Harbor, Grant crossed the James River and directed his main effort against Petersburg. In a surprise move aimed at preventing Lee from shifting troops to another sector, some 15,000 Union troops were transferred to the north side of the James. General Ord's 17th Corps stormed the heavily armed but badly undermanned Fort Harrison, capturing it without difficulty early in the morning of September 29. The gallantry of several regiments of black Union troops involved in the battle was recognized by awarding the Medal of Honor to fourteen black soldiers.

General Birney's Tenth Corps was thrown back at nearby Fort Gilmer. Lee brought up reinforcements from Petersburg, and tried several times to retake the fort. Fort Harrison was later renamed Fort Burnham in honor of Gen. Hiram Burnham, who was killed in the assault.

224   *THE EIGHTEENTH CORPS AT COLD HARBOR.*

VIEW OF UNION BREASTWORKS ON THE COLD HARBOR LINE, JUNE 1.
FROM A SKETCH MADE AT THE TIME.

Grant learned a costly lesson at Cold Harbor on June 3, 1864. Believing Lee's army to be "really whipped," he attacked the well-entrenched Confederate line. His troops, who had suspected otherwise, suffered 7,000 casualties in thirty minutes. Many men pinned to their uniforms slips of paper with their names and addresses so their bodies could be identified after the battle. In this engraving, Union troops are building breastworks two days before the battle.

A self-guided tour starts at the side gate of Fort Burnham. The short traverse to the left and the portion of the earthworks on the right were added by Union troops after the capture of Fort Harrison. These two features protected troops from deadly fire from Fort Gilmer to the north.

Enter the fort and stay on the path to the left. These earthworks make up the primary wall of Fort Harrison and are an extension of the outer defense line of Richmond. The wall from the bottom of the moat to the top was from eighteen to twenty-seven feet high and twelve to fifteen feet wide, two-thirds larger than it is now.

The structure you pass is a traverse built as an inner wall of Fort Burnham, affording greater protection from artillery fire from the Confederates' Fort Johnson.

The rectangular space ahead, enclosed on three sides and open in the rear, formed one of three similar sections of the Confederate fort. The other sections of Fort Harrison are not clearly visible because of changes made after Union occupation of the fort. The wall on the left is where Union troops first entered the fort. This section was considerably weakened when two large coastal artillery pieces were rendered inoperable. The solid mass of earth to the right was built to protect against heavy naval shells fired on the fort from Union gunboats on the James River.

A large traverse was built as protection from artillery fire. The opening beside the great traverse is an original roadway constructed after the capture of Fort Harrison to provide full access to the fortification.

At this point, Confederate Fort Harrison comes to an abrupt end and Union Fort Burnham begins. There is a contrast in the size of the walls. The Confederate walls took two years to build and are considerably larger than the Union walls.

The guardrail encloses the remainder of the freshwater well, dug by the Confederates, which the Union troops continued to use, building a small traverse around it to protect themselves from enemy gunfire.

On the trail to the left is a barbette-style gun emplacement built by Union troops. An artillery piece would be rolled up the ramp into position near the angle in the fort, with its barrel projecting above the parapet. While the parapet offered little protection for men firing the cannon, the position gave the piece freedom of horizontal sweep.

Along this wall are the caved-in remains of Union bombproofs used to protect the troops garrisoning the fort.

A self-guided trail through Fort Harrison provides details of the battle and the fort. At Fort Brady, an overlook affords a splendid view of the James River.

Parker's Battery. This small Confederate artillery work helped to immobilize Union Gen. Benjamin Butler's Army of the James during its attack on Richmond in May. The fighting continued into June and successfully bottled up Butler at Bermuda Hundred. The battery then became part of the Howlett Line, helping to defend Richmond until the capital was abandoned in April 1865.

VISITING RICHMOND

State Capitol, Capitol Square, one block south of Broad Street, between Ninth and Twelfth streets. Many important events of the war occurred in this building, designed by Thomas Jefferson: here Virginia ratified the Articles of Secession; Robert E. Lee assumed command of all Virginia forces; Jefferson Davis delivered his inaugural address at the base of the Washington Statue in the northwest corner of the Capitol grounds; and here the Confederate Congress met. Guided tours are conducted.

Monument Avenue. This fashionable boulevard, running east to west from Lom-

bardy Street, is lined with statues of Lee, Stuart, Jackson, Davis, and Commodore Matthew Fontaine Maury, the noted oceanographer.

Saint Paul's Episcopal Church, southwest corner of Grace and Ninth Sts., across from Capitol Square. (804) 643-3589. Known as the "Church of the Confederacy," Jefferson Davis received confirmation here early in the war. He was attending services on April 2, 1865, when he received a message from Lee that the Richmond-Petersburg defense had been broken. The Lee Memorial Window is notable. Guided tours by appointment.

Church Hill Restored Area. Surrounding St. Paul's is an area of more than seventy antebellum houses, most of them restored. Houses are open to the public during Historic Garden Week in mid-April. Information is available at Historic Richmond Foundation, Shelton House, 2407 East Grace St., or phone (804) 643-7407.

Battle Abbey, 428 North Blvd., phone (804) 358-4901. This building, now the headquarters of the Virginia Historical Society, was built in 1913 as a Confederate memorial hall. Displayed are battle flags, weapons, and portraits. A gigantic mural series by French artist Charles Hoffbauer depicts battles fought in Virginia. The finest Civil War research library in the state is here. Open every day except Sunday and major holidays.

Valentine, 1015 East Clay St., phone (804) 649-0711. A plaster cast of Edward V. Valentine's famous sculpture of the recumbent figure of Lee is in this 1812 house, now a museum. The collection is particularly strong on costumes. The museum includes the 1812 Wickham-Valentine house, a Federal home with a walled garden and period furnishings. Open daily except major holidays. Tours are given hourly.

Museum of the Confederacy, 1201 East Clay St., phone (804) 649-1861. The largest collection of Confederate artifacts in the nation is housed here, including the field uniforms and personal belongings of Lee, Jackson, Stuart, and Joseph E. Johnston. The art collection includes a series of oil paintings of the defenses of Charleston by

As the Confederate government and the army garrison evacuated Richmond, the city's factories, arsenals, and mills were ordered to be destroyed. This photograph shows the ruins of Haxall's Mills. Fires raged out of control, commissary depots were thrown open, and there was widespread pillaging. Whiskey stocks were broken into, and "the streets ran with liquor." A soldier said, "The old war-scarred city seemed to prefer annihilation to conquest."

Conrad Wise Chapman. Adjacent to the museum is the three-story home that served as the *White House of the Confederacy,* which is open by appointment while undergoing renovation. Open daily except major holidays. The museum is accessible to the disabled.

Hollywood Cemetery, 412 South Cherry St. at Albermarle St., phone (804) 648-8501. A number of noted Virginians, including James Monroe, John Tyler, and Jefferson Davis, are buried in the 115-acre cemetery, which was opened in 1853. Some 15,000 Confederate soldiers are interred on the grounds. The cemetery office at the gate offers an audiovisual program and a map-guide to the prominent graves.

Virginia War Memorial, 621 South Belvidere St., at the north end of the Robert E. Lee Bridge on U.S. 1. An eternal flame and a roll of honor with more than 12,000 names engraved on glass and the marble walls commemorate Virginia's sons killed in battle.

Meadow Farm Museum, in General Sheppard Crump Memorial Park, twelve miles northwest of Richmond via I-95 north, I-295 west, Woodman Road South exit, at Courtney and Mountain roads. Phone (804) 649-0566. A living-history farm museum that depicts rural life in Virginia before the Civil War. On the 150 acres are a farmhouse, barn, outbuildings, orchard, garden, and farm animals. Excellent for children, and accessible to the disabled. Open daily except Monday, closed January and February.

FAMILY MATTERS

When Jeb Stuart and his cavalry rode completely around the entire Union army during the Seven Days, the Union cavalry that pursued him was led by a Virginian who remained loyal to the Union, Brig. Gen. Philip St. George Cooke—Stuart's father-in-law.

The area around Richmond and Petersburg abounds in fine antebellum plantations, mansions, and estates. Some are open all year, others only during the annual Historic Garden Week in mid-April. Information and maps are available at the Metro Richmond Visitor Center, 1700 Robin Hood Rd., phone (804) 358-5511.

To capture the spirit of Richmond stay at the *Sheraton Jefferson,* Franklin and Adams Sts., 23220, phone (804) 788-8000, a historic turn-of-the-century hotel recently restored to its former elegance.

An excellent bed-and-breakfast in the Historic District is *Abbie Hill,* P.O. Box 4503, 23223, phone (804) 353-4656 or 353-5855.

Also recommended is the *Catlin-Abbot House,* 2304 East Broad St., 23220, phone (804) 780-3746, an 1845 home furnished with antiques and family heirlooms. A veranda overlooks the courtyard. Richmond has hotels and motels in all price ranges.

The seafood is recommended at the *Flying Cloud,* 2004 Dabney Rd. off Broad St., phone (804) 355-6412, and so are the authentic nautical artifacts.

The *Tobacco Company,* 1201 East Cary St., phone (804) 782-9431, serves hearty fare in an old tobacco warehouse decorated with antiques.

OTHER VIRGINIA SITES OF INTEREST

ABINGDON

An important Confederate railroad depot and supply base, Abingdon was at various times the headquarters of Generals John Hunt Morgan and John C. Breckinridge. Union troops captured the town in December 1864 and burned down a number of buildings.

During the war, the *Martha Washington Inn* (150 West Main St., 24210; phone

In Alexandria, Virginia, across the Potomac River from Washington, barricades are erected on Duke Street in 1861 to protect the Orange and Alexandria Railroad from the Confederate cavalry. For the first time in history, railroads played a vital role in war, transporting men, horses, and materiél to the front. From Manassas on, battle after battle was fought over rail junctions. On his March to the Sea, General Sherman made a point of destroying miles of railroad track in order to hobble the South.

[703] 628-3161) was pressed into service as a military hospital. Now a four-star inn, it has been restored to its original appearance. The dining room, *First Lady's Table,* does nice things with veal Zurich and chicken piccata.

ALEXANDRIA

Union troops occupied this town, directly across the Potomac from Washington, in May 1861, but not before it sent four companies into the Confederate army. Alexandria was an important Union supply base and port of embarkation.

Visitor Center. The historic sites may be seen on a walking tour starting at the Alexandria Tourist Council in the 1724 *Ramsay House,* the oldest house in town, at 221 King St. at Fairfax St., phone (703) 549-0205. The council has tour brochures. block tickets, highway maps, and parking permits. Open daily except Christmas and New Year's Day.

Christ Church, 118 North Washington St., phone (703) 549-1789. Robert E. Lee

was confirmed here, and it is believed to have also been the place where he was offered command of all of the state's military forces. The 1773 church is little changed since Colonial days. Open daily except major holidays.

Boyhood Home of Robert E. Lee, 607 Oronoco St., phone (703) 548-8454. The future general spent much of his boyhood in this 1795 house, now furnished with 19th-century pieces. Washington and Lafayette were among those who visited his father, "Light Horse Harry" Lee. Open daily from February through mid-December.

The Stabler-Leadbetter Apothecary Store, 105/107 South Fairfax St., phone (703) 836-3713. In business here since 1792, the shop is now a museum of early pharmacy artifacts. In October 1859, Jeb Stuart gave Lee a message here that directed him to proceed at once to Harpers Ferry to quell a disturbance by John Brown.

Fort Ward Museum and Historic Site, 4301 West Braddock Rd., phone (703) 838-4848. This was one of sixty-eight

The last capitol of the Confederacy, now the Danville Museum of Fine Arts and History, Danville, Virginia

forts and batteries defending the capital in the war. The northwest bastion of the old fort has been reconstructed, and other parts renovated. A Civil War museum is in the headquarters building. Open daily except major holidays.

An excellent European-style inn is the *Morrison House* (116 South Alfred St., 22314; phone [703] 838-8000), with a marble foyer and a mahogany-paneled library with fireplace. Each guest room is individually decorated in the style of the Federal Period. Have a Colonial dinner at *Gadsby's Tavern*, a fixture since 1792 across from the Old City Hall at 138 North Royal St., phone (703) 548-1288. Costumed waiters and waitresses serve such specialties as Sally Lunn bread and George Washington's favorite duck. Colonial singers Tuesday through Saturday. A small museum is in the restaurant.

Alexandria has twelve motels and a variety of good restaurants. Inexpensive and fun is the *Hard Times Cafe*, 1404 King St., phone (703) 683-5340.

CULPEPER

A railhead on the Orange & Alexandria Railroad, Lee often camped here. The hotel was Grant's headquarters before his 1864 campaign, and many buildings were used as hospitals.

Culpeper Cavalry Museum, 133 West Davis St., phone (703) 825-8628. Culpeper was called the "Cavalry Capital of the Civil War" and a thirty-minute slide program here explains why. The collection of cavalry equipment, weaponry, and other war artifacts is exceptional. Open Monday through Friday except major holidays.

Brandy Station Battlefield. Union cavalry surprised Jeb Stuart here on June 9, 1863, and for eleven hours the biggest cavalry battle of the war was fought over fields and through woods. The Confederates retained the field, but it was a victory for the Union horsemen, their first of the war. The battlefield is practically unchanged today. Historical markers are on *Fleetwood Hill,* the center of the fighting.

Five miles north of Culpeper at the junction with route 663, turn west to the battlefield.

Cedar Mountain Battlefield. Stonewall Jackson collided with the vanguard of Gen. John Pope's advancing army here on August 9, 1862, and Union regiments struck Jackson on both sides of the road. The Confederates were barely able to hold until reinforcements arrived and turned back Pope's troops. The battlefield is little changed from 1862. A highway plaque notes the site, five miles south of Culpeper on U.S. 15.

Fountain Hall Bed & Breakfast (609 South East St., 22701; phone [703] 825-8200) is in an 1859 Greek Revival home with period decor. A continental breakfast is included in the room rate.

There are motels a few miles south of Culpeper on U.S. 29.

DANVILLE

Near the end of the war, six tobacco warehouses here were used to hold Union prisoners. Some 1,400 of them died in a smallpox epidemic. When Grant broke

John Singleton Mosby

through the defenses of Petersburg, the Confederate government moved to Danville.

Last Capitol of the Confederacy. The antebellum home of Maj. William T. Sutherlin, now the *Danville Museum of Fine Arts and History* (975 Main St., phone [804] 793-5644), served as the last capitol of the Confederacy. Jefferson Davis lived here April 3–10, 1865. The parlor, the library, and the Davis bedroom have been restored, and there is a collection of silver, sculpture, and paintings. Open Tuesday through Friday and Sunday. Closed on major holidays.

Danville has motels on Piney Forest Rd. and Riverside Dr.

FAIRFAX

In a raid on Fairfax the night of March 8, 1863, Capt. John S. Mosby and thirty troopers captured Gen. Edwin Stoughton as he lay asleep in bed, and took thirty-two other Union prisoners, fifty-eight horses, and arms and equipment.

FARMVILLE

Sayler's Creek Battlefield Historical State Park. Nine miles southwest of Farmville on U.S. 360, then seven miles west on VA 307 and two miles north on VA 617. Phone (804) 392-3435. In the final major battle of the war in Virginia, Gen. Philip Sheridan encircled the rear third of Lee's retreating forces on April 6, 1865. Fighting continued through the afternoon, resulting in the capture of more than 7,000 Confederates, including eight generals. The fragments of units stumbled to catch up with the main body of the army, and Lee exclaimed: "My God! Has the army dissolved?" Some 220 acres of the battlefield have been developed into a state park. The battlefield may be toured by car or on self-guided trails. Open daily.

FRONT ROYAL

Once known as "Hell Town" for the wild and colorful characters who gathered here, Front Royal was famous in the war for the activities of Belle Boyd, a Southern spy. When Gen. Nathaniel Banks's regiment was occupying Front Royal, she invited Banks and his officers to a ball, and later slipped away on horseback to tell Stonewall Jackson what she had learned. The next morning, May 23, 1862, Jackson captured 750 of Banks's 1,000 men. Miss Boyd was imprisoned after the war, and later married a Union officer.

Warren Rifles Confederate Museum, 95 Chester St., phone (703) 636-6982. Memorabilia on display relate to Belle Boyd as well as to Lee, Jackson, Early, and other Confederate leaders. Open daily mid-April through October, other times by appointment.

Front Royal has five motels and two interesting inexpensive restaurants on South Royal Ave., *Constant Spring Inn,* phone (703) 635-7010, and *My Father's Moustache,* phone (703) 635-3496.

HAMPTON

On June 10, 1861, some 4,000 Union troops attacked 1,500 Confederates at Big Bethel, the first significant engagement of the war in Virginia. After two hours of confused fighting, the Union forces fled the field. (The battlefield is now under a reservoir and on an air force base.) Two months later, Hampton was burned by its residents to prevent occupation. Only five buildings survived.

Syms-Eaton Museum, 418 West Mercury Blvd., across from the Hampton Information Center. On display are uniforms and exhibits on Hampton during the war. Accessible to the disabled. Open daily except major holidays.

Fort Monroe, three miles southeast of Hampton, on VA 143. Known as "the Gibraltar of Chesapeake Bay," the fort was begun in 1819 and took fifteen years to build. Robert E. Lee was an army engineer on part of the construction. At various times during the war, the fort was the headquarters for Generals Benjamin Butler

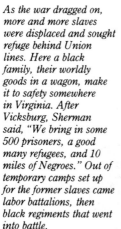

As the war dragged on, more and more slaves were displaced and sought refuge behind Union lines. Here a black family, their worldly goods in a wagon, make it to safety somewhere in Virginia. After Vicksburg, Sherman said, "We bring in some 500 prisoners, a good many refugees, and 10 miles of Negroes." Out of temporary camps set up for the former slaves came labor battalions, then black regiments that went into battle.

and George McClellan. Lincoln and Grant were visitors.

Casemate Museum, three miles southeast of Hampton, reached by I-64, then either VA 143 or VA 169. Phone (804) 727-3973. Falsely charged with plotting against the life of Lincoln, Jefferson Davis was imprisoned in this casemate of the fort following his capture in May 1865. A walking tour of the casemate leads to his cell. A museum displays war artifacts, uniforms, and three original Frederick Remington drawings. Open daily except major holidays.

HARRISONBURG

Battle of Harrisonburg. Two regiments of Confederates attacked a Union regiment here on June 6, 1862, in a fight for control of Chestnut Hill. Confederate General Turner Ashby was killed in the battle. Historical markers and a monument to Ashby are a half-mile south of town off I-81, county road 659, then left on county road 1003 for another half-mile.

Harrisonburg-Rockingham Historical Society, 301 South Main St., phone (703) 434-4762. A half-hour narration and a large electrified relief map give a clear description of Stonewall Jackson's 1862 Shenandoah campaign. Open Tuesday through Saturday except holidays.

Harrisonburg has six motels. An enjoyable, inexpensive restaurant is the *Train Station,* on Port Republic Rd., one block east of Exit 63, I-91, phone (703) 434-9843.

LEESBURG

Leesburg was a focal point for both Confederate and Union armies. Lee retrained his forces here in 1862 before his first invasion of the North. Col. John S. Mosby, the "Gray Ghost" of the Confederacy, operated in this area.

Jefferson Davis, former president of the Confederacy, was confined in this casemate cell at Fort Monroe, Virginia, following his capture in May 1865. During the early part of his confinement, he was kept in chains. Davis was paroled in May 1867 and never stood trial.

Battle of Ball's Bluff. A Union reconnaissance force of 1,000 crossed the Potomac here in October 1861, and met disaster. The Confederates drove them back over the bluffs to the river, where rifle fire from above killed the commander and half his force; others drowned, their bodies floating downriver to Washington. Oliver Wendell Holmes, Jr., who later became a justice of the U.S. Supreme Court, was among the wounded. A national cemetery and stone markers are on the battlefield. Drive north from Leesburg on the U.S. 15 bypass for two miles, then turn right on the unnumbered dirt road that dead-ends at the battlefield.

Loudoun Museum. 16 West Loudoun St., phone (703) 777-7427. A number of war artifacts are on display in this antebellum building. Open daily except major holidays.

There are three country inns, a motel, and several excellent restaurants in Leesburg.

This house was owned by Stonewall Jackson when he was a professor at Virginia Military Institute from 1859 to 1861, and has been restored to its original appearance. Many of the furnishings in the house were once owned by Jackson. He and many other Confederate soldiers are buried nearby, at the Stonewall Jackson Cemetery.

LEXINGTON

No town in Virginia was more dedicated to the Southern cause than Lexington, and no town today evokes a greater sense of Civil War history. Lexington sent an artillery battery and an infantry company into service. Union troops entered Lexington on June 10, 1864, and burned a substantial portion of the town, including buildings at the Virginia Military Institute.

Stonewall Jackson Home, 8 East Washington St., phone (703) 463-2552. Jackson lived here before the war, during the ten years he was a professor at the Virginia Military Institute. Many of the furnishings are original. An interpretive slide program precedes a tour of the house and garden. Open daily except major holidays.

Stonewall Jackson Cemetery, 300 block of South Main St. General Jackson, his family, and some 400 of his Confederate comrades in arms are buried here.

Washington and Lee University, South Jefferson and West Washington Sts., phone (703) 483-8400. Robert E. Lee served as the president of the college for the five years immediately after the war. Lee and most of his family are entombed in the *Lee Memorial Chapel* on the beautiful campus. The recumbent statue of Lee, by Edward Valentine, is magnificent. Art from the collections of the Lee and Washington families is on display. A museum in the basement of the chapel features items showing Lee's contribution to the college. Open daily except major holidays.

Virginia Military Institute, U.S. 11, phone (703) 463-6201. Established in 1839, this military college contributed a great number of officers and men to the Confederate army. An unusual statue depicting Stonewall Jackson standing in the wind is in the center of the campus. On the east side of the parade ground is Sir Moses Ezekiel's statue *Virginia Mourning Her Dead,* dedicated to the VMI cadets who fell in the Battle of New Market. Ezekiel, himself one of the cadets who fought at New Market, is buried under the statue. Mementos of the noted soldiers who were associated with the institute are in an on-campus museum. The museum is open daily except Thanksgiving and December 24–January 1. The cadet corps parades Friday afternoons from September to May, weather permitting.

The *Historic Country Inn,* (11 North Main Street, 24450; phone [703] 463-2044) is convenient to the historic district and greets guests with a tot of sherry or tea and sends them off with a complimentary continental breakfast.

The *Willson-Walker House* (30 North Main St., phone [703] 463-3020) is a chef-owned restaurant in a house built in 1820. It prides itself on its medallions of veal and fresh seafood.

PRESIDENTIAL MATERIAL

Two future Presidents of the United States fought in the Battle of Lynchburg, Virginia, in June 1864: Gen. Rutherford B. Hayes and Maj. William McKinley. Fighting for the Confederacy at Lynchburg was a former U.S. Vice-President, Gen. John C. Breckinridge. In all, seven former Union generals served as President; the others were Andrew Johnson, Ulysses S. Grant, James A. Garfield, Chester A. Arthur, and Benjamin Harrison.

LYNCHBURG

Three rail lines and a major canal made wartime Lynchburg a major supply depot. A brief military campaign centered around Lynchburg in June 1964.

Fort Early, Fort Ave. (U.S. 29 Business) and Vermont Ave. A partly restored redoubt is all that remains of the Battle of

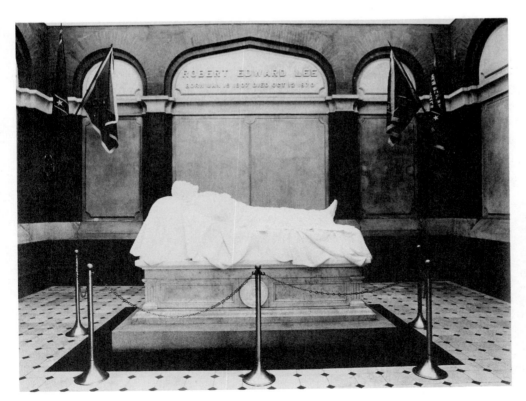

A recumbent statue of Robert E. Lee, carved by Edward Valentine, is on his tomb in the Lee Memorial Chapel of the Washington and Lee University campus, Lexington, Virginia. Lee was president of Washington College from 1865 to 1870; after his death the school's name was changed. His office at the college remains as he left it.

Formal parades are part of student life at Virginia Military Institute, Lexington, Virginia. Cadets from this college fought bravely at the Battle of New Market. Stonewall Jackson taught here before the war and Jackson mementos are on display.

Lynchburg. The fort was named for Gen. Jubal Early, who commanded the Southern defenses and lived in Lynchburg from 1869 until his death in 1894. A monument to Early is near the redoubt.

Jackson Funeral Boat. In Riverside Park, on a bluff overlooking the James, is part of the hull of the canal barge *Marshall*, which transported the body of Stonewall Jackson to Lexington.

MIDDLETOWN

Cedar Creek Battlefield. On October 19, 1864, Gen. Jubal Early surprised two Union corps and nearly routed them, but his starving soldiers began falling out of action to loot abandoned camps. Gen. Philip Sheridan was at Winchester when he learned of the battle. He mounted his horse, raced to the battlefield, and rallied the Union troops. This was the last battle fought for the control of the Shenandoah Valley. The undeveloped battlefield lies a half-mile south of Middletown on U.S. 11 (exit 77 from I-81).

Belle Grove, one mile south of Middletown on U.S. 11, phone (703) 869-2028. This limestone mansion, a National Trust property, was Union headquarters during the Battle of Cedar Creek. Guided tours. Open daily, April through October.

Strasburg Museum, five miles southwest of Middletown on I-81 on King St. in Strasburg. Relics from the war are on display in the old Southern Railway Depot. Open daily, May through October.

The *Wayside Inn* (at exit 77 from I-81, 22645; phone [703] 869-1797) has been in business since 1797, and the rooms are furnished with antiques.

NEW MARKET

New Market Battlefield Park, one mile north of I-81 exit 67, phone (703) 740-3101. A dramatic battle was fought here on May 15, 1864. Only a patched-together Confederate force stood between Staunton and a Union army commanded by Gen. Franz Sigel. In desperation, Confederate

General John Breckinridge, who was Vice-President under President James Buchanan from 1857 to 1861, was pressed to order the 257 teenage cadets from the Virginia Military Institute in Lexington to join the battle. Breckinridge agreed reluctantly, saying, "Major, order them up, and God forgive me for the order." They entered the fray fearlessly, capturing a battery, taking prisoners, and inspiring a Southern victory. Ten cadets were killed and forty-seven wounded. On the battlefield, the original *Bushong Farmhouse* and outbuildings have been restored and furnished in the period. The museum at the battlefield, called the *Hall of Valor*, has one of the finest war museums in the state, offers displays, dioramas, artifacts, and a motion picture that presents a clear, condensed explanation of the war in Virginia. Open daily except Christmas.

A Touch of Country (9329 Congress St., 22844; [703] 740-8030) is a bed-and-breakfast a short walk from the heart of New Market.

Virginia ham and barbecued short ribs are featured at the *Southern Kitchen,* on Main St., phone (703) 740-3514.

There are several motels and restaurants near town on U.S. 11.

NEWPORT NEWS

This city was only a village during the war, but it played an important role in the 1861–62 campaigns in Virginia.

Newport News Park, take the I-64 exit on VA 105 East to the intersection with VA 143, and turn left to the park entrance. Confederate General John B. "Jeb" Magruder prepared defense lines in what now is the largest municipal park east of the Mississippi. Levees also were built to flood the lowlands in the event of a Union advance. At Dam Number 1 in the park, on April 16, 1862, Vermont troops tried unsuccessfully to break the Confederate position. The park houses an interpretive center, and a self-guided walking tour explores the city.

Fort Eustis, at the northwest end of the city, on Mulberry Island. Take VA 105 west from I-64, phone (804) 878-1109. This site is now the headquarters of the U.S. Army Transportation Center. The *Transportation Museum* includes several Civil War exhibits. On a remote part of the base is *Fort Crafford,* a star-shaped earthwork fortification that anchored the right

Philip H. Sheridan

flank of the Confederate main defense line across the Peninsula. The earthworks and gun emplacements are well preserved. (Check at the museum to see if Fort Crafford is open to visitors.) Open daily.

The Mariners Museum, junction of U.S. 60 and Clyde Morris Blvd., three miles off I-64 exit 62A, phone (804) 595-0368. A large museum with some exhibits showing Civil War naval affairs. Ships' carvings, models, marine decorative arts, figureheads, etc. Research library. Gift shop. Guided tours. Open daily except Christmas.

War Memorial Museum of Virginia, 9285 Warwick Blvd., in Huntington Park on U.S. 60, phone (804) 247-8523. More than 60,000 artifacts including weapons, uniforms, vehicles, posters, insignia, and accoutrements from every war from the Revolution to Vietnam. Military history library. Film collection. Open daily except major holidays.

Monitor-Merrimac Overlook, take exit 6 from I-64, then drive south on VA 167 for 4.6 miles. On March 9, 1862, people gathered here to watch the ironclads USS *Monitor* and the CSS *Virginia* (formerly USS *Merrimac*) fight it out in Hampton Roads until the *Virginia* retired. The overlook is situated near the site of Camp Butler, a Union installation used in the last months of the war as an internment camp for Southern prisoners of war. Forts Monroe and Wool, the Norfolk naval yard, and other points of interest are visible from here, weather permitting.

PORTSMOUTH

Portsmouth Naval Shipyard Museum, 2 High St., on the Elizabeth River, phone (804) 393-8591. A large collection of items of naval equipment, including items pertaining to the *CSS Virginia,* the South's first ironclad warship. Open daily except Monday and major holidays.

In the harbor at Hampton Roads, Virginia, March 9, 1862, ironclad vessels clash for the first time. The USS Monitor, *left, and the* Merrimac *(rechristened the CSS* Virginia*) fought inconclusively for nearly two hours until injuries forced both commanders to withdraw. Although they were of little importance in determining the outcome of the war, ironclads were to change the course of naval history.*

During the Peninsula campaign in the spring of 1862, gunners of Mortar Battery No. 4, First Connecticut Heavy Artillery, pose with their massive 13-inch Seacoast Mortars in an emplacement near Yorktown, Virginia. McClellan's plan to take Richmond ended abruptly when Robert E. Lee took command of the Army of Northern Virginia and drove back the Union army toward Washington in a series of battles called the Seven Days.

WARRENTON

Union troops occupied Warrenton through most of the war, despite several raids by Mosby's partisan rangers. One of the three companies Warrenton contributed to the Confederate armies, the "Black Horse Cavalry," compiled a war record that earned it the title "the bravest of the brave."

Warren Green Hotel. From the upper porch in November 1862, Gen. George McClellan delivered his farewell address to the Army of the Potomac. The restored building on Hotel Street now houses county offices.

Mosby Home. The handsome 1850 home at 173 Main St., now privately owned, was the postwar residence of Colonel Mosby and later of Gen. Eppa Hunton, who commanded a brigade in Pickett's Charge at Gettysburg.

Warrenton Cemetery, Lee St. A tall shaft stands here, over the grave of Col. John Mosby. Some 600 unknown Confederate soldiers lie nearby.

The Inn at Little Washington (Middle and Main Sts., Washington, VA 22747, twenty-two miles west of Warrenton on U.S. 211; phone [703] 675-3800) is a four-star hostelry with the atmosphere of an English country house. The restaurant at the inn also has been awarded four stars by the Mobil Travel Guide. Outdoor dining, weather permitting. Prix-fixe dinner.

WAYNESBORO

Gen. Philip Sheridan's Union cavalry broke Gen. Jubal Early's lines here on March 2, 1865, and captured most of the town's thousand defenders in the last major battle fought for the control of western Virginia.

WILLIAMSBURG

On May 5, 1862, the first battle of the Peninsula campaign was fought just east of the first capital of Virginia. There was skirmishing in the streets and on the campus of the College of William and Mary. The Wren Building, the main building on the campus, was burned, and in 1895 the U.S. govern-

*Moore Home, Stonewall
Jackson's headquarters in
Winchester, Virginia*

*Logan Home, Philip
Sheridan's headquarters
in Winchester, Virginia*

Two Union cavalry officers rest in a Virginia field. The horse bears the rugged McClellan saddle, designed by the Union general, which was considered the best of the several types used during the war. An overcoat usually was strapped across the saddle bow, a blanket and poncho across the cantle. A cavalry trooper's ability to fight depended on his horse. Each man was his own groom and veterinarian, maintained his own tack, and kept his horse well fed.

ment made partial restitution. After the battle, Williamsburg was a key point in the Confederate defenses of the Peninsula. Williamsburg, superbly restored by John D. Rockefeller, Jr., is a major tourist attraction today.

WINCHESTER

Winchester, "the gateway to the Shenandoah Valley," saw more action than any other town west of Richmond, changing hands seventy-two times during the war. When the war ended, the town was practically in ruins.

Battlefields. Four major engagements were fought in and around the town: Kernstown, March 23, 1862; First Winchester, May 25, 1862; Second Winchester (also called Stephenson's Depot), June 14–15, 1863; and Third Winchester (also called Opequon Creek), September 19, 1864. No traces of the battles remain.

Jackson's Headquarters, 415 North Braddock St., phone (703) 667-3242. Stonewall Jackson made his headquarters in this French-style house between November 1861 and March 1862. Now a museum, it houses displays of Jackson and other Confederate memorabilia. Open daily April through October, by appointment the rest of the year.

Sheridan's Headquarters, Braddock and Piccadilly Sts. Gen. Philip Sheridan directed his 1864 Second Valley campaign from this imposing home. From here, on October 19, 1864, he began his famous ride to rally the Union army under attack at Cedar Creek. Earlier, the house was the headquarters of Generals Custer, Banks, and Milroy. Now it is the local Elks Club.

Stonewall Cemetery. Gen. Turner Ashby, Jackson's cavalry commander, is buried here, as well as some 3,000 other Confederate soldiers. Across the street is the *National Cemetery,* where lie between 2,110 and 2,381 unknown Union soldiers killed in the Winchester campaigns. The Stonewall Cemetery is part of Mount Hebron Cemetery on Boscawen Street.

There are eight motels in Winchester. The best restaurant in town is *The Elms,* 2011 Valley Ave., 22601; phone (703) 662-0535.

✦ 4 ✦

THE WAR IN THE MID-SOUTH

KENTUCKY

CUMBERLAND GAP NATIONAL HISTORIC PARK

Virginia, Kentucky, and Tennessee meet at Cumberland Gap, and it is a back door into all three states. Daniel Boone explored the pass, and it became a main artery of the great trans-Allegheny migration to the West. A strategic objective in the Civil War, the gap changed hands several times. On June 18, 1862, Gen. George W. Morgan captured the gap, forcing the Confederates to destroy their supplies and withdraw. Morgan withdrew that September, when Confederates invaded Kentucky. He managed to escape with all his stores and equipment, traveling 130 miles through the Kentucky mountains to the Ohio River. On September 9, 1863, Union forces recaptured the gap, opening a door to raids into southwestern Virginia. Two cannon now are mounted in the remains of Fort Gilmore, one of several small fortifications built during the war. The Visitor Center has a museum with interpretive and audiovisual exhibits and occasional living-history programs. The park is reached by U.S. 25E from Kentucky and Tennessee or U.S. 58 from Virginia. The Visitor Center is a half-mile south of Middlesboro on U.S. 25E, and is open from 8 A.M. until 5 P.M. daily except

Christmas. Overnight accommodations and restaurants are in Middlesboro. For further information, write to the Superintendent, Cumberland Gap National Historic Park, Middlesboro, KY 40965, or phone (606) 248-2817.

HODGENVILLE

Abraham Lincoln Birthplace National Historic Site. Abraham Lincoln was born February 12, 1809, in a log cabin on the Sinking Spring Farm, named after a small limestone spring nearby. When he was three years old, his father, Thomas Lincoln, moved the family to the Knob Creek Farm, ten miles to the northeast, and later to Indiana and Illinois. Today, 110 acres of the original Lincoln farm are in the 116-acre park.

The Visitor Center offers an audiovisual program and exhibits exploring Lincoln's background and environment. Thomas Lincoln's Bible is on display. The *Memorial Building* was built in 1911, financed by contributions from more than 100,000 people. Inside the granite and marble building is the log cabin traditionally believed to be the Lincoln birthplace. The cabin was here in 1860, then was disassembled, moved, and exhibited elsewhere many times before returning here permanently. Open daily except Christmas, the Memorial Building is accessible to the disabled. Three miles south of Hodgenville on U.S. 31E and KY 61. Motels are adjacent to the park, and there are restaurants in Hodgenville. For further information, write to the Superintendent, Route 1, Box 94, Hodgenville, KY 42748, or phone (502) 358-3874.

BARDSTOWN

Lincoln Homestead State Park, five miles north of Bardstown on KY 528, phone (502) 336-3502. Abraham Lincoln, Sr., the President's grandfather, settled here in 1782. In the compound, framed by split-rail fences, is a replica of the original cabin, furnished in the pioneer style, including several pieces made by Thomas Lincoln. Here, too, is the Berry House, the home of Nancy Hanks during her courtship by Thomas Lincoln. A replica of the blacksmith and car-

penter shop where Thomas Lincoln worked is in the compound. Open daily, May through mid-October. Picnic facilities.

My Old Kentucky Home State Park, one mile east on U.S. 150, phone (502) 348-3502. Many of the songs associated with the Old South were written by Stephen Foster, who occasionally visited his cousin Judge John Rowan at his stately home, Federal Hill. This house may have inspired Foster to write "My Old Kentucky Home." Attendants in period costumes give house tours. Open daily, March through the third week in December; daily except Monday, January through February. Closed New Year's Day. The first floor of the house is accessible to the disabled.

Old Bardstown Village and Civil War Museum, East Broadway, east of First St., phone (502) 348-6501. A reproduction of a late-18th-century frontier vil-

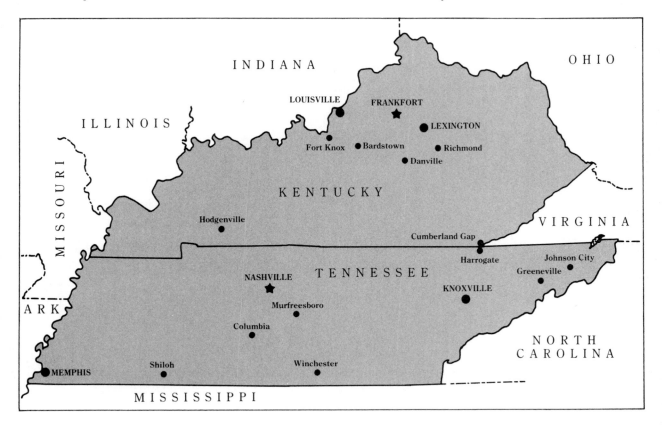

lage, including a wheelwright's shop, a moonshine distillery, a forge, and a spinning-and-weaving shop. The Civil War Museum has cavalry, infantry, and medical displays, as well as weapons, uniforms, and documents. It is wheelchair accessible. Open daily except Monday, April through October.

The Mansion, 103 N. Third St., phone (502) 348-2586. The home of Ben Johnson, a powerful political figure in the state, was the site of the raising of the first Confederate flag in 1861. Open daily. Tours by appointment.

An interesting place to stay in Bardstown is the *Old Talbott Tavern Inn* (107 West Stephen Foster Ave., 40004 [U.S. 62]; phone [502] 348-3494), in continuous operation since 1779. Young Abraham Lincoln stayed here with his parents during a court trial to establish ownership of their farm. The dining room serves Southern-style food.

DANVILLE

Perryville Battlefield State Shrine, ten miles west of Danville on U.S. 150, then north four miles on U.S. 68, phone (606) 332-8631. Confederate General Braxton Bragg invaded Kentucky in the fall of 1862, and Don Carlos Buell moved east from Louisville to prevent Bragg from joining up with Kirby Smith. The armies blundered into each other here, by Doctor's Creek, on October 8. The leading column, commanded by Philip Sheridan, first skirmished near the creek, then Bragg, unaware that he was outnumbered three to one, struck the Union left. Bragg was repelled, but Buell lost his opportunity for an important victory. Half of his army took no part in the battle, and Bragg was allowed to get away unmolested. By the end of the month, both armies were back in Tennessee. Perryville cost 4,241 Union and 1,822

Don Carlos Buell

Confederate casualties. Buell was soon replaced by William Rosecrans.

The 100-acre park looks much as it did at the time of the battle. Still standing are the *Crawford House,* Bragg's headquarters, and *Bottom House,* the center of some of the heaviest fighting. On a thirty-acre area of what was the north end of the battle line are monuments to the Confederate and Union dead. The Museum in the park has a diorama of the battle, and is open daily, April through October, open by appointment the rest of the year. The battle is reenacted annually on the first weekend in October.

Shaker Village of Pleasant Hill, Rte. 4, Harrodsburg. The wounded of both sides at Perryville were tended by Shakers from Harrodsburg, and the *Inn* (3500 Lexington Rd., 40330; phone [606] 734-5411) is indeed a pleasant place to stay. On the historic site are thirty restored 19th-century Shaker buildings maintained by a nonprofit educational corporation. There are seventy guest rooms with Shaker furnishings in the original family houses, and a tour is included in the rates. The dining room in the Trustees' House features Shaker dishes. A paddlewheel riverboat gives day cruises.

Another excellent place to stop in Harrodsburg is the *Beaumont Inn* (638 Beaumont Dr., Danville, KY, 40330; [606] 734-3381), an 1807 Greek Revival mansion that has been an inn since 1919. Kentucky was neutral in the war, but the owners of this house were not. An admirable collection of portraits of Robert E. Lee are displayed in the entrance hall. The dining room is also excellent.

FORT KNOX

Patton Museum of Cavalry and Armor, phone (502) 624-3351. Fort Knox is famous for the U.S. Bullion Depository, where part of the nation's gold reserves are stored, but it also is the army's home of armor and cavalry. The museum, named for Gen. George S. Patton, Jr., has cavalry material from the Civil War. For further information, write to the Public Affairs Office, Fort Knox, P.O. Box 995, 40121. The nearest accommodations and restaurants are in Elizabethtown or Shepherdsville.

FRANKFORT

Kentucky Military History Museum. In the Old State Arsenal on East Main Street (phone [502] 564-3265), exhibits show the state's involvement in military conflicts through the years. The collection includes weapons, flags, and uniforms. Open daily except major holidays.

HOPKINSVILLE

Jefferson Davis Monument State Shrine, eleven miles east of Hopkinsville, on U.S. 68 in Fairview, phone (502) 886-1765. The son of a Revolutionary War officer, Jefferson Davis was born here in 1808,

less than a hundred miles from where Abraham Lincoln was born. Davis graduated from West Point, became a successful cotton planter in Mississippi, was elected to the U.S. Senate, and was Secretary of War in Franklin Pierce's cabinet. Elected President of the Confederacy, Davis served for the duration of the war, then was captured in Georgia, and imprisoned for two years. His monument, a 351-foot cast-concrete obelisk, is the fourth tallest in the country. Dedicated in 1924, the monument was funded by a public subscription of $200,000. The elevator to the top is open daily, May through August, and daily except Monday in September and October.

Pennyroyal Area Museum, 217 East 9th St., phone (502) 887-4270. Civil War items, a miniature circus, an 1840 bedroom suite, and old railroad artifacts are among the exhibits. Open Monday through Friday, and Saturdays in the summer, closed on major holidays.

LEXINGTON

Ashland, Richmond Rd. (East Main St.) at Sycamore Rd., phone (606) 266-8581. This 1806 estate was the home of Henry Clay, statesman, orator, senator, and would-be President. In the family for four generations, Ashland is furnished with Clay possessions and furniture. Open daily except Mondays and major holidays. Closed January.

Hunt-Morgan House, 201 North Mill St. at West Second St. in the Gratz Park area, phone (606) 253-0362. Built in the early 1800s for John Wesley Hunt, the state's first millionaire, it later was occupied by his grandson, Gen. John Hunt Morgan, known as "the Thunderbolt of the Confederacy." The Federal-period house is notable for its cantilevered elliptical staircase. Open daily except Monday, closed late December through February and Thanksgiving Day.

Mary Todd Lincoln House, 578 West Main St., phone (606) 233-9999. The childhood home of Mary Todd Lincoln has been authentically restored with period furnishings and personal items. Open Tuesday through Saturday, April to mid-December.

Lexington Cemetery, 833 West Main St. on U.S. 421, phone (606) 255-7575. Buried here are Henry Clay; General John Hunt Morgan; Mary Todd Lincoln's parents; and 1,100 Union and 500 Confederate veterans. The gardens and other plantings in the 170-acre cemetery are exceptional.

Lexington has dozens of hotels and motels. Among its restaurants, a personal favorite is the *Coach House,* 855 South Broadway, 40504; phone (606) 252-7777.

RICHMOND

Courthouse, Main St. between North First and North Second Sts. This 1849 Greek Revival courthouse was used as a hospital by both Union and Confederate forces.

White Hall State Shrine, five miles north of town on I-75, off the Boonesborough-Winchester exit, phone (606) 623-9178. The restored forty-four-room Georgian home of Cassius M. Clay, emancipationist, diplomat, and publisher of *The True American,* an antislavery newspaper. Period furnishings and some personal mementos. Open daily, April through Labor Day, Wednesday through Saturday from Labor Day through October.

NORTH CAROLINA

DUNN

Bentonville Battleground State Historic Site, fifteen miles east of Dunn via NC 55 to Newton Grove, three miles north via U.S. 701 to NC 1008, then three miles east; phone (919) 594-0789. As Sherman's army marched into North Carolina, hundreds of North Carolinians deserted Lee's army to protect their homesteads. Gen. Joseph Johnston's small force attempted to stem the tide at *Averasboro* on March 16, and here on March 19–21 was fought the biggest battle ever fought in the state, and the last battle in which a Confed-

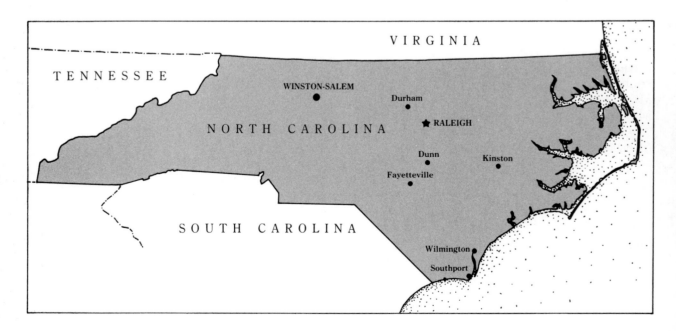

erate army was able to mount an offensive attack.

With fewer than 30,000 men, Johnston waited until miserable road conditions forced Sherman to divide his 60,000-man command into wings. On the evening of March 18, Johnston organized his forces into a sickle-shaped line along the Goldsboro Road and waited.

The next day Sherman's left wing stumbled into Johnston's trap. Initial Confederate attacks overran large sections of the Union lines. One Union division held on despite being surrounded. Failing to crush the Union lines, Johnston pulled back to his earlier position. Sherman's right wing arrived at the battle early the next day, and for two days cannon and rifle fire were constant. On March 21 a Union force led by Gen. J. A. Mower outflanked the Confederate positions and came within 200 yards of General Johnston's headquarters before being driven back. That evening Johnston withdrew to Smithfield, and Sherman marched on to Goldsboro, where supplies awaited him.

The battle was fought in an area of 6,000 acres, and more than 4,000 Union and Confederate troops were reported killed, wounded, or missing. The restored *Harper House* was used as a hospital for the wounded of both sides. On the battleground are original and reconstructed trenches. An audiovisual show at the Visitor Center explains the battle. The history trail has markers and exhibits, and the roads in the area also are marked with plaques highlighting events of the battle. Open daily April to October, daily except Monday from November through March. Closed major holidays.

DURHAM

Bennett Place State Historic Site, six miles west of Furham, then a half-mile south of U.S. I-85 on U.S. 70; phone (919) 383-9835. In April 1865, two battle-weary adversaries, Joseph E. Johnston and William T. Sherman, met under a flag of truce midway between their lines on the Hillsborough Road, seven miles from Durham Station. Needing a place to confer, Johnston suggested a simple farmhouse a short distance away. They met here three times, struggling to achieve equitable terms of surrender. On April 26 the farmhouse became the site of the largest troop surrender of the war.

Striving to avoid capture in Virginia, President Davis arrived in Greensboro, North Carolina, on April 11 and summoned Johnston to assess the strength of his army. Davis felt that the South could continue the war, but the confirmation of Lee's surrender prompted him to allow Johnston to confer with Sherman.

At their first meeting, Sherman showed Johnston a telegram announcing the assassination of Lincoln. Sherman was prepared to offer terms similar to those Grant gave Lee, but Johnston wanted "to arrange the terms of a permanent peace," political as well as military.

At the second meeting, on April 18, knowing that Johnston's surrender wasn't a military necessity, Sherman submitted a "memorandum or a basis of agreement," which Johnston accepted. This liberal document provided for an armistice terminable at forty-eight hours' notice, the disbanding of armies following the deposit of arms in state arsenals, recognition of state government, establishment of federal courts, restoration of political and civil rights, and a promise of general amnesty.

Unhappy with the terms, President Davis ordered Johnston to disband his infantry and make an escape with the cavalry. Johnston, realizing the further devastation a prolonged war would bring, disobeyed orders and met Sherman again at the farmhouse on April 26. The final agreement was simply a military surrender ending the war in the Carolinas, Georgia, and Florida, affecting 89,270 Confederate soldiers. The

"I AM TIRED AND SICK OF WAR. ITS GLORY IS ALL MOONSHINE. IT IS ONLY THOSE HAVE NEITHER FIRED A SHOT NOR HEARD THE SHRIEKS AND GROANS OF THE WOUNDED WHO CRY ALOUD FOR MORE BLOOD, MORE VENGEANCE, MORE DESOLATION. WAR IS HELL."

—WILLIAM T. SHERMAN, *1879*

mustering-out of Johnston's troops and the issuing of paroles took place in Greensboro.

Two surrenders followed: Richard Taylor surrendered in Alabama on May 4, and E. Kirby Smith at New Orleans on May 26. These, combined with Lee's surrender at Appomattox, meant that the Confederate forces were completely disbanded.

The buildings on the Bennett farm were destroyed by fire in 1921, and the present buildings were reconstructed from wartime photographs and sketches. An audiovisual presentation at the Visitor Center tells the complete story of the events that happened here. Open daily April through October, daily except Monday November through March. Closed Thanksgiving and December 24–26.

Bed-and-breakfast accommodations are available at *Arrowhead Inn,* a restored 1775 manor house on four landscaped acres near Durham's historic attractions. For information, write to Jerry and Barbara Ryan, 106 Mason Rd., Durham, NC 27712, or phone (919) 477-8430.

FAYETTEVILLE

The North Carolina Arsenal Site. Nine days after Fort Sumter fell, a contingent of old men and boys under Confederate General Draughon demanded the surrender of the arsenal. It later manufactured weapons for the Confederacy. Equipment captured at the Harpers Ferry Arsenal was stored here. General Sherman ordered the arsenal burned, blown up, and knocked down with battering rams. The site is a historical park with a self-guided tour. The *Arsenal House,* 822 Arsenal Ave., phone (919) 323-1776, now is the headquarters of the local arts council. Open daily except Christmas and Easter weeks. There are motels at the Fayetteville exits off I-95, and restaurants in the center of the city.

KINSTON

Governor Caswell Memorial–CSS *Neuse* State Historic Site, one mile west of Kinston on U.S. 70A, phone (919) 522-2091. The remains of a Confederate ironclad ramming vessel raised in 1963 may be viewed here. Though the ship was completed in 1864, the low water of the Neuse River prevented its entry into the war. In 1865, Comdr. Joseph Price ordered the vessel scuttled to avoid capture by Union troops. An audiovisual presentation in the Visitor Center tells the story of CSS *Neuse,* and there are related exhibits and demonstrations of nautical blacksmithing. Open daily April through October, daily except Monday, November through March. Closed major holidays.

In nearby Wilson on I-95, *Pilgrim's Rest Bed & Breakfast* is in the historic district, convenient to the art museum and antique shops. For information, write to Doug and June Stewart, 600 West Nash St., Wilson, NC 27893, or phone (919) 762-8562.

SOUTHPORT

Fort Fisher State Historic Site, six miles east of Southport via U.S. 421, then a one-hour ferry ride; fort: (919) 458-5538; ferry: (919) 457-6942. The largest earthwork fort in the Confederacy, Fort Fisher kept the port of Wilmington open to blockade runners until the last few months of the war. Some of the heaviest naval bombardment of land fortifications took place here on December 24–25, 1864, and January 13–15, 1865. When Fort Fisher fell after the second bombardment, its defeat helped seal the fate of the Confederacy. Shaded by gnarled live oaks, the path atop the remains of the earthwork gives a clear view of the Cape Fear River. A reconstructed gun emplacement and items recovered from sunken blockade runners are among the exhibits in the Visitor Center. An audiovisual

program tells the complete history of the fort. Open daily April through October, daily except Monday from November through March. Closed Thanksgiving and December 24–25.

Brunswick Town–Fort Anderson Historic Site, fourteen miles north of Southport on NC 133, then five miles south on a local road; phone (919) 371-6613. The location of a town burned by British sailors in the Revolution. Built across part of this site are the Civil War earthworks of Fort Anderson, which held out for thirty days after the fall of Fort Fisher. There are marked historical trailside exhibits, and an audiovisual presentation and exhibits are in the Visitor Center. Open daily April through October, daily except Monday November through March. Closed Thanksgiving and December 24–25.

Restaurants and accommodations are available in Wilmington, thirty miles to the north.

WILMINGTON

New Hanover County Museum, 814 Market St., phone (919) 763-0852. On display here is a seventeen-by-twenty-foot scale model of Wilmington in 1863. Recent exhibits have included "Lifeline of the Confederacy: Lower Cape Fear During the Civil War." Open Tuesday through Sunday, closed major holidays.

Guests may be served breakfast in bed, on the veranda, or in the garden at *The Worth House,* and horse-drawn carriages will pick them up for a tour of the historic district. For information, write to Terry Meyer and Kate Walsh, 412 South Third St., Wilmington, NC 28401, or phone (919) 762-8542. There are a number of hotels and motels in Wilmington. *Stemmerman's,* 138 South Front St., 28401; phone (919) 763-0248, is an excellent restaurant in an 1855 commercial building.

The last gap in the Union blockade was plugged on January 15, 1865, when a joint army-navy operation captured Fort Fisher, North Carolina, thus bottling up Wilmington, the South's principal port for blockade runners. The fighting was particularly fierce at the "Pulpit," shown after its capture. The Confederacy needed to import war materiél by ship, and a blockade of its ports was part of Union strategy from the start of the war.

TENNESSEE

FORT DONELSON

FORT DONELSON NATIONAL BATTLEFIELD AND CEMETERY DOVER, TENNESSEE

The capture of Fort Donelson in February 1862 gave the North its first major victory, an opening to the heart of the Confederacy, and a new hero, Gen. Ulysses S. Grant. Newspapers around the country dubbed him "Unconditional Surrender" Grant.

For a while the South had seemed invincible. The war had been stalemated since the Confederate victories at First Manassas and Wilson's Creek in the summer of 1861. In the West, attempts had failed to break the Confederate defense line, which extended from southwest Missouri to the Appalachian Mountains.

A reconnaissance in January convinced the Union command that the most vulnerable places in the defense line were Fort Henry and Fort Donelson, guarding the Tennessee and Cumberland rivers. A joint army-navy attack was planned, commanded by Flag Officer Andrew H. Foote and Grant, then an obscure brigadier general. It would be the first use of Foote's ironclad gunboats.

As Grant's troops marched overland from their camp downstream, the gunboats approached Fort Henry and opened fire. The Confederate commander, Lloyd Tilghman, decided he couldn't hold out for long. After trading shots with the gunboats for an hour, Tilghman surrendered the earthwork fort. Fewer than one hundred of its nearly 2,500-man garrison were taken prisoner, the rest escaped to Fort Donelson. Grant was chagrined to find that the fort had been taken before his troops arrived.

Fort Donelson, twelve miles away on the Cumberland, was a tougher nut to crack. Two batteries, mounting a total of eleven heavy guns, controlled the river. An outer defense line stretched along high ground from Hickman Creek on the right to the little town of Dover. Within the fort, Confederate infantrymen and artillerymen huddled in log cabins against the winter.

Grant had to spend several days at Fort Henry before it was secure and his troops ready. As his force set out on February 11, the weather turned unseasonably warm, and many soldiers threw away their heavy winter gear. By February 13 the 15,000 Union troops arrived at Fort Donelson. Sporadic clashes broke out, but neither side gained ground. Nightfall brought lashing sleet and snow.

February 14 dawned cold and quiet. The stillness was broken early in the afternoon by the fort's batteries exchanging "iron Valentines" with the gunboats, which were damaged and forced to withdraw. The generals in the fort—John Floyd, Gideon Pillow, Simon Buckner, and Bushrod Johnson—were elated. However, they soon realized that Grant was receiving reinforcements daily, extending his line almost to Lick Creek to complete the encirclement of the fort. They were in danger of being starved into submission.

The Confederate troops were massed against the Union right, hoping to clear a route to Nashville and safety. On February 15, fighting raged all morning, the Union army giving ground grudgingly. Just as it seemed that the way was clear, the Confederate troops were ordered back to their entrenchments; the order was a result of confusion and indecision among the generals. Grant launched a vigorous counterattack, closing the avenue of escape.

Generals Floyd and Pillow gave command of Donelson to Buckner and slipped away to Nashville in the night with about 2,000 men. Col. Nathan Bedford Forrest led his men across swollen Lick Creek. The next morning, February 16, Buckner asked for terms from Grant, who had been a classmate of his at West Point. Grant replied, "No terms except an unconditional and immediate surrender can be accepted." Buckner thought Grant was being ungentlemanly, but surrendered anyway.

The capture of Forts Henry and Donelson forced the South to give up southern Kentucky and much of middle and western Tennessee. The heartland of the Confederacy was now open to attack.

VISITING FORT DONELSON

Fort Donelson National Battlefield is located one mile west of Dover and three miles east of Land Between the Lakes, Tennessee, on U.S. 79. The Visitor Center is open from 8 A.M. to 4:30 P.M. daily except Thanksgiving Day, Christmas, and New Year's Day. In the center are a museum, a fifteen-minute slide presentation on the history of the fort and the battle, "touch" exhibits, and a bookstore. For information, write to the Superintendent, Fort Donelson, P.O. Box 434, Dover, TN 37058, or phone (615) 232-5706.

A self-guided driving tour includes these highlights:

Fort Donelson. Soldiers and slaves built this fifteen-acre fort over a period of seven months, using axes and shovels to make a wall of logs and earth ten feet high. The fort was intended to protect the Cumberland River from land attack.

Log Huts. Some hundred huts used for winter quarters stood within Fort Donelson at the time of the battle. Sometime after the surrender, Union troops burned the cabins as a sanitary measure during an outbreak of measles.

River Batteries. Here, inexperienced Confederate gunners faced Union ironclad and timberclad gunboats and defeated them in a land-naval battle that was heard thirty-five miles away.

Buckner's Final Defense. After the Confederates attempted to break out, Grant ordered Gen. C. F. Smith to attack the far right of the Confederate line. Smith's troops drove the Confederates back to this ridge, where they valiantly held their position until reinforcements arrived.

Jackson's Battery. Ordered to support the Confederate right wing, Jackson's four-gun battery moved to this position on the night of February 13. It was held in reserve here throughout the following day. Early on the morning of February 15, the battery was ordered to the Wynn Ferry Road sector.

Smith's Attack. Union troops swarmed up these snow-covered slopes on February 15 in a determined assault on the Confederate rifle pits.

Confederate Monument. This monument commemorates the Confederate soldiers who fought and died at Fort Donelson. It was erected in 1933 by the Tennessee Division of the United Daughters of the Confederacy.

French's Battery. Along with Maney's Battery to the west, the four-gun battery was placed here to prevent Union forces

FRIENDS INDEED

Ulysses S. Grant and Simon Bolivar Buckner were classmates at West Point and good friends before the war. When Grant was down on his luck in the 1850s, Buckner loaned him money. But it was Buckner, in command of Fort Donelson after his superiors had fled, who received Grant's demand for "unconditional surrender." He felt that the terms were "unchivalrous," but had no choice other than to accept. Later he met with Grant and found his old friend more than magnanimous. Grant, remembering Buckner's help of years before, offered his own funds to ease the Confederate general's personal hardship.

Dover Hotel, Fort Donelson National Military Park, Tennessee

from attacking down Erin Hollow and penetrating the fort's perimeter.

Forge Road. The Confederate mass attack on February 15 opened this avenue of escape, only to have it closed again through blunders and indecision on the part of the Southern generals and by a Union counterattack.

Dover Hotel (Surrender House). Before the war, the small town of Dover had shown promise. The surrounding region was prosperous from the production of iron ore. With a population of 800 in the 1860s, Dover was an important port on the Cumberland. After the fall of Fort Donelson, Dover was occupied by a Union garrison for the duration of the war. On two occasions, Confederate cavalry tried to drive the Union troops from the area. The second attempt, led by Gen. Joseph Wheeler in early 1863, cost Dover its future. All but four of the town's buildings were destroyed in what became known as the Battle of Dover.

The Dover Hotel was one building that survived. Built between 1851 and 1853, the hotel served during the Battle of Fort Donelson as General Buckner's headquarters. Here, on February 16, 1862, Buckner surrendered his army to General Grant. Also from here some 13,000 Confederate troops were loaded onto transports to be taken to prisoner-of-war camps. After the surrender, the hotel was converted into a Union hospital.

The Dover Hotel was restored in the late 1970s, the exterior looking now much as it did at the time of the battle. The front room on the ground floor is representative of a hotel lobby during the 1860s. The building is one of only two existing original structures where a major surrender took place during the war; the other is the Bennett House in Durham, North Carolina, where Gen. Joseph E. Johnston surrendered to Gen. William T. Sherman in April 1865.

One room at the hotel has been furnished with reproduction items to give the visitor an idea how the inside might have looked at the time. A short film depicts the surrender. The Dover Hotel is open daily from 11 A.M. to 4 P.M.

National Cemetery. After the Battle of Dover in 1863, the Union garrison built a fortification that became the center of activity for black freedmen in the area. A small community grew up around the fort as freedmen and their families sought the protection of the garrison. Four years later this same site was selected for the establishment of the Fort Donelson National Cemetery, and 655 Union dead were buried here, including 504 who were unknown. Today the cemetery also contains the remains of Civil War veterans and veterans of other wars, and their families.

There are food facilities in the nearby town of Dover. Overnight accommodations are in Clarksville, thirty miles northeast on U.S. 79, and Paris, thirty miles southwest on the same highway.

SHILOH

SHILOH NATIONAL MILITARY PARK

The first major battle in the West was one of the fiercest battles in history. In two days, April 6–7, 1862, nearly 24,000 men were killed or wounded or missing. Veterans called it Bloody Shiloh, and the name stuck. The Confederate failure here to destroy Grant's army opened the way to Vicksburg. Shiloh was a Northern victory, but a costly one. Neither side was brilliantly led.

During the winter before the battle, the Army of the Tennessee pushed south from St. Louis, capturing Forts Henry and Donelson on the Tennessee and Cumberland rivers. This forced Gen. Albert Sidney Johnston to abandon southern Kentucky and much of Tennessee, including Nashville.

Johnston established a new line of defenses covering the Memphis and Charleston Railroad, the only direct link to Richmond, then concentrated 44,000 men at Corinth, Mississippi. He knew he couldn't wait for another Union advance, and hoped to destroy the army, now commanded by Gen. Ulysses S. Grant, before it could be joined by Gen. Don Carlos Buell's Army of the Ohio.

Grant wasn't prepared for Johnston's withdrawal to the south. He delayed before moving his 40,000 troops south along the Tennessee toward Pittsburg Landing, twenty-two miles northeast of Corinth, where he waited for Buell. Concerned about the large number of raw recruits in his army, Grant drilled his men rather than fortifying his position.

Johnston planned to attack Grant on April 4, but postponed it for two days. His second-in-command, Gen. P. G. T. Beauregard, thought that the element of surprise was lost, but Johnston refused to call off the attack. Beauregard was mistaken. There were almost no Union patrols, and the senior field commander, Gen. William

Albert S. Johnston

T. Sherman, ignored reports of Confederate troops in the area.

When Johnston's army hit the Union camp early on the morning of April 6, they achieved complete surprise. Some Union troops fought to hold the line, while others fell back to re-form. Many inexperienced soldiers fled for safety to the Tennessee River. The Confederates rolled over one Union position after another.

Along the Sunken Road, Union troops commanded by Gen. Benjamin Prentiss finally stopped Johnston's advance around noon. Rather than look for a way around the Union stronghold, the Confederates charged it repeatedly. Fighting was so intense here that the area was called the Hornets' Nest.

Confederate General Daniel Ruggles brought up sixty-two cannon to bombard the Union position, the largest concentration of artillery ever seen on an American battlefield. As the guns hammered the Hor-

nets' Nest, the Confederate infantry swept forward, surrounding and capturing most of the Union defenders. But the defenders had bought precious time for Grant to establish a final defensive line near Pittsburg Landing.

On the right and left of the Hornets' Nest, Union forces fell back and the fighting became disorganized and confused. Gen. Albert Sidney Johnston was killed while trying to push home attacks on the river side of the battlefield to isolate the Union troops from Grant at Pittsburg. Beauregard assumed command of the Confederate forces.

By late afternoon, Grant's chief of artillery, Col. J. D. Webster, established a line of fifty-three cannon on the heights around the landing, and the troops within the defensive line there were safe. The Confederates hit the flanks of the line but were easily beaten off.

While Beauregard was attacking, the

Cavalrymen hurry to the front in the chaos of Shiloh, April 6, 1862. General Johnston's Confederate army had marched north from Mississippi, caught Grant unprepared, and nearly trapped him at Pittsburg Landing on the Tennessee River. During the night 25,000 fresh Union troops arrived, and the next day turned the tide. The battle made the reputation of General Sherman, whose stubborn defense gave Grant time to organize his troops.

first of Buell's army crossed the Tennessee and took up position on Grant's left. Fire from Union infantry, artillery, and river gunboats stopped the Confederate attempt to cross the rugged Dill Creek terrain. The fighting sputtered out as night fell. The gunboats continued to fire at fifteen-minute intervals, frustrating Beauregard's attempts to reorganize his army.

By dawn on April 7, the remainder of Buell's army was across the river. Union troops now numbered some 55,000. Unaware of Buell's arrival, Beauregard resumed the attack, attempting to drive Grant into the river.

The first Confederate assaults succeeded, but soon the stronger Union forces began to push the Confederates back. Realizing that he had lost the initiative, Beauregard tried to stem the Union drive by counterattacking at Water Oaks Pond. The advance was stopped, but the Union line didn't break.

Having sustained 15,000 casualties and running low on ammunition and food, Beauregard knew he could not win. He withdrew beyond Shiloh Church and began the weary march back to Corinth. The exhausted Union troops did not pursue. Bloody Shiloh was over.

The next day Grant sent Sherman south along the Corinth Road to try to catch the remnants of Beauregard's army. Ten miles out, he ran into a rear guard commanded by Col. Nathan Bedford Forrest, and abandoned the pursuit.

A month went by before Grant seized Corinth, and Beauregard had long since moved on. A Union amphibious force on the Mississippi destroyed the Confederate River Defense Fleet. From these bases Grant would push on down the Mississippi to besiege Vicksburg.

VISITING SHILOH

Shiloh National Battlefield Park is located on 3,800 acres, 110 miles east of Memphis,

THE DRUMMER BOY OF SHILOH

A legend that arose from the smoke of Shiloh became the inspiration for poems, books, songs, and a popular play, *The Drummer Boy of Shiloh.* Written in 1870 by Samuel J. Muscroft, the play was staged in cities and towns all over the Northern states for nearly forty years, and was second in popularity only to *Uncle Tom's Cabin.* In the play, the drummer, a mere lad, runs away from home to seek adventure in the ranks of the Union army, and is mortally wounded at Shiloh. Several Shiloh veterans claimed they were the inspiration for the drummer, and from time to time newspapers in various parts of the country would run a headline announcing, "Drummer Boy of Shiloh Dies." Historians now believe that the man with the strongest claim was John Clem (1851–1937), ten years old at Shiloh, who later served at Chattanooga.

Tennessee, and twenty-six miles north of Corinth, Mississippi. The battlefield is on TN 22, which runs from near Corinth to U.S. 64 at Crump, Tennessee. The park is open every day except Christmas from 8 A.M. to 5 P.M., from 8 A.M. to 6 P.M. Memorial Day to Labor Day.

The Visitor Center is near the entrance to the park. A twenty-five-minute motion picture that explains the background of the battle and describes the battle itself is shown every half hour. A small museum has battle flags, small arms, uniforms, other military artifacts, and historic photographs. The bookstore has a good selection of books about the battle and other aspects of the war. The center is accessible to the disabled. Occasional living-history demonstrations are given in the park, and a schedule of events is posted in the center. No food is sold at the park. A small picnic ground is near the Shiloh Church, but cooking is not allowed. A larger picnic ground near the entrance permits cooking. There are restaurants in the nearby town of Shiloh. Overnight accommodations can be found in Corinth, MS, twenty-two miles

Iowa Monument, Shiloh, Tennessee

southwest, and in Selmer, TN, fifteen miles northwest of the battlefield.

A self-guiding tour covers the points of interest of the battle. A visitor also should see the National Cemetery near Pittsburg Landing. If there are no living-history demonstrations in progress, the battlefield can be toured comfortably in three or four hours.

For further information, write the Superintendent, Shiloh National Battlefield Park, Shiloh, TN 38376, or phone (901) 689-5275.

The stops on the self-guided driving tour include the following:

Grant's Last Line. While the troops in the Hornets' Nest held the Confederates at bay, Grant formed a defensive line along this ridge. The line of artillery marks the final position of the Union army on April 6, and the attack on the morning of April 7 began here.

Hornets' Nest. Though stunned by the surprise attack at dawn and forced to abandon their first line and camps, Union troops bravely held this position for six hours against eleven Confederate attacks. This gave Grant time to prepare a strong defensive position closer to Pittsburg Landing.

Ruggles' Battery. After repeated infantry attacks against the Hornets' Nest had failed, Confederate General Daniel Ruggles brought up sixty-two guns to bombard the Union position. A final attack under cover of this artillery fire led to the capture of Union General Benjamin Prentiss and more than 2,100 of his troops.

Confederate Burial Trench. This is the largest of five trenches in which Confederate dead were buried. More than 700 soldiers lie here.

Water Oaks Pond. The Confederate counterattack through this wet-weather pond on April 7 stopped the Union advance but failed to break the Union line. With chances for victory gone, Beauregard withdrew to Corinth.

Shiloh Church. Here stood the original Shiloh Church, from which the battle took its name. Shiloh is a Hebrew word meaning "peace." The present church was built in 1949.

Fraley Field. At 5:15 on the morning of Sunday, April 6, Union scouts discovered the Confederate line of battle advancing to the west into Fraley Field, where the first shots of the battle were fired. A two-minute walk down the trail will take you to Fraley Field.

Union Defense Line. On this low ridge on the morning of April 6, Gen. Benjamin Prentiss formed his Sixth Division into a line of battle to try to halt the Confederate onslaught. His troops held for only a few minutes before being forced to retreat.

Union Camps Overrun. Along this road that ran in front of the Union camps, soldiers from Prentiss's division made a brief stand before being driven back to the Hornets' Nest. An upright cannon marks the spot where Col. Everett Peabody was killed while trying to rally his men.

Tent Hospital Site. Here Union surgeons established one of the first tent hospitals of the Civil War. By gathering tents from all over the battlefield and concentrating medical services, patient care was greatly improved and the death rate lowered.

Johnston's Death Site. The monument here stands near the place where the Confederate commander, Gen. Albert Sidney Johnston, was mortally wounded.

Peach Orchard. The orchard was in bloom as the Confederates charged repeatedly, trying to break the Union defensive position in the woods. The peach blossoms shaken down by gunfire reminded some soldiers of falling snow.

Bloody Pond. During the battle, soldiers of both sides came here to drink and to bathe their wounds. Both men and horses died in the pond, their blood staining the water a dark red.

The Left Flank. Here stood the defenders of the left flank of Grant's last line. Reinforced by Buell's vanguard, the defenders repulsed the last Confederate attack on April 6.

Pittsburg Landing. This was the Union base during the battle and, for many years, a landing for river steamers. Here, Buell's Army of the Ohio crossed the river to join Grant in the late afternoon and night of April 6. Thus reinforced, the union troops were able to force Beauregard to withdraw the next day.

National Cemetery. On a bluff overlooking Pittsburg Landing and the Tennessee River is the cemetery where 3,800 soldiers, two-thirds of them unknown, are buried.

SHILOH SURVIVORS

Among those who fought at Shiloh were John Wesley Powell, who lost an arm, but later went down the Colorado River by boat and became head of the U.S. Geological Survey; James A. Garfield, the twentieth President of the United States; Ambrose Bierce, satirist and short-story writer; and Henry Morton Stanley, the adventurer and reporter for the *New York Herald*, who later led an expedition to Africa in search of Dr. David Livingstone.

CORINTH, MISSISSIPPI

Shiloh is one of the most isolated battlefields of the war. However, nearby Corinth, Mississippi, is of interest. At the beginning of the war it was a mobilization center for Confederate troops. In March 1862, troops marched from here to fight at Shiloh, and Beauregard retreated here after the battle. During the early stages of the Vicksburg campaign, 120,000 Union troops lay siege to Corinth, occupying the town on May 30, 1862. The Confederates tried unsuccessfully to retake Corinth on October 3–4, 1862. The Union troops finally withdrew in January 1864. In December 1864, General Hood retreated through Corinth.

National Cemetery, on U.S. 72, less than a mile southeast of the railroad depot, was established in 1866 and now is the final resting place for more than 7,000 Union soldiers, 3,996 of them unknown. Remains were gathered from such battlefields as Iuka, Holly Springs, Guntown, and Corinth itself, and interred here. The graves represent 273 regiments from fifteen states. Three Confederate soldiers are buried near the flagpole.

Curlee House, 705 Jackson St., phone (601) 287-2231, is a restored antebellum home that served as headquarters for Generals Bragg, Van Dorn, and Halleck at various times during the war. It is open daily except Thursday, and is closed during January.

Battery Robinette, Linden Street. This Union fort was assaulted during the Battle of Corinth, October 3–4, 1862. Monuments mark spots where Confederate heroes died, and headstones commemorate color-bearers who fell while trying to plant a flag during the battle.

Union cavalry gallop into action in the Battle of Stones River, Murfreesboro, Tennessee, on New Year's Eve, 1862. Braxton Bragg's rebel troops nearly overwhelmed Gen. William Rosecrans's army, but Union reinforcements arrived during the night. "Common prudence," wrote Bragg, "left no doubt in my mind as to the necessity of my withdrawal. . . ."

The Northeast Mississippi Museum Association. Located at the corner of Fourth and Washington Sts., this museum has a collection of war artifacts and maps, and a rare collection of war photographs taken by Armstead White, a Southern rival of Mathew Brady. Margaret Rogers, at the museum, has maps for self-guided tours. With advance notice you can arrange for a guided tour. Open daily, 2 P.M. to 5 P.M. Phone (601) 286-6403.

An interesting place to stay is *The Generals' Quarters* (924 Fillmore St., phone [601] 286-3325), a vintage clapboard house furnished with antiques. A hearty Southern breakfast is included in the room rate. The dining room is open to the public every night except Monday.

STONES RIVER

STONES RIVER NATIONAL BATTLEFIELD AND CEMETERY MURFREESBORO

The struggle for the railroads and rich farms of middle Tennessee was decided here in the biting cold on the last day of 1862, when Union General William Rosecrans's 45,000-man Army of the Cumberland clashed with Gen. Braxton Bragg's 38,000-man Army of Tennessee. Despite his numerical advantage, Rosecrans was pressed hard by Bragg, and only sheer determination and the excellence of the Union artillery saved the day. The narrow victory gave the Union army the thin edge of a wedge into the heart of the Confederacy.

After his victories in early 1862 at Fort Donelson and Shiloh, General Grant occupied Nashville without a shot being fired. In October 1862, General Bragg retreated from Perryville, Kentucky, encamping his army for the winter at Murfreesboro, Tennessee. Rosecrans had followed Bragg from Kentucky as far as Nashville. He moved out of Nashville on December 26, intending to sweep Bragg aside and drive on to Chattanooga. Four days later he found Bragg's army at Murfreesboro.

The two armies camped within sight of each other. As night fell, the mood was tense but there was no firing. The Union and Confederate bands serenaded the soldiers before taps was sounded.

At dawn the Confederates charged, sending soldiers on the Union right flank reeling back through the dense cedar thickets that covered the area. The noise was so intense that the Confederates paused to stuff their ears with cotton.

By 10 A.M. the Union line had been driven back almost to the Nashville Pike, but it stiffened and held. "Old Rosy," as the general was fondly called by his men, ordered them "to contest every inch of ground." Contest they did. Gen. Philip Sheridan's division and Gen. George Thomas's troops beat off repeated attacks, using bayonets when their ammunition ran out.

Rosecrans sent in reserves, and by late afternoon a strong new line was established along the pike. The day's fighting sputtered to a close, and New Year's Day was spent in position, wondering what the day would bring.

No attack came on January 1, 1863, and the two armies remained facing each other across the field. Confident that Rosecrans would withdraw, Bragg was perplexed to find the Union army still on the line the next morning.

Late that afternoon, Bragg attacked with the brigades of Gen. John Breckinridge. They drove the first line of Union troops back to a shallow river crossing known as McFadden's Ford, but intense artillery fire halted the attack. Bragg left 1,800 Confederate soldiers lying on the field and in the river. The brave Confederate infantry was no match for the excellence of the Union artillery.

The battle ended with both sides claiming victory. Bragg had inflicted the most damage: 13,000 Union losses compared to his 10,000. But it was Bragg who retreated. On January 3 his army left for Tullahoma, Tennessee, forty miles away. Stones River was the beginning of the end of the proud Army of Tennessee.

Rosecrans occupied Murfreesboro and turned it into a huge supply base. Housing the supply base was the appropriately named Fortress Rosecrans, the largest earthwork fortification built during the war.

When summer came, Rosecrans's army left to launch a successful attack on the rail center in Chattanooga, severing transportation routes running southeast through Tennessee. The loss of produce from middle Tennessee was a severe blow to the Confederate army.

VISITING STONES RIVER

Stones River National Battlefield and Cemetery is located in the northwest corner of Murfreesboro, Tennessee, twenty-seven miles southeast of Nashville. The Visitor Center presents an audiovisual program on the battle, and has a museum containing uniforms, artifacts, and historical maps and photographs. No food is sold, but there is a picnic ground at the wheelchair-accessible park. Restaurants and motels are in Murfreesboro, five miles away. Information about special events at the park is posted at the Visitor Center. For further information, write to the Superintendent, Rte. 10, Box 495, Old Nashville Highway, Murfreesboro, TN 37130, or phone (615) 893-9501.

Plan to spend at least two hours seeing the park. About 60 percent of the historic features can be viewed from a car. The others are reachable by trails that are combinations of paving and wood chips. An audio guide to the battlefield is available at the Visitor Center.

While walking in the park, beware of exposed roots, uneven trails, poison ivy and sumac, slippery rocks, occasional snakes, and rocky outcroppings. The river is unsafe for wading or swimming. The forest is an important part of the park, and visitors are asked not to smoke outside their vehicles.

The driving tour begins across from the center and follows the phases of the battle:

DECEMBER 31, 1862

Chicago Board of Trade Battery (8 A.M.). Thousands of Union troops burst from the cedars across the field behind what is now the Visitor Center, followed by attacking Confederates. The Chicago Board of Trade Battery, so called because the Board of Trade provided the money for establishing and equipping the six-gun battery, sprang into action on this rise. Its charges of canister shot forced the Confederates to withdraw to the woods. A second battery joined in on the left, and the combined fire broke up the attack.

The Fight for the Cedars (10 A.M.). The deep Confederate penetration at this point forced Rosecrans to revise his plan to assault the Confederate right. He rushed reserves to this sector, and Union artillery along the Nashville Pike finally checked the drive.

Waters's Alabama Battery 12:30 P.M.). This Confederate artillery unit tried to bring its guns into action as it followed in the rear of Anderson's brigade. The dense cedar forest and limestone outcroppings prevented Capt. David D. Waters from bringing his four deadly artillery pieces into position to support the Confederate infantry, which was attacking the Union positions along the Nashville Pike. Without sufficient artillery support, the Confederate infantry assaults were doomed to failure.

Sheridan's Stand (10 A.M.). Near here the men of Generals Sheridan and Thomas fended off determined Confederate assaults. In an attempt to crack the Union line at this point, the Confederates wheeled up their guns to within 200 yards of Sheridan's position, but attack after attack still failed, with heavy losses on both sides. Sheridan eventually abandoned this position, but his delaying action during the withdrawal gave Union troops time to form a new line along the Nashville Pike.

Confederate High Tide (noon–4 P.M.). Gen. Thomas Crittenden's Union troops held this part of the line until late afternoon. When the battle suddenly overtook them, they took cover behind a rail fence and opened fire. The attack collapsed when the Confederates divided their forces. An hour later the Confederates again reached these cedars, and the Union troops retreated.

Rosecrans Establishes a New Line (5 P.M.). When the attacking Confederates saw the new Union battle line drawn along the Nashville Pike and into the Round Forest, they fell back into the Cedars. As long as the Union troops clung to the Round Forest, the Confederates could not gain victory.

To reach the next stop, visitors must cross the heavily traveled Old Nashville Highway.

Stones River National Cemetery. This hillside was an open field at the time of the Civil War. With the railroad at their backs, Union artillerymen and their guns were placed randomly across this hillside, from the Chicago Board of Trade Battery, on the right, to the Round Forest on the left, to support the infantry stretched along the Nashville Pike.

After the battle, most of the dead were buried on the field. When the National Cemetery was established in June 1865, the Union dead were disinterred and re-

buried here. Of the more than 6,100 Union burials, 2,562 were unable to be identified. Confederates were taken to their hometowns or to the nearest Southern community, or buried in unmarked mass graves.

Struggle for the Round Forest (9 A.M.–4 P.M.). This was the only Union position to hold throughout the first day of the battle. The first Confederate attack came at 10 A.M. across the field on the other side of the Nashville Pike, and was broken up by Union artillery. An hour later, another charge carried to within 150 yards of the Union line before being stopped. The monument, erected in 1863 by the survivors of Col. William B. Hazen's brigade, is the oldest Civil War memorial in the country.

A visitor at the Stones River National Battlefield examines a broken field piece. Rocky limestone outcroppings and dense cedar thickets made troop movements and communication difficult during this 1862–63 battle.

JANUARY 2, 1863

Breckinridge's Attack (4 P.M.–6 P.M.). As Union soldiers crouched here behind breastworks of stone and rail, a battered advance division fled back across the river, pursued by Gen. John C. Breckinridge's hard-charging Confederate brigades. Union batteries firing from the rise above McFadden's Ford halted Breckinridge's pursuit with shot, shell, and canister. Some 1,800 Confederates were killed or wounded in less than an hour in this final action of the battle.

Other Points of Interest. Redoubt Brannon, a part of Fortress Rosecrans, and the sites of the headquarters of Generals Bragg and Rosecrans are near the park and may be visited.

MURFREESBORO

In Murfreesboro, a city of 33,000, is *Oaklands,* at the end of North Maney Avenue, two miles north of I-24 (phone (615) 893-0022), a 19th-century mansion that blends architectural elements of four different periods. Before the war it was a social center, and later served as the command headquarters of Union Colonel W. W. Duffield, who surrendered the city to Gen. Nathan Bedford Forrest here. The style of the Civil

War period can be seen in the furnishings of the rooms and the design of the garden. A small medical museum is on the grounds. Open daily except Mondays and holidays.

On South Front Street is *Cannonsburgh Pioneer Village,* a reconstruction of life here in the early 1800s. It includes homes, a chapel, a grist mill, a school, a town hall, a blacksmith shop, and a general store. Open daily except Monday, May to September. Phone (615) 895-6565.

Clardy's Guest House (435 East Main St., 37130; phone [615] 893-6030) is a twenty-room Victorian mansion furnished in antiques and located in the historic district a few blocks from downtown. Guests are served a continental breakfast.

Murfreesboro is known as the antique center of the South, and the summer *Murfreesboro Antiques Show and Sale* attracts collectors and dealers from across the country.

Carter House, Franklin, Tennessee

Drawing room, Carter House, Franklin, Tennessee

OTHER TENNESSEE SITES OF INTEREST

COLUMBIA

The Athenaeum, 808 Athenaeum St., phone (615) 388-2354. During the war, this building of Moorish design was used as the headquarters of Union Generals Schofield and Negely. Open during the Fall Tour and by appointment at other times.

FRANKLIN

Gen. John B. Hood invaded Tennessee in the fall of 1864 with a Confederate army of 30,000. His first objective was to prevent the 23,000 Union troops of Gen. John Schofield from linking up with Gen. George Thomas's 40,000 at Nashville. Schofield beat him to Columbia by two days and slipped by him at Spring Hill. Hood pursued and outflanked Schofield, catching up with him just south of Franklin on the afternoon of November 30. Hood attacked the Union troops entrenched around the Carter House, breaking through the line. The gap was plugged, and further Confederate attacks were repelled. The battle raged for five hours, sputtering out as darkness fell. During the night, Schofield pulled out and joined Thomas in Nashville on December 1. The Confederates suffered 6,252 casualties, including six generals slain. Union casualties were 2,326.

Carter House, 1140 Carter Ave., phone (615) 791-1861. This 1830 house, the command post for the Union forces during the Battle of Franklin, is a Confederate museum displaying documents, uniforms, flags, guns, maps, and prints. A slide presentation describes the battle. There are guided tours of the house and grounds daily except holidays.

Carnton Mansion, one mile southeast of Franklin off U.S. 31, phone (615) 794-0903. An elegant 1826 estate, once noted for breeding fine thoroughbred horses, was on the southern part of the battlefield. Next to the family plots in the cemetery lie 1,481 Confederate soldiers. Open daily April

Andrew Johnson

through December, Monday through Friday the rest of the year.

Overnight visitors are welcomed at *Windsong Farm* (Rte. 3, Sweeney Hollow Rd., Franklin, TN 37064; phone [615] 794-6162), a large, U-shaped modern hillside farm home. Arabian horses and Angus cattle are in residence on the 100-acre estate. Breakfast included.

There are motels near the Franklin exit off I-65.

GREENEVILLE

Andrew Johnson National Historic Site, Depot and College Sts., Andrew Johnson came here as a tailor's apprentice from his native Raleigh, North Carolina, in 1826. After service in local, state, and federal governments, Johnson, then a U.S. senator, remained loyal to the Union when Tennessee seceded. During the war he served as military governor of Tennessee, and was Lincoln's Vice-President in 1864. He became President on April 15, 1865, following Lincoln's assassination. Opposition to the radical program of Reconstruction led to his impeachment in 1868.

Acquitted by one vote in the Senate, he served out his term. In 1875, Johnson became the only ex-President to be elected to the U.S. Senate. The Visitor Center houses the Johnson tailor shop with original furnishings and the tools of his trade, and a museum with memorabilia of his career. Opposite the wheelchair-accessible center is the home where Johnson lived as a tailor and as a congressman. Open daily except Christmas. For information, write to the Superintendent, Andrew Johnson National Historic Site, P.O. Box 1088, Greeneville, TN 37744, or phone (615) 638-3551.

The Park Service also administers the following sites:

Johnson Homestead, Main St. The Johnson family lived here from 1851 to 1875, except during the war and his term as President. The house is restored and furnished with family heirlooms. Open daily except Christmas.

National Cemetery, Main St. Johnson and his family are buried here. A marker capped with an eagle stands over the President's grave. Open daily.

A bed-and-breakfast within walking distance of the Johnson home, *Big Spring Inn,* 315 North Main St., Greeneville, TN 37743, phone (615) 638-2916, is a turn-of-the-century manor house furnished with antiques and handmade quilts, on two acres of trees and gardens. There are restaurants in town, and motels on the U.S. 11E bypass.

HARROGATE

Abraham Lincoln Museum, south of town on U.S. 25E, phone (615) 869-3611. On the Lincoln Memorial University campus, the museum has a research center and a collection of more than 250,000 items relating to Lincoln and the war. Open daily except major holidays. A Holiday Inn, phone (615) 869-3631, is about a half mile east on U.S. 25E.

JOHNSON CITY

Tipton-Haynes Living Historical Farm, off I-181 exit 31 at the south edge of town, phone (615) 926-3631. The museum at the Visitor Center on this restored 1784 farm has exhibits spanning American history from Colonial days through the Civil War. There are six original and four reconstructed buildings. Open daily April through October.

Jonesborough History Museum, 117 Boone St., phone (615) 753-5961. A collection of early abolitionist publications is one of the highlights of the museum. Open daily March through December, weekends January and February.

Historic District. In the center of town, a four-by-six-block area has a fine collection of Federal, Greek Revival, and Victorian buildings. A walking-tour brochure is available at the Visitor Center (see above). Phone (615) 753-5961. The town has several hotels and motels. An excellent choice for dinner is the *Parson's Table,* housed in an 1870 church, on U.S. 11 east in nearby Jonesboro, phone (615) 753-8002.

KNOXVILLE

East Tennessee had many Union sympathizers, and during the war Knoxville was seized by the Confederates and used as the headquarters of an army of occupation. The troops withdrew to Chattanooga in 1863, and a Union army moved in, only to be besieged by the Confederates. Large sections of the city were destroyed in the battle for Knoxville, but the Confederate attack was repelled and the city remained under Union control for the rest of the war.

Confederate Memorial Hall, 3148 Kingston Pike, S.W, phone (615) 522-2371. This fifteen-room antebellum mansion, Gen. James Longstreet's headquar-

Andrew Johnson Homestead, Greeneville, Tennessee

ters during the siege of Knoxville, has been restored and furnished with museum pieces. There is a collection of war relics and an extensive library of Southern literature. Guided tour. Open Tuesday through Friday.

The Graustein Inn, a few minutes from downtown Knoxville at 8300 Nubbin Ridge Rd., Knoxville, TN 37923, phone (615) 690-7007, has five guest rooms furnished with antiques. Breakfast served on the breakfast porch is included.

For dinner, try *Annie's,* 106 North Central Ave., phone (615) 637-4484, in a restored 1910 store in old Knoxville. The menu is continental, and a jazz combo performs Thursday through Sunday.

MEMPHIS

Memphis was briefly the Confederate capital of Tennessee as well as a military supply depot. Union troops seized the city in 1862 after a river battle involving thirty Union gunboats, and held it throughout the war.

Memphis Pink Palace Museum and Planetarium, 3050 Central Ave., phone (901) 454-5600. The wheelchair-accessible museum has an excellent collection of Civil War material. Open daily except Monday and holidays.

For overnight accommodations, the *Lowenstein-Long House* (217 North Waldran, Memphis, TN 38105; phone [901] 527-7174) is a turn-of-the-century mansion now on the National Historical Register. Guests have access to dining room, drawing room, parlor, conservatory, and the grounds. Breakfast is included in the room rate.

Justine's, 919 Leward Pl. at East St., phone (901) 458-2648, is in an antebellum mansion with lovely gardens, and specializes in fresh seafood.

NASHVILLE

Union troops seized Nashville in March 1862. A Confederate force commanded by General Hood moved to the hills south of the city in December 1864 in an attempt to recapture it, but two Union counterattacks virtually wiped out Hood's army.

Tennessee State Museum, James K. Polk State Building, 5th and Deaderick Sts., phone (615) 741-2692. Some exhibits focus on Nashville's role in the war. Open daily except major holidays. Accessible to the disabled.

Sam Davis Home, twenty miles south of Nashville, off I-24 in Smyrna, phone (615) 459-2341. Called "the most beautiful shrine to a private soldier in the country," this stately home and working farm is preserved as a memorial to Sam Davis, a Confederate scout caught behind Union lines and tried as a spy. He was offered his life if he revealed the name of his informant, but chose instead to die on the gallows. Davis's boyhood home is restored and furnished with many original pieces. He is buried here in the family burial grounds. Open daily except major holidays.

Miss Anne's Bed & Breakfast is filled with antiques, collectibles, and Miss Anne's collection of doll dishes. The grounds include a patio with grill and picnic table. For information, write to Miss Anne Cowell, 3033 Windemere Circle, Nashville, TN 37214, or phone (615) 885-1899.

WINCHESTER

Franklin County Old Jail Museum, 400 First Ave., N.E., phone (615) 967-0524. This restored 1897 jail houses a Civil War museum with a collection of artifacts. The nearest accommodations are in Monteagle, twenty miles northeast.

✦ 5 ✦

THE WAR IN
THE DEEP SOUTH

ALABAMA

CLANTON

Confederate Memorial Park, ten miles south on U.S. 31 to Mountain Creek. Phone (205) 755-1990. A Confederate cemetery situated on one hundred acres that once was the site of the Confederate Soldiers' Home. The wheelchair-accessible museum has mementos of the war as well as records, documents, and photographs relating to the home. Open daily except Christmas and New Year's Day.

DAUPHIN ISLAND

Fort Gaines, phone (205) 861-6992. This five-sided fort on the east end of the island was completed in the 1850s. Confederate forces manned the fort from 1861 until its capture by Union troops on August 23, 1864. The fort houses a Confederate museum. Open daily except Christmas. The nearest accommodations and restaurants are in Mobile, twenty miles north.

DECATUR

Mooresville, six miles east of Decatur on AL 20, phone (205) 355-1867. The oldest incorporated town in Alabama, Moores-

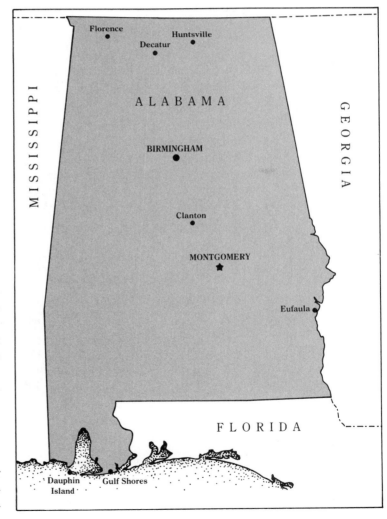

ville has many antebellum houses, including the home of President Andrew Johnson. An 1820 community brick church has a "slave balcony." Open daily except Sundays and major holidays.

EUFAULA

Shorter Mansion, 2340 North Eufaula Ave., phone (205) 687-3793. A Greek Revival mansion with antique furnishings, Confederate relics, and memorabilia of the six Alabama governors from Barbour County. Open daily except major holidays. Mini-tours are available by appointment.

Seth Lore and Irwinton Historic District. The second-largest historic district in the state, with 582 registered landmarks. A driving-tour brochure is available from the Chamber of Commerce and Eufaula Heritage Association, P.O. Box 486, 36027.

The Tavern Restaurant, 105 Riverside Dr., phone (205) 687-4451. Reputedly Eufaula's first permanent structure, which served as a Confederate hospital during the war. Open Monday to Friday. The *Lakeside Resort,* phone (205) 687-8011, is a 101-unit cottage colony five miles north on U.S. 431.

FLORENCE

Pope's Tavern, 203 Hermitage Dr., phone (205) 766-2662. Built in 1811 as a stage stop and tavern, the building served as a hospital for both sides during the war. Open Tuesday through Saturday, closed major holidays. Florence has several motels on Florence Boulevard.

GULF SHORES

Fort Morgan, twenty-one miles west of Gulf Shores on AL 180 (Fort Morgan Parkway), phone (205) 540-7125. After an

David G. Farragut

eighteen-day siege, this star-shaped fort surrendered to the Union fleet under Admiral David Farragut. The use of mines by the Confederates prompted Admiral Farragut's command, "Damn the torpedoes! Full speed ahead!" The fort is a fine example of brick architecture. The *Fort Morgan Museum* displays military artifacts. Open daily except Thanksgiving, Christmas, and New Year's Day. Gulf Shores is a beach resort area with a range of accommodations and restaurants.

HUNTSVILLE

Huntsville Depot, 320 Church St., phone (215) 539-1860. Opened in 1860 as the "passenger house" and eastern division headquarters for the Memphis & Charleston Rail Road Co., the depot was captured by Union troops and turned into a prison. Wartime graffiti can still be seen on the walls. Open daily except Monday. Wheelchair accessible.

MONTGOMERY

State Capitol, Bainbridge Ave. between Washington and Monroe Aves., phone (205) 261-3035. A bronze star between the columns of the capitol building marks the spot where Jefferson Davis was inaugurated President of the Confederate States of America on February 18, 1861, making Montgomery the Confederacy's first capital. From here the telegram was sent ordering the bombardment of Fort Sumter. In what is now the house of representatives chamber, the State Convention passed the Ordinance of Secession on January 11, 1861, and the Confederate government was organized in what is now the senate chamber. Open daily.

First White House of the Confederacy, 644 Washington Ave., phone (205) 261-4624. Across from the capitol, this 1835 two-story white frame house was the residence of President Davis and his family while Montgomery was the Confederate capital. In 1921 it was moved from its original location at Bibb and Lee streets, and now is a Confederate museum. It contains period furnishings, Confederate mementoes, and many personal belongings and paintings of the Davis family. Tours. Open daily except Thanksgiving, Christmas, and New Year's Day. Wheelchair access to first floor.

Teague House, 468 South Perry St., phone (205) 834-6000. This 1848 Greek Revival mansion was the headquarters of Gen. James H. Wilson after Federal forces captured the city on April 12, 1865. Open daily.

Alabama seceded from the Union in the present house of representatives chamber of the state capitol on January 11, 1861, and the Confederate government was organized in the present senate chamber. The capitol was built in 1851.

The First White House of the Confederacy. President Jefferson Davis and his family lived here in Montgomery, the first Confederate capital.

FLORIDA

APALACHICOLA

Fort Gadsden State Historic Site, twenty-four miles northeast of Apalachicola via U.S. 98 and FL 65, phone (904) 670-8988. During the War of 1812, the British built a fort here, but it was destroyed by American forces. In 1818, Andrew Jackson ordered the fort rebuilt as a supply base. Confederate troops occupied the fort from 1862 to 1863. Only part of the foundation of the fort remains, but a miniature replica and six exhibits about the fort's history are in the interpretive center.

The Gibson Inn, 100 Water St. at River Bridge, 32320, phone (904) 653-2191, is a restored 1907 Victorian hotel with a good restaurant.

BRADENTON

Gamble Plantation State Historic Site, about four miles northeast of Bradenton on U.S. 301, at 3708 Patten Ave. in Ellenton, phone (813) 722-1701. Maj. Robert Gamble owned and operated a 3,500-acre sugar plantation and refinery with 190 slaves. In May 1865, Judah P. Benjamin, secretary of state of the Confederacy, came here to hide from Union troops. He left just before a surprise raid by Union troops, fleeing first to Bimini, then to Nassau. Built between 1845 and 1850, the mansion, restored and furnished with period pieces and war relics, is the oldest building on Florida's west coast and the state's major Confederate shrine. House tours are given daily. Picnicking is allowed on the grounds.

FERNANDINA BEACH

Fort Clinch State Park, Atlantic Ave. off FL A1A, phone (904) 261-4212. Park rangers dressed in Union uniforms explain the role this old fort played in the war, protecting the entrance to St. Mary's River and the town of Fernandina. Built between

1847 and 1860, Fort Clinch was occupied by Confederates in 1862 and recaptured by Union forces the next year. Located on 1,085 acres at the state's northeasternmost point, the brick ramparts afford a splendid view of the Georgia shoreline and the ocean. Open daily.

DRY TORTUGAS

Fort Jefferson National Monument. The largest of the 19th-century coastal forts is on Dry Tortugas, a cluster of seven coral reefs some seventy miles west of Key West. Pirates sailed from Dry Tortugas until they were driven out after Florida became a state in 1821. Realizing that Dry Tortugas was the key to controlling navigation in the Gulf, the Department of War built Fort Jefferson on Garden Key. The fort, one half-mile in perimeter, was the largest of the chain of fortifications built from Maine to Texas during the first half of the 1800s. Its eight-foot-thick walls stood fifty feet high. Three gun tiers were built to hold 450 cannon. A 1,500-man garrison was planned, but the fort was never completed. Union troops occupied the fort throughout the war, but saw no action, and it became a prison for deserters.

In 1865, four of the Lincoln assassination conspirators were imprisoned at the fort after their conviction: Michael O'Loughlin, Samuel Arnold, Edward Spangler, and Dr. Samuel Mudd. Sentenced to life imprisonment for setting the broken leg of John Wilkes Booth, Lincoln's assassin, Mudd was pardoned in 1869 for fighting a yellow fever epidemic that killed thirty-eight prisoners and guards. Fort Jefferson was abandoned in 1874 after a severe hurricane and another yellow fever outbreak.

Visitors reach the fort by tour boat or seaplane from Key West, Naples, and Fort Myers. The tour operators supply drinking water and provisions, since no fresh water, food facilities, accommodations, or supplies of any kind are on the island. Visitors are given a slide orientation program, and the self-guided tour includes Dr. Mudd's cell. Nature is a bigger attraction here than history. The coral reef supports a wealth of sea life, and in April thousands of sooty terns gather on Bush Key for their nesting season. For further information, write the Superintendent, Everglades National Park, Box 279, Homestead, FL 33030, or phone (305) 247-6211.

LAKE CITY

Olustee Battlefield State Historic Site, fifteen miles east of Lake City on FL 90. The only major battle in Florida was fought near here on February 20, 1864, in a pine forest. A Union expeditionary force commanded by Gen. Truman Seymour landed at Jacksonville on February 7, to stop shipment of food supplies from central Florida to other Confederate states and thereby induce Unionists in eastern Florida to form a loyal state government. By February 11, Union cavalry rode to within three miles of Lake City, where they skirmished with entrenched Confederates. On February 20 the Union force of 5,500 men and sixteen cannon met a large Confederate

force some two miles east of Olustee. For five hours they fought in a forest of virgin pine before Seymour's troops broke off and retreated. Confederate cavalrymen pursued them, returning with 150 prisoners. The Union casualties were 1,861 against the Confederates' 946. Union troops occupied Jacksonville and other northern Florida ports until the end of the war. The battlefield is open daily; the Visitor Center, Thursday through Monday. A museum at the center has exhibits depicting battle scenes. The battle is reenacted annually in late February.

PENSACOLA

Fort Pickens, Gulf Islands National Seashore, south on U.S. 98 and FL 399 to Pensacola Beach, then west on Fort Pickens Road; phone (904) 934-2600. After the loss of Fort Sumter, a few Southern forts remained under Union control, notably Fort Pickens, built on a barrier island outside Pensacola Bay. Pickens and nearby Fort McRee and Fort Barrancas were involved early in the war. In January 1861, Lt. Adam Slemmer withdrew his tiny garrison from Barrancas to Pickens and abandoned the other forts to the Confederates. The Union never let go of Pickens. On November 22 and 23, 1861, the guns of Fort Pickens joined those of two warships in driving the Confederates out of the other two forts. Fort Pickens helped make the Union blockade of the Gulf Coast effective throughout the rest of the war. Fort McRee was lost to neglect after the war. Fort Pickens was restored and is now the headquarters for the Florida unit of the Gulf Islands National Seashore. Open daily. Wheelchair accessible. A museum has Civil War exhibits and material relating to Geronimo's imprisonment here.

Fort Barrancas. Built from 1839 to 1844 on the site of early Spanish fortifications, Fort Barrancas and the attached

Water Battery have been restored from old drawings and documents. The fort comprises sixty-five acres in the middle of the Pensacola Naval Air Station. In the Visitor Center is a small museum displaying material relating to the fort. Open daily. One-half mile away is the fort's Advance Redoubt, which is open during the summer. The station is in Warrington, ten miles west on Navy Boulevard. For further information, phone (904) 455-5167.

Pensacola Historic Museum, 405 South Adams St. at Zaragoza, phone (904) 433-1559. During the war, Pensacola was captured by Union troops and used as a base for the blockade of the Confederate Gulf Coast. The museum is in the oldest Protestant church still standing in the state, which was used by the occupying troops as a barracks and a hospital. In addition to exhibits, the museum offers a historical library, genealogy records, and an extensive collection of old photographs. Open daily except Sunday and holidays.

New World, 600 South Palafox, 32501, phone (904) 432-4111, is a charming sixteen-room inn with an excellent restaurant on the premises called *Michael's,* phone (904) 432-4311. Pensacola has many motels, including a cluster on Plantation Rd., and restaurants in all price ranges.

GEORGIA

ANDERSONVILLE

ANDERSONVILLE NATIONAL HISTORIC SITE

No battle was fought at Andersonville, but nearly 13,000 Union prisoners of war died there during the fourteen months that this was the most notorious military prison in the South. They were killed not by rifle fire or artillery bombardment, but by disease,

malnutrition, poor sanitation, overcrowding, and exposure to the elements.

Camp Sumter, as Andersonville was officially known, was the largest military prison in the South. It was built in early 1864, after the Confederate government decided to move the large number of prisoners in and around Richmond to a place of greater security and more abundant food.

Initially the prison pen covered about sixteen and a half acres of land enclosed by a fifteen-foot-high stockade of pine logs. It was enlarged to twenty-six and a half acres in June 1864. The prison proper was in the shape of a parallelogram 1,620 feet long and 779 feet wide. Sentry boxes—prisoners called them "pigeon roosts"—stood at thirty-yard intervals along the top of the stockade. Inside, about nineteen feet from the wall, was the "deadline," which pris-

Meager rations are issued to the nearly 33,000 Union prisoners at the infamous Andersonville Prison in Georgia. In the military cemetery at Andersonville are the graves of 12,912 prisoners who died in captivity.

oners were forbidden to cross under penalty of death.

A branch of the Sweetwater Creek, called Stockade Branch, flowed through the prison yard and supplied water to most of the prison. Two entrances, the north and south gates, were on the west side of the stockade. Eight small earthen forts located around the exterior were equipped with artillery to put down disturbances within the compound and to defend against Union cavalry attacks.

The first prisoners arrived at Andersonville in February 1864. During the next few months, some 400 more arrived each day. By the end of June, 26,000 men were confined in a prison originally designed to hold 10,000. In August 1864, the prison population was more than 32,000.

There were reasons for the overcrowding. The South was handicapped by deteriorating economic conditions, an inadequate transportation system, and, more impor-

tant, the need to concentrate all its resources on its army. The Confederate government simply wasn't able to provide its military prisoners with adequate housing, food, clothing, and medical care. Another complicating factor was the breakdown of the prisoner-exchange system.

One prisoner, John Ransom, a Michigan cavalryman, described prison life at Andersonville in his diary: "There is so much filth about the camp that it is terrible trying to live here. With sunken eyes, blackened countenances from pitch pine smoke, rags, and disease, the men look sickening. The air reeks with nastiness."

Most of the prisoners were sent to other military prisons, in South Carolina and coastal Georgia, after General Sherman occupied Atlanta on September 2, 1864. Union cavalry were now within striking distance, but never came.

Capt. Henry Wirz, Andersonville's commandant, was arrested when the war ended and charged with conspiring with high Confederate officials to "impair and injure the health and destroy the lives . . . of Federal prisoners" and "murder, in violation of the laws of war." Such a conspiracy was never proven, if it ever existed, but public anger and indignation in the North over the conditions at Andersonville demanded retribution.

Wirz was tried by a military tribunal as a war criminal, and found guilty. On November 10, 1865, he was hanged in Washington. Ironically, a monument to Wirz now stands in the town of Andersonville, erected by the Georgia Division of the United Daughters of the Confederacy.

In the summer of 1865, Clara Barton came to Andersonville with a detachment of soldiers and laborers, and a former prisoner, Dorence Atwater, to identify and mark the graves of the dead prisoners. Fearing the loss of the death records when the war ended, Atwater made his own copy of the register in hopes of notifying the relatives of the dead. Thanks to Atwater's list and the Confederate death records captured at the end of the war, only 460 of the Andersonville graves had to be marked "unknown U.S. soldier."

Andersonville National Cemetery was established on July 26, 1865. The prison site reverted to private ownership in 1875. In 1890 it was purchased by the Georgia Department of the Grand Army of the Republic, a Union veterans' organization. The veterans couldn't finance the improvements needed to protect the property, and sold Andersonville for one dollar to the Woman's Relief Corps, the national auxiliary of the G.A.R.

The Woman's Relief Corps made many improvements with the idea of creating a memorial park. Pecan trees were planted to produce nuts for sale to help maintain the site. The Corps built the Provident Spring House in 1901 to mark the site where, on August 9, 1864, a spring burst forth during a heavy summer rainstorm— an occurrence many prisoners attributed to Divine Providence.

In 1910 the Woman's Relief Corps donated the prison site to the people of the United States. It was administered by the War Department and its successor, the Department of the Army, through 1970, when it was made a national historic site.

Now Andersonville is a memorial to all Americans ever held as prisoners of war. Congress stated that the purpose of the park was "to provide an understanding of the overall prisoner-of-war story of the Civil War, to interpret the role of prisoner-of-war camps in history, to commemorate the sacrifice of Americans who lost their lives in such prison camps, and to preserve the monuments located [within the site]."

Clara Barton

VISITING ANDERSONVILLE

Andersonville National Historic Site is situated on 475 acres, fifty miles south of Macon and ten miles northeast of Americus on GA 49. The Visitor Center contains exhibits on the prison, the cemetery, Civil War prisons in general, and the systems of exchange and parole used during the war. Abbreviated records of the Union soldiers interned here are available at the Visitor Center. A twelve-minute slide presentation and a relief map introduce visitors to the site. A bookstore contains a selection of publications on Civil War prisons and the war in general. No food is sold at the park, but there is a picnic area. Schedules of daily activities and special events are posted at the center. For further information, write to the Superintendent, Andersonville National Historic Site, Rte. 1, Box 85, Andersonville, GA 31711, or phone (912) 924-0343.

The *National Cemetery* is the resting place of 12,912 who died here. Other interments of military personnel have brought the total to more than 16,000. Records of Civil War and subsequent interments and the locations of graves in the cemetery are located at the Visitor Center.

The cemetery here is hauntingly beautiful, and to wander among the white headstones is an emotionally moving experience. Most visitors tour Andersonville by car with an audiotape and player available from the center. After leaving the cemetery, which is next to the center, the sites include:

POW Museum. A short slide presentation and exhibits depict the plight of American prisoners of war from the Revolution to Vietnam.

The Dead House. Men who died in the stockade were removed to a small house built of tree branches outside the South Gate. From there they were carried by wagon to the cemetery for burial.

Providence Springhouse. A lovely springhouse marks the spot where lightning struck within the stockade, releasing a nat-

Graves of Union prisoners, Andersonville National Historic Site

Providence Springhouse, Andersonville National Historic Site

ural spring of potable water. The prisoners believed it was the work of Divine Providence.

The Star Fort. This earthwork, along with several others around the perimeter of the stockade, was constructed to quell disturbances inside the prison and to guard against Union cavalry attacks.

Third Hospital Site. This, the last prison hospital, was a large stockade structure with tents for sick prisoners. Because of the Union blockade of Southern ports, a shortage of transportation, and great demands on existing supplies, few medicines were available. As a result, Confederate doctors could do little to relieve patients' suffering.

The Inner Stockade. The outer row of posts marks the location of the stockade fence. It was built of twenty-foot pine logs sunk five feet into the ground.

Escape Tunnels and Wells. Prisoners dug many tunnels in their attempts to escape. Nearly all of the men who made it outside the stockade were recaptured and returned. Not all of the holes in this area are escape tunnels, however. Many are the remains of wells dug by prisoners searching for fresh drinking water.

Visitors should be wary of snakes and poison ivy, as well as fire ants that live in red sandy mounds and have a painful sting. Don't go barefoot. Sandburs grow wild in the grass.

IN AND AROUND ANDERSONVILLE

Across the highway from the prison is the town of Andersonville, the railroad stop where the prisoners arrived. The village also was the supply center for the prison. Capt. Henry Wirz, the camp commandant, had his offices here. A Welcome Center and museum are housed in a quaint 18th-century railroad depot in the center near the *Wirz Monument.* The *Civil War Village of Andersonville* is nearby in a five-acre park complete with log cabin, barn, farm ani-

*Wirz Monument,
Andersonville, Georgia*

CHICKAMAUGA AND CHATTANOOGA

CHICKAMAUGA AND CHATTANOOGA NATIONAL MILITARY PARK
GEORGIA AND TENNESSEE

In the fall of 1863 the prize sought by both sides in the conflict was Chattanooga, a key rail center and gateway to the heart of the Confederacy, and to win it, more than 100,000 men clashed on these fields and hills in some of the hardest fighting of the war.

The campaign began the previous June, when Union General William Rosecrans's Army of the Cumberland left Murfreesboro, Tennessee, to attack Gen. Braxton Bragg's Army of Tennessee. Bragg was dug in twenty miles southwest of Murfreesboro, defending the road to Tennessee.

These two armies had fought at Stones River (Murfreesboro) six months before. A three-day battle ended when the Confederates retreated. Rosecrans again had the upper hand. Through a series of skillful marches, he forced Bragg's 43,000-man army to withdraw into Chattanooga.

Bragg dug in, guarding the Tennessee River crossings northeast of the city, where he expected Rosecrans to attack. But in early September, Rosecrans led his 60,000 troops across the Tennessee well below the city, forcing Bragg to withdraw southward.

Eluding Rosecrans, Bragg concentrated his forces at La Fayette, Georgia, twenty-six miles south of Chattanooga. Reinforcements arrived from Virginia, east Tennessee, and Mississippi, swelling Bragg's ranks to 66,000. After two unsuccessful attempts to destroy isolated segments of the Union army, Bragg moved his army to the west bank of Chickamauga Creek along a line from Reed's Bridge to just opposite Lee and Gordon's Mill. He hoped to put his army between Rosecrans and Chattanooga.

mals, and a sugarcane mill. Paths lead through the trees and across a footbridge spanning a brook. A restaurant and several antique shops are nearby. Open daily except Christmas from 9 A.M. to 5 P.M. (until 6 P.M. from May through September). The first weekend in October is the annual *Andersonville Historic Fair,* which features Civil War reenactments, military bands, and old-time craftsmen.

Two bed-and-breakfasts are within an easy drive of Andersonville. The *Plains Bed and Breakfast* (280 West Church St., Plains, GA 31709; phone [912] 824-7252) is a restored Victorian house where Lillian Carter lived before she gave birth to the future President Jimmy Carter. Among the fine homes in the Historic District of Marshalville is *Suite Revenge* (400 West Main St., P.O. Box 306, Marshalville, GA 31057; phone [912] 967-2252). Other accommodations are available in Americus, ten miles south on GA 49.

Shortly after dawn on September 19, Union infantry encountered Confederate cavalry at Jay's Mill, touching off a general battle that spread south for nearly four miles. The armies fought desperately all day and gradually Bragg pushed the Union army back to La Fayette Road.

The next day he again tried to drive between Rosecrans and Chattanooga, but failed to crack the Union line. Then, in the heat of battle, a mistaken order opened a gap in the Union ranks. Gen. James Longstreet's Confederates smashed through the hole, routing Rosecrans and half his army.

Gen. George H. Thomas took command of the remaining Union troops and formed a new battle line on Snodgrass Hill. His men held their ground against repeated assaults, earning for Thomas the sobriquet "Rock of Chickamauga." After dark, Thomas withdrew his men from the field.

The defeat forced the Union troops to retreat into Chattanooga. Bragg pursued, occupying Missionary Ridge, Lookout Mountain, and the Chattanooga Valley. By placing artillery on the heights overlooking the river and blocking the roads and rail lines, Bragg prevented supplies from entering the city. Unless something was done quickly, Rosecrans's army would be starved into surrendering.

Reinforcements were dispatched. Gen. Joseph Hooker arrived from Virginia late in October with 20,000 troops. Gen. William T. Sherman brought 16,000 more from Mississippi in mid-November. In October, Gen. Ulysses S. Grant had assumed overall command, replacing Rosecrans with Thomas as commander of the Army of the Cumberland.

Soon after Grant arrived the situation began to change. On October 28, Union troops opened a short supply route, called the "Cracker Line," from Bridgeport, Alabama. On November 23, Thomas attacked and routed the Confederates from Orchard Knob. On the twenty-fourth, General Hooker, aided by a heavy fog that clung to the slopes of Lookout Mountain, pushed the Confederates out of their defenses around the Cravens House. On the twenty-fifth, Grant launched Sherman's troops against the right flank of Bragg's army, concentrated on Missionary Ridge. Hooker attacked the Confederate left. Thomas's

CIVIL WAR PRISON CAMPS

Neither the North nor the South expected a long conflict or anticipated the need to care for thousands of prisoners. In the South, prisoners were housed initially in old warehouses and barns. As the number of prisoners increased, special prisons were built in a number of places, including Florence, South Carolina; Salisbury, North Carolina; and Millen and Andersonville, Georgia.

In the North, army training camps were converted into military prisons. Stockades were placed around such camps as Butler, Illinois; Elmira, New York; and Chase, Ohio; to provide security. Some Confederate prisoners were kept in forts, like McHenry at Baltimore and Warren in the harbor at Boston.

Of the more than 211,400 Union soldiers captured, 30,208 died in prison camps. Union forces captured some 462,000 Confederates, including those belonging to the armies surrendered at the end of the war. Of these, 25,976 died in prison camps, most of the deaths occurring during the latter part of the war.

Between August 1862 and November 1863, captured men either were exchanged or paroled on their oath of honor not to reenter their armed forces. This permitted the captured men to return to training camps as noncombatants. More important, the prisoners did not have to be provided for. But by October 1863, disagreement had arisen over the exchange system, and it soon broke down.

The most common problems confronting prisoners in both the North and the South were overcrowding, poor sanitation, and the lack of a proper diet. Additional hardships came from mismanagement by prison officials. The end of the war saved many prisoners, but for many others it came too late.

Some of Sherman's veterans of western fighting, the 21st Michigan Infantry, pose for the photographer in a Tennessee camp. In four months of campaigning from Chattanooga to Atlanta, Sherman's Army of the Tennessee constructed more than 300 miles of rifle pits, and fired nearly 150,000 artillery rounds and more than 22 million rounds of small-arms ammunition.

troops were held in reserve in the center, at Orchard Knob.

The attack soon ran into trouble. Hooker was delayed crossing Chattanooga Creek. Sherman's attack was stopped by the Confederate line. To relieve the pressure on Sherman, Grant ordered Thomas to assault the rifle pits at the base of Missionary Ridge. After this was accomplished, something amazing happened. The men of Thomas's Army of the Cumberland spontaneously scaled the heights of Missionary Ridge in one of the great charges of the war. The Confederate line collapsed, and Bragg's troops fled to the rear. During the night they retreated into Georgia.

The siege and battle for Chattanooga were over. Union armies now controlled the city and nearly all of Tennessee. Chattanooga would be the base for Sherman when he started his drive for Atlanta and the sea.

VISITING CHICKAMAUGA AND CHATTANOOGA

Chickamauga and Chattanooga National Military Park is composed of a number of separate areas: *Chickamauga Battlefield,* seven miles south of Chattanooga on U.S. 27; *Point Park* and *Lookout Mountain* battlefield; *Orchard Knob;* and *Missionary Ridge,* which contains a series of small units called reservations along its summit. All of these areas, along with *Signal Point Reservation* to the north, can be toured easily in a day.

The Visitor Center, located at the north entrance to the 5,400-acre Chickamauga battlefield on U.S. 27, is the logical starting point for visitors. The center's museum contains the Fuller Collection of American Military Shoulder Arms, consisting of 385 weapons. An audiovisual presentation depicts the fighting here and in the other related areas. A bookstore has a selection of volumes on the battles. No food is sold at the center, but a picnic area and restaurants are on the highway nearby. The center and the park are accessible to the disabled. Outside the center is an artillery display, illustrating the cannons used by the light field artillery during the war.

U.S. 27 extends more than three miles through the battlefield, where events have been commemorated by monuments, markers, tablets, and artillery pieces. Woods and fields are kept as close as possible to the way they were in wartime, and some old buildings still stand.

Park Service personnel give guided tours of the battlefield, evening programs, and, in the summer, musket- and cannon-firing demonstrations. Details of special events are posted in the center. For further information, write to the Superintendent, Chickamauga and Chattanooga National Military Park, Fort Oglethorpe, GA 30742, or phone (404) 866-9241.

The major points of interest along the seven-mile self-guided driving tour include:

Battle of Chickamauga. Unlike many other Civil War battles, which were fought in open fields, Chickamauga was fought in dense woods and thick underbrush. Generals had trouble keeping track of their troops, much less directing them. The monuments and markers along the tour road mark the locations of units and batteries engaged in the battle. Metal tablets—blue for Union, red for Confederate—are positioned so that visitors view the field much the way it was seen by the soldiers positioned here in 1863.

The Battle Line. The final day of the battle opened near this spot and spread along what is now the tour route. At about 9:30 A.M., Confederates under Gen. Leon-

Union troops arrive at the summit of Lookout Mountain in this period engraving. The action became known as the "Battle Above the Clouds," although the fiercest fighting took place 500 feet from the summit.

idas Polk attacked Thomas's corps, who were lined up behind log barricades. The pressures created by these attacks caused Rosecrans to shift troops to Thomas's aid. This weakened the Federal right flank and set the scene for Longstreet's breakthrough.

Mix-up in the Union Command. Shortly before 11 A.M. on September 20, Rosecrans received an erroneous report that Gen. John M. Brannan's division was out of position, creating what was believed to be a gap in the Union line. It was while Gen. Thomas J. Wood's division was shifting to fill Brannan's spot that Longstreet's troops struck. A part of Brannan's line is marked by monuments, tablets, and cannon. The figures near the base of the Georgia Monument across the road represent the three arms of the land-based military: infantry, artillery, and cavalry.

Confederate Breakthrough. Just as the last element of Wood's division pulled out of line and before Gen. Jefferson C. Davis's division could fill the gap its departure created, Longstreet's troops charged from the woods to the rear, past the *Brotherton Cabin,* and across the field to the Union line in the trees. The attack drove the divisions of Davis and Gen. Philip H. Sheridan and a part of Wood's division from the field. The Brotherton Cabin stands now as it did in 1863.

The Cost of Chickamauga. Chickamauga was one of the bloodiest battles of the war. Confederate losses totaled more than 18,000 out of some 66,000 engaged. Union losses were 16,000 out of 58,000. In

The Tennessee River from Lookout Mountain

one day the 22nd Alabama Regiment lost 55 percent of its soldiers and almost half of its officers; seventeen of twenty-three officers of the 20th Georgia fell in action. "We advanced under a perfect shower of bullets," recalled Col. James L. Abernathy of the Eighth Kansas Infantry, "sometimes driving the enemy and in turn being driven by them, until we had fought over the ground over and over again, and almost half of our number lay dead or wounded." The markers across the road mark troop positions on September 19.

Wilder Tower. This imposing, eighty-five-foot monument honors Col. John Wilder and his brigade of mounted infantry who occupied this part of the battlefield when Longstreet's troops broke through the Union line on September 20. Armed with seven-shot Spencer repeating carbines, Wilder's 2,000-man brigade poured deadly fire into Longstreet's veterans, but were unable to stop them. The monument stands on the ground where Rosecrans maintained his headquarters on September 19 and early on the morning of September 20. A platform at the top affords an excellent view of the battlefield and the surrounding area.

Retreat of the Union Right. Many Union units moving through this area were surprised by Longstreet's attack and driven off the field, including Rosecrans and two of his corps commanders. Beyond the woods to your right is the Brotherton cabin, point of the Confederate breakthrough. To the left, on the knoll beyond the field, a monument marks the site of Rosecrans's headquarters at that time.

Snodgrass Hill. Here Gen. George H. Thomas became the Rock of Chickamauga. When Longstreet's attack struck the Union center, the Union troops there fell back to this hill, where Thomas organized them into a determined defending force. The log cabin here marks the site of the 1863 home of the Snodgrass family.

TRUER WORDS

Chickamauga is a Cherokee word meaning "river of death."

LOOKOUT MOUNTAIN

Lookout Mountain was the scene of one of the key engagements in the battle for Chattanooga. The Visitor Center, across the road from the entrance gate, contains an information area, an eight-minute slide orientation program, and a bookstore. From June through August, park rangers present a variety of daily tours, historical talks, and demonstrations. Details are posted in the center.

From the upper level to the Ochs Museum and Overlook is a descent of 500 feet. There are several tiers of steps along the trail, which is not accessible to the disabled, and is physically testing to those not in good condition.

The stops along the walking tour include:

The Entrance Gate. Constructed in 1905 by the U.S. Corps of Engineers, the gate is the largest replica of the Corps' insignia in the world.

Gun Batteries. The three gun batteries inside the park mark a very small segment of the siege lines that once encircled Chattanooga. The first consists of two "Parrott rifles," named for their inventor, Robert Parrott of New York. These guns each weighed 1,750 pounds, and their barrels were grooved, or rifled, to increase firing accuracy. Their maximum range was two miles at an elevation of five degrees. They are easily recognized by the heavy metal placed on the breech for reinforcement against cracking from extreme heat.

The second, known as *Garrity's Battery*, overlooks the valley below. These twelve-pound howitzers, known as "Napoleons" because Emperor Napoleon III of France sponsored their development, were the

A Federal gun crew poses with a massive 200-pound Parrott gun on Missionary Ridge, overlooking the Tennessee River at Chattanooga after the decisive battle that opened the way for Sherman's march to Atlanta. Batteries like this were used to prevent enemy use of the river for troop and supply transport. The North had clear superiority in artillery throughout the war, in part because of its greater industrial capacity.

standard cannon used by both armies during the war. These guns could fire a twelve-pound cannonball 1,700 yards. They were effective for close-range fighting, but could not be tilted down, because the charge would roll out before it was fired.

The third, *Corput's Battery,* is near the western overlook, from which Sunset Rock may be seen. Gen. James Longstreet used this rock as an observation point while watching a nighttime attack in Wauhatchie Valley.

New York Peace Memorial. On top of the shaft of this large monument, Union and Confederate soldiers shake hands under one flag signifying peace and brotherly love. The monument is ninety-five feet high, fifty feet in diameter at the base, and constructed of Tennessee marble and pink Massachusetts granite.

The Ochs Museum and Overlook. Dedicated November 12, 1940, the museum was named in honor of Adolph S. Ochs, onetime Chattanooga resident and

owner-publisher of *The New York Times.* The exhibits and pictures in the museum depict the story of the battle for Chattanooga and its importance in determining the outcome of the war. (Umbrella Rock, to the front and left of the museum, is unsafe to climb.)

Cravens House. The fiercest fighting on the mountain took place around this house. Confederate officers used the building for headquarters, and Union gunfire badly damaged it.

Bluff Trail. This is the main hiking trail in the park, reached by way of metal steps to the left of the museum. At this exact spot, Kentucky Volunteers climbed the mountain to reach the point and plant their flag. Many trails lead away from this one, and all are clearly marked.

RELATED SITES

Orchard Knob Reservation. The site of Grant's headquarters, from which he directed the Army of the Cumberland as it advanced against Missionary Ridge on November 25, 1863.

Missionary Ridge. A low-lying mountain barrier east of Chattanooga, Missionary Ridge is approximately twenty miles long and 400 feet above the city. Fortified by the Confederates, the ridge was almost impregnable, but it fell to the hard-charging veterans of the Army of the Cumberland.

The ridge is accessible by car via Crest Road. Along the road are several park areas, the most significant of which are Bragg, Ohio, De Long, and Sherman reservations.

Bragg Reservation. This marks the site of Bragg's headquarters during the siege. The monument here honors Illinois troops who fought in the battle.

Ohio Reservation. Ohio troops who participated in the Chattanooga Campaign are honored here.

De Long Reservation. A large monument honors the Second Minnesota Regiment, which fought gallantly at the Battle of Chickamauga and was among the first to reach the crest of Missionary Ridge.

Sherman Reservation. Sherman's troops tried in vain to break through the Confederate defenses here.

Signal Point Reservation, north of, and directly opposite Lookout Mountain, is one of the many sites used by the U.S. Signal Corps during the war. Exhibits are displayed along the terrace.

CHATTANOOGA

Lookout Mountain Incline Railway, 3917 St. Elmo Ave., phone (615) 821-8224. The steepest passenger incline railroad in the world climbs up the 2,225-foot Lookout Mountain. Near the top, the grade is 72.7 percent. The round trip aboard the glass-roofed trains takes about thirty minutes. An observation deck is at the top. Open daily.

Confederama, Garden Road on the west slope of Lookout Mountain, phone (615) 821-2812. An automated three-dimensional display recreates the Battle of Chattanooga, employing 5,000 miniature soldiers, flashing lights, smoking cannons, and cracking rifles. Wheelchair accessible. Open daily except Thanksgiving and Christmas.

On Lookout Mountain just below Ruby Falls and Point, the *Alford House Bed & Breakfast* is furnished with antiques, including a collection of glass baskets. An antique and gift shop offers discounts to guests. For information, write to Ms. Rhoda Alford, 2510 Lookout Mountain Pkwy., Chattanooga, TN 37419, or phone (615) 821-7625.

Railroad buffs will enjoy the *Choo-Choo,* Terminal Station, Choo-Choo Blvd., 37402; phone (615) 266-5000. This handsome converted 1905 station offers several choices of accommodations, including Victorian sleeping cars. The largest model railroad in the country is in the main station. Guests can drink in the authentic Wabash Cannonball Club Car and dine on Southern country dishes in the Trans-Continental in the station.

THE FIRST NATIONAL MILITARY PARK

Between 1890 and 1899, Congress authorized the establishment of the first four national military parks: Chickamauga and Chattanooga, Shiloh, Gettysburg, and Vicksburg. The first and largest of these, the one upon which the establishment and development of most of the other national military and historical parks was based, was Chickamauga and Chattanooga.

The park owes its existence largely to the efforts of Gen. H. V. Boynton and Ferdinand Van Derveer, both veterans of the

Army of the Cumberland; during a visit to the area in 1888, they saw the need for a national park to preserve and commemorate these battlefields.

The men spent the better part of two years gathering support for the park idea among both Union and Confederate veterans. Early in 1890, Ohio Congressman Charles H. Grosvenor introduced a bill drafted by Boynton to establish the park. President Benjamin Harrison signed the bill into law on August 19 of that year.

Both congressional military affairs committees had pointed out that there was probably no other field in the world that presented more formidable natural obstacles to large-scale military operations than the slopes of Lookout Mountain and Missionary Ridge. They noted that there had been scarcely any changes at Chickamauga since the battle, except for the growth of underbrush and young trees, which could easily be removed.

The fields of Chickamauga, the committees felt, offered unparalleled opportunities for historical and professional military study. From observation towers it would be possible to comprehend the grand strategy of the campaign over a front that extended 150 miles. No battlefield park of this quality and magnitude could be found in any other nation of the world.

The park was officially dedicated with impressive ceremonies on September 18–20, 1895. Most of the 1,400 monuments and historical markers on the battlefields were planed and placed by Boynton and other veterans of the battles.

Over the years the park had a close relationship with the military. In 1896, Congress declared all military parks national fields "for military maneuvers for the army and national guard." In 1898, Chickamauga and Chattanooga National Military Park was used as a training area for troops destined to fight in the Spanish-American War. Camp Thomas, named for Gen. George H.

Thomas, the Rock of Chickamauga, was established on the battlefield and became a sprawling city of some 45,000 soldiers. Four years later, all military activity was transferred to the newly established Fort Oglethorpe, adjacent to the park.

FORT PULASKI

FORT PULASKI NATIONAL MONUMENT
COCKSPUR ISLAND, GEORGIA

After the War of 1812, construction began on a system of thirty coastal fortifications from Maine to Key West and along the Gulf Coast. Fort Pulaski, named after the Revolutionary War hero Casimir Pulaski, was started in 1829 and required a million dollars, twenty-five million bricks, and eighteen years to complete. As a young officer in the Army Corps of Engineers, Robert E. Lee worked on the island's drainage system. The fort was considered invincible, "as strong as the Rocky Mountains." When war came, however, its armament was not complete, nor was the fort garrisoned.

On January 3, 1861, two weeks after South Carolina seceded from the Union, Georgia Governor Joseph E. Brown ordered the state militia to seize Fort Pulaski on Cockspur Island, recently built to guard the river approaches to the thriving seaport of Savannah. After Georgia seceded on January 19, the fort was transferred to the Confederacy, but it would not be held by the South for long.

In the summer of 1861, President Lincoln ordered the navy to blockade Southern ports. As the blockade tightened, it began to strangle the Confederate economy. On November 7, a combined army and navy expedition attacked at Port Royal Sound, South Carolina, about fifteen miles north of Fort Pulaski. Confederate troops fled as Union warships bombarded Fort Walker and Fort Beauregard, allowing Union

Fort Pulaski

troops to land unopposed on Hilton Head Island. A base was established on Hilton Head for operations against Fort Pulaski and the entire South Atlantic coast.

On November 10, the Confederates abandoned Tybee Island at the mouth of the Savannah River, unthinkingly giving the enemy the only site from which Fort Pulaski could be taken. Moving quickly, the Union forces cut the fort's communications with the mainland, then put troops ashore on Tybee Island to prepare for siege operations.

Capt. Quincy A. Gillmore, an engineer, assumed command of the troops on Tybee Island in February 1862. He believed that an overwhelming bombardment would force the Confederates to give up Fort Pulaski. Over the next two months, Gillmore erected eleven artillery batteries containing thirty-six guns and mortars along the northwest shore of the island. On April 10, after his formal demand to surrender was refused, Gillmore opened fire.

The Confederates were not overly alarmed, as the Union guns were a mile away, more than twice the effective range of heavy ordnance of that time. But the fort didn't know that the Union artillery included ten new experimental rifled cannon. Projectiles from these thirty-pound Parrott guns soon began to bore through the fort's seven-and-a-half-foot-thick walls with devastating effect.

By noon of the second day, the bombardment had opened wide gaps in the southeast angle, and explosive shells passing through the holes threatened the main powder magazine. Convinced that the situation was hopeless, and concerned about his men, the commander of the fort, Col. Charles H. Olmstead, surrendered thirty hours after the bombardment began. One Confederate soldier was killed during the bombardment.

The quick fall of Fort Pulaski surprised and shocked the world and made Gillmore an instant hero. He was quickly promoted to brigadier general. One Union officer wrote: "The result of this bombardment must cause a change in the construction of fortifications as radical as that foreshadowed in naval architecture by the conflict of the *Monitor* and *Merrimac.* No works of stone or brick can resist the impact of rifled artillery of heavy calibre."

Olmstead and his garrison of 384 officers and men were sent north and imprisoned on Governor's Island in New York City. Olmstead was exchanged in the fall of 1862 and served with distinction until the end of the war, although his decision to surrender haunted him the rest of his life. He later wrote: "We were absolutely isolated, beyond any possibility of help from the Confederate Authorities, and I did not feel warranted in exposing the garrison to the hazard of the blowing up of our main magazine—a danger which had just been proved well within the limits of probability. There are times when a soldier must hold his position to the last extremity, which means *extermination* but this was not one of them. . . . That the fort could and would be absolutely destroyed by the force of the enemy was a demonstrated fact . . . while our own power to harm them had been reduced to a minimum. . . . I am still convinced that there was nothing else that could be done."

Union troops garrisoned Fort Pulaski through the rest of the war, and later it was used to house political prisoners. After 1880, a caretaker and lighthouse keeper were the fort's only occupants. They were removed after a few years, leaving Fort Pulaski to the encroaching vegetation and animal life. The island was made a national monument in 1924, and restoration of the fort began in the early 1930s.

VISITING FORT PULASKI

Fort Pulaski National Monument is on Cockspur Island in the delta area of the Savannah River, fifteen miles east of Savannah, Georgia, on U.S. 80. A causeway links the island to the mainland. The Visitor Center contains a small museum depicting the significance of the fort, its place in the evolution of seacoast fortification and ordnance, and its restoration. Artifacts dating from the era of Spanish exploration to the 20th century are on display. A bookstore offers a wide selection of Civil War material. There are interpretive talks, walks, weapon demonstrations, and guided and self-guided tours. A schedule of events is posted in the center. The fort is open daily from 8:30 A.M. to 5:30 P.M., with extended hours in the late spring and summer (closed Christmas and New Year's Day). The center and most of the fort are accessible to the disabled. No food is sold, but there are picnic grounds nearby. There are restaurants in Savannah and on Tybee Island, four miles away. Hiking and nature trails, ranging from a quarter-mile to two miles in length, lead around the fort. For further information, write to the Superintendent, Fort Pulaski National Monument, Box 98, Tybee Island, GA 31328, or phone (919) 786-5797.

Stay off mounds and the topmost walls of the fort. Don't run on the terreplein (upper level) of the fort. Come down from the terreplein if there is lightning. Mosquitoes, gnats, and horseflies are present in the spring and summer; protective clothing and a repellent are suggested. Stay on the trails when walking or hiking, and beware of poisonous snakes. (The yellow rat snakes—brown or black with dull white or yellow markings—are harmless to humans but useful in exterminating rats and mice in the fort.)

The sites to see in the fort include:

The Moat. The water in the ditch that surrounds the fort is seven feet deep and varies in width from thirty-two to forty-eight feet. The water is brought through a canal from the Savannah River and is controlled by tide gates. A variety of small marine life and an occasional alligator inhabit the moat.

The Demilune. This huge triangular earthwork was built after the Civil War to protect the rear or "gorge" wall of the fort. During the war, this area was flat and surrounded by a parapet, and contained outbuildings and storage sheds. The earthen mounds overlay four powder magazines and passageways to several gun emplacements.

The Drawbridge. A part of the fort's overall defense, the drawbridge is constructed in such a way as to make forced entry difficult. As the drawbridge is raised, a strong wooden grille, called a portcullis, drops through the granite lintel overhead, and bolt-studded doors are closed behind the portcullis. An inclined granite walk leads between two rows of rifle slits, past another set of doors, and into the fort.

Gorge Wall. This is the rear section of the fort and contains the sally port, or fort entrance. Officers lived in most of the rooms here. Several are furnished to represent various aspects of life at the fort.

The Northwest Magazine. On the morning of April 11, 1862, Union artillery projectiles breached the southeast angle and crashed into the walls and roof of this magazine, which contained 40,000 pounds of gunpowder. Rather than be blown up by its own gunpowder, the garrison surrendered. The walls of the magazine are from twelve to fifteen feet thick, or roughly four times thicker than the rest of the walls of the fort.

Confederate Defense System. The Confederate defenders of the fort built earthen traverses between the guns and over the magazine, and dug ditches and pits in the parade ground to catch rolling cannon shot. They also erected a heavy timber "blindage" to cover the interior perimeter of the fort as a protection against shell fragments.

The Prison. During the winter of 1864, the northeast, southeast, and part of the south casements were used as a military prison holding Confederate officers under miserable conditions. After the war, several political prisoners were held here.

The Breach. The seven-and-a-half-foot-thick walls at this angle were demolished by Union rifled artillery on April 10–11, 1862, forcing the Confederates to surrender the fort. The walls were repaired within six weeks after the surrender by troops of the 48th New York Volunteers.

Southwest Bastion. This bastion, which burned in an 1865 fire, has been left unrestored to show various construction details of the fort. Brick arches under the terreplein carry weight to counter-arches in the floor, which, in turn, are supported by a timber grillage and pilings driven seventy feet into the mud of Cockspur.

Cistern Room. The cistern exposed here is one of ten that were used to store fresh water. Rain filtered through the sod of the terreplein ran down lead pipes in brick piers and thence to the tanks. The whole system could hold more than 200,000 gallons.

Exhibits and Rest Rooms. This section of the gorge wall contains various exhibits on soldier life and artillery in the war.

Damaged Wall. Craters made by Union artillery pock the south and southeast walls. Rifled cannon shot fired from Tybee Island penetrated the walls twenty to twenty-five inches. Some of the 5,275 shots fired can still be seen in the wall.

Three miles east of Fort Pulaski on U.S. 80 is *Tybee Island,* a V-shaped sandbar fronting the Atlantic and the Savannah River. The north end of the beach is marked by old coastal defenses and a lighthouse on the tip. Of interest is the *Tybee Museum,* opposite the lighthouse. Housed

"WE HAVE
DEVOURED THE
LAND AND OUR
ANIMALS EAT UP
THE WHEAT AND
CORN FIELDS
CLOSE. ALL THE
PEOPLE RETIRE
BEFORE US AND
DESOLATION IS
BEHIND. TO
REALIZE WHAT
WAR IS, ONE
SHOULD FOLLOW
OUR TRACKS."

—GENERAL
WILLIAM T.
SHERMAN, *on the
campaign near
Atlanta, 1864*

in a coastal battery, the building has walls of solid concrete and granite. The Civil War Room contains relics of Union and Confederate forces and secession documents. The Old Tybee Room has uniforms and weapons dating from antebellum days through World War II. Open daily. Phone (912) 786-4077.

IN AND AROUND SAVANNAH

On November 16, 1864, General Sherman cut his communications, burned much of Atlanta, and began his march to the sea. "I can make Georgia howl," he promised. His 62,000 tough soldiers fell on Georgia like a plague of locusts. Practically unopposed, Sherman cut a path of destruction fifty to sixty miles wide, right across the state. The soldiers lived off the land, rifling corncribs, smokehouses, and barns, looting houses, tearing up railroads, and demolishing bridges. Following the army was a mob of "bummers" intent only on looting. Southern newspapers called Sherman "the spirit of a thousand fiends centered in one," and the "Attila of the West."

At Milledgeville, then Georgia's capital, Union soldiers built bonfires with Confederate money. They also found several escaped prisoners from Andersonville. An officer wrote that these living skeletons "sickened and infuriated the men who thought of the tens of thousands of their imprisoned comrades, slowly perishing with hunger in the midst of . . . barns bursting with grain and food to feed a dozen armies." Georgia would howl even louder.

Sherman left Milledgeville to march to Savannah, 175 miles away. As he closed in on Savannah in mid-December, the 10,000 Confederate soldiers defending the city departed. The only resistance Sherman encountered was at Fort McAllister. Occupying Savannah, Sherman telegraphed President Lincoln: "I beg to present you, as a Christmas gift, the city of Savannah,

with 150 heavy guns and . . . about 25,000 bales of cotton." Sherman stayed in Savannah two months before marching north to take the war to South Carolina.

Savannah today is an architectural jewel. More than a thousand buildings of historic or architectural significance have been restored in the city's Historic District, the largest in the country. South of the Historic District is the Victorian District, an outstanding collection of post–Civil War Homes.

The points of interest in Savannah include:

Historic Savannah Waterfront Area. The riverfront bluff has been restored to preserve and stabilize the historic waterfront area, a nine-block brick concourse of parks, studios, museums, shops, pubs, and restaurants.

U.S. Customs House. This 1850 building at Bull and East Bay streets was erected on the site of the colony's first public building. A tablet on Bull Street marks the site where John Wesley, the founder of Methodism, preached his first Savannah sermon, and a tablet on Bay Street marks the location of the headquarters of James Oglethorpe, the colonial governor of Georgia and founder of Savannah.

Factors Walk. This row of business houses "on the Bay" between Bull and East Broad streets was named for the cotton factors who operated here in the 19th century. It is accessible via a network of iron bridgeways over cobblestone ramps.

Great Exposition, 303 West Broad St. in Battlefield Park, next to the Savannah Visitor Center, phone (912) 238-1779. A 19th-century railroad shed has been renovated to house a historical orientation center. Among the attractions are the *Savannah-Spirit of the South Theater,* where the history of the city is dramatized using motion pictures, special effects, and music, and the *Grand Museum Hall* displaying artifacts, antiques, and reproductions from the city's past, including Civil War arms and uniforms. Open daily except Christmas and New Year's Day.

Georgia Historical Society, 501 Whitaker St., phone (912) 651-2128. A research library and the archives for Savannah and Georgia history and genealogy. Open daily.

Green-Meldrim House, 14 West Macon St. General Sherman stayed here during the occupation of Savannah. The house now is the parish house of St. John's Church. Open daily except Sunday, closed the first two weeks in January, major holidays, and occasionally for parish activities.

Ships of the Sea Museum, 503 East River St., on the river, phone (912) 232-1511. A collection of ship models, figureheads, scrimshaw, sea artifacts, ship's carpenter's tools, and a chandlery, including some material pertaining to the war. Open daily except for major holidays.

Fort McAllister Historic Park, twenty-five miles south of Savannah, via GA 144 from I-95 or U.S. 17. This fort stands on the left bank of the Great Ogeechee River, commanding the river's mouth. The fall of Fort McAllister, on December 13, 1864, marked the end of Sherman's march to the sea. Communication was opened between the Union army and the fleet, making the further resistance of Savannah useless. The fort had performed well in the past. It protected the blockade-running CSS *Nashville* from pursuit by Union gunboats in July and November 1862, and successfully resisted the attacks of *Monitor*-type ironclads in 1863. The USS *Montauk* shelled Fort McAllister with the heaviest shells ever fired by a naval vessel, and the fort sustained only minor damage. Sherman called the capture of the fort "the handsomest thing I have seen in this war."

The Green-Meldrim House was used by Sherman during the occupation of Savannah, 1864–65.

Union losses were twenty-four killed, one hundred wounded, mostly by mines outside the fort. The Confederate garrison of 230 suffered sixteen killed and fifty-four wounded in the fifteen-minute battle.

The earthworks are restored to their wartime appearance and condition. A museum contains mementos of the fort and the *Nashville.* Open daily except Thanksgiving and Christmas. For further information, write the Superintendent, Rte. 2, P.O. Box 394-A, Richmond Hill, GA 31324, or phone (912) 727-2339.

Savannah Tours. The beautiful city is well worth touring, and the *Historic Savannah Foundation Tour* takes visitors on a two-hour trip through the Historic District, with admission to two house museums. The foundation also offers a three-hour Low Country Tour, walking tours, a "haunted house" tour, and bicycle rentals. Write Savannah Foundation Tours, Box 1733, Savannah GA, 31402. Phone (912) 233-TOUR for scheduled tours; 233-7703 for special tours.

For those preferring to tour by themselves, *Savannah Tours on Tape* offers cassette-guided driving, walking, and bicycling tours of the Historic District and the surrounding countryside. Rental includes player, tape, and maps. (Cassettes also are available in French, Spanish, and German.) Cassettes may be rented at the Savannah Visitor Center and major hotels.

Harbor Boat Tours. The *Cap'n Sam, Oh Suzanna,* and *Waving Girl* make regular tours daily of the harbor from Captain Sam's Dock at the foot of the Bull Street ramp. Call (912) 234-7248 for departure times.

Savannah has many beautiful, restored houses that serve as inns. Among the best: *Ballastone* (14 East Oglethorpe Ave., 31401; phone [912] 236-1484) is an 1835 Victorian mansion, and each of its nineteen guest rooms has a unique period decor. The courtyard garden has a fountain.

The *East Bay Inn* (225 East Bay St., 31401; [912] 238-1225) was built as a warehouse in 1853, furnished with antiques, and overlooks the historic waterfront.

In an early-19th-century Victorian building in the Historic District is the elegant *Mulberry Inn* (601 East Bay St., 31401; phone [912] 238-1200). The decor is Old Savannah, with many objets d'art, paintings, and antiques.

The most famous restaurant in Savannah is *Pirates' House* (20 East Broad St., phone [912] 233-5757), offering a number of regional specialties, including gumbo. In an 1832 building on the grounds of the Pirates' House, *45 South* (phone [912] 233-1881) offers a continental menu. The *Garibaldi Café* (315 West Congress St., phone [912] 232-7118) is housed in a former 1871 firehouse in the Historic District. The decor is Italian café; the seafood is delicious.

A delightful and inexpensive dining experience awaits visitors at *Mrs. Wilkes' Boarding House,* 107 West Jones St., phone (912) 232-5997. Southern cooking is served boardinghouse style. No reservations accepted.

KENNESAW MOUNTAIN

KENNESAW MOUNTAIN NATIONAL BATTLEFIELD PARK MARIETTA, GEORGIA

An army of 100,000, led by Gen. William Tecumseh Sherman, marched south from Chattanooga, Tennessee, early in May 1864, ordered by Grant to attack the Confederate army in Georgia, "break it up, and go into the interior of the enemy's country as far as you can go, inflicting all the damage you can upon their resources." Opposing him was wily, cautious Gen. Joseph E. Johnston and his 65,000-man army. Sher-

man's first objective: the vital railroad and war manufacturing center of Atlanta.

A series of flanking maneuvers and minor battles set the stage for the confrontation at Kennesaw Mountain. The armies first met at Rocky Face, near Dalton, Georgia. Sherman approached Rocky Face with two-thirds of his men on May 9. The rest marched fifteen miles southward through Snake Creek Gap, threatening Johnston's rail link with Atlanta, so Johnston broke off and dug in at Resaca. After repulsing Sherman's attacks on May 13–15, Johnston fell back along the railroad to Cassville. By late May he was entrenched in the Allatoona Mountains, prepared at last to make a stand, but Sherman swung wide to the southwest. Johnston sidestepped to meet him with stubborn fighting at New Hope Church on May 25, Pickett's Mill on May 27, and Dallas on May 28. Johnston entrenched across Lost Pine and Brushy mountains while Sherman returned to the

railroad at Acworth. The Confederate position was anchored by Kennesaw Mountain, a lofty, humped ridge with rocky slopes rising above the surrounding plain. The armies held these positions for nearly a month.

Sherman extended his lines southward to flank the Confederates. Johnston countered by shifting 11,000 men under Gen. John Bell Hood to strike at Sherman. A fierce attack at Kolb's Farm on June 22 checked Sherman's advance, but failed to throw him back.

Immobilized by muddy roads, Sherman decided to make a frontal attack. He believed the line was thin and that one sharp thrust would break through and destroy Johnston's army. He planned diversionary moves against Kennesaw Mountain and the Confederate left, while striking Johnston's center with a two-pronged assault.

Early on June 27, the attack brigades surged forward after an artillery bombard-

Sherman left Chattanooga on May 6, 1864, and headed south with orders from Grant "to move against Johnston's army, to break it up, and to go into the interior of the enemy's country . . . inflicting all the damage you can." Their armies tangled at the Battle of Kennesaw Mountain on June 27, 25 miles north of Atlanta. Eventually, after an unsuccessful attack launched from the position shown, Sherman wheeled around Johnston and then moved closer to Atlanta.

The Confederate enginehouse at Atlanta stands in ruins in September 1864. The major railroads in the deep South converged here, making Atlanta a prime military objective. After fierce fighting, Sherman telegraphed Lincoln on September 2, "Atlanta is ours, and fairly won." The victory helped Lincoln gain reelection. On November 15, Sherman cut his communications, burned a large part of the city, and began his march to the sea.

ment. Sherman miscalculated the Confederate strength, and both assaults were bloody failures. Astride Burnt Hickory Road, three Union brigades totaling 5,500 men crossed swampy, heavily wooded terrain. Sheets of fire drove them to cover before they reached their objective, a mountain spur called Pigeon Hill. Confederates on Little Kennesaw rolled boulders down on them. The attack was called off.

At Dallas Road, 8,000 Union infantrymen in five brigades hit the two best divisions in Johnston's army, commanded by Generals Patrick Cleburne and Benjamin Cheatham. The assault waves were shot to pieces. Hand-to-hand fighting at the Confederate earthworks was so intense that the place was called "Dead Angle." The battle was over by noon. Sherman had lost 3,000 men, Johnston 500.

In a twist of fate, the Confederate diversionary movement left an important road intersection open to capture, placing Sherman closer than Johnston to the Chattahoo-

chee River crossings. Sherman resumed his flanking strategy, and Johnston abandoned the Kennesaw lines during the night of July 2.

Sherman crossed the Chattahoochee near Roswell on July 9. Johnston withdrew to the fortifications of Atlanta. Exasperated by Johnston's retreats and seeming lack of aggressiveness, Jefferson Davis relieved him of command on July 17, replacing him with General Hood.

As Sherman closed in on Atlanta, Hood tried without success on July 20 to destroy Gen. George Thomas's army as it crossed Peachtree Creek. At the Battle of Atlanta, two days later, Hood struck at Gen. James McPherson's army and was again thrown back with heavy losses. Sherman tried to outflank Atlanta's defenders by maneuvering west of the city. Hood lashed out with an attack at Ezra Church, but was defeated again.

Sherman besieged Atlanta during August. Both sides used cavalry raids to break the other's grip, without success. Sherman's troops were cutting the railroads linking Atlanta with the rest of the South, seizing the last one on August 31. After losing a two-day battle near Jonesboro, Hood ordered the city evacuated and all property destroyed. The resulting fire raged out of hand and destroyed most of Atlanta. Sherman entered the city on September 2 and telegraphed Washington: "Atlanta is ours, and fairly won."

The fall of Atlanta was a crippling blow to the South's will and capacity to wage war. On November 8, Lincoln was reelected, pledging a fight to the finish. A week after the election, Sherman left Atlanta in ruins to begin his devastating march to the sea.

VISITING KENNESAW MOUNTAIN

Kennesaw Mountain National Battlefield Park is located three miles north of Marietta, Georgia, and is easily accessible from U.S. 41 and I-75. The Visitor Center contains exhibits and presents an audiovisual introduction to the battle; during the summer months, living-history programs are presented. A schedule of events is posted in the center, which is fully accessible to the disabled. (Note, however, that several of the stops on the self-guided tour require walking over moderately steep terrain.) The battlefield may be toured comfortably in half a day.

No food is sold at the park, but picnicking is permitted in designated areas. Restaurants and overnight accommodations can be found in Marietta, two miles south of the battlefield on I-75. The park is open daily except Christmas and New Year's Day. Through the week, visitors may drive or hike to the top of Kennesaw Mountain. On weekends, driving is not permitted, but a bus leaves for the top every half hour. Hiking trails of two, five, ten, and sixteen miles start at the center. The trails have no water, shelter, or food concessions along the way. Stay on the trails and be alert to venomous snakes, biting insects, and poisonous plants. Do not climb on cannon, monuments, or earthworks.

For further information, write to the Superintendent, Kennesaw Mountain National Battlefield Park, Box 1167, Marietta, GA 30061, or phone (404) 427-4686.

A self-guided tour starting at the center includes these points of interest:

Kennesaw Mountain. An observation overlook near the summit offers a sweeping view of the northern Georgia terrain where the armies of Sherman and Johnston struggled in the late spring and summer of 1864. To the south is the skyline of Atlanta. A short, moderately steep trail leads to the mountaintop. Along the way are exhibits and gun emplacements dug by Confederate gunners to command the Western & Atlantic (now Seaboard) Railroad.

Twenty-four-Gun Battery. From this entrenched position, twenty-four Union cannons bombarded Confederate positions on Little Kennesaw for nearly a week. One Confederate remarked afterward that the mountain should have been renamed "Bald Mountain." The battery has been under development and may not be open to visitors.

Pigeon Hill. A foot trail leads to a Confederate entrenchment on this mountain spur where one of Sherman's two major attacks was repulsed.

JOSEPH E. JOHNSTON

Some historians believe Joseph E. Johnston to be the greatest strategist of the Confederacy. He was a hero of First Manassas, commanded the Army of Northern Virginia until he was wounded and replaced by Lee, and bedeviled Sherman in the Atlanta campaign. After the war, Johnston and Sherman became good friends. When Sherman died, Johnston stood in the rain bareheaded at the funeral procession in New York City. He contracted pneumonia and died a few weeks later.

Cheatham Hill. To protect the hill now named for Gen. Benjamin Cheatham, the Confederates created a salient. The fiercest fighting of the battle raged here. Along the short trail to the imposing Illinois Monument are Confederate earthworks and markers where prominent Union soldiers fell. Near the base of the monument is the entrance to a tunnel begun by Union soldiers intending to blow up the Confederate position with a mine. Also nearby are Union entrenchments dug under fire and held for six days.

Kolb's Farm. Damaged by gunfire, Peter Kolb's log house has been restored to its original 1836 appearance, although it isn't open to visitors. On the afternoon of June 22, 1864, General Hood's troops were repulsed in an ill-fated attack just to the north of Powder Springs Road. Gen. Joseph Hooker used the Kolb house for his headquarters after the encounter.

IN AND AROUND MARIETTA

Big Shanty Museum, 2829 Cherokee St., Kennesaw, six miles north of Marietta via GA 293 or I-75 or U.S. 41. Housed here is the Louisville & Nashville steam locomotive *General,* stolen in 1862 by Union raiders in an attempt to cut Confederate supply lines. The raiders were chased and captured by the train crew. A narrated slide presentation and exhibits explain the details of the escapade. The story of the *General* was dramatized in Walt Disney's film *The Great Locomotive Chase.* Open daily.

The Marlow and Stanley Houses (192 Church St., Marietta, GA 30060; phone [404] 342-4802) are Victorian inns near the square. Breakfast is included in the room rates.

Thirty-five miles north of Marietta via I-575 and GA 53 and worth the drive is the *Tate House* (P.O. Box 33, Tate, GA 30177; [404] 735-3122), a pink marble Victorian mansion that accommodates guests and has a superb chef-owned restaurant. The Georgia mountain trout is superb. The restaurant is closed Monday and Tuesday.

Kolb House, Kennesaw Mountain

OTHER GEORGIA SITES OF INTEREST

ATHENS

Double-barreled cannon. On the city hall lawn at College and Hancock avenues is a unique weapon cast in 1863 at the Athens Foundry, believed to be the only double-barreled cannon in the world.

Antebellum houses. Athens has a number of architecturally important antebellum buildings, including the *Taylor-Grady Home,* 634 Prince St.; *Ross Crane House,* 247 Pulaski St.; *Lucy Cobb Institute,* 200 North Milledge Ave.; *Joseph Henry Lumpkin House,* 248 Prince St.; *Old Franklin Hotel,* 480 East Broad St.; and *Governor Wilson Lumpkin House,* South Campus, University of Georgia. The Taylor-Grady Home is open Monday through Friday, except Christmas and New Year's Day (404) 549-8688. The *Church-Waddell-Brumby House,* 280 East Dougherty St., phone (404) 546-1805, the oldest residence in the city, now is the *Athens Welcome Center,* open daily. A tour of historic homes in mid- or late May is sponsored by the Athens-Clarke Heritage Foundation, 489 Prince Ave., Athens, GA 30601, phone (404) 353-1801.

The Serpentine (1416 South Milledge Ave., 30605; phone (404) 493-1930), near the University of Georgia, offers bed, a full breakfast, and, for an extra charge, dinner. *Morrison's Cafeteria,* in the Georgia Square Mall, 3700 Atlanta Hwy., phone (404) 353-0030, serves up excellent meals at low prices.

ATLANTA

State Capitol, Capitol Square, phone (404) 656-2846. A number of Confederate regimental and battle flags are on display in the Hall of Flags.

The General, *Big Shanty Museum, Kennesaw (Big Shanty), Georgia*

Atlanta Historic Society, 3101 Andrews Dr., N.W., phone (404) 261-1837. In *McElreath Hall,* headquarters of the society, are the archives and library. Many of the exhibits here focus on Atlanta's role in the war. On the grounds, the *Tullie Smith House Restoration* is an 1840 farmhouse with slave cabins, craft demonstrations, and exhibits. Open daily. Partially accessible to the disabled. Guided tours are given on the hour and half hour.

Grant Park. In this large park off Cherokee Ave., S.E. (phone [404] 658-7625), are traces of breastwork, a temporary fortification, built for the defense of Atlanta. Also in the park is the *Cyclorama,* a hundred-year-old circular painting, 400 feet long and 50 feet high, coupled with a three-dimensional diorama that depicts the Battle of Atlanta. This and one in Gettysburg are the only two cycloramas in the United States.

Stone Mountain Park. This 3,200-acre state park, sixteen miles east of Atlanta on U.S. 78, surrounds the world's largest granite monolith, which rises 825 feet from the plain. On the mountain's face

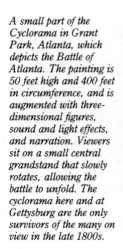

A small part of the Cyclorama in Grant Park, Atlanta, which depicts the Battle of Atlanta. The painting is 50 feet high and 400 feet in circumference, and is augmented with three-dimensional figures, sound and light effects, and narration. Viewers sit on a small central grandstand that slowly rotates, allowing the battle to unfold. The cyclorama here and at Gettysburg are the only survivors of the many on view in the late 1800s.

is a gigantic deep-relief carving of Robert E. Lee, Stonewall Jackson, and Jefferson Davis. The work was first undertaken by sculptor Gutzon Borglum after World War I, continued by Augustus Lukeman, and finally completed by Walter Hancock. Sound-and-light presentations make dramatic use of the sculpture. The top of the mountain is accessible by foot or cable car. Facing the sculpture is the *Memorial Hall,* which contains a Civil War museum. Nearby is the *Antebellum Plantation,* a nineteen-building complex restored and furnished with 18th- and 19th-century heirlooms. Other attractions include the *Scenic Railroad,* with full-size replicas of Civil War trains making five-minute trips around the base of the mountain, and the riverboat *Scarlett O'Hara,* which plies the 363-acre lake in the park. For further information, write P.O. Box 778, Stone Mountain, GA 30086, or phone (404) 498-5600.

The *Shellmont* (821 Piedmont Ave., N.E., Atlanta, GA 30308; phone [404] 872-

9290) is a restored Victorian home and carriage house offering bed and breakfast in midtown Atlanta.

Bed & Breakfast Atlanta is an agency coordinating placement with some hundred hosted homes, guest houses, and inns in Atlanta. Phone (404) 875-0525 9 A.M. to noon and 2 P.M. to 5 P.M., Monday through Friday.

A touch of ersatz history and some tasty game dishes are waiting at *Pittypat's Porch* (25 International Blvd. in the Peachtree Center, phone [404] 525-8228), a restaurant named after the aunt in *Gone With the Wind.*

One favorite low-priced restaurant, near the Georgia Tech campus is the *Varsity,* 61 North Ave. at the junction of I-75 and I-85. Fried peach pies are a special treat.

AUGUSTA

Confederate Powder Works Chimney. The chimney, at 1717 Goodrich St., is a memorial honoring Augusta's war dead, and all that remains of what once was the second-largest powder factory in the world.

S & S Cafeteria, 1616 Walton Ave., (404) 736-2972, is a bargain. *Town Tavern,* 15 Seventh St., (404) 724-2461, is an excellent restaurant housed in a refurbished old warehouse.

COLUMBUS

Fort Benning National Infantry Museum, five miles south of Columbus on U.S. 27, phone (404) 545-2958. Exhibits of infantry weapons, equipment, and uniforms from the Revolution to the present. The fort, the largest infantry post in the country, is named after Confederate General Henry L. Benning of Columbus. The museum is open daily except Monday and major holidays.

Confederate Naval Museum, 201 4th St., phone (404) 327-9798. The salvaged remains of the Confederate gunboats *Jack-son* and *Chattahoochee* are on display. Other exhibits feature relics, ship models, and material pertaining to Confederate naval operations. Open daily except Monday and major holidays.

LA GRANGE

There are no battlefields, museums, or historic buildings here, but La Grange had a unique distinction during the war: it was the only place in the Confederacy that organized its own female military company. La Grange, the story goes, was so loyal to the Confederacy that every man enlisted. A women's home guard was formed, named for the Revolutionary heroine Nancy Hart. When the defenseless city was about to be invaded by Wilson's Raiders, the Nancy Harts marched out to do battle. The Union colonel, coincidentally named La Grange, was so touched that he marched on without burning the city.

A restored 1892 Victorian home fur-

The mammoth memorial carving of (from left to right) Jefferson Davis, Robert E. Lee, and Stonewall Jackson, at Stone Mountain, Georgia

nished with antiques, *In Clover,* 205 Broad St., (404) 882-0883, serves up continental dishes at attractive prices.

MACON

During the war, Macon manufactured small weapons, cannon, and shot, and the city held $1.5 million in Confederate gold. Union troops were repulsed in July and November 1864, finally surrendering to Wilson's Raiders in April 1865.

City Hall, 700 Poplar St., phone (912) 744-7000. This was the state capitol from November 18, 1864, to March 11, 1865, during the last session of the Georgia General Assembly under the Confederacy. Open Monday to Friday, closed holidays.

Old Cannonball House and Macon-Confederate Museum, 856 Mulberry St., phone (912) 745-5982. This 1853 Greek Revival house was hit by a Union cannonball in 1864. The museum contains war relics and artifacts as well as historical items. Open daily except Monday. Closed on major holidays.

Hay House, 934 Georgia Ave., phone (912) 742-5982. This 1855 Italianate twenty-four-room villa is an architectural treasure filled with period furniture and art objects. Open Tuesday through Sunday, closed holidays.

There are a number of interesting buildings from the Civil War period in Macon. *Sidney's Old South Historic Tours* (phone [912] 743-3401), operated by the Macon-Bibb County Convention and Visitors' Bureau, offers excellent tours of these architecturally historic structures, daily except Sunday. Visitors seeking a guide for a private tour will find one at *Discover Macon Tours* (phone [912] 743-3851), operated by the Middle Georgia Historical Society.

The *1842 Inn* (353 College St., Macon, GA 31201; phone [912] 741-1842) is an el-egant antebellum restoration with twenty-two guest rooms. Continental breakfast is included in the room rate.

La Point Maison (618 College St., Macon, GA 31201; phone [912] 742-4674) offers guests two carriage suites and continental breakfast in the historic district.

Dinner is delightful at *Beall's 1860* (315 College St., phone [912] 745-3663), a restored 1860 mansion.

MADISON

Madison was spared by General Sherman on his march to the sea, and the town has a wealth of well-preserved antebellum residences.

The Madison-Morgan Cultural Center, 434 South Main St., phone (404) 342-4743. This 1895 school building usually has exhibits on wartime Madison. Wheelchair accessible. Open daily except holidays.

The Boat House (383 Porter St., Madison, GA 30650; phone [404] 342-3061) is a bed-and-breakfast in an 1850 house in the historic district.

Davis Bros. Cafeteria (Davis Bros. Quality Inn), two miles south at the junction of U.S. 129, phone (404) 342-1440, offers old-time dishes at old-time prices.

MILLEDGEVILLE

Georgia Military College, 201 East Greene St., phone (912) 453-3481. Milledgeville was the state capital from 1804 through 1868, and a Gothic Revival building on the campus once housed the legislature. The college's museum has material relating to the college and the Civil War. There are frequent student parades during the school year.

Milledgeville is short on accommodations and restaurants. There is a *Holiday Inn* (U.S. 441 North, four miles north, phone [912] 452-3502).

MISSISSIPPI

BRICES CROSS ROADS

BRICES CROSS ROADS NATIONAL BATTLEFIELD SITE BALDWYN, MISSISSIPPI

In the spring of 1864, Gen. William T. Sherman, now in command of the Union's armies in the West, drove south from Tennessee toward Atlanta. The Confederates decided to strike at Sherman's vulnerable supply line. To lead the attack they chose one of the most brilliant and singular warriors of this or any other war: Nathan Bedford Forrest, an unschooled farmboy who became a millionaire before he was forty, at which age he joined the army in 1861, and rose from private to major general.

The attack was to come from northern Mississippi and hit the one-track railroad that carried Sherman's supplies from Nashville to Chattanooga. On June 1, General Forrest left Tupelo, Mississippi, and three days later was in Russellville, Alabama, a day's march from the Tennessee River.

Forrest was known for his ability to move fast and fight hard. A self-schooled tactician, the hard-bitten cavalryman is remembered for saying that to win a battle, one must "git there fustest with the mostest." He usually did just that.

Sherman knew his supply line was vulnerable, and sent Gen. Samuel D. Sturgis from Memphis into Mississippi. Alerted to Sturgis's move, Forrest hurried back to Tupelo, concentrating his force of 3,500 men along the railroad around Baldwyn, between Guntown and Booneville. Forrest's scouts spotted Sturgis's force of 8,100 encamped at Stubbs Farm, some nine miles from Brices Cross Roads. Both armies marched at dawn.

Forrest planned to attack at Brices Cross Roads, but Sturgis's cavalry had passed through before he arrived. On the Baldwyn Road, Forrest met the Union advance pa-

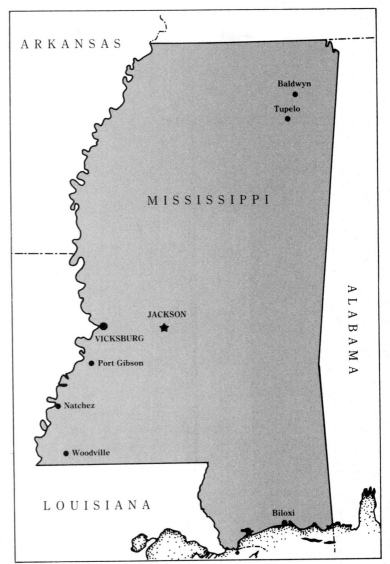

trols a mile from Brices Cross Roads. The Confederates checked the Union advance and by noon were attacking vigorously. Torrential rains the night before had made the roads nearly impassable, and Union reinforcements were exhausted when they arrived at the battlefield.

Forrest pressed the attack, pushing the Union line back to Brices Cross Roads by midafternoon. Sturgis began a cautious withdrawal, but was delayed when a supply wagon overturned on the bridge at Tishomingo Creek. Then, fording the treacherous Hatchie River, some Union soldiers panicked and the retreat became a rout. Most of the artillery and supply wagons were abandoned, and more than 1,500 Union troops were captured.

Although Brices Cross Roads was a brilliant tactical victory for Forrest, it brought no relief to the Confederacy. Sherman continued to forestall attacks on the Nashville–Chattanooga railroad by sending small commands into northern Mississippi. Inexorably, his army pushed on to Atlanta.

VISITING BRICES CROSS ROADS

Brices Cross Roads National Battlefield Site is located six miles west of Baldwyn on MS 340. The park is small, but affords a view of much of the scene of action. There are no facilities or personnel at the park, but at the Tupelo Visitor Center of the Natchez Trace Parkway, park interpreters can answer questions about the battle.

The nearest accommodations and restaurants are in Tupelo, Mississippi, twentyfive miles northeast on U.S. 45.

TUPELO

TUPELO NATIONAL BATTLEFIELD SITE

After the Battle of Brices Cross Roads, General Sherman was determined to prevent Forrest from attacking the Nashville–Chattanooga Railroad, which brought food and ammunition to the Union army. Sherman ordered his commander in Memphis "to make up a force and go out to follow Forrest to the death, if it costs 10,000 lives and breaks the Treasury."

Sherman wrote that General Forrest "whipped Sturgis fair and square, and now I will put against him A. J. Smith and Mower

and let them try their hand." On July 5, 1864, Smith moved south from La Grange, Tennessee, with twenty-four cannon and more than 14,000 troops. The marching column was nearly fifteen miles long. Commanding half the force was Gen. Joseph A. Mower, whom Sherman called "a young and game officer."

Knowing they would be provoked into giving battle, Generals Forrest and Stephen Lee moved to a fortified position at Okolona, eighteen miles south of Tupelo, and began concentrating troops there.

Union cavalry discovered that Tupelo was unprotected, and on July 13 the main Union force headed there. If they took Tupelo, they would gain a hold on the Mobile & Ohio Railroad and force Forrest and Lee to attack them in a fortified position.

Forrest quickly brought up his main force to attack the Union column before it reached Tupelo. Several attacks were repelled. At dusk on July 13, the Union forces reached Harrisburg, a tiny village now within the Tupelo city limits. They camped there, awaiting attack the next day.

The battle opened early in the morning. Forrest attacked repeatedly for three hours. He resumed the attack in the afternoon, but heavy Union fire again drove his force back. A final, unsuccessful attempt to break the Union line was made at night.

Despite having repulsed the attacks with few losses, General Smith was alarmed. Ammunition was running low. There was little but coffee and worm-infested hardtack to eat, and many of his troops were suffering from heat exhaustion. The next morning, abandoning his wounded, Smith marched four miles north and encamped.

The Confederates struck again, but, as General Smith reported, their attacks "were gallantly made, but without order, organization, or skill." Smith's troops threw off the Confederates after a swirling, confused fight. A Confederate officer later wrote that Forrest's troops "went in by

Brices Cross Roads

piecemeal and were slaughtered by whole-sale."

The Union forces withdrew the next morning. The Confederates followed for two days, but did not attempt another attack. Smith had not followed Forrest "to the death," but Sherman's supply line was safe. By the time Forrest attacked again, Sherman was beyond Atlanta, marching through Georgia.

Both Tupelo and Brices Cross Roads were part of a new phase of the war. After Grant took overall command in the spring of 1864, the Union armies worked in concert. Grant drove toward Richmond, Sherman toward Atlanta, and small Union commands prevented the Confederates from harrassing them.

President Lincoln liked what was happening, and said, "Those not skinning can hold a leg." At Tupelo and Brices Cross Roads in Mississippi, Sturgis, Smith, and Mower held a leg while Sherman did the skinning in Georgia.

VISITING TUPELO

Tupelo National Battlefield Site is located in Tupelo, Mississippi, on MS 6, about a mile west of the intersection with U.S. 45. This is where the Confederates formed to attack the Union position. There are no park personnel at the site, but at the Tupelo Visitor Center on the Natchez Trace Parkway, a mile west of the battlefield, interpreters can answer questions about the battlefield.

VICKSBURG

VICKSBURG NATIONAL MILITARY PARK

Many of the major battles of the war were simply occasions for slaughter, haphazard affairs with no lasting benefits for either side. By contrast, Gen. Ulysses S. Grant's Vicksburg campaign was as complex and subtle as a chess game. At stake was control of the Mississippi River. President Lincoln called Vicksburg the key to the Mississippi, observing that "the war can never be brought to a close until that key is in our pocket."

Between Cairo, Illinois, and the Gulf of Mexico, the Mississippi meanders along a course more than a thousand miles long. The Union needed the Mississippi to send troops and supplies into the deep South. The Confederacy needed it to bring troops and supplies from Texas, Arkansas, and most of Louisiana. Nearly half the land area of the Confederacy lay west of the Mississippi.

Early in the war, the Confederacy erected fortifications at strategic points along the river. Fighting their way south from Illinois and north from New Orleans, Union forces captured fort after fort. By late summer of 1862, only Port Hudson and Vicksburg stood between them and domination of the Mississippi.

Vicksburg was the stronger and more important of the two. Situated on a high bluff overlooking a bend in the river, it was protected by artillery batteries along the riverfront and by a maze of swamps to the

north and south. The Confederacy believed it was impregnable.

On October 16, the War Department announced sweeping changes in the organization of the Union Army. The Departments of Ohio, Cumberland, and Tennessee were combined into the Military Division of the Mississippi, under the command of Grant, who was charged with clearing the Mississippi of Confederate resistance. That same month Gen. John C. Pemberton, a Pennsylvanian by birth, took command of some 50,000 widely scattered Confederate troops defending the Mississippi, under orders to keep the river open.

During the winter, Grant conducted a series of unsuccessful amphibious operations aimed at Vicksburg. By spring he had decided to march his 45,000-man army down the west bank of the Mississippi, cross the river well below Vicksburg, swing around, and attack from the south.

On March 31, 1863, Grant marched south from his encampment at Milliken's Bend, twenty miles northwest of Vicksburg. By April 28 he was at Hard Times, on the river above Grand Gulf. The next

A Union cannon

day, Adm. David Porter's gunboats bombarded the Confederate forts at Grand Gulf to prepare the way for a crossing, but the attack was repulsed.

Things were not going well for Grant. His supply lines were being harassed and broken by Confederate cavalry. Determined to take Vicksburg, he decided on a bold gamble.

He marched down the west bank below Vicksburg, and ordered Admiral Porter to steam his gunboats south from Memphis, crossing beneath the guns of Vicksburg at night. The boats were sighted and two transports sunk, but the others got through to rendezvous with Grant, and transported his army across the river at Bruinsburg.

Cut off from the supply line, Grant's army had to live off the land. Striking rapidly eastward to secure the bridgehead, Grant ran into part of Pemberton's forces near Port Gibson on May 1. The Confederates were overwhelmed and fell back toward Vicksburg. Grant defeated another small Confederate force near Raymond on May 12. He then captured Jackson, the state capital, on May 14, scattering the defending troops.

Turning his army westward, Grant advanced on Vicksburg along the line of the Southern Railroad of Mississippi. At Champion Hill on May 16, and at Big Black River Bridge on May 17, he attacked and overwhelmed Pemberton's disorganized troops, driving them back into the Vicksburg fortifications. Grant's army was before Vicksburg.

Believing that Champion Hill and Big Black River Bridge had broken Confederate morale, Grant planned an immediate attack. The first assault hit the Stockade Redan on May 19 and was thrown back. A second attack on May 22 also failed.

Realizing that Vicksburg couldn't be taken frontally, Grant began siege operations. Batteries of artillery were established to hammer the fortifications from the

land, while Admiral Porter's gunboats cut off supplies and communications and blasted the city from the river.

For forty-seven days and nights, Vicksburg was pounded by mortar and cannon fire. The people of the city very nearly starved, spending much of their time hiding in caves cut into the windblown loess on which the city was built. Grant dug tunnels under Confederate positions and planted mines, but this didn't breach the defensive lines.

By the end of June, with little hope of relief and no chance of breaking out of the Union cordon, Pemberton knew it was only a matter of time before he must "capitulate upon the best attainable terms." On the afternoon of July 3, he met with Grant to discuss terms for the surrender of Vicksburg.

Grant demanded unconditional surrender, but Pemberton refused, and the meet-

Dapper in their straw hats, two officers of the Union gunboat Hunchback *pose with a 12-pound Dahlgren boat howitzer. A 3.4-inch rifle barrel gave the gun an accurate range of 1,000 yards. When war came, the North had 90 warships; the South had none. The Union navy moved to blockade the 3,500 miles of Southern coastline and to control the Mississippi and other major rivers, a task that proved more formidable than the admirals had imagined.*

ing broke up. Later that afternoon, Grant modified his demand and agreed to let the Confederate soldiers sign paroles not to fight again until exchanged. Officers could retain sidearms and a mount. Pemberton accepted these terms, and at 10 A.M. on July 4, 1863, Vicksburg was officially surrendered.

Port Hudson surrendered four days later. The Mississippi River was open and the Confederacy was severed. Grant had achieved the Union's great objective in the West, and for the first time since the war began, the Mississippi was free of Confederate troops and fortifications. President Lincoln said gratefully, "The Father of Waters again goes unvexed to the sea."

VISITING VICKSBURG

Vicksburg National Military Park borders the eastern and northern sections of the city. The park entrance and Visitor Center are on Clay St. (U.S. 80), a mile from Interstate 20. The center is open daily except Christmas, and museum exhibits and au-

diovisual aids portray the history of the campaign. No food is sold in the park, but picnicking is allowed in designated areas. The center and the stops on the tour are accessible to the disabled. Information on special activities and programs is posted in the center. For further information, write to the Superintendent, 3201 Clay St., Vicksburg, MS 39180, or phone (601) 636-0583.

A sixteen-mile, self-guided driving tour of the battlefield begins at the center. Allow three hours for the tour and another hour for the USS *Cairo* Museum and some other nearby sites. Along the way, there are metal markers painted either red or blue. Red markers signify interpretive information pertaining to Confederate lines or emplacements; blue markers denote information on the Union forces. The sites include the following:

Battery DeGolyer. From this position, a battery of guns from the Eighth Michigan Artillery commanded by Capt. Samuel DeGolyer hammered the Confederate

The Shirley House, a survivor of the siege of Vicksburg, Mississippi

Aerial view of Vicksburg National Military Park

Great Redoubt, directly ahead. At one time, as many as twenty-two Union artillery pieces were mounted here. Captain DeGolyer was mortally wounded while directing the fire of this battery.

Shirley House. Union troops called this "the white house," and it is the only surviving wartime structure in the park. During the siege it served as headquarters for the 45th Illinois Infantry, whose members built hundreds of bombproof shelters around it to protect themselves from Confederate artillery fire. The house has been restored to its 1863 appearance.

Third Louisiana Redan. Here was one of the major Confederate fortifications guarding the Jackson Road approach to Vicksburg. Deciding that the fort was impregnable to direct assault, Grant ordered his troops to dig mines under the fort and blow it up. The first mine was detonated on June 25, the second on July 1. Neither succeeded in breaking the Confederate line.

Ransom's Gun Path. To provide additional artillery support for Union infantry manning this sector of the siege lines, men of the Second Illinois Artillery dismantled two twelve-pound cannon and, aided by General Ransom's infantry, dragged the guns over rough terrain to an earthen parapet just a hundred yards from the Confederate position. There the guns were reassembled and returned to action.

Stockade Redan Attack. From this and nearby points on May 19, General Sherman launched an infantry attack against the Stockade Redan (see below). The Union troops were repulsed with heavy losses. Three days later, as part of a general assault on the Confederate lines, troops again unsuccessfully attacked the redan.

"HERE BROTHERS
FOUGHT FOR
THEIR
PRINCIPLES
HERE HEROES
DIED TO SAVE
THEIR COUNTRY
AND A UNITED
PEOPLE WILL
FOREVER
CHERISH
THE PRECIOUS
LEGACY OF
THEIR NOBLE
MANHOOD."

—*Pennsylvania
Monument at
Vicksburg*

Thayer's Approach. During the afternoon of May 22, Union troops commanded by Gen. John M. Thayer stormed up this hill toward Confederates dug in at the top. They were stopped by enemy fire and the steepness of the hill. Thayer's men later began digging a six-foot-deep approach trench toward the Confederate position. The Union soldiers used the tunnel beneath the road to avoid crossing the ridge, where they would be exposed to enemy fire.

Battery Selfridge. Naval cannon were used exclusively here, and were manned by navy gunners. The battery is named in honor of Lt. T. O. Selfridge, one of the naval officers stationed here and the officer in command of the ironclad USS *Cairo* when she was sunk in the Yazoo River on December 12, 1862. A plaque here tells of the navy's role in the siege of Vicksburg.

Vicksburg National Cemetery. This cemetery was established in 1866. In addition to the nearly 17,000 Union soldiers buried here, of whom some 13,000 are unknown, the cemetery is the final resting place for veterans of later American wars. It was closed to further burials in 1961. Many of the Confederates who died during the siege are buried in the Vicksburg City Cemetery.

Fort Hill. This fort anchored the left flank of the Confederate line. So formidable were its defenses that no Union attack ever was made against it. Confederate gunners

posted here assisted the river batteries in sinking the gunboat *Cincinnati* on May 27, 1863.

Stockade Redan. This was the principal Confederate work guarding the Old Graveyard Road approach to Vicksburg. Union failures on May 19 and 22 to overrun this fortification helped persuade Grant to stop making direct assaults.

Great Redoubt. Like the Third Louisiana Redan (see above), this massive Confederate earthwork guarded the Jackson Road. The Union attack here on May 22 was repulsed with heavy losses. Later, Union artillery kept the redoubt under almost continuous bombardment.

Second Texas Lunette. Manned by the Second Texas Volunteer Infantry, this Confederate fortification guarded the Baldwin Ferry Road approach to Vicksburg. On May 22 it was the scene of furious fighting as Confederates beat back repeated Union attacks. During the siege, Union soldiers dug approach trenches to within fifteen feet of the lunette.

Railroad Redoubt. Confederates built this work to protect the Southern Railroad of Mississippi. On the morning of May 22, Union troops assailed this stronghold and forced out the defenders. A detachment of Col. Thomas Waul's Texas Legion counterattacked and, in a savage hand-to-hand fight with bayonets, clubbed muskets, and artillery shells used as grenades, threw back the Union attackers.

Fort Garrott. Here, on June 17, Confederate soldiers suffered heavy casualties from the accurate fire of Union sharpshooters. Col. Isham W. Garrott, whose 20th Alabama Regiment occupied the fort, became so exasperated at the damage being inflicted on his men that he picked up a musket to return the fire. A rifle ball pierced his heart, and he died without

FORGOTTEN BATTLEGROUNDS

During the war, battles, engagements, and skirmishes were fought at more than ten thousand locations, many of them with memorable names now forgotten, such as Wet Glaze, Missouri; Convalescent Corral, Mississippi; Gum Swamp, North Carolina; Droop Mountain, Virginia; and Bear Wallow, Kentucky.

learning he had been promoted to brigadier general.

Hovey's Approach. This restoration of part of the two approach trenches dug by Gen. Alvin P. Hovey's Union troops provides an excellent example of how the siege of Vicksburg was conducted. The zigzag design helped to nullify the effect of Confederate enfilading fire and minimized casualties among the Union troops occupying the trenches.

There are three sites to visit that are not on the tour: *Louisiana Circle* and *South Fort,* both sites of Confederate fortifications, and *Navy Circle,* marking the southern anchor of the Union lines. All are located south of Vicksburg along Warrenton Road (U.S. 61) near the interstate bridge. Interpretive markers explain their significance.

USS *Cairo* Museum, reached from the park tour road or through the city via Fort Hill Drive and Connecting Avenue, phone (601) 636-2199. On December 12, 1862, the Union ironclad gunboat *Cairo,* along with several other vessels, steamed up the Yazoo River, north of Vicksburg, to destroy Confederate batteries and clear enemy obstructions from the channel. Suddenly, two explosions in quick succession tore gaping holes in the boat's bottom. Within minutes the ironclad lay on the bottom of the river, only the tops of her smokestacks and flagstaffs above the water. The *Cairo* had become the first vessel in history to be sunk by an electrically detonated mine.

On the sunken *Cairo* was preserved, as in a time capsule, information about naval construction as well as naval stores, armament, and the personal gear of her crew. The vast array of artifacts recovered from the gunboat before and after she was salvaged in the early 1960s provided new insights into naval life during the Civil War years. The restored gunboat and more than

a thousand of her artifacts are on display at the museum, adjacent to the Vicksburg National Cemetery. An audiovisual program tells of the sinking, and of the role played by gunboats in the war. The museum is open daily except Christmas. Tours of the vessel are conducted Friday through Sunday from June through August. The museum and the vessel are accessible to the disabled.

Illinois Monument, National Military Park and Cemetery, Vicksburg, Mississippi

A Christmas ball was interrupted at the Balfour House when the Battle of Vicksburg began. The mistress of the house, Mrs. Emma Balfour, was the author of the famous Siege Diary. *After the city fell, Gen. James B. McPherson made his headquarters here. When the house was being restored, a cannonball was found embedded in a wall. The Balfour House, now a bed and breakfast, may be toured.*

IN AND AROUND VICKSBURG

Visitors have much to see and do in Vicksburg, and a few days here will be well spent. No other place in the country gives such a sense of what the Civil War was, or what it meant to the people caught up in it. Ironically, Vicksburg is no longer on the Mississippi. The river, in one of its periodic changes of course, left the city on the Yazoo, although still accessible from the Mississippi. The *Tourist Information Center* on U.S. 80 East (P.O. Box 110, Vicksburg, MS 39188; phone [601] 638-9421 or [800] 221-3536) has information, maps, and brochures on what to see and do. It is accessible to the disabled. Guides are available for a fee. Open daily except Thanksgiving, Christmas, and New Year's Day. Places to visit in the city include the following:

Old Court House Museum, Court Square, 1008 Cherry St., phone (601) 636-0741. Built in 1858 with slave labor, this building is on a hilltop overlooking the Yazoo Canal. Grant raised the U.S. flag here on July 4, 1863, signifying the end of the siege. The museum has nine display rooms of Americana. One, the Confederate Room, contains weapons and documents of the siege. Open daily except New Year's Day, Thanksgiving, and December 24–25. Hours vary.

Toys and Soldiers Museum, 1100 Cherry St. at Grove, phone (601) 638-1986. Sebastian sculptures, Civil War artifacts, old model trains, old toys—more than 25,000 figures on display. Open daily March through December. Closed New Year's Day. Hours may vary.

Four elegant antebellum houses are now bed-and-breakfast inns:

Cedar Grove (2200 Oak St., Vicksburg, MS 39180; phone [601] 636-1605) is a mansion hit by a shell from a Union gunboat during the siege, and the cannonball is still lodged in the parlor wall. General Grant reputedly slept here on his first night in Vicksburg. The house is on three acres of formal gardens and courtyards.

Anchuca (1010 First East St., Vicksburg, MS 39180; phone [601] 636-4931 or [800] 262-4822) is a Greek Revival mansion furnished with period antiques and gas-burning chandeliers. The house has a landscaped garden and a swimming pool. Besides the house, guests use a cottage and the old slave quarters. Jefferson Davis once addressed the citizens of the city from the balcony.

Grey Oaks (4142 Rifle Range Rd., Vicksburg, MS 39180; phone [601] 638-6968) wasn't built until 1940, but its architecture reminds visitors of Tara in *Gone With the Wind*. On seven beautiful acres, its rooms are furnished with antiques.

Duff Green (1114 First East St., Vicksburg, MS 39180; phone [601] 636-6968) is a mansion in the Palladian style that was shelled during the siege, then used as a military hospital for the rest of the war.

All the above bed-and-breakfast houses may be toured. Other antebellum houses that welcome visitors include *McRaven Home,* at the east end of Harrison St., which was the most heavily shelled house during the siege; *Balfour House,* 1002 Crawford St., where on December 24, 1862, Confederate officers and their ladies were being entertained at a Christmas ball when the battle began; *Martha Vick House,* 1300 Grove St., built by the daughter of the founder of Vicksburg, Newett Vick, displays an outstanding art collection.

The house and garden tours of the *Spring Pilgrimage* in late March or early April attract many visitors.

From the foot of Clay Street, the authentic riverboat *Spirit of Vicksburg,* (phone [601] 634-6059) makes tours on the river, and is a reminder of the days when Mississippi was the link between North and South.

Though it is not of Civil War interest, visitors enjoy the old-time candy store and soda fountain at the *Biedenharn Candy Company Museum* (1107 Washington St., phone [601] 634-6514), where Coca-Cola was first bottled in 1894. Open daily except holidays.

OTHER MISSISSIPPI SITES OF INTEREST

The town of Corinth figured largely in the war, and it is worth visiting to see the museum, Union Fort, the cemetery, and the antebellum house that served as headquarters for Generals Bragg, Van Dorn, and Halleck. Because of the town's proximity to Shiloh, which is located twenty-six miles to the north, touring details are presented in the Tennessee chapter, on page 119.

BILOXI

Beauvoir, five miles west of Biloxi on West Beach Blvd. (U.S. 90), phone (601) 388-1313. For ten years after his release from Fortress Monroe, Jefferson Davis sought a permanent home. In 1877, Davis, then sixty-nine, was invited to visit Beauvoir, Mrs. Sarah Dorsey's home on the Gulf Coast. Davis was so charmed with Beauvoir that he arranged to buy it, and he lived here with his wife, Varina, and daughter, Winnie, until his death in 1889. He wrote two books here, the two-volume *Rise and Fall of the Confederate Government* and the *Short History of the Confederate States of America.* After his death, Mrs. Davis wrote *Jefferson Davis: A Memoir by His Wife.* She struggled to keep Beauvoir until Winnie's death in 1898. Although under financial pressure, Mrs. Davis turned down a $100,000 offer from a promoter who wanted to turn Beauvoir into a hotel, and sold it to the Mississippi Division of the United Sons of the Confederate Veterans for $10,000.

From 1903 until 1955, Beauvoir was the Jefferson Davis Memorial Home for Confederate Soldiers and Sailors. The tomb of the *Unknown Soldier of the Confederate States of America* is in the *Confederate Veterans Cemetery,* where more than 700 veterans who lived here are buried. The house, gardens, and grounds are carefully restored, and the original furniture and possessions of the Davis family are on display. The ground floor is a Davis family museum. A *Confederate Museum* is in the old hospital building. Davis's desk and books are in the *Library Pavilion.* The museum and the ground floors of the house are accessible to the disabled. There is a gift shop. Open daily except Christmas.

Biloxi Lighthouse, West Beach Blvd. (U.S. 90) at the foot of Porter Ave., phone (601) 388-1313. When Biloxi was threatened by Union ships, a man climbed the sixty-five-foot-high lighthouse tower, removed the lens, and buried it. Open daily from Memorial Day to early September, Wednesday through Sunday the rest of the year.

GULF ISLANDS NATIONAL SEASHORE

Fort Massachusetts. After Mississippi seceded, state militia took control of Fort Massachusetts on West Ship Island, renaming it Fort Twiggs in honor of the New Orleans Confederate general. After repeated threats by Union forces, the Confederates relinquished the fort in September 1861. Some 4,300 Confederate prisoners were held in a camp in the area east of the fort. Commercial boats run to the fort from Biloxi and Gulfport from March to October. Open daily. Guided tours. For further information, write to the Park Office, 3500 Park Rd., Ocean Springs, MS 39564, or phone (601) 875-0821.

JACKSON

State Historical Museum, 400 High St., phone (601) 354-6222. Housed in the *Old State Capitol,* the scene of the Secession Convention in January 1861, are dioramas and exhibits tracing the history of the state and a collection of Jefferson Davis memorabilia. Besieged by General Sherman in 1863, the city was destroyed and the state government's records went up in smoke. The ruins of Jackson were nicknamed "Chimneyville." This building was one of the few that survived. Near the museum is the *Confederate Monument,* built in 1891 with contributions from the women of Mississippi. The museum is accessible to the disabled. Open daily except major holidays.

The Oaks, 823 North Jefferson St. The 1846 Greek Revival cottage of James H. Boyd was occupied by General Sherman during the siege of 1863. Period furnishings. Open daily except Monday and major holidays.

Manship House, 420 East Fortification St., phone (601) 354-7303. Charles Henry Manship, mayor of Jackson during the war, lived in this Gothic Revival cottage. Period furnishings. Accessible to the disabled. Open daily except Monday and holidays.

Battlefield Park, Porter St. between Langley Ave. and Terry Road. Original cannon and trenches from the defense of Jackson.

Millsaps Buie House (628 North State St., Jackson, MS 39202, phone [601] 352-0221) offers guests private patios or balconies in a restored 1888 Victorian house with period furnishings.

Try tasty redfish at *Poets* (1855 Lakeland

Dr. [601] 982-9711), where the decor features an antique bar and Tiffany lamps.

NATCHEZ

Rosalie, 100 Orleans St., phone (601) 445-4555. This antebellum home was the Union army headquarters during the occupation of Natchez. The original furnishings date from 1857. Open daily except Thanksgiving and December 24–25.

Historic Springfield Plantation. Built in 1786–1790, this is believed to be the first plantation mansion in Mississippi, and it is beautifully preserved. The owner was Thomas Marston Green, Jr., a wealthy planter from Virginia. This was the site of Andrew Jackson's wedding. Displays include Civil War equipment and railroad memorabilia. Open daily except Christmas. Twenty miles northeast of Natchez via U.S. 61, Natchez Trace Parkway, then twelve miles north on MS 553. Phone (601) 842-1572.

Tour of Historic Homes and Gardens. The *Natchez Pilgrimage* offers tours to fifteen antebellum mansions open all year to visitors. During the Natchez Pilgrimages held annually in early April and mid-October, the number of mansions on the tour increases to thirty. For further information, write P.O. Box 347, Natchez, MS 39120, or phone (601) 647-6742. The tour office is in the *Canal Street Depot,* at the corner of Canal and State streets, which also houses the *Natchez Tourist Headquarters.*

Monmouth (36 Melrose Ave., 39120, phone [601] 442-5852 or [800] 828-4531), the home of General John Anthony Quitman, hero of the Mexican War, is one of the mansions on the tour offering bed and breakfast. The house contains a Civil War museum. Guests stay in the remodeled slave quarters of the 1818 estate.

For a change of pace, dine at the *Cock of the Walk* (15 Silver St., phone [601] 446-8920), on the Mississippi River in the

Beauvoir, Jefferson Davis's last home, in Biloxi, Mississippi

Natchez-under-the-Hill area. Try the catfish and hush puppies.

Cajun cooking in an elegant setting may be found at the *Carriage House* (401 High St. behind Stanton Hall, phone [601] 445-5151).

Motels and budget restaurants are clustered on U.S. 61 on the eastern edge of town.

PORT GIBSON

Grand Gulf Military Park. Most of Grand Gulf was gone when the war began. Mississippi River floods destroyed fifty-five of the seventy-six city blocks from 1855 to 1860. When the Confederacy decided to fortify the banks, the population was only 160. Adm. David G. Farragut steamed his squadron upriver in the spring of 1862. Baton Rouge and Natchez fell, but Vicksburg wouldn't surrender. Confederate troops and artillery were sent here to Grand Gulf, where intermittent fighting between the Union warships and the shore batteries continued until a Union force was landed at Bayou Pierre and assaulted and burned the town. Later, Adm. D. D. Porter's ironclads opened fire on Fort Cobun and Fort Wade on April 29, 1863. After more than five hours, two ironclads were disabled and the guns of Fort Wade silenced. The remaining sites in the park include fortifications, an observation tower, a cemetery, a sawmill, a dog-trot house, a memorial chapel, a water wheel and grist mill, a carriage house with vehicles used by the Confederates, and a four-room cottage reconstructed from the early days of Grand Gulf. A museum at the Visitor Center displays artifacts of the war. Open daily except major holidays. Ten miles northwest of Port Gibson off U.S. 61, phone (601) 437-5911.

The Ruins of Windsor. On Old Rodney Road, twenty-three stately columns are all that remain of a four-story mansion built by 600 slaves at a cost of $175,000 in 1860, spared by Grant, but destroyed by fire thirty years later. Its size and nearness to the Mississippi made it a natural marker for steamboat pilots, including Mark Twain.

More stately mansions from the war remain in Port Gibson, which was spared, the story goes, by General Grant, who supposedly said, "It's too pretty to burn." An antebellum home that now welcomes overnight guests is the *Oak Square Country Inn* (1207 Church St., MS 39150, phone [601] 437-4350). A southern-style breakfast is included in the room rate.

The nearest motels are thirty miles north on U.S. 61 in Vicksburg.

WOODVILLE

Rosemont Plantation. Jefferson Davis and his parents, Samuel and Jane Davis, moved to Woodville and built this house in 1810 when the boy was two years old. He grew up here and returned to visit his family throughout his life. Many family furnishings remain, including a spinning wheel. Five generations of the Davis family are buried on this 300-acre plantation. Open Monday through Saturday, March through December. The plantation is east of Woodville on MS 24, a continuation of Main Street.

Burning of Bowling Green. One of the greatest of the plantation houses here, Bowling Green was destroyed by Union troops in 1864. Only three pillars and the carriage house remain. The Woodville Civic Club offers an audio reenactment by appointment. Phone (601) 888-6809. The club is located east of Woodville on MS 24, a continuation of Main Street.

The nearest accommodations and restaurants are in Natchez, thirty-five miles north on U.S. 61.

SOUTH CAROLINA

FORT SUMTER

FORT SUMTER NATIONAL MONUMENT CHARLESTON

At four-thirty on the morning of April 12, 1861, a mortar shell arched above Charleston Harbor and exploded directly over Fort Sumter. Within minutes, forty-three guns and mortars opened fire from shore batteries, pounding the fort constantly for thirty-four hours. On April 14 the commander of Fort Sumter, Maj. Robert Anderson, agreed to evacuate the fort. The next day President Lincoln called out 75,000 militia. The Civil War had begun.

In retrospect it seems inevitable that the war would have started here. On December 20, 1860, South Carolina became the first state to secede from the Union, and no city in the South was more militant than Charleston. Fort Sumter was a bone in the South's—and the city's—throat. The *Charleston Mercury* declared, "The fate of the Southern Confederacy hangs by the ensign halliards of Fort Sumter."

Fewer than a hundred Union troops under Major Anderson manned the harbor defenses—Sumter, Moultrie, and two smaller forts—which, to defend properly, required more than a thousand men. On the night of December 26, Anderson moved all his men to Fort Sumter.

Claiming this was an act of war, South Carolina demanded the surrender of Fort Sumter. President James Buchanan ignored the demand, content to pass the buck to President-elect Lincoln, who would be inaugurated in March. The South interpreted this as a belligerent action, and the rush to secession was on. By February 1, six more states had left the union. Their representatives met at Montgomery, Alabama, organized a provisional government, and chose Jefferson Davis President of the Confederate States of America.

Lincoln made it clear in his inaugural address on March 4, 1861, that he considered secession unlawful, and he pledged "to hold, occupy, and possess the property and places belonging to the Government." He also pledged not to attack the South, saying, "You can have no conflict without yourself being the aggressor." The South reacted by authorizing the enlistment of 100,000 men for a year's service.

The Confederacy ordered Gen. P. G. T. Beauregard to order Fort Sumter to surrender. Major Anderson refused. Under bombardment, Anderson's troops could only man a few of Sumter's guns, and the supply of gunpowder was low. Confederate shelling set fire to the barracks on the second day, and the flames soon raged out of control, threatening the powder magazine. The situation inside the fort was chaotic, and Anderson was forced to give in.

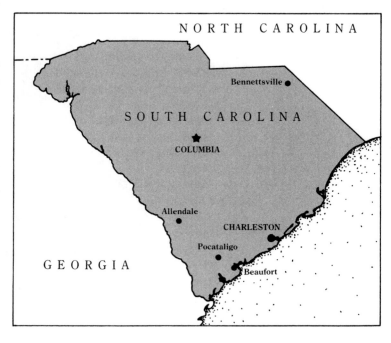

The next afternoon, with the permission of the Confederates, the garrison fired a fifty-gun salute to the American flag. As Major Anderson marched his men to a waiting ship, the Confederate troops stood by with bared heads in tribute to the garrison's courage. Ironically, while none of the garrison had been killed during the bombardment, Private Daniel Hough was accidentally killed during the salute, becoming the first casualty of the war.

Fort Sumter was to remain a Confederate stronghold until the end of the war, despite frequent Union attempts to recapture the fort.

VISITING FORT SUMTER

Fort Sumter stands on a man-made granite island four miles from downtown Charleston at the entrance to the harbor. Its brick walls are forty feet high and eight to twelve feet thick, and were designed to mount 148 cannon and house a 650-man garrison. It was still being completed when South Carolina seceded. The fort is a national monument administered by the Park Service. Extensive repairs and restoration have been made over the years. The fort can be reached only by boat. Park Service tour boats leave from the City Marina on Lock-

Damage to the interior of Fort Sumter is apparent in this photograph, taken on April 15, 1861, two days after Robert Anderson surrendered the garrison. In Washington that day, President Lincoln issued a public proclamation calling for 75,000 militia to still the insurrection in South Carolina, drawing instant support from the Northern states.

Aerial view of Fort Sumter, Charleston, South Carolina

wood Drive, just south of U.S. 17, and from the naval museum at Patriots Point in Mount Pleasant. During the summer there are three round drips daily from each location. For boat schedules, write to Fort Sumter Tours, Inc., P.O. Box 59, Charleston, SC 29402, or phone (803) 722-1691. The fort is open every day except Christmas. From June 15 to Labor Day, the hours are 9 A.M. to 6 P.M.; the hours vary at other times of the year. Phone (803) 883-3123 for information on hours. A visit to Fort Sumter takes two hours and fifteen minutes, including the boat trip. One hour is spent at the fort. A Park Service ranger conducts a tour, allowing visitors time to visit the museum and gift shop. For further information, write to the Superintendent, 1214 Middle St., Sullivan's Island, SC 29482, or phone (803) 883-3123.

Things to see at Fort Sumter include the following:

Sally Port. The wall at the entrance to the fort from the boat landing is only about half its original height. Built after the Civil War, the sally port replaced a gun embrasure.

Left Flank Casements. Just inside the entrance are two tiers of casements (gun rooms), which continue around most of the fort.

Ruins of Enlisted Men's Barracks. A three-story building here had a mess hall on the first floor and sleeping quarters on the upper floor. On the right was another barracks.

Ruins of Officers' Quarters. A three-story building housed officers, administrative offices, storerooms, the guardhouse, and powder magazines. An explosion in the small-arms magazine on December 11,

The Confederate flag flies over Fort Sumter, in the harbor of Charleston, South Carolina.

1863, killed eleven and wounded forty-one Confederates.

Parade. In 1899, Battery Huger was built over part of the parade, and the remainder was filled with sand. Two feet of this fill was removed by the Park Service in 1959.

Left Face of the Fort. Casements here were destroyed by Union guns on Morris Island from 1863 to 1865. Several projectiles still protrude from the wall. Outside the casement ruins are two fifteen-inch Rodman guns, an eight-inch Columbiad, and a ten-inch mortar.

Right Face of the Fort. Union troops on Morris Island fired the eleven 100-pound Parrott guns displayed here against Fort Sumter. The army moved them here after the Civil War.

Right Gorge Angle. Here Capt. Abner Doubleday, credited with inventing the game of baseball, returned Confederate fire during the bombardment on April 12, 1861.

Mountain Howitzer. Light fieldpieces like this twelve-pound "mountain howitzer" were used by the Confederates to defend the fort against a surprise landing by Union forces.

Esplanade. This twenty-five-foot-wide promenade ran the full length of the gorge exterior. Extending from the sally port was a 171-foot wharf, the original entrance to the fort.

The museum displays photographs and artifacts covering the bombardment of the fort and the use of it by the Confederacy, including a U.S. flag that flew over the fort before the war, and the flag of the Palmetto Guard. The gift shop has a good selection of scholarly books on Sumter and the war. No food is sold at the fort and there are no picnic areas. The fort is semi-accessible to the disabled, but it is particularly difficult to visit the museum.

VISITING FORT MOULTRIE

Although of less Civil War significance than Fort Sumter, Fort Moultrie is worth a visit. It was here in 1776 that Col. William Moultrie and his men drove off a squadron of nine British warships at the Battle of Sullivan's Island, and the fort was used by the army until 1947. The fort, smaller than Fort Sumter, is the third on this site. The tour with a park ranger shows the visitor parts of the fort that relate to different periods of its history, including the Civil War. The Visitor Center has a gift shop, a small museum, and a twenty-minute movie that alternates with a slide presentation, both giving the history of the fort. No food facilities are available. The wheelchair-accessible fort is located on Sullivan's Island and can be reached by car by taking SC 703 from U.S. 17 in Mount Pleasant and following the signs to the center on Middle Street.

IN AND AROUND CHARLESTON

Charleston is a beautiful, aristocratic city where doll-like, pastel-hued houses peek out from behind lacy iron gates. More than 800 of the city's buildings were erected before the Civil War. Visiting Charleston is taking a trip back in time; the historic area hasn't changed much since the unpleasantness at Fort Sumter. To capture the spirit of Charleston, see the multimedia presentation *Charleston Adventure,* shown continuously at the Visitor Center in the Arch Building, 85 Calhoun St., (803) 723-5225. A must is a horse-drawn carriage tour, or a stroll through the historic area with an audiotape tour, both available at *Charles Towne Tours,* phone (803) 723-5133.

Sites of particular Civil War interest include the *Old Slave Mart Museum and* *Gallery,* 6 Chalmers St., phone (803) 722-0079; the *Charleston Museum,* 360 Meeting St., phone (803) 722-2996, which displays a full-size replica of the Civil War submarine *Hunley,* the first submarine ever to torpedo and sink a warship. The *Citadel* is a military college established in 1842, which has an excellent museum of military

ANDERSON AFTER SUMTER

After Maj. Robert Anderson, the commander of Fort Sumter, arrived in the North following the surrender, President Lincoln made him a general, but he never took an active part in the war again. A Southerner and sympathetic to the Southern viewpoint, Anderson suffered from anxiety and failing health, and he retired in 1863. Ironically, his father, an officer during the Revolution in command at Charleston, also had been forced to surrender. On April 14, 1865, Anderson returned to Fort Sumter to raise the same flag he had lowered exactly four years before.

Robert Anderson

THE WAR AT SEA

To counter the strength of the Union navy, the Confederacy continually experimented with ironclads, mines (called torpedoes), and even submarines. Horace L. Hunley built a prototype submarine and took it to Charleston in 1863. Called the *Hunley,* it was propelled by eight men operating hand cranks, and could make four miles an hour. On February 17, 1864, it attacked the Union sloop *Housatonic* in Charleston Harbor and sent her to the bottom, making it the first warship in history to be sunk by a submarine. The crew of the *Hunley* perished in the explosion.

artifacts and equipment. There is a dress parade every Friday at 3:45 P.M. during the school year. To reach the Citadel, follow Ashley Avenue to Hampton Park and Moultrie Street. The Maritime Museum, at Patriots Point, has excellent material on Confederate raiders. Phone (803) 884-2727. Near the museum are the aircraft carrier *Yorktown,* the submarine *Clamagore,* the nuclear-powered ship *Savannah,* the destroyer *Laffey,* and the Coast Guard cutter *Comanche.*

Part of the Charleston experience is staying in an antebellum guest house. Among the finest are the *Battery Carriage House,* across from Battery Park at 20 South Battery, SC 29401, phone (803) 845-7638; *Guilds Inn,* a restored Colonial building at 101 Pitt St. in Mount Pleasant, SC 29464, phone (803) 881-0510; and *Lodge Alley Inn,* built in 1773, at 195 East Bay St., SC 29401, phone (803) 722-1611. There are a number of other fine historic bed-and-breakfasts in the city. For information, phone the Historic Charleston Bed and Breakfast at (803) 722-6606. Many motels are on U.S. 17, northwest of Charleston.

Moultrie Tavern, at 18 Vendue Range in the historic district, offers entrées based on authentic period recipes, such as Confederate game pie (a mixture of rabbit, duck, and quail), Marse Robert (Smithfield ham and breast of chicken with a cornbread dressing), and gumbo. The period decor is authentic, and there is a collection of Civil War artifacts. Guests wearing Civil War uniforms or costumes are given a discount. Two other restaurants are recommended: *Le Madeleine* in a 1780 brick building at 158 Church St., phone (803) 723-1700; and the elegant *Le Midi* at 337 King St., phone (803) 577-5571. Wherever you dine, do not leave Charleston without sampling the crab soup.

To see what life was like before the war, visit one of the following nearby plantations:

Magnolia Plantation (ten miles northwest of the city on SC 61, phone [803] 571-1266) has been in the same family since the arrival of Thomas Drayton in 1671. The plantation house, the third on the original foundation, dates from the Reconstruction era and is open for tours. The garden is famous for its camellias and azaleas.

Middleton Place (fourteen miles northwest of the city on SC 61, phone [803] 556-2060) was the home of Henry Middleton, president of the First Continental Congress, his son Arthur, a signer of the Declaration of Independence, and his great-grandson William, a signer of the Ordinance of Secession. Here are the oldest formal landscaped gardens in the country, laid out in 1741. In the original plantation house are priceless silver, china, furniture, and rare works of art. Visitors to the plantation can help dip candles, grind corn, take a mule-drawn wagon ride, and try to milk a cow.

Boone Hall (eight miles north of the city off U.S. 17 on Long Point Road in Mount Pleasant, phone [803] 884-4371) was a 17,000-acre cotton plantation established in 1681. Ancient live oak trees line the road for nearly a mile into the plantation complex. The original cotton-gin house still stands, and nearby are six rude houses on

Slave Row. The main house, built from brick made on the plantation and woodwork and flooring from the original house, is open for tours.

OTHER SOUTH CAROLINA SITES OF INTEREST

ALLENDALE

Rivers Bridge State Park, fifteen miles east of Allendale via U.S. 301, phone (803) 267-3675. In January 1865, Gen. William T. Sherman's army left Savannah and started north into South Carolina. A Confederate force of 1,200, under Gen. Lafayette McLaws, was at the main crossing of the Salkehatchie River at Rivers Bridge,

one of the sixteen bridges along the causeway stretching through the Salkehatchie Swamp. Sherman moved so rapidly that the Confederates had no time to burn the bridges before falling back to breastworks on the far bank of the river. Sniper and artillery fire kept the Union troops from crossing, and they began felling trees to build other bridges. On February 4, two companies of Union infantry crossed the river six miles upstream of Rivers Bridge, followed by a full regiment and two brigades. Late in the afternoon they advanced on the right flank of the Confederate breastworks. General McLaws ordered a withdrawal, and Sherman continued to march north. A museum contains Confederate artifacts.

Before leaving Atlanta to march to the sea, Sherman promised Grant: "I can make Georgia howl!" After capturing Savannah, Sherman headed north into South Carolina, the first state to secede, with a vengeance. Charleston felt his wrath, as the ruins seen from the city's Circular Church indicate. Columbia, the state capital, would be next. Throughout Sherman's campaign, the Confederacy was unable to mount more than token resistance.

The nearest accommodations are in Aiken and Orangeburg.

BEAUFORT

When Union troops captured this charming town, the second oldest in the state, nearly the entire population packed up and left.

Beaufort Museum, in the Beaufort Arsenal (1795) at 713 Craven St., phone (803) 525-7471. Civil War artifacts. Open Monday through Saturday except holidays.

National Cemetery. Confederate and Union soldiers are interred in this 1863 cemetery on Boundary Street.

Beaufort, midway between Savannah and Charleston, is well worth exploring. A delightful place to stay is the *Bay Street Inn* (601 Bay St., phone [803] 524-9030), an antebellum town house on the water in the historic district. Several good restaurants are an easy stroll away.

BENNETTSVILLE

Jennings-Brown House, 121 South Marlboro St., phone (803) 479-7748. This 1826 house was the Union headquarters when Bennettsville was captured in 1865. Restored and furnished with antiques. The nearest accommodations are in the nearby towns of Cheraw and Dillon.

COLUMBIA

On February 17, 1865, while Sherman's troops occupied Columbia, a fire broke out, destroying an area of eighty-four blocks and 1,386 buildings. Among the buildings that survived are the unfinished new State House and the home of the French consul.

State House, Main and Gervais Sts., phone (803) 734-2430. Only the outer walls of the State House were completed when Sherman shelled the city; metal stars on the west and southwest walls mark where artillery shells hit. The dome varies from the original plans, which were destroyed in the fire. Open Monday through Friday.

Sherman's Battery, across the Congaree River off U.S. 378, at 321 Moffatt Dr. A boulder marks the location of the guns that shelled the State House.

Hampton-Preston Mansion, 1615 Blanding St. Wade Hampton purchased this 1818 mansion, and the Hampton family and later his daughter, Mrs. John Preston, lived here. In February 1865 it was the headquarters of Union General J. A. Logan. Open daily except Monday and major holidays.

Classen's Inn (2003 Greene St., SC 29205; phone [803] 765-0440) is a luxurious twenty-nine-unit inn located in a renovated 1928 bakery. The inn is next to the University of South Carolina, minutes from the capitol in downtown Columbia, and walking distance to the restaurants of Five Points. There are several budget motels on the outskirts of the city.

POCATALIGO

Sheldon Church Ruins, seven miles south of Pocataligo on U.S. 21. The ghostly ruins, with roofless walls and pillars, of a church burned first by the British and later by Sherman.

The nearest accommodations and restaurants are in Beaufort.

◆ 6 ◆

THE WAR WEST OF THE MISSISSIPPI

ARKANSAS

PEA RIDGE

PEA RIDGE NATIONAL MILITARY PARK

Throughout the war, the South repeatedly tried to gain control of the border state of Missouri. An early effort by the pro-Confederacy governor of Missouri and the state militia was thwarted at the Battle of Wilson's Creek. Another attempt was not long in coming. It reached its climax here, in the northwest corner of Arkansas, at the Battle of Pea Ridge (also called the Battle of Elkhorn Tavern).

This campaign began late in 1861, when Gen. Samuel R. Curtis assumed command of the Federal Southwestern District of Missouri and zealously began pushing pro-Confederate forces out of the state. In February 1862, the Missouri State Guard, commanded by Gen. Sterling Price, crossed into Arkansas.

In the Boston Mountains, south of Fayetteville, Price joined forces with Gen. Ben McCulloch's Confederates. Gen. Earl Van Dorn took command of the combined force of 16,000, and headed north on March 4, intending to strike at St. Louis. Between

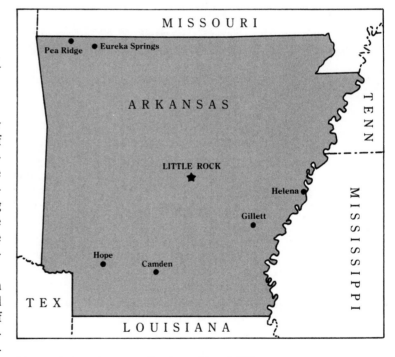

him and the city was Curtis, with 10,500 Union troops, many of them German imigrants who spoke no English. They would meet at Pea Ridge.

Curtis's army dug into the bluffs overlooking Little Sugar Creek, not far from Elkhorn Tavern and Pea Ridge. Van Dorn knew that a frontal attack against Curtis's position would be suicidal. He swung north

187

Samuel R. Curtis

to get Curtis, planning to attack at dawn on March 7.

Weary from a three-day march over difficult terrain, Van Dorn's troops arrived hours late, and the attack was postponed. This gave Curtis time to pull his men away from Little Sugar Creek, face about, and prepare for Van Dorn's attack in the open.

To make up for lost time, Van Dorn did not consolidate his forces, but launched a two-pronged assault. From the Round Top and west of Pea Ridge, the Confederates drove down upon the village of Leetown, where they ran into intensive fire that killed two generals. The ranking colonel was captured and their command structure decimated, and the Confederates scattered, some simply deserting. Later, more regrouped and made their way toward Elkhorn Tavern, two miles to the east.

The other prong of the attack fared better. Price's Missourians attacked east of the ridge and slowly but steadily pushed the Union troops back. At nightfall, Price held Elkhorn Tavern and the crucial Telegraph and Huntsville roads. The survivors of the Leetown battle joined them during the night.

On the morning of March 8, Curtis counterattacked near Elkhorn Tavern. His massed artillery punished the Confederates, and his concerted infantry and cavalry attacks began to crumble their defenses.

Ammunition was running short, but still the Confederates held. They might have won if an expected wagon train had moved up with the reserve ammunition. For some reason, however, the wagons turned and drove away.

Van Dorn disengaged and marched eastward down the Huntsville Road, away from Elkhorn Tavern. A few hundred stragglers headed down Old Telegraph Road. Curtis thought they were the main force and pursued them. This allowed Van Dorn to continue an orderly retreat.

The Battle of Pea Ridge was over, and Missouri was safe. Most of the Union and Confederate troops soon moved east of the Mississippi to fight in other campaigns.

VISITING PEA RIDGE

Pea Ridge National Military Park is located on 4,300 acres on U.S. 62, thirty miles northeast of Fayetteville and ten miles north of Rogers, Arkansas. The park is open daily, except Christmas and New Year's Day, from 8 A.M. to 5 P.M., with extended hours during the summer. A twelve-minute slide presentation describing the battle and its significance is shown every half-hour at the Visitor Center. A museum contains arms, uniforms, artifacts, and historical photographs relating to the battle. There is a gift shop, but no restaurant. A picnic ground with cooking facilities is in the park, and there are restaurants and fast-food outlets in Rogers. The park is accessible to the disabled. A leisurely tour and a visit to the center should take from two to three hours. Information about special events and reenactments are posted in the center. For further information, write to the Superintendent, Pea Ridge National Military Park, Pea Ridge, AR 72751, or phone (501) 451-8122.

A self-guided tour goes along a seven-mile loop of the battlefield. Part of it follows the Old Telegraph Road. In 1858 the Butterfield Overland Mail Company routed its stagecoaches over it to Fort Smith, then westward to California. The road received its name in 1860, when a telegraph line was strung along it. The road was used before the Battle of Pea Ridge by both Union and Confederate armies. Stops along the tour route include the following:

General Curtis Headquarters Site. Union General Samuel R. Curtis located his headquarters in this vicinity just before the battle. His army was entrenched along the bluffs overlooking Little Sugar Creek, about two miles south of here. Curtis believed that any Confederate attack would come from the south against his fortified line. Events, however, did not develop as he anticipated and he nearly lost his army.

Winton Spring. In 1862 the Ruddick family lived on the hill overlooking this spring. The house you see now dates from the early 1900s, and probably stands on the site of the old Ruddick cottage. Union troops drew water from this spring.

Leetown. A short distance to the left of this road is the site of a small hamlet called Leetown. Except for a few grave markers, the village now is gone. In 1862 the villagers learned much of the terrors of war while the battle raged around them for two days.

Leetown Battlefield. The thunder of battle filled the air in these fields in 1862. Smoke, confusion, and the mingled shouts and curses of the soldiers added to the frenzied scene. Union artillery and supporting infantry were formed along the south fence-line of the field. Confederate troops, pressing their attack through the woods north of the field and across Round Top to the right front, failed to defeat their opponent. Two Confederate commanders, Gen. Ben McCulloch and Gen. James McIntosh, were killed near the field's north boundaries. Learning of their deaths, the Confederates withdrew to the north and east to Elkhorn Tavern.

The Indians at Pea Ridge. Pea Ridge was the only major battle of the war in which American Indian troops were used. One thousand Cherokees from the Indian Territory (now Oklahoma) fought with the Confederates in this battle. The Indians participated in a successful charge against a three-gun Union artillery battery that had fired on them from the field to the left. Many of the Indians, never having seen artillery before, referred to the captured cannon as "shooting wagons." But soon afterward, fire from Union batteries poured into the Indian ranks and so demoralized them that they took cover in the woods. Their later participation in the battle was limited to scouting and patrolling.

Pea Ridge—West Overlook. From this point can be seen the Boston Mountains, on the horizon to the front. Bentonville, Arkansas, from which the Confederates advanced to Pea Ridge, is fourteen miles to the right.

Pea Ridge—East Overlook. About 150 yards down this gravel path is the best view of the battlefield in the park. From that point, about 60 percent of the field can be seen. A recorded message in the shelter tells in detail about the campaign.

Elkhorn Tavern. A landmark in this area for many years, the original building was the center of fighting that marked the start and the finish of the battle. From the Telegraph Road, north of the tavern, the Confederates made their first assault on Union forces, gradually pushing them back about a half-mile to the rear of this stop. On the second day, after a fierce artillery duel, the Union troops gained the upper hand as the Confederates ran out of artillery ammunition. Left with no other choice, General Van Dorn withdrew most of his troops over the Huntsville Road eastward from the tavern, thus ending the battle.

Fighting at Elkhorn Tavern. About a hundred yards from the tavern, along the Old Telegraph Road, are displays explaining the fighting in this area.

Confederate Artillery. A Missouri battery held this portion of the Confederate line during the morning of March 8. It and other Confederate batteries returned the fire from the Union line a quarter-mile to the south.

Federal Artillery. On the morning of March 8, Union artillery massed on this line in a desperate attempt to drive the Confederates from the vicinity of Elkhorn Tavern. This line extended from the guns on the hill to the right to a point almost directly behind the Visitor Center. Under fire of these guns, the Confederates withdrew from the field at about ten that morning.

From here, return to U.S. 62 at the park entrance, turn right, and drive 2.8 miles west to where a sign will direct you to the Union entrenchments above Little Sugar Creek.

MILITARY HISTORY

Many historians believe the Civil War marked the beginning of modern warfare: the first war with trenches and wire entanglements; the first with observation balloons and the telegraph; the first with railroads and armored ships; the first with repeating infantry weapons and the submarine. In this war, both the Union and the Confederacy employed the military draft for the first time in America.

Little Sugar Creek Trenches. On the bluff above Little Sugar Creek, six-tenths of a mile from U.S. 62, the earthworks built by Union soldiers still stand. A trail from the parking lot leads to the crest of the bluff.

FAYETTEVILLE

Prairie Grove Battlefield State Park. More than 18,000 Union and Confederate forces clashed here on December 7, 1862, and after a day of inconclusive fighting, the Confederates withdrew. The total casualties were 2,500. *Hindman Hall Museum* houses the Visitor Center, and has several exhibits, artifacts of the war, a battlefield diorama, and an audiovisual presentation on the battlefield and the park. The historic structures include the *Battle Monument;* a chimney from *Rhea's Mill;* the *Morrow House;* the *Latta House;* the *Dogtrot Cabin;* and the *Borden House,* the scene of the heaviest fighting. Accessible to the disabled. Guided tours and picnicking are available. Open daily in the summer, the rest of the year by request. For further information, write to the Superintendent, P.O. Box 306, Prairie Grove, AR 72753, or phone (501) 846-2990.

There are budget motels on the outskirts of Fayetteville. An interesting place to dine is the *Old Post Office* (1 Center Square, phone [501] 443-5588), serving up seafood and prime ribs in a 1909 post office.

EUREKA SPRINGS

In this nearby Victorian resort town in the Ozarks, the *Palace Hotel & Bath House* (135 Spring St., Eureka Springs, AR 72632; phone [501] 253-7474) is an elegant, eight-room hotel with antique furnishings and a full bath house with massage personnel. Breakfast is included in the room rates.

The *Plaza Restaurant* (55 South Main St., phone [501] 253-8866) offers a continental menu and a good wine list.

OTHER ARKANSAS SITES OF INTEREST

CAMDEN

McCollum-Chidester House, 926 Washington St., N.W., phone (501) 836-9243. Once a stagecoach stop, this 1847 house was used at different times as the headquarters of Confederate General Sterling Price and Union General Frederick Steele. Mementos of the war are on display. The building was the setting for some scenes in the television miniseries "North and South."

Leake-Ingram Building. Near the McCollum-Chidester House, on the same grounds, is a small white 1850 building, a law office before the war, a Freedmen's Bureau during Reconstruction. It houses a collection of books and memorabilia of the Old South. Tours are given of both houses, which are open Wednesday through Saturday, April through October.

Poison Spring Battleground Historical Monument, seven miles northwest of Camden on AR 24, then two miles west on AR 76. Here, Confederate troops ended General Steele's part in the Red River campaign into southwest Arkansas, sending him retreating north. Exhibits and dioramas trace troop movements.

Fort Lookout, end of Monroe St. Rifle trenches and cannon pits can still be seen at this site of a fort overlooking the Ouachita River.

Confederate Cemetery, Adams Ave. and Pearl St. Many unknown soldiers and more than 200 Civil War veterans are buried here.

GILLETT

Arkansas Post National Memorial. Arkansas Post, the first permanent French settlement in the lower Mississippi Valley, began as a trading post in 1686. Relocated several times to escape the spring floods of the Mississippi, by the late 18th century it was on the edge of the Grand Prairie, fifty river miles above the confluence of the Arkansas River and the Mississippi. The Confederates built Fort Hindman here in 1862. On January 10, 1863, union gunboats began bombarding the fort, and Gen. John A. McClernand led an attack on it the next day. After three hours the Confederate garrison of 5,000 surrendered the fort. The Arkansas Post campaign had not been authorized, and it did little to help Grant's drive to capture Vicksburg. McClernand's attack destroyed most of the community of Arkansas Post, and a later flood demolished the fort. The battlefield is gone, and only a few rifle pits survive. The site of Fort Hindman is underwater. The Visitor Center has exhibits and audiovisual programs. Open daily 8 A.M. to 5 P.M., except Christmas. The memorial is on AR 169, seven miles south of Gillett via U.S. 165 (the Great River Road). For further information, write to the Superintendent, Arkansas Post National Memorial, Route 1, P.O. Box 16, Gillett, AR 72055, or phone (501) 548-2432.

HELENA

Phillips County Museum, 623 Pecan St., adjacent to the public library, phone (501) 338-3537. Collection of Civil War artifacts and relics. Open daily except Sunday and holidays.

Historic homes. Antebellum homes in the Helena area may be seen through *Beauchamp By The River Tours,* 804 Columbia St., phone (501) 338-3607.

Visitors may also stay in a historic mansion. The *Edwardian* (317 Biscoe St., AR

72342; phone [501] 338-9155) has twelve guest rooms, many antiques, and can arrange tennis and golf for guests. Complimentary continental breakfast.

Confederate State Capitol. Built in 1836, this was the state capitol after Union troops occupied Little Rock from 1863 to 1865. Guided tours of the capitol and other historic buildings in the *Old Washington Historic State Park* (nine miles northwest of Hope on AR 4) are given daily except Tuesday and major holidays. For further information, write to the Superintendent, P.O. Box 98, Washington, AR 71832, or phone (501) 983-2684.

Motels and fast-food restaurants are on AR 4 between the park and the town.

LOUISIANA

BATON ROUGE

Port Hudson State Commemorative Area, fourteen miles north of Baton Rouge on U.S. 61, phone (504) 654-3775. After Adm. David Farragut's squadron passed the ports guarding New Orleans, the South's hold on the Mississippi was limited to Port Hudson and Vicksburg. Farragut tried and failed to storm Port Hudson, and a Union force of 20,000 laid siege to the port and its 7,000 defenders in the last week of May 1863. Two head-on Union assaults on May 27 and June 14 met with stubborn resistance and suffered heavy casualties, so Union General Nathaniel Banks decided to starve the defenders into submission. The garrison, subsisting on a diet of mules and rats, anxiously hoped Gen. Joseph Johnston would rescue them after defeating Grant at Vicksburg. When news of the fall of Vicksburg reached Port Hudson on July 9, the garrison surrendered, ending the longest siege in American military history. The 650-acre park encompasses part of the battlefield. Interpretive programs describe the siege. Forty-foot observation towers give good views of the area and the river. Cannon and trenches dot the battlefield. There are seven miles of hiking trails. Open daily. Accessible to the disabled.

Within the city limits, *Mt. Hope Plantation* (8151 Highland Rd., LA 70808; phone [504] 766-8600) is an inn on nearly five acres and listed in the National Register of Historic Buildings. The best restaurant in the city is the chef-owned *Chalet Brandt* (7655 Old Hammond Highway, phone [504] 927-6040), which specializes in seafood and veal. The most interesting is *Lafitte's Landing*, thirty miles south on I-10 and across the Sunshine Bridge on Donaldsonville (Sunshine Bridge Access Rd.; phone [504] 473-1232). In this restored 1791 Acadian

cottage, the chef-owner serves up Cajun and Creole specialties.

LAFAYETTE

Lafayette Museum, 1122 Lafayette St., phone (318) 234-2208. A collection of Civil War antiques and artifacts is housed in the home of Alexandre Mouton, the first Democratic governor of Louisiana. Open daily except Mondays, holidays, and during Mardi Gras.

MANY

Battle of Pleasant Hill Reenactment, eighteen miles north of Many on LA 175. Gen. Nathaniel Banks's attempt to march to Texas and occupy the state was turned back near here. This important battle left little for the visitor to see, but every March it is reenacted in a three-day event, which also includes a parade, a Confederate ball, and a beauty pageant. For information, write to the Sabine Parish Tourist Commission, 920 Fisher Rd., Many, LA 71449, or phone (318) 256-5880.

NEW ORLEANS

After failing to neutralize Fort Jackson, Fort St. Philips, and the defenses of New Orleans, Adm. David Farragut decided to run their batteries. He told his officers, "Conquer or be conquered." At two in the morning of April 24, 1862, his squadron steamed upriver. In the battle, one ship was sunk, another rammed, and Farragut's flagship was briefly grounded and set on fire, but he was successful. The mayor refused to surrender the city, and on April 25 Farragut sent a detachment of marines to raise the flag. Two days later, Gen. Benjamin Butler's troops arrived to begin a heavy-fisted occupation that lasted until the end of the war. One Butler ruling held that any woman insulting a Union soldier would be treated as a prostitute plying her trade. After Butler attended a dinner at the home of a prominent local family, the hostess insisted he had made off with some of her silver. Butler quickly was nicknamed "Spoons." The South hated Butler for his conduct in New Orleans.

The Beauregard-Keyes House, 1113 Chartres St., phone (504) 523-7257. General P. G. T. Beauregard lived in this 1826 cottage for eighteen months after the war. It was later restored by the novelist Frances Parkinson Keyes, who made it her home. Costumed docents give tours. Family heirlooms are on display. Gift shop. Open daily except Sunday and holidays.

The Old U.S. Mint, Esplanade and Decatur Sts., phone (504) 568-6968. Coins for both the Confederacy and the Union were minted in this Greek Revival building, and an exhibit depicts this activity. Visitors may make an appointment to see the *Louisiana State Museum's Historical Center,* a research facility now housed in the mint. Many of its 40,000 documents, maps, and photographs pertain to the war years. The mint is open Wednesday through Sunday except major holidays; Monday and Tuesday by appointment.

U.S. Customs House, Decatur and Canal Sts., phone (504) 589-2976. This building was begun in 1849, interrupted by the war, and completed in 1881. During the occupation of New Orleans, part of the building was General Butler's headquarters, and another part was a prison for Confederate soldiers. A great dome was planned for the custom house, but the weight of the granite and marble caused the foundation to settle, and the dome was forgotten. The building recently was renovated and restored. Exhibits depict the war years and the occupation. Open daily.

Confederate Museum, 929 Camp St., phone (504) 524-9077. Uniforms, weapons, medical instruments, and battle flags are displayed. The main hall contains a selection of Jefferson Davis memorabilia. Open daily except Sunday and during Mardi Gras.

Like Charleston and Savannah, but on a grander scale, New Orleans retains a strong feeling of the Old South, and visitors who take the time to explore the city are rewarded handsomely. Wander through the *French Quarter* and see *Jackson Square* and *The Cabildo, Saint Louis Cathedral* (and *Pirate's Alley* behind it), have a *café du monde* (half coffee with chicory, half hot milk) and a beignet (sugared fritter) in the *French Market*. In the evening, stop by *Preservation Hall* to hear some traditional jazz. Ride the streetcar that's been running out St. Charles Street to the *Garden District* since 1835, and stroll through *Audubon Park and the Zoological Garden*. Take a Mississippi River cruise on a stern-wheeler such as the *Cotton Blossom* or the *Natchez*. Visit some of the great plantations along the Great River Road: *Oak Alley, Nottoway,* or *San Francisco,* all open to visitors.

Historic places with overnight accommodations include the elegant *Maison de Ville* (727 Toulouse St., New Orleans, LA 70130; phone [504] 561-5858), in the French Quarter, where Tennessee Williams wrote part of *A Streetcar Named Desire.*

The Frenchmen (417 Frenchmen St., New Orleans, LA 70116; phone [504] 948-2166) is two antebellum town houses with a pool and patio.

In the Garden District, the *St. Charles Guest House* (1748 Prytania St., New Orleans, LA 70130; phone [504] 523-6556) is a low-key alternative to the bustle of the French Quarter.

The restaurants of New Orleans are legendary. For breakfast: *Brennan's,* 417 Royal St., phone (504) 525-9711. For historic atmosphere: *Antoine's,* since 1840 at 713 St. Louis St., phone (504) 581-4422.

For traditional cooking: *Galatoire's,* 209 Bourbon St., phone (504) 525-2021. For Creole cooking: *Le Ruth's,* 636 Franklin St., off the West Bank Expressway in suburban Gretna, phone (504) 362-4914.

MISSOURI

WILSON'S CREEK

WILSON'S CREEK NATIONAL BATTLEFIELD REPUBLIC, MISSOURI

Both the North and the South wanted the border state of Missouri, strategically located on the Mississippi and Missouri rivers, and rich in manpower and natural resources. Most Missourians wanted the state to stay neutral, but there was a strong pro-Confederacy element led by the governor, Claiborne F. Jackson. The issue came to a head quickly and was decided at the Battle of Wilson's Creek, which the Confederates called the Battle of Oak Hills. It kept Missouri in the Union, but the fighting would go on for the rest of the war. Savage guerrilla warfare nearly tore Missouri apart.

When President Lincoln called for troops to put down the rebellion, Missouri was asked to supply four regiments. Governor Jackson refused, ordering state militia to muster at Camp Jackson, outside St. Louis, in preparation for seizing the U.S. Arsenal there.

Capt. Nathaniel Lyon, the commander of the arsenal, was loyal to the Union and secretly moved most of the weapons to Illinois. He then marched 7,000 men to Camp Jackson on May 10, 1861, and forced its surrender. He tried unsuccessfully to come to terms with the governor, then led an army up the Missouri River and captured Jefferson City, the state capital. After an unsuccessful stand at nearby Booneville, the governor retreated to the southwest part of the state with the militia.

Now a general, Lyon installed a pro-Union state government, picked up reinforcements, and moved southwest. By July 13 he was camped at Springfield with some 6,000 troops, including the First, Second, Third, and Fifth Missouri Infantry; the First Iowa Infantry; the First and Second Kansas Infantry; several companies of regular army troops; and three batteries of artillery.

Gen. Sterling Price, commander of the Missouri State Guard, was training 5,000 troops seventy-five miles southwest of Springfield. Troops commanded by Generals Ben McCulloch and N. Bart Pearce joined Price there in July, bringing the Confederate force to 12,000.

On July 31 the Confederates marched northeast to attack Lyon's Union forces. Hoping to surprise the Confederates, Lyon marched from Springfield on August 1. The next day he mauled the vanguard of the Confederate force at Dug Springs. Realizing that he was outnumbered, Lyon withdrew to Springfield. The Confederates followed. By August 6 they were encamped near Wilson's Creek.

Though still outnumbered, Lyon moved to attack the Confederate encampment. He led 5,400 troops out of Springfield the night of August 9, ordering Col. Franz Sigel to take 1,200 troops on a wide swing to the south to flank the Confederate right. Lyon planned to strike from the north with the main body of troops. Surprise was critical.

General McCulloch, now commanding the Confederate forces, also was planning a surprise attack, but called it off because of rain. On the morning of August 10, Lyon caught McCulloch flatfooted. The Union troops overran several Confederate camps and advanced to the crest of a hill, now known as Bloody Hill. Lyon was stopped there by fire from the Pulaski Arkansas Battery, giving the Confederate infantry

time to form a line on the south slope of the hill.

The battle for Bloody Hill raged for more than five hours. Meanwhile, artillery fire halted Sigel's flanking maneuver at the Sharp farm. Confederate infantry counterattacked, and Sigel and his men fled.

On Bloody Hill, General Lyon, already wounded twice, was killed leading a charge. Maj. Samuel Sturgis assumed command, but by 11 A.M., his ammunition nearly exhausted, he ordered the Union troops to fall back to Springfield.

The Confederates did not pursue. General Lyon had lost the battle and his life, but achieved his ultimate goal: Missouri remained under Union control. The Union lost 1,317 men at Wilson's Creek; the Confederates 1,222.

Wilson's Creek did not end the fighting in Missouri. The Confederates made two large-scale attempts to control the state, both directed by General Price. He led the Missouri State Guard north shortly after the battle here, and captured the garrison at Lexington. He remained in Missouri until early 1862, when a Union army drove him into Arkansas. Another attempt was halted in northwest Arkansas at the Battle of Pea Ridge.

General Price returned to Missouri in September 1864 with 12,000 troops. Before his campaign ended in disaster, he marched some 1,500 miles, fought forty-three battles or skirmishes, and destroyed $10 million worth of property. At Westport on October 23, 1864, Price was defeated in the largest battle fought west of the Mississippi. He retreated southward, ending organized Confederate military operations in Missouri.

VISITING WILSON'S CREEK

Wilson's Creek National Battlefield is located on 1,750 acres, three miles east of Republic and ten miles southwest of Springfield, Missouri. The Visitor Center, which is accessible to the disabled, features a film, battle map, and museum that provide an introduction to the park, the battle, and its relevance to the war. A bookstore has books about the battle and the war in general. No food is sold in the park, but there is a picnic ground where cooking is allowed. Food facilities are available in the town of Republic, three miles west. The park is open from 8 A.M. to 7 P.M. daily, except Christmas and New Year's Day. On summer weekends, living-history demonstrations are featured at the Ray House and Bloody Hill. Special programs are presented on Memorial Day, July 4, August 10, and Labor Day. For further information, write to the Superintendent, Postal Drawer C, Republic, MO 65738, or phone (417) 732-2662.

The self-guided driving tour is a 4.9-mile, one-way loop road. Each stop has wayside exhibits with maps, artwork, and historical information. There are walking trails at Gibson's Mill, the Ray House, the Pulaski Arkansas Battery and Price's Headquarters, Bloody Hill, and the Historic Overlook. Exhibits are provided at specific locations along these trails. The one-way tour road is eighteen feet wide: the twelve-foot-wide left lane is for vehicular traffic, and the six-foot-wide right lane is for walking, jogging, and bicycling. Stops along the tour include the following:

Gibson's Mill. This area marks the northern end of the Confederate camps, where Missouri State Guard Gen. James S. Rains established the headquarters of his 2,500-man division near the mill. Gen. Nathaniel Lyon's dawn attack quickly drove Rains's division down the creek to the south. (The trail leads to the sites of the Gibson house and mill.)

Ray House and Cornfield. The Ray house was used as a Confederate field hospital during and after the battle. Col. Richard Weightman died in the front room, and the body of General Lyon was brought here at the end of the fighting. The small stone building at the foot of the hill is the Ray springhouse, the family source of water and the only other surviving wartime structure in the park. The only major fighting to take place on this side of Wilson's Creek occurred on the hill northwest of here, in the Ray cornfield, from which Union troops were driven back across the stream. The wooded hill on the western horizon beyond Wilson's Creek is Bloody Hill, where the most intense fighting took place.

Pulaski Arkansas Battery and Price's Headquarters. From the wooded ridge to the northwest, the cannon of the Pulaski Arkansas Battery opened fire on Bloody Hill, halting the Union advance and giving the Confederate infantry time to form into a line of battle and attack Lyon's forces. This battery from Little Rock fired on Lyon's forces on Bloody Hill throughout the battle.

Sigel's Second Position. On the ridge across Wilson's Creek to the left, Col. Franz Sigel's artillery heard Lyon's attack to the north and opened fire on the 2,300 Confederate cavalry camped in this field. The cavalry was routed, and fled into the woods to the north and west. Crossing to this side of the creek, Sigel halted about a hundred yards in front of this location and formed his 1,200-man force to oppose a Confederate cavalry regiment positioned at the north end of this field. After a twenty-minute artillery bombardment, the cavalry withdrew and Sigel continued his advance.

Sigel's Final Position. Sigel halted his advance on this hillside and formed his men into a line of battle across the Wire Road. Here he was attacked and defeated by Confederate troops, whom he mistook for a Union regiment, owing to the similarity of their uniforms to those of Lyon's First Iowa Infantry. This critical error turned the tide of the battle in favor of the Confederates.

Gibor's Battery. Near here, Capt. Henry Gibor placed his battery in position with the Confederate line of battle. The battery dueled with Union artillery on the crest of Bloody Hill. Three times the Confederate infantry mounted attacks through these fields and woods, but the Union line held. On their fourth assault they found that the Union troops had abandoned the crest and were retreating.

Bloody Hill. Throughout the battle, General Lyon's 4,000-man command held this high ground against repeated attacks. At the peak of the fighting, the entire south slope was covered with battle smoke. When the fighting ended, more than 1,700 Union and Confederate soldiers had been killed or wounded here, including General Lyon.

Historic Overlook. The Union army passed through this field, both advancing on and retreating from Bloody Hill. To guard against a Confederate attack, the 2nd Missouri Infantry Regiment and Du Bois's artillery battery were formed in a line of battle in this area. The John Ray house is clearly visible to the southeast.

SPRINGFIELD

Springfield's strategic location made it a military objective. Occupied by the Confederates in the Battle of Wilson's Creek, it was recaptured by the Union in 1862. Numerous Confederate attempts to regain Springfield were unsuccessful. A reminder of Springfield's dual nature in the war is the presence of a separate Confederate cemetery within the National Cemetery here. A scout and spy for Union headquarters was James Butler "Wild Bill" Hickok, later a famous frontier lawman.

Museum of Ozarks History, 603 Calhoun St., phone (417) 869-1976. In the historic Bentley House, a restored eighteen-room Queen Anne mansion, are artifacts and exhibits relating to Springfield's role in the war.

Drury College, 900 North Benton Ave. Historical markers on the campus indicate Civil War entrenchments.

The *Walnut Street Bed & Breakfast* (900 East Walnut St., Springfield, MO 65805; phone [417] 864-6346), a gracious 1894 Victorian house in the historic district, is considered one of the city's finest homes. Furnished with antiques.

The *Shady Inn* (524 West Sunshine St., phone [417] 862-0969), done up in Old English decor, offers prime ribs, seafood, and a piano bar.

There are motels on Glenstone Ave. You can find fried chicken, homemade desserts, and bargain prices at *Heritage Cafeteria* (310 South Glenstone Ave., phone [417] 881-7770).

OTHER MISSOURI SITES OF INTEREST

BLUE SPRINGS

Missouri Town, 1855, east side of Lake Jacomo in Fleming Park, phone (816) 881-4431. A re-creation of life in western Missouri on the eve of the war. Original buildings from 1820–60 have been brought here and restored. Site interpreters are garbed in period dress. Open daily mid-April through mid-November, weekends the rest of the year.

Lone Jack Civil War Museum, ten miles east of Blue Springs on U.S. 50, phone (816) 881-4431. After occupying Independence, 1,000 Confederate troops from Missouri and Arkansas met a similar number of state militia here on August 16, 1862, in any indecisive engagement, each side suffering some 200 casualties. Four Union cannon were lost and recaptured four times during the five-hour pitched battle. The militia and the Confederates occupied the town. The battle dead of both sides are buried here, and the museum displays artifacts of the battle and of Missouri's war days. The battle was named after a single jack pine tree that was near the center of the fighting.

Accommodations and restaurants are in Independence and Kansas City.

HANNIBAL

Civil War Fort, one mile northwest of Hannibal via U.S. 61N, second exit to Huck Finn Shopping Center, on a service road. In the hometown of Samuel Clemens, Tom Sawyer, and Huck Finn, a fort was manned by Union troops guarding the Hannibal–St. Joseph Railroad Bridge at South River Crossing. A museum at the fort displays cavalry equipment, buggies, and other artifacts. Nearby is a railroad station with railroad memorabilia. Open daily April through November.

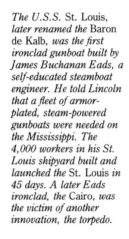

The U.S.S. St. Louis, later renamed the Baron de Kalb, was the first ironclad gunboat built by James Buchanan Eads, a self-educated steamboat engineer. He told Lincoln that a fleet of armor-plated, steam-powered gunboats were needed on the Mississippi. The 4,000 workers in his St. Louis shipyard built and launched the St. Louis in 45 days. A later Eads ironclad, the Cairo, was the victim of another innovation, the torpedo.

The *Fifth Street Mansion Bed & Breakfast* (213 South Fifth St., Hannibal MO 63401; phone [314] 221-0445), listed on the National Register of Historic Places, has unusual fireplaces and is furnished with antiques. The Mark Twain historic district is within walking distance.

The *Missouri Territory* (600 Broadway, phone [314] 248-1440), in the Old Federal Building, is the best restaurant in town.

INDEPENDENCE

Best known as the hometown of Harry S. Truman, Independence was ravaged by raiders and occupied by both Union and Confederate troops in the war.

1859 Marshal's Home and Jail Museum, 217 North Main St., phone (816) 252-1892. Some of the raiders ended up in the dungeonlike cells here. A museum of regional history, the marshal's living quarters, and a one-room 1870 schoolhouse also may be visited. Open daily May through Labor Day, Tuesday through Saturday the rest of the year, closed on major holidays.

The *Woodstock Inn* (1212 West Lexington St., Independence, MO 64050; phone [816] 833-2333) is convenient to the points of interest, and has eleven tastefully appointed guest rooms. A full breakfast is included in the room rate.

JEFFERSON CITY

Missouri State Museum, in the Capitol Building, at High St. and Broadway, phone (314) 751-4127. Civil War exhibits, including battle flags of Missouri regiments. Wheelchair accessible.

LEXINGTON

Battle of Lexington State Historic Site, on MO 13 north of Lexington, phone (816) 259-2112. After the Battle of Wilson's Creek, the Union forces retreated to Rolla, leaving the south and west of the state open to the pro-Southern State Guard, commanded by ex-Governor Sterling Price. By September 12, 1861, General Price and 12,000 men had advanced to the fortified Union outpost at Lexington. Col. James Mulligan commanded 3,500 Union troops at the outpost. Another 20,000 Union troops were nearby, but did not respond to repeated appeals for help. After an initial attack failed, Price waited until September 18 for an ammunition train to arrive before trying again. An attack brought Price's Confederates to within 125 yards of the Union position. The next day his men used huge hemp bales from a nearby warehouse as a mobile breastworks. Two or three men would butt the bales forward with their heads while riflemen crouched behind the bales fired on the Union lines. When the Confederates were close enough to take the breastworks with a final rush, Mulligan surrendered. A walking tour of the battlefield begins at the restored *Anderson House,* the center of the battle, and includes the *Union Entrenchments,* the *Union Gun Employment,* and the scene of the hand-to-hand combat on the battle's final day. Guided tours are given. The park is open daily except major holidays.

Lexington Historical Museum, 13th and Main Sts., phone (816) 259-2112. Built as a church in 1848, the museum contains much material on the Battle of Lexington. It also has a good collection of Pony Express artifacts and an excellent photographic library. Open daily mid-April to mid-October, Monday through Saturday the rest of the year, and closed on major holidays.

Lafayette County Courthouse, 11th and Main Sts., phone (816) 259-4315. A Civil War cannonball is embedded in the east column of this 1847 courthouse, the oldest courthouse in constant use west of the Mississippi. Open Monday through Friday, except holidays.

Linwood Lawn, two miles southeast of town, off U.S. 24. This twenty-six-room Italianate mansion on 236 acres was built at a cost of $85,000 in 1850. Its features include a hand-carved spiral staircase and elaborate chandeliers specially designed for each room. Open by appointment from mid-April to mid-October.

NEVADA

Nevada was the headquarters for Confederate guerrillas during the Civil War, and was known as the "Bushwhackers' Capital." The town was burned to the ground in 1863 by Union troops, and was not rebuilt until after the war.

Bushwhacker Museum, 231 North Main St. at Hunter St., three blocks north of U.S. 54, phone (417) 667-5841. Operated by the Vernon County Historical Society, the museum is housed in a building used as a jail from 1860 to 1960. The exhibits include Civil War relics.

ST. LOUIS

Jefferson Barracks Historical Park, ten miles south of the city on I-55 to the South Broadway exit, South Broadway at Kingston, phone (314) 544-5714. An important Union post during the war, the barracks was established in 1826 and used through 1946. The county now maintains 424 acres of the original tract. The restored buildings include the stable, a laborer's house, two powder magazines, and the ordnance room. Displays at the Visitor Center depict the history of the barracks. Picnicking sites are available. The buildings are open Wednesday through Sunday, except major holidays.

Missouri Historical Society, Jefferson Memorial Building in Forest Park, Lindell Blvd. and De Ballviere, phone (314) 361-1424. Exhibits of Civil War arms and uniforms. Archives. Wheelchair accessible. Open daily except Monday and major holidays.

Grant's Farm, 10501 Gravois Rd., phone (314) 843-1700. An 1856 log cabin on a 281-acre wooded tract once owned by Ulysses S. Grant. The farm now has a deer park where many animals—deer, buffalo, and longhorn cattle—may be seen in their natural habitat. There is a Clydesdale stallion barn and a carriage house with horse-drawn vehicles. The farm may be toured by miniature train (reservations required). Open daily except Monday June through August, Thursday through Sunday mid-April through May and September through mid-October.

Soldiers' Memorial Military Museum, 1315 Chestnut St., phone (314) 622-4550. Memorabilia from pre-Civil War through Vietnam. Open daily except major holidays. Accessible to the disabled.

Old Courthouse, 11 North 4th St. at Market St., phone (314) 425-4465. The first two trials of the Dred Scott case were held in this building, begun in 1842 and completed in 1864. There are exhibits about the city, dioramas, and films. Guided tours are available. Open daily except major holidays.

The Winter House (2156 Lafayette Ave., St. Louis MO 63104; phone [314] 772-4429) is an 1876 turreted Victorian bed-and-breakfast convenient to the city's points of interest. Cats are in residence. A continental breakfast is included in the room rate.

The *Lt. Robert E. Lee* (on the riverfront at 100 Leonor K. Sullivan Blvd., phone [314] 241-1282) offers seafood, steak, a Dixieland band on Fridays and Saturdays, and models of Mississippi riverboats.

TEXAS

AUSTIN

Texas Confederate Museum, first floor of the Old Land Office, 112 East 11th St., phone (512) 472-2596. Displays of Confederate relics including battle flags, uniforms, guns, and documents. Open Monday through Friday except holidays.

A convenient bed-and-breakfast is the late-Victorian *McCallum House.* Write to Roger Danley, 613 West 32nd St., Austin TX 78705, or phone (512) 451-6744.

Breakfast is served in bed on request at the *Brook House,* a 1920s estate. Write to Sandy Hasgler, 609 West 33rd St., Austin, TX 78705, or phone (512) 459-0534.

BROWNSVILLE

The last battle of the Civil War was fought at *Palmito Hill,* a few miles east of Brownsville on the Rio Grande, on May 12–13, 1865, more than a month after Lee's surrender. No trace of the battlefield remains.

EL PASO

Texas troops of the Confederate army captured Fort Bliss in 1861 as part of a campaign to win New Mexico. The campaign failed, the troops gradually withdrew, and the fort and El Paso returned to Union hands.

Fort Bliss Museum, east of El Paso on U.S. 54, between Fred Wilson Rd. and

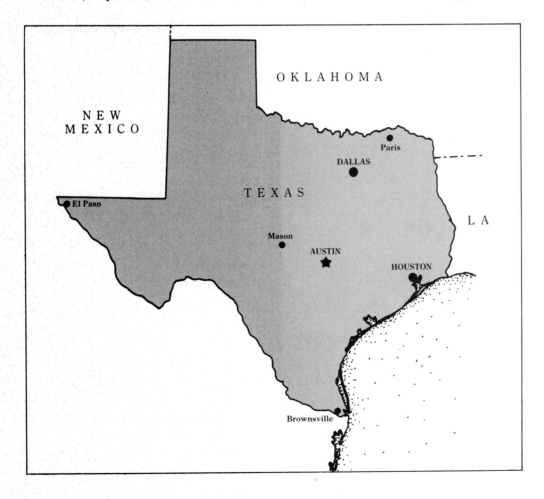

Montana Ave. (U.S. 62, 180), phone (915) 568-4518. Five adobe buildings replicate the army post of the war years and contain items relating to the history of the fort, army uniforms and weapons, and civilian artifacts. Open daily except major holidays.

Ysleta, the oldest mission in Texas, built in 1682, now houses the *Tiguas Indian Reservation Restaurant* (122 South Old Pueblo Rd., eighteen miles southeast of El Paso via I-10, Zaragosa Road exit, phone (915) 859-3916), decorated in Indian artifacts and serving Tex-Mex specialties.

MASON

Fort Mason. This was Robert E. Lee's last command before the war, a reconstructed four-room officers' quarters on the crest of Fort Hill.

In nearby historic Fredericksburg, *The Schmidt Barn* is a bed-and-breakfast in a 125-year-old farm barn converted into a guest house. Deer and other wildlife abound on the surrounding property. Write to Dr. Charles Schmidt, Rte. 2, Box 112A3, Mason, TX 78624, or phone (512) 997-3234.

PARIS

Maxey House State Historical Structure, 812 South Church St., phone (214) 785-5716. Sam Bell Maxey, a major general in the Confederate army and a U.S. Senator, built this two-story, High Victorian home in 1867. It was occupied by his descendants until 1966, and is decorated with family heirlooms and furniture. Accessible to the disabled. Open Wednesday through Sunday, except holidays.

✦7✦

THE WAR IN THE NORTH

DELAWARE

DELAWARE CITY

Fort Delaware State Park, Rte. 13 south to DE 72 to ferry dock in Delaware City, phone (302) 834-7941. From 1861 to 1866, some 33,000 Confederate troops, high-ranking officers, and political prisoners were held here on Pea Patch Island. At any one time, as many as 12,500 prisoners were in residence, many living in wooden barracks outside the fort walls. The damp, insect-infested terrain fostered epidemics, and some 2,700 prisoners perished here during the war, 2,400 of whom are buried just across the river in a national cemetery at Finn's Point, New Jersey. The suffering at Fort Delaware earned it the title "Andersonville of the North." The fort currently is

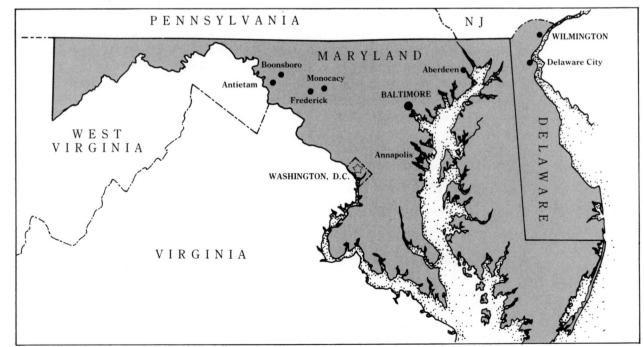

The box in Ford's Theatre where Lincoln was shot.

being restored. A museum houses scale models of the fort and Civil War relics. On the third weekend in June there is a costumed re-creation of life at the fort during the war, with tactical demonstrations, a medicine show, a fashion show, and lectures. Boat trips depart for the island from Delaware City on Saturdays, Sundays, and holidays from the last weekend in April to the last weekend in September. Snacks are available at a concession stand. The nearest accommodations are in New Castle and Wilmington.

DISTRICT OF COLUMBIA

FORD'S THEATRE

On the night of April 14, 1865, John Wilkes Booth, a well-known actor and Southern sympathizer, slipped into the presidential box at Ford's Theatre in Washington and shot Abraham Lincoln in the back of the head. Then he stabbed Maj. Henry Reed Rathbone, who was in the presidential party, and jumped from the box to the stage. Booth's spur caught in the bunting that decorated the box, and he landed off balance, breaking a small bone in his left leg. He managed to hobble across the stage, leave the theater, mount his horse in the back alley, and flee the city. The unconscious President was carried to a house across the street at 453 (now 516) Tenth St., and laid in the back bedroom. His wife, Mary, and son, Capt. Robert Todd Lincoln, waited in the front room. Lincoln died at 7:22 the next morning.

Booth had been planning for months to kidnap Lincoln, whom he saw as the source of the South's problems. He recruited several conspirators, including John Surratt, whose mother, Mary, ran a boardinghouse where most of the plotting was done. By early 1865, David Herold, George Atzerodt, and Lewis Powell had joined Booth. An attempt to kidnap Lincoln on March 17 failed. John Surratt had a change of heart and left the area. After Lee surrendered,

Booth put together his final plan: Powell would kill Secretary of State William Henry Seward, Atzerodt would shoot Vice-President Andrew Johnson, and Booth would assassinate Lincoln. But only Booth was successful.

Washington was celebrating the end of the war when the Lincolns decided to attend a performance of a popular comedy entitled *Our American Cousin* at Ford's Theatre, starring the famous actress Laura Keene. The Lincolns invited General and Mrs. Grant to join them, but the Grants had to leave Washington. At the last minute, the Lincolns invited Clara Harris, daughter of New York Senator Ira Harris, and her fiancé, Major Rathbone.

The first person to enter the presidential box after the shooting was Charles Augustus Leale, a twenty-three-year-old doctor. He and Dr. Charles Sabin Taft treated Lincoln and had him carried out of the theater

John Wilkes Booth

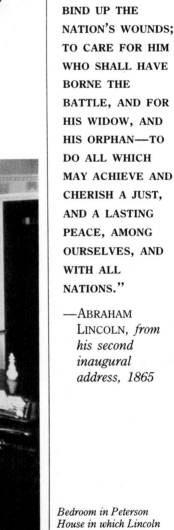

"WITH MALICE TOWARD NONE; WITH CHARITY FOR ALL; WITH FIRMNESS IN THE RIGHT, AS GOD GIVES US TO SEE THE RIGHT, LET US STRIVE ON TO FINISH THE WORK WE ARE IN; TO BIND UP THE NATION'S WOUNDS; TO CARE FOR HIM WHO SHALL HAVE BORNE THE BATTLE, AND FOR HIS WIDOW, AND HIS ORPHAN—TO DO ALL WHICH MAY ACHIEVE AND CHERISH A JUST, AND A LASTING PEACE, AMONG OURSELVES, AND WITH ALL NATIONS."

—ABRAHAM LINCOLN, *from his second inaugural address, 1865*

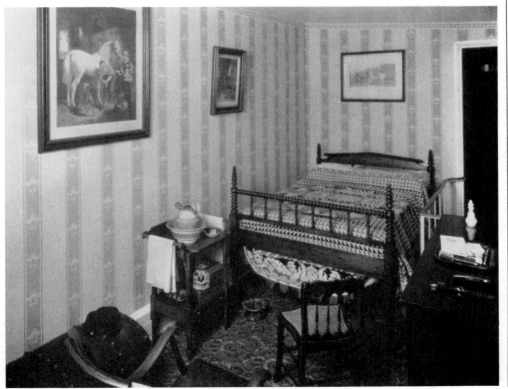

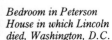

Bedroom in Peterson House in which Lincoln died, Washington, D.C.

Ford's Theatre,
Washington, D.C.

"I DESIRE SO TO
CONDUCT THE
AFFAIRS OF THIS
ADMINISTRATION
THAT IF AT THE
END, WHEN I
COME TO LAY
DOWN THE REINS
OF POWER, I
HAVE LOST EVERY
OTHER FRIEND ON
EARTH, I SHALL
AT LEAST HAVE
ONE FRIEND LEFT,
AND THAT FRIEND
SHALL BE DOWN
INSIDE ME."

—ABRAHAM
LINCOLN, *1864*

and across the street to the home of William Peterson, a tailor. Leale, Taft, and nearly a dozen other doctors attempted to make Lincoln comfortable, though they realized from the first that the wound was mortal. Through the long night, Dr. Leale held Lincoln's hand, knowing that if the President regained consciousness, he would be blind. Leale wanted him to know that a fellow human being was nearby.

As Lincoln lay dying, Secretary of War Edwin Stanton was in the back parlor, beginning his investigation into the events surrounding the assassination. Aided by Charles A. Dana, Stanton questioned eyewitnesses, sent out orders for the arrest of Booth, and issued the news of the events to the press. His investigation would lead to the trial of the conspirators. At the moment of Lincoln's death, Stanton reportedly said, "Now he belongs to the ages."

In the chaos following the shooting, Booth rode through Washington, then south into Maryland, stopping at the Surratt Tavern around midnight to rendezvous with his accomplice, David Herold, and pick up weapons. Booth hoped for a quick escape to the South, where he was expecting a hero's welcome. In intense pain, he stopped at the home of Dr. Samuel Mudd to have his broken leg set before continuing. On April 26, Union troops surrounded a tobacco barn near Port Royal, Virginia, where Booth and Herold were hiding. After Herold surrendered, the barn was set on fire to force Booth out, but he was shot and killed while still in the barn.

The other conspirators were soon arrested, and their trial began May 10. On June 30, Atzerodt, Herold, Powell, and Mrs. Surratt were sentenced to death, and they were hanged on July 7. Samuel Arnold and Michael O'Laughlin, who were involved in the original kidnapping conspiracy, and Dr. Mudd were given life sentences. Edman Spangler, a stage hand at the theater who held Booth's horse, was given six years of hard labor. All four were sent to Fort Jefferson in Florida to serve their sentences. O'Laughlin died of yellow fever in 1867; the others were pardoned in 1869 by President Andrew Johnson.

Tragedy followed all the people in the presidential box. Criticism of Mary Todd Lincoln's public conduct did not end with the assassination. Three of her four sons died in her lifetime. In 1875 she was judged insane and admitted to a sanitarium for several months. She died at the home of her sister in Springfield, Illinois, on July 16, 1882. Clara Harris Rathbone was shot dead by her husband in 1883, and he died in an insane asylum in 1911.

VISITING FORD'S THEATRE

Ford's Theatre National Historic Site, which includes the theater at 511 10th St., N.W., and the House Where Lincoln Died at 516 10th St., is administered by the National Park Service and is open daily from 9 A.M. to 5 P.M., except December 25. The

Sgt. Boston Corbett claimed he shot John Wilkes Booth, but doubts persist. Corbett was armed with a carbine; the autopsy report on Booth said he was killed by a pistol ball. Nor did anyone see Corbett fire. A religious fanatic, Corbett moved to Kansas after the war and was a doorkeeper in the state capitol until he went berserk on the job and brandished a revolver. Declared insane and institutionalized, Corbett later escaped and vanished.

theater is closed to tours when rehearsals or matinees are in progress, generally Thursday, Saturday, and Sunday. However, the Lincoln Museum, in the theater's basement, and the House Where Lincoln Died remain open. For further information on the theater, phone (202) 426-6924. For further information on the site, write to the Superintendent, National Capital Parks-Central, 900 Ohio Drive, S.W., Washington, DC 20242.

Ford's Theatre as it exists today is the result of two separate strands coming together. The first is the Lincoln Museum. Its initial collection of Lincoln-related items was assembled by Osborn Oldroyd and brought to Washington in 1893. The government purchased the collection in 1926 and installed it in the theater six years later. After World War II, public interest developed in restoring the theater to its 1865 appearance. The restored theater and the newly constructed museum opened on February 13, 1968.

Besides being a memorial to Lincoln, Ford's is also an active, legitimate theater,

Peterson House, where Lincoln died, Washington, D.C.

presenting a full schedule of plays during the year. The Ford's Theatre Society is responsible for the productions, which represent the cultural and ethnic diversity of the country. For box office information, phone (202) 347-4833.

THE HOUSE WHERE LINCOLN DIED

Front Parlor. Here Capt. Robert Todd Lincoln, summoned from the White House after the shooting, spent most of the night trying to comfort his mother. The room now is furnished to correspond to its 1865 appearance, but none of the furniture is original to the house. At the time of the assassination, folding doors opened to the Back Parlor.

Back Parlor. Here Stanton began his investigation of the assassination. Cpl. James Tanner sat at a center table, taking shorthand notes of the interviews with the eyewitnesses.

Back Bedroom. The original bed in this room, similar to the bed now on display, wasn't long enough to accommodate Lincoln, and he had to be laid diagonally across it. The pillow and the bloodstained pillowcases are some of the ones that were used for Lincoln.

JOHN WILKES BOOTH ESCAPE ROUTE

In Waldorf, Maryland, fifteen miles south of Washington on U.S. 301, are two sites connected with Booth's flight from Washington.

At the *Surratt House and Tavern* (9110 Brandywine Rd., Clinton (once named Surrattsville), phone [301] 868-1121) six rooms furnished with period furniture are shown to visitors by guides in period costumes. There are candlelight tours and special events and exhibits throughout the year. In late April there is a Civil War encampment on the grounds, with living-history demonstrations of the camp life of soldiers. Open Thursday through Sunday, March to mid-December.

Unaware that Booth had just shot Lincoln, Dr. Mudd set Booth's leg at this site, the *Dr. Samuel Mudd House* (just off MD 382 in St. Catherine, phone [301] 934-8464 or 645-6870). Tours are conducted by docents, some of whom are Dr. Mudd's descendants. Open Saturday and Sunday, April through November.

Detail of Daniel Chester French's statue of Lincoln, Lincoln Memorial, Washington, D.C.

Surratt house and tavern,
Clinton, Maryland

OTHER DISTRICT OF COLUMBIA SITES OF INTEREST

Students of the war will find many points of interest in Washington in addition to such standbys as the Capitol, the White House, and the Smithsonian Institution. These include the following:

Lincoln Memorial, West Potomac Park at 23rd St., N.W. Daniel Chester French's nineteen-foot statue of the seated Lincoln looks across a reflecting pool at the Washington Monument and the Capitol. The Gettysburg Address and the Second Inaugural Address are engraved on the walls. The memorial is particularly impressive at night, and is open twenty-four hours a day. Accessible to the disabled.

Armed Forces Medical Museum. 6825 18th St., N.W., phone (202) 576-2348. Interesting material on the treatment of the wounded during the Civil War. Open daily except for major holidays. Facilities for the disabled. Special tours by appointment. The museum is at the Armed Forces Institute of Pathology, Building #54, Walter Reed Army Medical Center.

Fort Stevens Park, Piney Branch Rd. and Quackenbos St., N.W., phone (202) 426-6829. Confederate troops under Gen. Jubal Early were stopped here on July 11–12, 1864, in their attempted invasion of Washington. President Lincoln risked his life at the fort trying to get a look at the fighting. Open daily.

Emancipation Statue, Lincoln Park, East Capitol St., N.E., between 11th and 12th Sts. On the eleventh anniversary of Lincoln's assassination, this bronze statue

The Capitol as it appeared in September 1860.

by Thomas Bell was unveiled. Frederick Douglass was in attendance.

Navy Museum, Building 76, Washington Navy Yard, 9th and M Sts., S.W., phone (202) 433-2651. The role of the navy in the war is part of the story presented here. Dioramas show achievements of early naval heroes and the development of naval weapons. More than 5,000 objects are on display, including paintings, models, flags, and decorations. Accessible to the disabled. Open daily except major holidays.

When General Grant was summoned to Washington to take command of the Union armies, he stayed at the Willard Hotel, as did many Presidents on the eve of their inaugurations. The 1847 hotel, now the *Willard Inter-Continental* (1401 Pennsylvania Ave., N.W., 20408; phone [202] 628-

9100), has been restored to its original elegance, with all the modern conveniences and comforts. The famous "Peacock Walk" runs the length of the hotel, connecting Pennsylvania Avenue and F Street.

A superbly located bed-and-breakfast is *The Reeds,* a Victorian town house ten blocks northeast of the White House. It is furnished with antiques and has lovely gardens. Write to Mrs. Jacqueline Reed, P.O. Box 12011, Washington, DC 20005, or phone (202) 328-3510.

Washington is graced with a number of fine restaurants. One that amuses is the *Old Ebbitt Grill* (675 15th St., N.W., phone [202] 347-4801), housed in an old vaudeville theater. The decor is Victorian, and the restaurant is lit by gaslight.

The *Hawk 'n Dove* (329 Pennsylvania Ave., S.E., phone [202] 543-3300) is a pub restaurant in a Civil War–period building on

Capitol Hill. The walls are decorated with Confederate and Union money.

Washington is an excellent starting point for a two-day, two-hundred-mile Civil War automobile tour. Drive west on U.S. 66 for twenty-seven miles to *Manassas National Battlefield Park,* Virginia. Then drive northwest on VA 234 nine miles to U.S. 15, turn right and continue nineteen miles to *Leesburg.* Turn west on VA 7 and drive twenty-four miles to *Berryville.* Turn north on U.S. 340 and continue nineteen miles to *Harpers Ferry,* West Virginia. Leave Harpers Ferry on U.S. 340 East and cross the Potomac River to MD 67. Turn north and drive fourteen miles to *Boonsboro,* Maryland, then turn southwest on MD 34 and drive six miles to *Antietam National Battlefield Site and Cemetery.* Return to Boonsboro, turn southwest on U.S. 40A, and drive fourteen miles to Frederick. From Frederick, take I-270 southeast thirty-five miles, cross I-495 (Capital Beltway), and continue to Washington.

FORD AND HIS THEATER

John T. Ford was a successful theatrical entrepreneur from Baltimore who decided to expand his operations to Washington. He leased the First Baptist Church and turned it into a music hall, opening in 1861 with a two-and-a-half-month run of the Christy Minstrels. Everything was going well for Ford when his theater burned down on December 30, 1862. He raised money for a new theater on the same site, opening it on August 27, 1863. The building and its equipment were up-to-date, and Ford hired only first-rate actors. Ford was enjoying his second success when Lincoln was assassinated.

Ford's Theatre was closed by the government during the investigation of the assassination and the trial of the conspirators. After they were hanged, Ford was given permission to reopen, but he received threats that the theater would be burned down if it was reopened, and the War Department closed it. The government bought the theater from Ford for $100,000 in 1886, and used it until 1931 as office space.

ILLINOIS

CHARLESTON

Moore Home State Historic Site, nine miles south of Charleston on an unnumbered road. For directions, phone (217) 345-6489. Before leaving for his presidential inauguration, Abraham Lincoln ate his last meal here with his stepmother and her daughter, Mrs. Matilda Moore. A small museum is in the house. Open Tuesday through Saturday except holidays.

Lincoln Log Cabin State Historic Site, one mile south of the Moore Farm, phone (217) 345-6489. The Thomas Lincoln Log Cabin has been reconstructed on its original foundation as it was when it was built in 1837 by Abraham Lincoln's father. A small museum in the house displays Lincoln family memorabilia. There is a summer living-history program. In the nearby Shiloh Cemetery are the graves of Thomas Lincoln and Sarah Bush Lincoln, the President's stepmother. Open daily except major holidays.

Coles County Courthouse, Charleston Square. Lincoln practiced law in Charleston and debated Stephen A. Douglas here on September 18, 1858.

Accommodations and restaurants are in the nearby communities of Arcola and Mattoon.

DECATUR

Lincoln came here with his family in 1830, when he was twenty-one, to settle on the Sangamon River, a few miles to the west. He worked as a farmer and rail-splitter, and made his first political speech in what is now Lincoln Square.

Ulysses S. Grant poses grimly for Mathew Brady at his field headquarters. Grant was an enigma. He had a reputation as a hard drinker, a heartless butcher of men, a straight-ahead-and-damn-the-expense general. Yet he was temperate throughout his command, he led a brilliant Vicksburg campaign, and he outmaneuvered Lee from the Wilderness to the defenses of Petersburg. Lincoln had indeed found a commanding general.

Lincoln Trail Homestead State Park, ten miles west of Decatur on U.S. 36, then south on County 27, phone (217) 963-2729. A marker denotes the site of the Lincoln family homestead.

Lincoln Log Cabin Courthouse, Fairview Park, junction of U.S. 36 and IL 48, phone (217) 422-5911. A replica of the first courthouse in the county. When he was riding the circuit, practicing law from town to town, Lincoln defended clients in the original courthouse, located in what now is the heart of the city. Open daily.

The best restaurant in town is the *Blue Mill* (1099 West Wood St. at Oakland Ave., phone [217] 423-7717); the best value, *Bishop Buffet Cafeteria* (Hickory Point Mall, seventeen miles north on I-72 exit 28B, phone [217] 875-2757).

GALENA

In this river town, sentiments were divided when war came, but two companies were formed to support the Union. Ulysses S. Grant, who had recently moved to Galena from St. Louis, was the drillmaster of the troops. Galena has changed little over the years. Ninety percent of its buildings are listed on the National Register.

Ulysses S. Grant Home State Historic Site, 500 Bouthillier St., phone (815) 777-9129. Given to General Grant upon his return from the war in 1865, the house contains original furnishings and items used by the Grants in the White House. Guided tours are given. Open daily except major holidays.

Galena–Jo Daviess County History Museum, 211 South Bench St., phone (815) 777-9129. The collection includes "Peace in Union," Thomas Nast's famous painting of the surrender at Appomattox, as well as Civil War costumes. Open daily except major holidays.

Now restored, the historic *DeSoto House* (230 South Main St., Galena, IL 61036; phone [815] 777-0900) provided overnight accommodations when Grant first came to Galena, and still does.

A restored 1858 Italianate mansion is the home of the *Stillman County Inn* (513 Bouthillier St., phone [815] 777-0557), a good choice for steak or seafood.

PETERSBURG

Lincoln's New Salem State Historic Site, two miles south of Petersburg on IL 97, phone (217) 632-7953. The town that Lincoln lived in from 1831 to 1837, at the beginning of his political career, has been reconstructed on 620 acres from original maps and family archives. The only original building is the *Onstott Cooper Shop*. Reconstructed buildings include *Rutledge Tavern,* the *Lincoln-Berry Store,* the *Denton Offut Store* (where Lincoln first worked, a carding mill, and a grist mill. Most of the buildings have period furnishings. Ann Rutledge, believed to be Lincoln's first love, is buried in *Oakland Cemetery* on Oakland Avenue in Petersburg. Self-guided tours are available. Most buildings have attendants in period clothing. A replica of the riverboat *Talisman* gives short excursions from May through October. A museum exhibits Lincoln memorabilia. Open daily except major holidays.

Kelso Hollow Amphitheater. In the summer, three plays about the life, legend, and legacy of Lincoln are presented: *Your Obedient Servant, A. Lincoln* blends his speeches, letters, and comments with the words of those who knew him, accompanied by folk songs and period music; *Abraham Lincoln Walks at Midnight* shows the Lincoln legend through the words of Illinois poets Vachel Lindsay, Edgar Lee Masters, and Carl Sandburg; and *Even We*

Here explores the legacy of Lincoln from World War I to the 1969 landing on the moon. Performances run from mid-June to mid-August, nightly except Mondays. The amphitheater is at the *New Salem Historic Site*. For information, from September to May, write to Station A, Box 2178, Champaign, IL 61820, or phone (217) 367-1900. From June through August, write to Box 401, Petersburg, IL 62675, or phone (217) 632-7755.

Menard County Courthouse, 102 South 7th St., phone (217) 632-2415. Lincoln's papers are on display here. Open Monday through Friday except holidays.

Mary Todd Lincoln

Abraham Lincoln lived here for more than a quarter-century. He practiced law, married, raised a family, and led the campaign to make Springfield the state capital.

Lincoln Home National Historic Site, 426 South 7th St., phone (217) 492-4150. Lincoln and his family lived here for seventeen years before he became President. It was the only home he ever owned. The interior has been furnished with period artifacts and Lincoln family furnishings. The Visitor Center presents a movie on Lincoln's years in Springfield, and houses exhibits and a bookstore. Open daily except major holidays.

Lincoln's Tomb State Historic Site, Oak Ridge Cemetery, at the end of Monument Ave., phone (217) 782-2717. The tomb has a 117-foot spire, four heroic bronze groups at the base, and a ten-foot statue of Lincoln at the south end of the shaft. Niches inside the tomb commemorate important events in Lincoln's life. Lincoln, his wife, Mary Todd Lincoln, and three of their four sons are buried here. (Robert Todd Lincoln, the fourth son, is buried in Arlington National Cemetery.) Attendants describe the tomb and its significance. Self-guided tours are available. Open daily except major holidays.

Old State Capitol State Historic Site, City Square, between Adams, Washington, 5th, and 6th Sts., phone (217) 785-7960. Lincoln made his famous "House Divided" speech and argued cases before the state supreme court in the old capitol, which has been reconstructed on the original site. The *Illinois State Historical Library* is in the building. Open daily except major holidays.

Lincoln-Herndon Building, 6th and Adams Sts., phone (217) 782-4836. Lincoln

Interior of Lincoln Home, Springfield, Illinois

practiced law here for ten years. The building also housed the old federal court. Open daily except major holidays.

Lincoln Depot, Monroe St. between 9th and 10th Sts., phone (217) 544-8695. Now restored, this is the depot where Lincoln gave his farewell address when he departed for Washington on February 11, 1861. Exhibit area and audiovisual presentation. Open daily from June through August.

Daughters of Union Veterans National Headquarters, 503 South Walnut St., phone (217) 544-0616. Collection of Civil War documents and relics. Open Tuesday and Thursday, and by appointment.

Just two blocks from Lincoln's home is the hundred-year-old *Mischler House* (718 South 8th St., Springfield, IL 62703; phone [217] 523-3714), a bed-and-breakfast comfortably furnished with antiques. *Baur's* (620 South First St., phone [217] 789-4311), a short walk from the capitol, is where knowledgeable legislators go to dine. Many antiques.

A FAMILY AFFAIR

Abraham Lincoln had four brothers-in-law in the Confederate army, and three of his sisters-in-law were married to Confederate officers.

Vandalia Statehouse State Historic Site, 315 West Gallatin St., phone (618) 283-1161. This two-story 1836 Greek Revival building was the state capitol when Lincoln and Stephen Douglas served in the House of Representatives. Contains many antiques and furnishings of the period. Guided tours are available. Open daily except major holidays.

Little Brick House Museum, 621 Saint Clair St., phone (618) 283-0024. Lincoln memorabilia here include photographs, portraits, statues, speeches, and letters. Open daily from June through August, other times by appointment.

INDIANA

Corydon Civil War Battle Site, IN 135 South (Business), phone (812) 738-4865. On July 9, 1863, a Confederate raiding party under Gen. John Hunt Morgan occupied the town briefly and held the home guard captive, the only battle fought on Indiana soil during the war.

Overnight accommodations are available at the Victorian *Kintner House* bed-and-breakfast (101 South Capitol Ave. at Chestnut, Corydon, IN 47933; phone [812] 738-2020), a good base for exploring Corydon's historic district. There is no smoking on the premises.

Lincoln Boyhood National Memorial

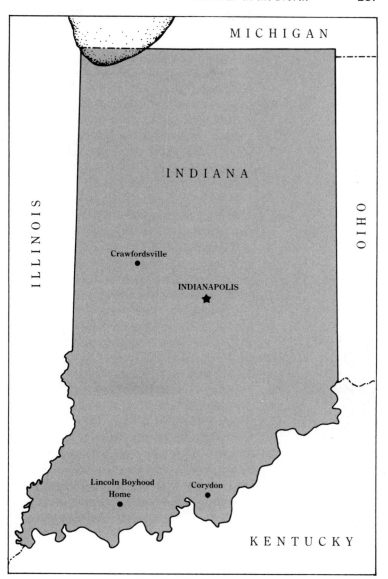

CRAWFORDSVILLE

General Lew Wallace Study, East Pike St. and Wallace Ave., phone (317) 362-5769. Now a city museum, this 1898 house contains the war relics and personal items of the general, diplomat, painter, and author of *Ben Hur.* Open Tuesday through Sunday, early April through October.

LINCOLN BOYHOOD NATIONAL MEMORIAL

Abraham Lincoln spent his boyhood years (1816–1830) here, reading, clerking at James Gentry's store, and helping on the family farm. Lincoln's mother, Nancy Hanks Lincoln, died of milk sickness on October 5, 1818, at the age of thirty-four, and is buried here. When Lincoln was twenty-one, the family moved to Illinois. The *Memorial Visitor Center,* constructed of Indiana limestone and sandstone, contains the *Abraham Lincoln Hall,* a museum, and a bookstore. A film is shown of Lincoln's years in Indiana. On the original Thomas Lincoln tract is the *Lincoln Living Historical Farm,* with a furnished log cabin similar to the original, a smokehouse, a stable, a chicken house, and a workshop. The fields are planted with crops of the period. Nightly, except Mondays, from mid-July through early September, a musical called *Young Abe Lincoln* is presented in a nearby covered amphitheater. All facilities are wheelchair accessible. The center is open daily except major holidays, the farm from mid-April through October. Visitor Center, phone (812) 937-4541; theater, phone (812) 937-4493. The complex is four miles west of the town of Santa Claus on IN 162.

The only motel nearby is *Stone's* (RR1, Dale, 47523; two miles south off I-64, exit 57, phone [812] 937-4448), with thirty-three units and a café.

MARYLAND

ANTIETAM

ANTIETAM NATIONAL BATTLEFIELD
SHARPSBURG

Robert E. Lee's first attempt to carry the war into the North ended in failure in rolling Maryland farm country near the village of Sharpsburg. His 40,000-man Army of Northern Virginia clashed savagely with Gen. George B. McClellan's Army of the Potomac, 87,000 strong, on September 17, 1862, the bloodiest day in American history. The Union lost 12,410 men, the Confederacy 10,700. Lee's defeat probably cost the South diplomatic recognition by Great Britain. McClellan's victory gave President Lincoln the opportunity to issue the Emancipation Proclamation.

After his great victory at Manassas in August 1862, Lee boldly marched his army into Maryland. Lee and President Davis had several objectives: Lee badly needed men and supplies, and hoped to find them among Southern sympathizers in the border state; a victory on Northern soil might persuade Great Britain to recognize the Confederacy, and would strengthen the Peace Party in the North, which wanted to end the war.

Near Frederick, Maryland, Lee had an extraordinary stroke of bad luck. An officer lost a copy of Lee's battle plan, Special Order No. 191, which had been wrapped around some cigars. It was brought to McClellan, who said, "If I cannot whip Bobbie Lee, I will be willing to go home."

After leaving Frederick, the Confederate army marched westward twelve miles to the passes of South Mountain. Lee dispatched Stonewall Jackson to capture Harpers Ferry. Without Jackson's forces, Lee could only delay the Union troops coming through Turner's, Fox's, and Crampton's gaps.

McClellan forced his way through, and by the afternoon of September 15, both armies had established battle lines west and east of Antietam Creek, near Sharpsburg. McClellan lost the opportunity to strike Lee while Jackson was away. Harpers Ferry surrendered that day, and Jackson reached Sharpsburg on September 16. Lee consolidated his position along the low ridge that runs north and south of the village.

At dawn on September 17, Gen. Joseph Hooker's artillery began a murderous fire on Jackson's troops in the Miller cornfield, north of town. "In the time I am writing," reported Hooker, "every stalk of corn in the northern and greater part of the field was cut as closely as could have been done with a knife, and the slain lay in rows precisely as they had stood in their ranks a moment before."

Hooker's troops advanced, driving the Confederates before them. Jackson reported to Lee that his men were "exposed for near an hour to a terrific storm of shell, canister, and musketry."

Jackson was reinforced, and was able to drive back the Union troops. An hour later, Union troops under Gen. Joseph Mansfield counterattacked, and by nine o'clock they had regained some of the lost ground. In an effort to extricate some of Mansfield's troops from their isolated position near the Dunker Church, Gen. John Sedgwick's division of Edwin V. Sumner's corps advanced into the West Woods. Confederate troops were waiting, and hit Sedgwick on both sides. The casualties were appalling.

LAST BUT NOT LEAST

The last Union veteran, Albert Woolson, died in 1958; the last Confederate veteran, Walter Williams, died in 1959 at the age of 117.

Another division of Sumner's corps, commanded by Gen. William H. French, moved up to support, but for some reason veered south into Gen. D. H. Hill's Confederate troops. They were posted along an old sunken road that separated the Roulette and Piper farms.

Fighting raged for nearly four hours at the sunken road, which would be remembered as Bloody Lane. French, supported by Gen. Israel B. Richardson's division, tried to drive back the Confederates. The battle here became increasingly confusing, and ended when both sides were too exhausted to fight anymore.

Southeast of Sharpsburg, Gen. Ambrose E. Burnside had been trying all morning to get across Antietam Creek. The creek was fordable in several places, but Burnside insisted on sending his men across a stone bridge. Some 400 Georgians on the other side drove them back time after time.

At about one in the afternoon, Burnside finally crossed the bridge, now known as the Burnside Bridge. He spent two hours re-forming the lines of his troops before advancing up the slope toward the battlefield. By late afternoon, Burnside had driven the Georgians back almost to the village. This threatened to cut off the line of retreat for Lee's embattled Confederates.

Lee was saved by Gen. A. P. Hill's division, which had been left behind at Harpers Ferry by Jackson to salvage the captured Union property. After a forced march, Hill arrived about four o'clock and immediately sent his troops into battle. Burnside's troops were driven back to the heights near the stone bridge. The Battle of Antietam was over.

The next day, Lee began withdrawing his army south across the Potomac. McClellan made no attempt to stop him, a decision

Robert E. Lee's first invasion of the North ended tragically at Antietam on September 17, 1862, the bloodiest day in American history. Among the more than 23,000 men who fell were these soldiers of Stonewall Jackson's brigade, slain attempting to rally before General Hooker's ferocious charge along the Hagerstown Pike, 500 yards north of Dunker Church. The Union victory enabled Lincoln to issue the Emancipation Proclamation.

Lincoln came to visit the Antietam battlefield and confer with General McClellan. Alexander Gardner photographed the six-foot-four President towering over the diminutive general at Fifth Corps headquarters. Corps commander Fitz John Porter, hand on sword, is to the right of the President. Lincoln was disappointed: Although the invasion of the North had been repulsed, McClellan had allowed Lee's army to return unhindered to Virginia.

that soon would cost him command of the Army of the Potomac. Five days after the battle, Lincoln issued the Emancipation Proclamation, declaring free all slaves in states still in rebellion against the United States. Now the war had a dual purpose: to preserve the Union and to end slavery.

VISITING ANTIETAM

Antietam National Battlefield lies north and east of Sharpsburg along MD 34 and 65, and both routes intersect either U.S. 40 or 40A and I-70. The Visitor Center, north of Sharpsburg on MD 65, is open daily except Thanksgiving, Christmas, and New Year's Day. The center has a museum and offers an audiovisual orientation program, hourly on the hour, and a slide presentation every half hour. Musket and cannon demonstrations and historical talks are given regularly

from May through September. A schedule of activities is posted in the center. All center activities and most tour-route exhibits are accessible to the disabled. There is no restaurant on the battlefield, but several are in Sharpsburg. There are interpretive markers at *Turner's, Fox's,* and *Crampton's* gaps, scenes of preliminary fighting, and at the *Shepherdstown Ford* in West Virginia, where Lee's army recrossed the Potomac. For further information, write to the Superintendent, Box 158, Sharpsburg, MD 21782, or phone (301) 432-5124.

The battle of Antietam was fought over an area of twelve square miles. It consisted of three basic phases—morning, midday, and afternoon. During the morning phase, three piecemeal Union attacks drove back Jackson's line but did not break it. The midday phase saw two Union divisions break D. H. Hill's line in the sunken road, but

McClellan's failure to follow up cost him the advantage that had been gained. In the afternoon phase, Burnside's slow pincer movement beyond the lower bridge was broken by the timely arrival of A. P. Hill. The self-guided driving tour is arranged according to the sequence of the battle:

MORNING PHASE (6 A.M.–9 A.M.)

Dunker Church. This was the focal point of repeated clashes, as both armies sought to occupy and hold the high ground around it. Leveled by a storm in 1921, the church was rebuilt in 1962.

North Woods. Union General Hooker launched the initial attack from this point. The attack was stopped by Jackson's troops in the Miller cornfield, a half-mile to the south.

East Woods. Union General Joseph Mansfield was fatally wounded here as he led his Twelfth Corps into battle.

The Cornfield. More fighting took place here in the Miller cornfield than anywhere else at Antietam. The battle lines swept back and forth across the field for three hours.

West Woods. Union General John Sedgwick's division lost more than 2,200 men in less than half an hour in an ill-fated charge into these woods against Jackson's troops.

Mumma Farm. Burned by the Confederates to prevent their use by Union sharpshooters, the Mumma farm buildings were the only civilian property purposely destroyed during the battle.

After the Battle of Antietam, soldiers and wagons cross the stone bridge, later named the Burnside Bridge. Confederate snipers kept General Burnside's troops from crossing this bridge for three critical hours during the battle, a delay that allowed Lee to reinforce his threatened line. Burnside apparently was unaware that Antietam Creek was easily fordable above and below the bridge. Burnside was one of several generals who ineptly led the Army of the Potomac.

*Burnside Bridge,
Antietam*

MIDDAY PHASE (9:30 A.M.–1 P.M.)

Roulette Farm. Union troops under Generals French and Richardson crossed these fields on their way to meet the Confederates posted in the sunken road.

Sunken Road (Bloody Lane). For nearly four hours, Union and Confederate infantry contested this sunken country road, resulting in more than 5,000 casualties.

AFTERNOON PHASE (1 P.M.–5:30 P.M.)

Lower Bridge (Burnside Bridge). The fighting here was a key factor in McClellan's failure at Antietam. Called Burnside Bridge after the Union general whose troops were held off most of the day by a few hundred Georgia riflemen, it is the battlefield's best-known landmark.

The Final Attack. After taking the Lower Bridge and re-forming his corps, Burnside marched his men across these hills toward Sharpsburg, threatening to cut off Lee's line of retreat. Just as the Union troops reached this area, A. P. Hill's Confederate division arrived from Harpers Ferry and drove them back.

Antietam National Cemetery. The remains of 4,776 Union soldiers, including 1,836 who are unknown, are buried in this hilltop cemetery near the village. Most of the Confederate dead are buried in Hagerstown and Frederick, Maryland; in Shepherdstown, West Virginia; and in local church and family cemeteries.

There are two excellent inns in Sharpsburg. *Piper House Inn* (Write Doug and Paula Reed, Rte. 65, MD 21782, phone [301] 797-1862) is a restored farmhouse on the battlefield near Bloody Lane. The inn was Longstreet's headquarters during the battle. It has four guest rooms, each with private baths, and serves a continental breakfast. *The Inn at Antietam* (Write Mrs. Betty Fairbourne, 220 East Main St., MD 21782, phone [301] 432-6601) is a restored Victorian mansion next to the National Cemetery, also serves a continental breakfast. Other accommodations are available in Frederick, about twenty miles west of Sharpsburg.

MONOCACY

MONOCACY NATIONAL BATTLEFIELD FREDERICK

Gen. Jubal Early's bold attempt to capture Washington was thwarted at the Battle of Monocacy, fought just south of Frederick, Maryland, on July 9, 1864, by green troops commanded by Generals Lewis Wallace and James B. Ricketts. General Early won the battle, but it cost him a day's march and gave reinforcements time to arrive at the capital's defenses. Early was thrown back at Fort Stevens in the District of Columbia, and retreated to Virginia, ending the last Confederate campaign to carry the war to the North.

The attack on Washington was part of a plan to divert Union forces away from Lee's army at Petersburg. Pushing northward through the Shenandoah Valley, Early arrived at Winchester on July 2 with 18,000 men. He plundered stores at Harpers Ferry, then crossed into Maryland at Sharpsburg, near the site of the Battle of Antietam two years earlier. Confederate cavalry collected $20,000 for the promise not to burn Hagerstown. Early himself received $200,000 to spare Frederick.

Responding to Early's movement, General Grant dispatched a division under Ricketts on July 6, followed by a full corps under H. G. Wright a few days later. But the only Union troops near Early were Wallace's ragtag group of 2,300 in Baltimore. Unsure whether Early would attack Washington or Baltimore, Wallace marched, determined to delay Early until reinforcements arrived.

The logical place to stop Early was Frederick Junction (also called Monocacy Junction), three miles southeast of Frederick. The Georgetown Pike to Washington, the National Road to Baltimore, and the Baltimore & Ohio Railroad, all crossed the Monocacy River there. Wallace needed to stretch his forces over six miles of river-front to protect both turnpike bridges, the railroad bridge, and several fords. Shortly after he arrived, Wallace learned that Ricketts's troops were on their way by rail from Baltimore. The combined forces were dug in on July 9.

One Confederate division encountered Wallace's troops on the Georgetown Pike, another clashed with Ricketts on the National Road. Early decided not to attack frontally, and crossed the river at the McKinney-Worthington Ford to attack Wallace's left flank. Fierce fighting broke out when Early confronted Ricketts's troops at a fence separating the Worthington and Thomas farms. A three-pronged Confederate attack pushed Ricketts back toward the National Road, where he was joined by Wallace.

By late afternoon the Union troops were retreating toward Baltimore, leaving behind 1,600 dead, wounded, and captured. The battle cost Early a day lost and 1,300 killed

Lewis Wallace

and wounded. The next day the Confederates started to march to Fort Stevens in the District of Columbia, only to find Wright's corps arriving there. That night, Wright pushed Early back. The next morning, Early withdrew across the Potomac at White's Ford.

Reporting on the campaign, General Early wrote, "Some of the Northern papers stated that . . . I could have entered the city; but on Saturday I was fighting at Monocacy, thirty-five miles from Washington, a force which I could not leave in my rear; and after disposing of that force and moving as rapidly as it was possible for me to move, I did not arrive in front of the fortifications until after noon on Monday, and then my troops were exhausted."

General Grant later wrote, "General Wallace contributed on this occasion, by the defeat of the troops under him, a greater benefit to the cause than often falls to the lot of a commander of an equal force to render by means of a victory."

Wallace gave orders to collect the bodies of the dead in a burial ground on the Monocacy battlefield, where he proposed a monument that would read: "These men died to save the National Capital, and they did save it."

Visiting Monocacy

The National Park Service is in the process of completing the acquisition of 1,670 acres within the boundaries of Monocacy National Park. As of this writing, the battlefield has no visitor center.

To reach the battlefield from Frederick, take MD 355 south, watching for battlefield monuments along the way. Just beyond the railroad overpass, turn left on a short road to the tracks. A small, two-story house marks the spot where a large blockhouse, burned during the battle, guarded the approaches to the river.

This point was the scene of the main bat-

tle activity. A monument to the New Jersey 14th Regiment is a short distance along the access road. Back on MD 355, continue south, crossing the Monocacy River. Araby Road, on the right, is roughly the route that Union forces took in retreat. Monuments here pay tribute to the Pennsylvania and Vermont troops. The battlefield can be toured in less than an hour.

For further information, write to the Superintendent, Antietam and Monocacy National Battlefields, P.O. Box 158, Sharpsburg, MD 21782, or phone (301) 432-5124.

Visiting Frederick

During the war, Frederick was a focal point for strategic operations by both sides. During the first Confederate invasion of the North, attacks were made at nearby South Mountain and Sharpsburg. Wounded men by the thousands were cared for in Frederick. Troop movements passed through here throughout the war, and cavalry skirmishes took place in the streets. The town paid a $200,000 ransom to Gen. Early before he fought the Battle of Monocacy a few miles to the south. A thirty-three-acre area has been designated a Historic District.

Walking tours of Frederick begin at the Visitor Center (19 East Church St., phone [301] 663-8703) operated by the Tourism Council of Frederick County. Visitors also may take a nostalgic, horse-drawn tour of the historic district conducted daily from April through December by *Frederick Carriage & Livery*, phone (301) 695-7433. Sites of Civil War interest include the following:

Barbara Fritchie House and Museum, 154 West Patrick St., phone (301) 663-3833. Mrs. Fritchie reportedly spoke her mind to Stonewall Jackson and his "rebel hordes," in an incident memorialized in a poem by John Greenleaf Whittier. On display at her home is clothing made by

Miss Fritchie, as well as her rocker and Bible, the bed in which she died, and other items of interest. Open daily except Tuesday; closed during the winter.

Roger Brooke Taney Home, 123 South Bentz St., phone (301) 663-8703. Taney was Chief Justice of the Supreme Court from 1835 to 1864, and swore in seven Presidents, including Lincoln. He is perhaps best remembered for issuing the Dred Scott Decision. The 1799 house also includes the Francis Scott Key Museum. Taney is buried in the cemetery of St. John's Catholic Church at East Third and East streets. The house is open by appointment only.

Evangelical Reformed Church, West Church St. near New Market St., phone (301) 662-2762. Before the Battle of Antietam, Stonewall Jackson slept through a pro-Union sermon here. Barbara Fritchie was a member of the congregation.

Mount Olivet Cemetery, south end of Market St. The last resting place of Barbara Fritchie and Francis Scott Key.

Historical Society of Frederick County Museum, 24 East Church St. A collection of interesting material relating to the town's role in the war. Open Thursday to Saturday from March to Christmas, Thursday and Friday the rest of the year.

Spring Bank (7945 Worman's Mill Rd., Frederick, MD 21701; phone [301] 694-0440) is a bed-and-breakfast in the 1880 home of a gentleman farmer. Now on the National Register of Historic Places, it is on ten acres, three miles north of the historical district. Excellent restaurants are nearby.

Five miles south of Frederick on MD 85 is the *Inn at Buckeystown,* 3521 Buckeystown Pike, Buckeystown, MD 21717, phone (301) 874-5755. This is a restored Victorian house with a full restaurant.

Barbara Fritchie House and Museum, Frederick, Maryland

OTHER MARYLAND SITES OF INTEREST

ABERDEEN

U.S. Army Ordnance Museum, Aberdeen Proving Grounds, phone (301) 278-3602. Broad collection of ordnance used in America's wars. Open daily except Monday and holidays.

ANNAPOLIS

U.S. Naval Academy. The Naval Academy Museum has an excellent collection of material relating to the navy's role in the Civil War. Open daily. Just inside Gate No.

3 entrance, on Hanover St. near Maryland Ave., phone (301) 233-6933.

BOONSBORO (WASHINGTON COUNTY)

Washington Monument State Park, three miles southeast of Boonsboro off U.S. 40A, phone (301) 293-2420. The History Center displays Civil War mementos and firearms, daily by appointment.

Gathland State Park, eight miles south of Boonsboro off MD 67, then one mile east, phone (301) 293-2420. A monument erected in 1986 to honor Civil War correspondents stands on a site once owned by George Townsend, a Civil War reporter. The Visitor Center at the park contains original Civil War papers. Open daily.

At Fort Corcoran in Washington, D.C., a chaplain conducts mass for the 69th New York State Militia, a unit composed largely of Irish immigrants. The youthfulness of the armies was astonishing: Of the 2,300,000 men in the Union Army, 70 percent were under the age of 23. Some 100,000 were 16; another 100,000 were fifteen. Some 300 were 13 or less, and the records show that there were 25 under the age of 10.

NEW YORK

AUBURN

Seward House, 33 South St., phone (315) 252-1283. The home of William Henry Seward, governor of New York, U.S. senator, Secretary of State under Presidents Lincoln and Johnson, and the man responsible for the purchase of Alaska. Original furnishings, Civil War mementos, Lincoln letters. Open Tuesday through Saturday, April through December except holidays.

Harriet Tubman Home, 180 South St., phone (315) 253-2621. Born into slavery, Harriet Tubman escaped in 1849 and rescued more than 300 slaves on the Underground Railroad. During the war, Miss Tubman assisted the Union army. Open by appointment only.

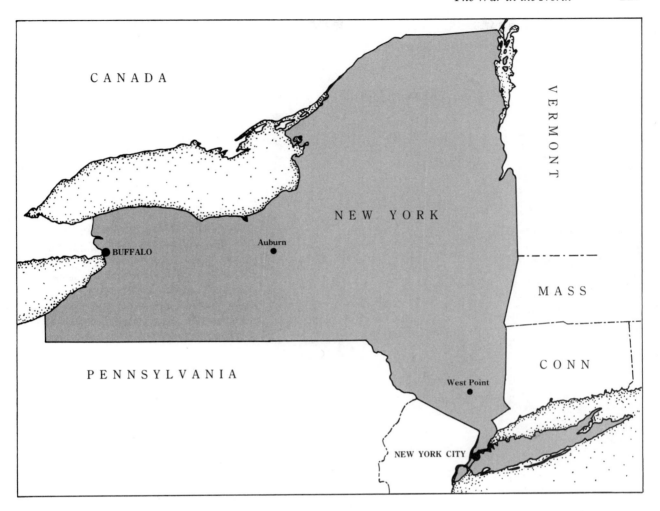

The *Springside Inn* (41 West Lake Rd., P.O. Box 327, Auburn NY 13021; phone [315] 252-7247), built in 1830 on Owasco Lake, has eight guest rooms, a popular restaurant, and a summer dinner theater. Located five miles south of Auburn on NY 38.

NEW YORK CITY

General Grant National Memorial, Riverside Drive and West 122nd St., phone (212) 666-1640. Ulysses S. Grant and his wife are buried here. Open Wednesday through Sunday except major holidays.

WEST POINT

U.S. Military Academy Museum, Cullum Road, off NY 218, on the west side of the Hudson River, north of New York City. The museum behind the Visitor Center at South Gate, has an excellent Civil War collection. Open daily except Christmas and New Year's Day.

Battle Monument, Thayer and Washington roads. A single column, inscribed with the names of 2,230 soldiers, arranged by regiment, honors the officers killed in the Civil War.

Grant's Tomb, New York City, New York

Overlooking the Hudson River inside the South Gate, the *Hotel Thayer* (Thayer Rd., West Point, NY 10996; [914] 446-4731) is popular with visitors to the academy. A lower-priced motel, *West Point* (361 Main St., Highland Falls, phone [914] 446-4180) is a half-mile south on NY 21B, just off NY 9W. The motel has a café.

OHIO

LANCASTER

Sherman House Museum, 137 East Main St., phone (614) 654-9923. Gen. William Tecumseh Sherman was born in this 1811 house, as was his descendant, Senator John Sherman, who sponsored the Sherman Anti-Trust Act. The Civil War museum is accessible to the disabled. Open Tuesday through Sunday, March through December. Closed most holidays.

R.J. Pitcher's Inn (123 North Broad St., OH 43130, phone [614] 653-5522) is a good value for the traveler, and so is the restaurant in the inn, which specializes in pasta and prime rib.

PENNSYLVANIA

GETTYSBURG

GETTYSBURG NATIONAL MILITARY PARK

The high water mark of the Confederacy came on July 3, 1863, the third day of this awesome battle. In a last-ditch attempt to throw the Union army off Cemetery Ridge. Gen. George E. Pickett led some 12,000 troops across an open field toward the center of the Union line, but only one in three returned. Robert E. Lee's final attempt to take the war to the North had failed.

A month before, fresh from its dramatic victory at Chancellorsville, Lee's Army of Northern Virginia marched westward from Fredericksburg, Virginia, through the gaps of the Blue Ridge Mountains, and north into Maryland and Pennsylvania. Gen. Joseph Hooker followed with the Army of the Potomac, but was replaced by George Meade before making contact with the enemy.

Lee, however, didn't know where the Union army was, because his "eyes," Jeb Stuart's cavalry, were off on a brash raid around the Union forces.

The two armies met by chance at Gettysburg on June 30. Some of Lee's troops had come into the small town in the hope of finding a supply of shoes, and encountered a Union patrol. The main battle opened on July 1, when Confederates attacked the troops on McPherson Ridge, west of town. The Union troops held until the afternoon, but were overpowered and driven back to Cemetery Hill. They dug in during the night as the rest of the Union army arrived and took up positions.

On July 2 the battle lines were drawn up in two sweeping arcs. The main bodies of both armies were nearly a mile apart on parallel ridges, the Union forces on Cemetery Ridge, the Confederates on Seminary ridge.

The first day of fighting at Gettysburg left a field at the Rose Farm scattered with the bodies of troops from Sickles's 3rd Corps, their shoes lost to scavenging Confederate soldiers. Ironically, the epic battle began with a search for supplies for Lee's tatterdemalion troops. One of A. P. Hill's divisions heard of a supply of shoes in Gettysburg, and Hill authorized that division to go there on July 1 to "get those shoes."

George Pickett's fresh division and six brigades, nearly 15,000 troops, attack the center of the Union line in a futile attempt to win the Battle of Gettysburg, July 3, 1863. A Union soldier said he saw "an overwhelming resistless tide of an ocean of armed men sweeping upon us." Later Robert E. Lee rode among the survivors saying, "It was all my fault."

Lee ordered an attack on both Union flanks. Gen. James Longstreet's thrust on the Union left turned the base of the hill called Little Round Top into a shambles, left the Wheat Field littered with dead and wounded, and overran the Peach Orchard. Farther north, Gen. Richard S. Ewell's evening attack on the Union right at East Cemetery Hill and Culp's Hill was briefly successful, but he couldn't follow through to advantage. At the end of the day, a Union officer summed up the Union situation to General Meade, saying, "They have hammered us into a solid position they cannot whip us out of."

On July 3, Lee's artillery opened a two-hour bombardment of the Union lines on Cemetery Ridge and Cemetery Hill. Union cannon responded, and a duel for supremacy on the battlefield raged. The Union defensive remained intact. In a desperate attempt to recapture the success of the day before, Pickett made his fateful charge against the Union center. When it was thrown back, the Battle of Gettysburg was over. In three days the armies had suffered a total of 51,000 casualties.

It was a black day for the South. As Lee licked his wounds, Grant was accepting the surrender of Vicksburg. The North now controlled the Mississippi River, splitting the Confederacy in two. Lee's army staggered back into Virginia, physically and spiritually exhausted. He would never again mount a comparable offensive. Meade was criticized for not pursuing Lee, but is remembered as the general who defeated Lee when it counted most.

VISITING GETTYSBURG

Gettysburg National Military Park is located on 3,850 acres on the southern edge of town, and more than thirty-five miles of road run through it. On the battlefield are 1,300 monuments, markers, and tablets of granite, marble, and bronze, and 400 cannon. The Visitor Center, located between the Emmitsburg and Taneytown roads, has orientation displays, exhibits, and the "electric map" presentation that shows, through the use of colored lights, troop movements during the battle. The center is accessible to the disabled. Although there is no food sold at the center, picnicking is permitted at designated areas in the park. A schedule of special events is posted at the center. Also at the center is a representative of the Gettysburg Travel Council who can provide information about accommodations, restaurants, campgrounds, museums, and other facilities in the area. For additional information, write to the Superintendent, Gettysburg National Military Park, Gettysburg, PA 17325, or phone (717) 334-1124.

Across the parking lot is the *Cyclorama Center,* which has exhibits, including Lincoln's original Gettysburg Address, and a ten-minute film, "From These Honored Dead." The Gettysburg Cyclorama, a spectacular 356-foot-long painting by Paul Philippoteaux of Pickett's Charge, is displayed with a sound-and-light program inside a large circular auditorium. Both the film and

HOPE AND GLORY

The man who led the charge at Gettysburg, General George E. Pickett, sought glory all his military career. In the Mexican War he distinguished himself by his headlong bravery. He was wounded leading a charge at Gaines' Mill. At Gettysburg his division was chosen to lead the attack on Cemetery Ridge. He told his men, "Charge the enemy and remember old Virginia!" Pickett himself did not charge; he and his aides watched the battle from a nearby farm. Less than half of Pickett's division returned from the ridge. Among the casualties were all of his regimental commanders and sixteen of the seventeen field officers under them. Lee subsequently ordered Pickett to prepare his division to repel a Union counterattack. "General Lee," Pickett replied, "I have no division now." For the rest of his life, Pickett blamed Lee for the disastrous charge. Five years after the war, Pickett and John Mosby, the Confederate guerrilla leader, visited Lee. Later, Pickett bitterly told Mosby, "That old man had my division slaughtered at Gettysburg." Mosby considered that for a moment before replying. "Well," said Mosby, "it made you immortal."

Three lean, battle-hardened prisoners are photographed after the Battle of Gettysburg. In Lee's army in 1863, a month's worth of rations consisted of less than a pound of bacon, 18 ounces of flour, 10 pounds of rice, and a small amount of peas and dried fruit. Lee hoped to capture food supplies in his northern invasion.

"WE HAD THEM WITHIN OUR GRASP. WE HAD ONLY TO STRETCH FORTH OUR HANDS AND THEY WERE OURS. AND NOTHING I COULD SAY OR DO COULD MAKE THE ARMY MOVE."

—ABRAHAM LINCOLN, *on the failure to pursue Lee's army after the Battle of Gettysburg, 1863*

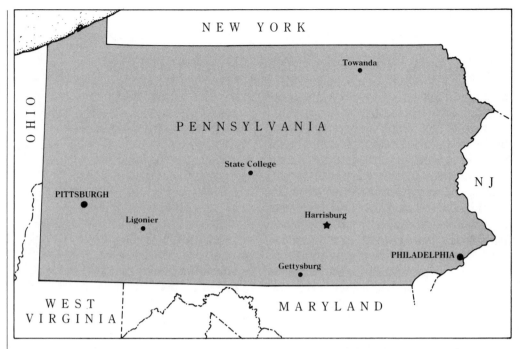

the Cyclorama program are presented regularly.

Most visitors take a self-guided tour of the battlefield. Licensed battlefield guides also conduct auto tours. A leisurely drive around the battlefield will take about three hours, including stops at the following sites:

High Water Mark. Here at the Copse of Trees and the Angle, Pickett's charge was halted on July 3. This was the climax of the battle.

Pennsylvania Memorial. On a field noted for its monuments, this one is outstanding. Statues of officers and bronze name plates call the roll of nearly 35,000 Pennsylvanians who fought here.

Little Round Top. Quick action by Meade's chief engineer, Gen. Gouverneur Warren, alerted Union commanders to the impending Confederate attack on July 2 and foiled Southern hopes for early victory.

Devil's Den. Longstreet's July 2 attack cleared Union troops from these boulders. Confederate sharpshooters, one of whose barricades can still be seen, fired on Little Round Top from here.

The Wheat Field. Clash after clash of troops on July 2 left these fields soaked with blood without giving either side a significant gain.

The Peach Orchard. On July 2, General Sickles's Union salient extended from Devil's Den to here, then angled northward on the Emmitsburg Road. From this high ground, Union batteries bombarded Confederates to the south and west before Longstreet's attack shattered their line.

Pitzer Woods. After a skirmish at noon on July 2, the Confederates occupied these woods. Four hours later they attacked and

PICKETT'S CHARGE

Only fifteen of the forty-six regiments that made the famous charge at Gettysburg were actually commanded by General Pickett, and of those, thirteen were led by Virginia Military School graduates, only two of whom survived the charge.

smashed Sickles's line along the road one-third of a mile to the east.

Virginia Memorial. General Lee watched the gallant charge of July 3 from here. When it failed, he rode forward to the fields in front of this spot and rallied his men.

North Carolina Memorial. Along and in front of this ridge, Lee marshaled his forces, among them thousands of North Carolinians, for the supreme effort on July 3.

McPherson Ridge. Just beyond McPherson's barn, the Battle of Gettysburg began early on July 1. Gen. John F. Reynolds, whose Union infantry held this line, was killed in the woods to the left.

Eternal Light Peace Memorial. This memorial was dedicated in 1938, on the seventy-fifth anniversary of the battle, to "Peace Eternal in a Nation United." The arrival of Gen. Robert Rodes's Confederate division on this hill at one in the afternoon of July 1 threatened Federal forces west and north of Gettysburg.

Oak Ridge. Union troops here held stubbornly against Rodes's advance from Oak Hill to the north on July 1.

Barlow Knoll. When Jubal Early's Confederates smashed Union defenders here on the afternoon of July 1, the Union line north of Gettysburg collapsed.

From Barlow Knoll, take U.S. 15 toward Gettysburg to the point where it curves right. Just past the curve, turn left on Stratton Street. Continue to East Middle Street, then turn left and drive east one block to East Confederate Avenue (Liberty Street), turn right, and proceed to Culp's Hill View.

Culp's Hill View. At dusk on July 2, Gen. Edward Johnson's Confederates unsuccessfully attacked Union troops on Culp's Hill ahead of this stop, advancing over the fields to the left.

Spangler's Spring. Though repulsed at Culp's Hill, the Confederates seized this spring and the Union earthworks to the north, only to lose them the next morning.

Cemetery Hill. Here Union troops rallied late on July 1. The next evening they repelled a Confederate assault that reached the crest of the hill east of this road.

National Cemetery. When the armies marched away, they left behind more than 51,000 casualties. The wounded and dying were crowded into nearly every building in

Pennsylvania Monument, Gettysburg

town. Most of the dead lay in hasty and inadequate graves, and some had not been buried at all.

The governor of Pennsylvania commissioned a local attorney, David Wills, to purchase land for a proper burial ground for the Union dead. Within four months of the battle, reinterment began on seventeen acres that later became Gettysburg National Cemetery. At the dedication, on November 19, 1863, the principal speaker, Edward Everett, delivered a two-hour oration rich in historical detail and classical allusion. Then spoke President Lincoln, whose two-minute address transformed Gettysburg from a scene of carnage into a symbol, giving meaning to the sacrifice of the dead and inspiring the living.

Soldiers' National Monument, commemorating the Union dead who fell at Gettysburg, stands near the spot where President Lincoln delivered his Gettysburg Address.

More than 3,700 Union soldiers killed at Gettysburg are buried here. Deceased vet-

erans of other wars, including Vietnam, now bring the total to more than 7,000.

East Cavalry Battlefield Site also may be visited by driving three miles east of Gettysburg on PA 116. Here Union cavalry under Gen. D. M. Gregg intercepted and defeated Jeb Stuart's cavalry.

Perhaps the best way to tour the battlefield is on foot, as tens of thousands of soldiers once did. There are three walking tours to choose from:

High Water Mark Trail, about a mile long, begins at the Cyclorama Center. Along the way are regimental monuments, part of an artillery battery, the land that was defended by Union soldiers in repulsing Pickett's charge, and General Meade's headquarters.

Big Round Top Loop Trail, also a mile long, begins at Tour Stop 3 and reveals something of the plants, animals, and rocks of the hardwood forest. Along the way are stone breastworks built by the armies. Allow about an hour.

For a much longer hike, inquire at the

Spectators crowd Lincoln as he delivers his address at the dedication of the military cemetery at Gettysburg, November 19, 1863. Edward Everett, the noted orator, spoke for two hours before Lincoln made the "few appropriate remarks" requested. In just ten sentences, he unforgettably captured the bravery and sacrifice of the men who had died in the pivotal battle.

B-4975

center about the nine-mile *Billy Yank Trail* or the 3.5-mile *Johnny Reb Trail,* both used by the Boy Scouts as part of their Heritage Trails Programs.

In addition, there are paths to *Devil's Den* and to the *Point of Woods* near the Virginia Memorial where Lee spoke to his defeated men, and a self-guided tour through the *National Cemetery.*

IN AND AROUND GETTYSBURG

An excellent way to see the historic sights in the town of Gettysburg is to take a walking tour. Begin at the *Western Maryland Railroad Passenger Depot* (35 Carlisle St.), which now houses the Gettysburg Travel Council Office (phone [717] 334-6274). The exterior of the depot looks the same today as it did on November 18, 1863, when President Lincoln arrived to deliver his address the next day at the dedication of the National Cemetery.

Head south to *Lincoln Square* along Carlisle Square, which was clogged with troops of the 11th Corps marching to the northern sector on the first day of the battle. Later in the day, the Confederates forced them back through the square, capturing the town and thousands of prisoners. Maj. C. W. McCreary of the first South Carolina Infantry signaled the capture by raising the Palmetto banner in the square. Four roads radiate out from the square in the center. All roads seem to lead to this spot, which is one reason the battle was fought here.

Continuing to the left around the square, you come to the *Willis House,* where Lincoln stayed overnight, completing the first draft and writing the entire second draft of the Gettysburg Address. The house tour includes the preserved Lincoln bedroom, a collection of Lincoln items, and an audiovisual display. In the house is a large plaque inscribed with the Gettysburg Address. Most of the buildings around the square were here at the time of the battle, and are so marked.

THE GETTYSBURG ADDRESS

Four score and seven years ago our fathers brought forth on this continent a new nation, conceived in liberty and dedicated to the proposition that all men are created equal.

Now we are engaged in a great civil war, testing whether that nation, or any nation so conceived and so dedicated, can long endure. We are met on a great battlefield of that war. We have come to dedicate a portion of that field, as a final resting place for those who here gave their lives that that nation might live. It is altogether fitting and proper that we should do this.

But in a larger sense, we cannot dedicate—we cannot consecrate—we cannot hallow—this ground. The brave men, living and dead, who struggled here, have consecrated it, far above our poor power to add or detract. The world will little note, nor long remember, what we say here, but it can never forget what they did here. It is for us, the living, rather to be here dedicated to the unfinished work which they who fought here have thus far so nobly advanced.

It is rather for us to be here dedicated to the great task remaining before us—that from these honored dead we take increased devotion to that cause for which they gave the last full measure of devotion—that we here highly resolve that these dead shall not have died in vain—that this nation, under God, shall have a new birth of freedom—and that government of the people, by the people, for the people, shall not perish from the earth.

Turn west on Chambersburg Street and continue a half-block to the *Christ Lutheran Church,* which served as a hospital during the battle. Thaddeus Stevens, violent abolitionist and Lincoln supporter, once lived in the house across the street. Three blocks farther along is a statue of a young Union soldier, representing the 26th Pennsylvania Emergency Infantry Regiment, which was hastily formed in part by students from Pennsylvania College and the Lutheran Theological Seminary. For several hours this raw regiment kept Gen. Jubal Early's troops from marching on Harrisburg.

Turn left on West Street, and left again a block later on West Middle Street. The street was the curved portion of the Confederate "fishhook" battle line during the second and third days of the battle. The block looks much the same as it did then.

Walk two blocks east to South Washington Street, then turn right and proceed one block to West High Street. Note the large brick building on the right at the intersection. At the second-floor level, a Whitworth cannon artillery bolt is embedded in the masonry. The building, now a private home, was the birthplace of both the Lutheran Theological Seminary and Pennsylvania (now Gettysburg) College. Farther along West High Street, both the *Saint Francis*

Gettysburg, Pennsylvania

Xavier Catholic Church and the *United Methodist Church* across the street served as military hospitals during the battle.

Continue east and cross Baltimore Street. At the intersection is the *Prince of Peace Episcopal Church,* built as a memorial to all the soldiers who fought here. On the other side of the street is the *United Presbyterian Church,* where Lincoln attended services. The pew in which he sat is marked, as is the pew used by President Eisenhower, who belonged to this church when he lived nearby.

Continuing on East High Street, you will come to the *Adams County Library,* which was the county jail at the time of the battle. Across the street is the *Gettysburg Public School Building,* built in 1857, where wounded from both sides were cared for. The *United Church of Christ (Trinity Reformed),* at the corner of East High and South Stratton streets, also was used as a hospital. The use of churches and schools as hospitals continued from July to October. The walls and floors had to be cleaned of bloodstains before they could be restored to their former use.

Turn left on South Stratton Street and cross East Middle Street one block to the north. The curved part of the Confederate "fishhook" battle line was one block east of here, running south toward Culp's Hill and Spangler's Spring.

A block to the north is the *Saint James Lutheran Church.* An earlier structure also was used as a military hospital. Jennie Wade, the only civilian casualty during the battle, was a member of the congregation. Near here, on North Stratton Street, the body of an unknown Union soldier was found after the battle. In his clenched hand was a photograph of his three children. The picture was widely disseminated until his widow in New York State identified the children and the body of Sgt. Amos Humiston. The incident caught the public imagination, and contributions flowed in. The money was used to establish a home for the orphans of Union soldiers who fought here.

Turn left on York Street and start back toward Lincoln Square. A stone house a quarter of the way on the right marks the site of *Samuel Gettys' Tavern,* owned by the father of James Gettys, the founder of Gettysburg. Farther along, the Gettysburg National Bank is on the site of the old *Globe Hotel.* During the battle, Confederates liberated all the whiskey from the hotel. As you approach the square, you will pass a building with a cannonball embedded under one of the second-floor windows.

Back at the square, you may wish to continue north on Carlisle and visit the campus of *Gettysburg College.* The large white brick building is called the *Old Dorm.* During the battle it served as an observation post for the Confederates on the first day of the battle and the Union on the second and third days.

Dayhoff's Carriages offers tours of historic Gettysburg by horse-drawn carriage, leaving from the parking area of the Dutch Cupboard Restaurant, 533 Baltimore St., daily from mid-June to October, weekends in April, May and October. Phone (717) 337-2276.

OTHER THINGS TO SEE AND DO IN GETTYSBURG

General Lee's Headquarters, 401 Buford Ave. This is the house in which Lee planned Confederate strategy for the battle. A collection of historical items is on display. Open daily, mid-March to mid-November.

Soldier's National Museum, 777 Baltimore St., at the Gettysburg Tour Center. Dioramas of major battles, the famous Charley Weaver Collection with sound accompaniment, and a display of war uniforms, arms, and other artifacts are here. The building was Gen. O. O. Howard's headquarters during the battle. Open daily, mid-March to November.

VETERAN'S DAY

John Burns was a seventy-two-year-old veteran of the War of 1812 when the armies came to his little hometown of Gettysburg. He got out his old rifle, put on a blue swallowtail coat and silk top hat, and set out to fight for the Union. He fought with the 150th Pennsylvania Volunteer Infantry, then with the famed Iron Brigade. Wounded three times, Burns returned home after the battle.

National Civil War Museum, 297 Steinwehr Ave. The entire story of the Battle of Gettysburg and the war era is presented in wax figures. Wheelchair accessible. A tape and player may be rented here for a self-guided auto tour of the battle area.

Lincoln Train Museum, a half-mile south of town via U.S. 15 on Steinwehr Ave. An audiovisual simulation of twenty miles of Lincoln's train trip to Gettysburg is featured, and a display of more than a thousand model trains and railroad memorabilia. Open daily, spring through fall.

"The Conflict," 213 Steinwehr Ave., phone (717) 334-8003. A three-screen, four-segment, multi-image program depicts the war, and a program about Gettysburg. Six projectors blend camera and artwork of the period with modern panoramic photography. The program is narrated by eleven voices. A military bookstore is on the premises. Open daily.

A. Lincoln's Place Theater, 777 Baltimore St., for reservations, phone (717) 334-6049. A forty-minute live portrayal of President Lincoln is presented here. Open daily, spring through fall.

Gettysburg Battle Theatre, 571 Steinwehr Ave. A miniature battlefield with 25,000 figures. A thirty-minute multimedia program shows the battle strategy. Open daily, March through November.

National Tower, one mile south of Gettysburg, off U.S. 97. Four observation decks, two of which are enclosed, on a 300-foot-high tower, permit a 360-degree view of the battlefield. There is also a twelve-minute sight-and-sound program, and displays. Picnicking is available on the grounds. Wheelchair accessible. Braille, and text for the deaf. Open daily, March to November.

Gettysburg abounds in antique shops, art galleries, and bookstores specializing in the war. There is a wider selection of wares here, vintage and reproduction, than anywhere else in the country. Three shops are particularly recommended:

American Print Gallery (219 Steinwehr Ave., phone [717] 334-6188) features a wide selection of limited edition prints, bronzes, and original oils by top historical artists.

The Horse Soldier (Old Gettysburg Village, 777 Baltimore St., phone [717] 334-0347) offers guns, swords, accoutrements, documents, vintage photographs, books, and genealogy research.

Sword & Saber (three miles south of town on Rte. 97, phone [717] 334-0205) specializes in original Confederate and Union paper, relics, and swords. The shop is in a building that once was the Shaffer Farm Hospital; General Sickles's leg was amputated here on July 2.

Visitors wishing to be photographed in Union or Confederate uniforms or vintage costumes may do so at *Old Time Photographs,* located in Old Gettysburg Village.

For those seeking to stay in a historic house, there are several choices.

Brafferton Inn (44 York St., Gettysburg, PA 17325; phone [717] 334-6211), is a restored stone house built in 1786, with eight guest rooms furnished with antiques.

Gettystown Inn (89 Steinwehr Ave., Gettysburg, PA 17325; phone [717] 334-2100) is within walking distance of most of the battlefield park's major attractions. A war-era home, it offers seven rooms with period furniture.

Doubleday Inn (104 Doubleday Ave., Gettysburg, PA 17325; phone [717] 334-9119) is behind original breastworks on the battlefield, and was the center of the Union line on July 1. Restored, with period antiques and private baths, it has a collection of Gettysburg memorabilia and books.

Farnsworth House (401 Baltimore St., Gettysburg, PA 17325; phone [717] 334-6227) once was occupied by Confederate sharpshooters, and there are more than a hundred bullet holes in the 1810 house. Guests are served breakfast in a shaded garden by a brook. At dinner the dining room is open to the public. The chef, who owns the house, specializes in vintage recipes, including Colonial game pie. Dinner guests may tour the house.

Three excellent restaurants offer period dining. *Dobbin House* (89 Steinwehr Ave., phone [717] 334-2100), specializing in recipes from the 1700s, is in the oldest building in Gettysburg (1776).

Eight miles west of Gettysburg, on PA 116, is the *Fairfield Inn* (Main St., Fairfield, PA 17320; phone [717] 642-5410), built in 1757 as a stagecoach stop. The specialties include seafood pies, beef, and bird. The inn also accepts overnight guests.

In late June and early July, Gettysburg stages *Civil War Heritage Days.* The events include a full-scale, living-history recreation of army encampments, as well as lectures by historians, a Civil War collec-

DAY IS DONE

Gen. Daniel Butterfield, Meade's chief of staff at Gettysburg, left a legacy to the army when he composed the plaintive bugle call "Taps."

After having destroyed in two years 60 vessels valued at more than 6½ million dollars, the Confederate commerce raider Alabama *put into Cherbourg, France, for repairs on June 11, 1864. When the* Kearsarge *appeared the following week, Raphael Semmes, captain of the* Alabama, *challenged the Union sloop to a duel. All the previous victories had been over unarmed merchantmen, and the Yankee gunners demolished the* Alabama, *wounding 40 before they sank it.*

tors' show, 1860s-style concerts, a fire-fighters' festival, fireworks, and a parade.

Other annual events of interest include the *Spring Outdoor Antique Show,* the third Saturday in May; the *Civil War Collectors Show,* the first weekend in July; and the *GBPA Civil War Book Fair* the first weekend in July.

AN IMAGE OF WAR

The USS *Kearsarge* sank the CSS *Alabama* in an hour-long engagement in the English Channel off Cherbourg, France, in June 1864. Among the French who gathered along the beach to watch was a young artist, Edouard Manet, who later painted the battle scene. The painting now hangs in the Philadelphia Museum of Art.

OTHER PENNSYLVANIA SITES OF INTEREST

HARRISBURG

State Museum of Pennsylvania, Third and North Sts., phone (717) 787-4978. On exhibit is Rothermel's *The Battle of Gettysburg,* one of the world's largest framed paintings. Open daily except Monday, holidays, and election day.

LIGONIER

Forbes Road Gun Museum, four miles north of Ligonier, on PA 711, phone (412) 238-9544. In the collection here are many Civil War firearms. Open daily.

A bed-and-breakfast near the reconstructed English fort is the *Grant House.* Nature trails and white-water rafting are nearby. Write to Mrs. Marilyn Grant, 244 West Church St., Ligonier, PA 15658, or phone (412) 238-5153.

PHILADELPHIA

Civil War Library and Museum, 1805 Pine St., phone (215) 735-8196. In a four-story brick 19th-century town house is a library with 12,000 books and periodicals treating the events leading up to the war, as well as the war itself and early reconstruction. A splendid collection of arms, uniforms, battle flags, memorabilia, and artifacts. Special rooms house exhibits on Lincoln, Grant, and Meade. The building is the headquarters of the Military Order of the Loyal Legion of the United States. Open Monday through Friday, weekends by appointment. Phone in advance.

The twelve-room *Society Hill Hotel* is near Independence Hall and the historic district. The hotel's restaurant and outdoor café have a European atmosphere. Write to Ms. Arlene Mand, 301 Chestnut St., Philadelphia, PA 19106, or phone (215) 925-1919.

The nearby *City Tavern* (2nd and Walnut Sts., phone [215] 923-6059), originally built in 1773, provides classic American dining in a colonial setting.

PITTSBURGH

Soldiers and Sailors Memorial Hall and Military History Museum, 5th Ave. and Bigelow Blvd., phone (412) 621-4254. Weapons, uniforms, and memorabilia from American wars. Lincoln's Gettysburg Address is inscribed above the stage in the auditorium. Open daily.

The Priory (614 Pressley St., Pittsburgh, PA 15212; phone [412] 231-3338) has rooms and suites around a courtyard. Complimentary breakfast and evening refreshments. Courtesy limousine to the city.

STATE COLLEGE

Pennsylvania Military Museum, four miles east of State College on U.S. 322 in Boalsburg, phone (814) 466-6263. Dioramas and exhibits covering American wars. Accessible to the disabled. Open daily except Monday, election day, and holidays.

On the Penn State campus, the *Nittany Lion* (North Atherton St. [U.S. Business 322] State College, PA 16803; phone [814] 237-7671) is an inn with an excellent restaurant, tennis courts, golf privileges, and a sauna.

TOWANDA

Tioga Point Museum, in the Spaulding Memorial Building, 724 South Main St., Athens, fifteen miles north of Towanda on U.S. 220 and PA 199, phone (717) 888-7225. Civil War mementos are on display. Open Monday, Wednesday, and Saturday except major holidays.

WEST VIRGINIA

HARPERS FERRY

HARPERS FERRY NATIONAL HISTORICAL PARK

The radical abolitionist John Brown made Harpers Ferry famous in 1859 by raiding its arsenal in an attempt to obtain arms for his dream of a slave uprising. During the war the town was an important arms-producing center and a strategic transportation link between east and west. Stonewall Jackson captured the Union garrison in the town on the eve of the battle of Antietam. After the war, Harpers Ferry went into decline, partly a victim of its superb location.

Harpers Ferry is on a point of land at the confluence of the Potomac and Shenandoah rivers, surrounded by the Blue Ridge Mountains. This was the western frontier when a trader, Peter Stephens, came in 1733 and set up a primitive ferry service. Fourteen years later, Robert Harper, who gave the town his name, took over the ferry and built a mill.

By the mid-1800s, Harpers Ferry had developed from a tiny village into an industrialized community of 3,000. In the 1790s, President Washington urged Congress to

set up a national armory here. The armory supported the economy of the village and attracted various small industries to nearby Virginius Island.

Hall's Rifle Works, established on the island in 1819, produced breech-loading flintlock rifles using interchangeable parts, an invention of John Hall that was the first successful application of the principle that led to modern mass production.

The town's growth was assured with the coming of the Chesapeake & Ohio Canal and the Baltimore & Ohio Railroad in the 1830s. But trouble came on the night of October 16, 1859, in the form of a wild-eyed man who looked like an Old Testament prophet.

John Brown was sternly religious, a militant abolitionist who attracted national attention as a leader in the bloody sectional strife in Kansas. Then he developed a scheme to liberate slaves by violence and set up a stronghold of free Negroes in the mountains of Maryland and Virginia.

Harpers Ferry was chosen as the starting point for the insurrection because it was near the Mason-Dixon line, the surrounding mountains were suitable for guerrilla warfare, and in the U.S. armory were enough rifles to equip a small army.

Brown and his twenty-two-man "army of liberation" seized the armory and several other strategic points before the startled townspeople knew what was going on. The alarm was sounded and the state militia was summoned, upon which the raiders barricaded themselves with forty hostages in the armory's fire-engine house, now known as "John Brown's Fort."

On October 18, Col. Robert E. Lee and Lt. J. E. B. Stuart arrived from Washington with a contingent of U.S. Marines, stormed

The federal arsenal at Harpers Ferry, West Virginia, shown in a view from Maryland Heights, was the target of John Brown's unsuccessful raid in October 1859. Brown and his men planned to seize weapons with which to arm a slave uprising, but he was captured by Col. Robert E. Lee's troops, tried for treason, and hanged. Brown's bold act further split the country on the issue of slavery and hastened the start of the war.

Radical abolitionist John Brown had the eyes of a fanatic set in the face of an Old Testament prophet. Before he was hanged for treason, he declared, "I did no wrong, but right." To the North Brown was a martyr; to the South, a maniac.

the armory, and captured Brown and his men. Ten of Brown's men, including two of his sons, and one marine were killed in the brief skirmish.

Brought to trial for murder, treason, and conspiring with slaves to create insurrection, Brown was guilty. He was hanged at nearby Charles Town on December 2, 1859.

On the day of his execution, Brown wrote a prophetic message to the world and handed it to his jailer. It said, "I, John Brown, am now quite certain that the crimes of this guilty land will never be purged away but with blood. I had, as I now think, vainly flattered myself that without very much bloodshed it might be done."

Brown's execution further polarized the nation. The North saw Brown as a martyred saint. The South saw him as a demon, proof that no compromise was possible on the issue of slavery. Sixteen months later the war began.

The war did not treat Harpers Ferry

kindly. The armory and arsenal buildings were burned in 1861 to keep them from falling into Confederate hands. Union and Confederate troop movements through town were frequent, and both sides occupied the town intermittently throughout the war.

Discouraged by war damage and growing unemployment, many people moved away. Hopes of an economic revival died in a series of devastating floods in the late 1880s.

VISITING HARPERS FERRY

Harpers Ferry National Historical Park is twenty miles west of Frederick, Maryland, on U.S. 340. In 1944, Congress authorized a national monument here, setting aside 1,500 acres for that purpose, and in 1963 it was designated a National Historical Park. The acreage has been increased to 2,224, and restoration is still going on.

Begin at the Visitor Center, open all year except Christmas and New Year's Day, where a movie depicts the town's history. Park personnel in military uniforms or period clothing explain the significance of the town. Conducted walks, demonstrations, and short talks by historians help the visitor to visualize and understand the old armory complex, the raid, and the mysterious ruins on Virginius Island.

In the fall and spring, activities are restricted to the weekends, although the Visitor Center and several of the historic buildings remain open all week. In October the 1860 presidential election is reenacted.

The places of Civil War interest are located in the Maryland Heights area. A self-guided tour, making all the stops, should take between three and four hours. Park personnel are at many of the stops to explain what went on there. Other stops have audio stations. Walking tours may be made of Bolivar Heights and Virginius Island. Information on these tours is available at the Visitor Center. A stroll along the C&O

Canal towpath is a pleasant change from the bustle of town.

For further information, write to the Superintendent, Harpers Ferry National Historic Park, Harpers Ferry, WV 25425, or phone (304) 535-6371.

Watch your step. The early settlers used brick and natural stone when constructing steps and sidewalks. These are sometimes uneven and slippery. Walk carefully, and use handrails where provided. Auto traffic on the narrow streets often is very heavy. Beware of the rivers. They are deceptively calm-looking, but have deep holes and swift undercurrents. The water may be polluted, and swimming is not advised. Boaters and fishermen should wear life jackets. Be careful when climbing. Mountain climbers must register at the ranger station before climbing the cliffs on Maryland Heights. First aid is available at the ranger station next to the Military Office on Shenandoah Street. In an emergency, dial 911.

Points of interest on the tour of Maryland Heights include the following:

Stagecoach Inn. Built in 1826–34, this building once housed an inn operated by Maj. James Stephenson. Now restored, it serves as the park Visitor Center.

Blacksmith Shop. The smith who worked here became an endangered species in the middle of the 19th century as machines replaced the craftsman.

Provost Office. During the war the provost guard, headquartered here, enforced military rules and regulations.

Dry Goods Store. Built in 1812, this was the home of the Master Armorer from

View of Harpers Ferry, West Virginia, from the Maryland shore

"[TURN] THE SHENANDOAH VALLEY [INTO] A BARREN WASTE . . . SO THAT CROWS FLYING OVER IT FOR THE BALANCE OF THIS SEASON WILL HAVE TO CARRY THEIR PROVENDER WITH THEM."

—Grant's orders to Gen. Philip Sheridan, 1864

1818 to 1858. Today it is restored to represent a typical dry-goods store of the 1850s.

Master Armorer's House. Built in 1858 as a home for the chief gunsmith of the armory, this restored dwelling now is a museum where the story of gunmaking is told.

Museum. Exhibits of many of the park's valuable artifacts are displayed here. The exhibits are changed periodically.

John Brown Museum. These restored buildings house a theater and museum relating the events of the John Brown raid.

John Brown's Fort. This was the fire-engine house used by John Brown for refuge during his 1859 raid. The building was moved here from its original site just down Potomac Street. A monument marks the original site.

Arsenal Square. Here are the foundations of the two U.S. arsenal buildings that were burned when Union troops evacuated the town at the beginning of the war in 1861.

The Point. Three states—West Virginia, Virginia, and Maryland—and two rivers, the Potomac and the Shenandoah, meet here. This was the heart of the town before the war.

Whitehall Tavern. This structure served as a "watering hole" for the armory workers.

Confectionery. Built in stages from 1844 to 1857, this was the home and business of Frederick Roeder, a German immigrant, strong Unionist, and respected citizen of the town.

Civil War Museums. This exhibit and the one directly across the street tell how peaceful citizens and thriving businessmen were replaced by marching troops and destruction as four years of war took their toll.

Pharmacy. A post–Civil War exhibit, the pharmacy represents the town's efforts to recover from military occupation and destruction.

The Stone Steps. Cut into natural rock at the beginning of the 19th century, these

John Brown's Fort, where the abolitionist made his last stand. The building was moved to a nearby site in the National Historical Park, Harpers Ferry, West Virginia.

steps allowed access to the upper levels of the town.

Harper House. Built by Robert Harper between 1775 and 1782, this is the oldest surviving structure in the park. The furnished interior, typical of a tenant house, reveals the crowded conditions of the town in the 1850s.

St. Peter's Catholic Church. Built in the 1830s and remodeled in the 1890s, the church still is in use today. (Not part of the park.)

Jefferson Rock. Thomas Jefferson visited here in 1783. He thought the view from this point was "stupendous" and "worth a voyage across the Atlantic."

Armory Worker's House. Built between 1822 and 1831 by an armory worker, this is the only surviving example in the park of a typical workman's dwelling.

Lockwood House. Built in 1848 as the office and home for the armory paymaster, in 1865 it became the classroom building of the future Storer College, one of the earliest integrated institutions of higher learning in the country.

Brackett House. Completed in 1858, this structure served as a home for the armory superintendent's clerk. It is named for the Reverend Nathan Brackett, who was instrumental in establishing Storer College.

Morrell House. The armory paymaster's clerk lived in this 1858 house, which later was used by Storer College.

Anthony Hall. This building, completed in 1848, once housed the armory superintendent. After the war it became the main building of Storer College. It now is a training center for National Park personnel.

John Brown Wax Museum. Outside the park area, on High Street, the museum contains figures of John Brown and other

THE LONG MARCH

In the 1862 Shenandoah Valley campaign, Stonewall Jackson marched his 16,000 men more than 600 miles in thirty-five days. They fought five major battles, defeating four separate Union armies totaling 63,000 men.

period personalities, and is open daily from April to November, Saturdays and Sundays in February and March.

There are several interesting places to stay in Harpers Ferry. The *Fillmore Street Bed and Breakfast,* an 1890 Victorian house built on land deeded to the first owner by Jefferson Davis when he was Secretary of War, is an easy walk from most of the points of interest. Write to Alden and James Addy, P.O. Box 34, Harpers Ferry, WV 25425, or phone (304) 535-2688.

The View Bed and Breakfast is a contemporary home on East Ridge Drive with a spectacular view of the Potomac and Maryland Heights, which visitors can enjoy from the patio or Jacuzzi. Write to Bill and Etta Mae Hannon, P.O. Box 286, Harpers Ferry, WV 25425, or phone (304) 535-2688.

An excellent choice for dinner is *The Anvil,* downtown on Washington St., phone (304) 538-2582.

OTHER WEST VIRGINIA SITES OF INTEREST

CHARLES TOWN

Jefferson County Courthouse, North George and East Washington Sts., phone (304) 725-9761. The courtroom in which John Brown was tried and found guilty after his raid on Harpers Ferry may be seen in this 1836 building. Open Monday through Friday except holidays.

Site of the Old Jail, South George and West Washington Sts. A plaque on the post

"I HAVE NO
PURPOSE,
DIRECTLY OR
INDIRECTLY, TO
INTERFERE WITH
THE INSTITUTION
OF SLAVERY IN
THE STATES
WHERE IT EXISTS.
I BELIEVE I HAVE
NO LAWFUL RIGHT
TO DO SO, AND I
HAVE NO
INCLINATION TO
DO SO."

—ABRAHAM
LINCOLN, *in his
first inaugural
address, March
4, 1861*

office denotes where Brown was held while awaiting trial for treason and murder.

Site of the Gallows, South Samuel and Hunter Sts. A pyramid of three stones, believed to have been taken from Brown's cell, marks the spot where he was hanged. About 1,500 troops were around the scaffold, some commanded by Stonewall Jackson. One of the Virginia militiamen present was John Wilkes Booth.

Jefferson County Museum, North Samuel and East Washington Sts., phone (304) 725-8628. A collection of Brown memorabilia is on display here. Open Monday through Saturday from April through November.

The Carriage Inn (201 East Washington St., Charles Town, WV 25414, phone [304] 728-8003) is a bed-and-breakfast in a large Colonial home in the historic district. All the guest rooms have canopy beds, fireplaces, and private baths.

GAULEY BRIDGE

At the confluence of the New and Gauley rivers, Gauley Bridge was the key to control of the Kanawha Valley. Gen. William S. Rosecrans defeated Gen. John B. Floyd here in 1861, assuring Union control of what was then western Virginia. Near the present bridge are the stone piers of the old bridge, destroyed by the retreating Confederates.

Contentment, six miles east of Gauley Bridge on U.S. 60, phone (304) 465-5032. This 1830 mansion once was the home of Confederate Colonel George W. Imboden. The Fayette County Society Museum in the house displays Civil War items. Open daily June through September, by appointment the rest of the year.

HILLSBORO

Droop Mountain Battlefield State Park, three miles south of Hillsboro on U.S. 219, phone (304) 653-4254. On November 6, 1863, Gen. William W. Averell ended the last major rebel resistance in the state. The troops of Confederate General John Echols camped in Hillsboro before the battle. An observation tower affords an excellent view of the 287-acre battlefield.

PHILIPPI

The first land battle of the war was fought here on June 3, 1861, when Confederate forces clashed with Union troops protecting the Baltimore & Ohio Railroad, whose main line between Washington and the West ran near the town. The battle, a running rout of the Confederates, was known locally as the "Philippi Races."

Barbour County Historical Society Museum, Depot St., phone (304) 457-3700. Civil War artifacts are among the material displayed in this restored B&O Railroad Station. Accessible to the disabled. Open daily, closed during the winter.

SUMMERSVILLE

In July 1861, twenty-year-old Nancy Hart led a Confederate raid here, captured a

---

STONEWALL JACKSON

In January 1862, Stonewall Jackson struck at Romney, West Virginia, capturing a large quantity of stores and cutting off Union troops in the state. Jackson's troops were unhappy in Romney and, without his knowledge, petitioned the Secretary of War to be recalled to Winchester. The move nullified Jackson's campaign, and he angrily resigned his commission. Gen. Joseph Johnston, his superior, and the governor of Virginia were able to persuade Jackson to stay in the Confederate army.

small Union force, and burned the town. Miss Hart was captured, but she charmed her jailer into letting her examine his gun, and shot him dead. She escaped, but returned to Summersville after the war.

Carnifex Ferry Battlefield State Park, twelve miles west of Summersville on WV 39, then southeast to the park, phone (304) 372-3773. Gen. William S. Rosecrans's 5,000-man army defeated Gen. John B. Floyd's smaller force here on September 10, 1861. The *Patterson House Museum* in the 158-acre park displays Civil War artifacts. Open daily, May through early September.

The *Country Road Inn* (eight miles southwest of town on WV 39, phone [304] 872-1620) is a chef-owned Italian restaurant well worth the drive.

WESTON

Jackson's Mill Museum, four miles north of Weston, off U.S. 19. Stonewall Jackson lived and worked as a boy in this town originally surveyed by his grandfather. Exhibits show the grist-mill and sawmill operations of the period. Open daily June through August.

WHITE SULPHUR SPRINGS

In August 1863 the Confederates won one of their few victories in West Virginia in this village, home of the splendid resort *Greenbrier Hotel,* a half-mile west on U.S. 60 (Station A, White Sulphur Springs, WV 24986, phone [304] 536-1110). "Old White" as the hotel then was known, was the headquarters and hospital of first the Confederates then the Union forces. It's now one of America's great resorts.

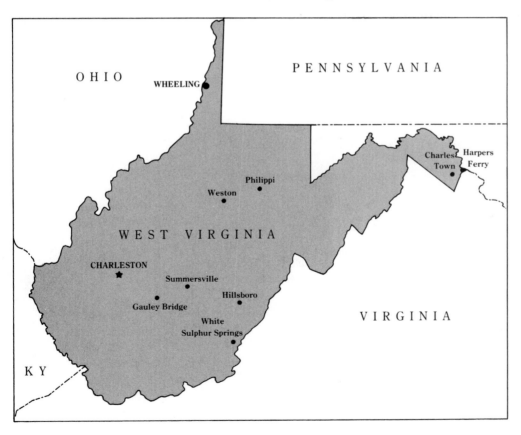

~ 8 ~

CIVIL WAR PUBLICATIONS

A surprising number of publications serve those with a serious interest in the Civil War. Some are broad in editorial scope, others concentrate on a particular aspect of the war, and all carry advertisements describing goods and services of interest to their readers.

The magazine with the largest circulation is *Civil War Times Illustrated,* with some 160,000 readers. Previous issues have featured articles on Union spy Pryce Lewis, the Atlanta campaign, General Grant's drinking habits, and Kirby Smith's exploits in Kentucky. Published monthly by Cowles Magazines, 2245 Kohn Rd., P.O. Box 8200, Harrisburg, PA 17105-8200. A one-year subscription is $20; a single copy is $2.95.

Blue & Gray Magazine is published, in its own words, "for those who still hear the guns." A series of articles featured various aspects of particular battles, including Stones River, Kennesaw Mountain, and Gettysburg. Published monthly by Blue & Gray Enterprises, Inc., 130 Galloway Rd., Galloway, Ohio 43119. A one-year subscription is $16.50; a single copy is $2.95.

Civil War is the bimonthly magazine of the Civil War Society. A multipart article on the Battle of Seven Pines, "Like an Avalanche," and a special issue on the Confederate navy appeared recently. Published by The Country Publishers, Inc., 133 East Main St.; P.O. Box 798, Berryville, VA 22611. A one-year subscription is included in the society's $39 membership; a single copy is $4.95.

The Civil War News is a newspaper published nine times a year for people with an active interest in the war. Features include book reviews; news for collectors; listings of reenactors, historians, and preservationists; and a calendar of events. A one-year subscription is $15. A sample issue may be obtained by writing to P.O. Box C, Arlington, MA 02174.

Military Images is a heavily illustrated bimonthly offering in-depth study of the common soldier and his uniforms, equipment, and fighting organizations, as seen in original photographs. A one-year subscription is $18. Write to RDD 2, P.O. Box 2542, East Stroudsburg, PA 18301.

Reenactors find news of events in the *Camp Chase Gazette,* published ten times a year. A one-year subscription is $18. Write to 3984 Cincinnati-Zanesville Rd., N.E., Lancaster, OH 43130.

Upcoming Civil War events and reenactments also are featured in *The Union Times,* along with general articles, book reviews, and unit history columns. Published eight times a year by UADF, 7214 Laurel Hill Rd., Orlando, FL 32818. A one-year subscription is $10.

Preceding spread: Bloody Lane at the Antietam National Battlefield, Sharpsburg, Maryland, where the greatest casualties of the war occurred. Antietam was the most fatal single-day battle in American history.

Opposite: Allan Pinkerton (at left with President Lincoln and General McClernand) was the head of General McClellan's secret service. Pinkerton repeatedly gave McClellan inflated estimates of Confederate troop strength. Convinced that he was outnumbered, McClellan, overly cautious by nature, refused to commit the Army of the Potomac to battle despite Lincoln's urging.

Collectors of Civil War memorabilia find much of interest in the *North South Trader's Civil War.* The monthly magazine features articles on dug and non-dug artifacts, reenactments, skirmishes, and shows. A one-year subscription is $20. Write to 918 Caroline St., Fredericksburg, VA 22401.

The *Civil War Book Exchange & Collector's Newspaper* is published six times a year. A one-year subscription is $15. Cutter & Locke, Inc., 4 Water St., P.O. Box C, Arlington, MA 02174.

Another publication for the collector is *The Courier.* A free sample copy can be obtained by writing to P.O. Box 1863, Williamsville, NY 14221.

A magazine that takes sides is the *Confederate Veteran,* published bimonthly by the Sons of Confederate Veterans as a service to their membership. Southern military leaders are profiled, battles dissected, and news and events of the society are prominently featured. Nonmembers may subscribe for $12 by writing Confederate Veteran, P.O. Box 820169, Houston, TX 77282-0169.

Also waving the Stars and Bars is the *Southern Partisan,* a quarterly review that describes itself as "the new voice of the Old South." The *Partisan* recently founded the Southern Heritage Association for the purpose of keeping Confederate flags flying on the Alabama and South Carolina state houses, and to defend the state flags of Georgia, Mississippi, and Florida. Membership dues are $25, which include a quarterly newsletter; subscription is only $12. P.O. Box 11708, Columbia, SC 29211.

The *Journal of Confederate History,* winner of the 1988 Southern Heritage Award, takes a more scholarly approach to the Confederacy. A one-year subscription to the book-length quarterly is $48 from The Guild Bindery Press, P.O. Box 2071, Lakeway Station, Paris, TN 38242.

The *Lincoln Herald* is devoted to historical research in the field of Lincolniana and the Civil War. Published quarterly since the early 1900s by the Lincoln Memorial University Press, Harrogate, TN 37752-0901. A one-year subscription is $20.

Another specialized magazine is *The Artilleryman,* published quarterly by Cutter & Locke, Inc., 4 Water St., P.O. Box C, Arlington, MA 02174. A one-year subscription is $15.

Grave Matters is a newsletter for necrolithographers and those in search of Civil War burial sites. Information and a sample copy may be obtained from Steve Davis, 1163 Warrenhall Lane, Atlanta, GA 30319.

━ 9 ━
BUILDING A PERSONAL CIVIL WAR LIBRARY

More books have been written on the Civil War than on any other American history subject— more than 60,000, although most are out of print. The number of titles essential to a personal library is surprisingly small, however, probably less than fifty. These will serve the needs of the amateur student of the war, and form a sound nucleus for additional acquisitions. All the books, except those so noted, are in print, and many are available in paperbound editions.

There is no better first book than James M. McPherson's magnificent *Battle Cry of Freedom* (Oxford University Press, 1988; Ballantine Books, 1989, paper). It does the seemingly impossible, in that it tells the story of the war in all its complexity in a single, highly readable volume. McPherson isn't simplistic, nor does he sacrifice detail or narrative flow. His canvas is broad, and the many complex issues of the period are presented clearly and made understandable.

A worthy companion volume is *The American Heritage Picture History of the Civil War,* by Bruce Catton and the Editors of American Heritage (American Heritage, 1960; Bonanza Books, 1982). Its rich collection of vintage visual material captures the flavor of the war years. Of particular value are the bird's-eye drawings of the major battles.

The best-known writer on the war is Bruce Catton, and his reputation is well deserved. An excellent selection would be his three-volume *Centennial History of the Civil War (The Coming Fury, Terrible Swift Sword,* and *Never Call Retreat)* (Doubleday, 1969). Catton is a marvelous writer, and his account of the military campaigns is as compelling as a good novel.

Catton leaned slightly to the Union viewpoint, so it is both helpful and informative to balance his Centennial history with an equally readable account of the military history of the war from an angle more sympathetic to the Confederacy: Shelby Foote's trilogy *The Civil War: A Narrative* (Random House, 1974). A Southern novelist and historian, Foote is especially compelling as he chronicles the campaigns of Lee and the Army of Northern Virginia.

The two series by historian Allan Nevins are modern classics and must-reads for any serious student of the Civil War: *Ordeal of the Union* and *The War for the Union* (Scribner's, 1947, 1953), both comprising four volumes.

The Civil War (Time-Life Books, 1985 *et seq.*) is a twenty-eight-volume overview of the war, well written and beautifully illustrated. Although a few volumes are sold in bookstores, the complete series is available only by mail from Time-Life Books.

If your budget and bookshelf space are unlimited, try to locate a used or reprinted edition of *War of the Rebellion: Official Records of the Union and Confederate Armies* (U.S. Government Printing Office), all 128 volumes, originally published between 1880 and 1901. Round it out with the thirty-volume *Official Records of the Union and Confederate Navies in the War of the Rebellion* (U.S. Government Printing Office), published between 1894 and 1922. Failing this, consider the four-volume *Battles and Leaders of the Civil War,* edited by Clarence C. Buel and Robert U. Johnson (Century, 1887–88), which contains participants' personal accounts of battles and campaigns, published twenty years after the war in *Scribner's Magazine.* By comparison, a model of compactness and clarity is *Decisive Battles of the Civil War* by Lt. Col. Joseph B. Mitchell (Ballantine, 1988).

There are several important reference works to add to your growing library. Two excellent books are *The Civil War Dictionary* by Mark M. Boastner III (Times Books, 1988) and the *Historical Times Illustrated Encyclopedia of the Civil War,* edited by Patricia L. Faust (Harper & Row, 1986). Another work worth considering is *The Encyclopedia of Southern History,* edited by David C. Roller and Robert W. Twyman (Louisiana State University Press, 1979). An indispensable aid for tracking military operations is E. B. Long's *The Civil War Day by Day: An Almanac 1861–1865* (Bison Books, 1983). Equally indispensable is *The West Point Atlas of the American Civil War* (Praeger, 1962).

To learn what it was like to be a common soldier in the war, add two volumes by Bell Irvin Wiley, *The Life of Johnny Reb* and *The Life of Billy Yank* (Louisiana State University Press, 1971). Using letters, diaries, and memoirs, Wiley has re-created life in the ranks. Life on the homefront is depicted in the popular *Mary Chesnut's Civil War,* a delightful diary edited by C. Vann Woodward (Yale University Press, 1981). A Southerner, Mary Chesnut witnessed many important events of the war.

No Civil War library would be complete without books about Abraham Lincoln. The most readable one-volume biography is *With Malice Toward None: The Life of Abraham Lincoln* by Stephen B. Oates (New American Library, 1978). More detailed is Carl Sandburg's epic *Abraham Lincoln: The Prairie Years* and *The War Years* (Harcourt Brace, 1954), and the four-volume *Lincoln the President* by James G. Randall (Dodd, Mead, 1944–45). In addition to providing a wealth of information about Lincoln himself, *The Abraham Lincoln Encyclopedia* (Quality Paperbacks, 1984), edited by Mark E. Neely, Jr., sheds light about the sectional conflict and the conduct of the war.

Civilians are casualties of war as well as soldiers. Here a refugee family leaves a war area with its belongings loaded on a cart. Virginia was particularly hard hit—60 percent of the Civil War's battles were fought there. Troop movements were constantly hampered by roads clogged with refugees, both white and black. Food shortages became a political and military problem. By war's end the South was an economic disaster, its way of life gone forever.

The final grand review of Union troops passes down Pennsylvania Avenue toward the Capitol in Washington, May 23–24, 1865. Some 600,000 soldiers had perished in the war. "Neither party," Lincoln said earlier, "expected for the war the magnitude or the duration that it has already attained. Both sides read the same Bible and prayed to the same God, and each invokes His aid against the other. . . . The Almighty has His own purposes."

An excellent biography of the Confederate President from a Southern viewpoint is Hudson Strode's three-volume *Jefferson Davis, American Patriot* (Harcourt Brace, 1955). Vital to an understanding of the Confederacy is Davis's two-volume *Rise and Fall of the Confederate Government* (Appleton, 1881).

David Southall Freeman's four-volume *R. E. Lee: A Biography* (Scribner's, 1935) is a classic, as is his three-volume opus, *Lee's Lieutenants: A Study in Command* (Scribner's, 1986). Together they form a brilliant portrait of the Army of Northern Virginia. A contrapuntal portrait of the Army of the Potomac is Bruce Catton's stellar trilogy, *Mr. Lincoln's Army, Glory Road,* and *A Stillness at Appomattox* (Doubleday, 1956). Intelligent criticism of Lee's strategy can be found in *The Marble Man: Robert E. Lee and His Image in American Society* (Louisiana State University Press, 1977) by historian Thomas L. Connelly.

Ulysses S. Grant wrote a superb autobiography, *Personal Memoirs of U. S. Grant* (Quality Paperbacks, 1982), finishing it while dying painfully of throat cancer. Excellent biographies of Grant include Bruce Catton's two-volume study, *Grant Moves South* and *Grant Takes Command* (Little, Brown, 1960, 1969); J. F. C. Fuller's *The Generalship of Ulysses S. Grant* (Indiana University Press, 1968); and William S. McFeely's *Grant: A Biography* (Norton, 1982).

Other military leaders wrote personal memoirs, including the two-volume *Memoirs of W. T. Sherman* (Quality Paperbacks, 1984); *Personal Memoirs of P. H.*

Sheridan, also in two volumes (Appleton, 1902); Joseph E. Johnston's *Narrative of Military Operations . . . During the Late War Between the States* (Greenwood, 1973); James Longstreet's *From Manassas to Appomattox* (Lippincott, 1903); George B. McClellan's *McClellan's Own Story* (Webster, 1887); and George G. Meade's two-volume *The Life and Letters of George Gordon Meade* (Scribner's, 1913).

The Civil War was the first conflict to be extensively photographed, and at least one collection of photographs belongs in any library. Two excellent ones are the ten-volume *Photographic History of the Civil War* (T. Yoseloff, 1957), edited by Francis T. Miller, which is hard to find; and the six-volume *The Image of War 1861–1865* (Doubleday, 1981). An excellent addition is the *Pictorial History of the Confederacy,* edited by Lamont Buchanan (Crown, 1957).

From this point, your library will start to reflect your personal interests in the war. A particular general, battle, or campaign may have caught your fancy. Some of my favorite books may suggest a starting point. Margaret Leech's *Reveille in Washington, 1860–1864* (Car-

roll & Graf, 1986), for instance; or James I. Robertson, Jr.'s *The Stonewall Brigade* (Louisiana State University Press, 1963). *Landscape Turned Red: The Battle of Antietam* by Stephen W. Sears (Ticknor & Fields, 1983; Popular Library, 1985, paper) and *Gettysburg: The Second Day* by Harry W. Pfanz (University of North Carolina Press, 1987) are exceptional.

Another series from Time-Life Books, *Collector's Library of the Civil War,* offers leather-bound, gilt-edged reprints of some of the classic war memoirs, including *Campaigning with Grant, Hardtack and Coffee,* and *Mosby's Rangers.* (Write to Time-Life Books, Richmond, VA 23261-2066.)

Some exceptional novels about the war include Stephen Crane's classic *The Red Badge of Courage* (Modern Library, 1942) and Michael Shaara's *The Killer Angels* (Ballantine, 1987, paper), a moving portrait of Lee at Gettysburg. McKinley Kantor's *Andersonville* (New American Library, 1957) justly won a Pulitzer Prize. Douglas C. Jones wrote a novel about the Battle of Pea Ridge, *Elkhorn Tavern* (Tor, 1989, paper). Margaret Mitchell's sweeping *Gone With the Wind* be-

Uniforms and weapons may change, but a soldier's life is the same as in the days of Caesar's legions: the tedious routine of camp life, wearisome marches, and moments of unspeakable horror. Here soldiers of a New York regiment endure the tedium. One washes mess gear, another contemplates something in the distance, a third practices the soldier's rule (Why stand when you can lie down?), while a fourth is ready for sentry duty.

Maj. Gen. Philip Sheridan (standing), commander of Grant's cavalry, and his generals pose in front of his tent. "Sheridan's Ride" became a legend in the war. He was away from his army when Early broke through the Union line at Cedar Creek in the Shenandoah Valley. Hearing the news, Sheridan galloped to the scene, rallying his retreating troops along the way. Defeat was turned into victory, and the Confederate hold on the valley was broken.

George G. Meade

longs on the shelf. Don't forget the book that helped set the stage for the war: *Uncle Tom's Cabin,* by Harriet Beecher Stowe (Bantam, 1981, paper).

BOOK DEALERS

The average bookstore carries only some of these titles. To build a library, especially if you want original editions, you will have to seek out specialized bookstores, either in person or by mail. The Civil War magazines and newspapers mentioned above carry advertisements for books. Here is a selected list of publishers and bookstores that specialize in Civil War books.

Wallace Pratt
1801 Gough St.
San Francisco, CA 94109
(free catalog)

Stone Mountain Relics, Inc.
968 Main St.
Stone Mountain, GA 30083
(404) 469-1425

Mathew B. Brady

Abraham Lincoln Book Shop
18 East Chestnut St.
Chicago, IL 60610
(312) 944-3085

Articles of War
8806 Bronx Ave.
Skokie, IL 60077
(312) 674-7445
(free catalog)

Camp Pope Bookshop
P.O. Box 2232
Iowa City, IA 52254
(Catalog $1)

"Old Army" Books
P.O. Box 24652
Lexington, KY 40524-4652
(free catalog)

The Mt. Sterling Rebel
P.O. Box 481
Mt. Sterling, KY 40353
(606) 498-5821
(free catalog)

Butternut and Blue
3411 Northwind Rd.
Baltimore, MD 21234
(301) 256-9220
(free catalog)

Heritage Books, Inc.
1540 East Pointer Ridge Pl.
Suite 205
Bowie, MD 20715
(free catalog)

Bill Mason Books
6209 Winans Dr.
Brighton, MI 48116
(313) 231-1643

Olde Soldier Books, Inc.
18779B North Frederick
Ave.
Gaithersburg, MD 20879
(301) 963-2929

Ron R. Van Sickle
Military Books
22 Montgomery Village
Ave.
Gaithersburg, MD 20879
(301) 330-2400

David E. Doremus Books
100 Hillside Ave.
Arlington, MA 02174
(617) 646-0892
(Catalog and mailings $2)

Frank E. Reynolds,
Old Books
P.O. Box 805
Newburyport, MA 01950
(Catalog $1)

The Galvanized Yankee
Bookshop
P.O. Box 37
South Conway, NH 03813
(List 75¢)

Longstreet House
P.O. Box 730
Hightstown, NY 08520
(free list)

The Military Bookman
29 East 93rd St.
New York, NY 10128
(212) 348-1280
(Catalogs by subscription)

McGowan Book Company
P.O. Box 222
Chapel Hill, NC 27514
(919) 968-1121
(free catalogs)

The Carolina Trader
P.O. Box 769
Monroe, NC 28110
(free catalog)

Broadfoot Publishing Co.
P.O. Box 508
Rte. 4
Wilmington, NC 28405
(919) 686-4816
(free catalog)

Morningside Bookshop
P.O. Box 1087
260 Oak St.
Dayton, OH 45401
(513) 461-6736

ABCDEF Books
726 North Hanover St.
Carlisle, PA 17013
*(Catalog $1, book-search
service)*

The Conflict
P.O. Box 689
213 Steinwehr Ave.
Gettysburg, PA 17325
(717) 334-8003

Farnsworth House Military
Impressions
401 Baltimore St.
Gettysburg, PA 17325
(717) 334-8838

J. Michael Santarelli
226 Paxson Ave.
Glenside, PA 19036
(free list)

Heritage Trails
P.O. Box 307
Turbotville, PA 17772
(717) 649-5846
(free lists)

Bohemian Brigade Book
  Shop
8705 Vultee La.
Knoxville, TN 37923
(615) 694-8227
(catalog $1)

The Guild Bindery Press
P.O. Box 2071
Lakeway Station
Paris, TN 38242
(901) 644-9292

Bacon Race Books
3717 Pleasant Ridge Rd.
Annandale, VA 22003

The Historical Store, Ltd.
203J Harrison St., S.E.
Leesburg, VA 22075
(703) 771-1110

Old Favorites Bookshop
610 North Sheppard St.
Richmond, VA 23221
(free list)

Owens Civil War Books
2728 Tinsley
Richmond, VA 23235
(804) 272-8888
*(Free catalogs; book-search
service)*

Wolf's Head Books
P.O. Box 1020
Morgantown, WV 26507
(304) 296-0706
*(free catalog; book-search
service)*

"[THE CIVIL WAR]
CREATED IN THIS
COUNTRY WHAT
HAD NEVER
EXISTED BEFORE
—A NATIONAL
CONSCIOUSNESS.
IT WAS NOT THE
SALVATION OF
THE UNION; IT
WAS THE REBIRTH
OF THE UNION."

—WOODROW
  WILSON, *1915*

The body of a Confederate sharpshooter lies in the Devil's Den, a pocket of stubborn resistance during the Battle of Gettysburg. The young soldier, one of more than 50,000 killed or wounded during the three days of fighting, probably was slain during a Union charge on Little Round Top. Experts believe the body and the rifle were moved by the photographer and repositioned for dramatic effect, a common practice during the war.

➤ 10 ➤

THE WAR ON
VIDEO- AND AUDIOTAPE

Videotapes about the Civil War succeed in capturing the look and sound of battle, although they bring no new insights into what the war or the individual battles were all about. They are unavailable for rental in video shops, and can only be purchased by mail from the producer or distributor.

The full scope of the war is presented in three well-produced library sets, each accompanied by a study guide. They are *Embattled Nation,* with individual tapes on First Manassas, Gettysburg, and Appomattox; *Grant in the West,* featuring Shiloh and Vicksburg; and *Mr. Lincoln's Army,* which covers Antietam, Chancellorsville, and Spotsylvania. The tapes combine action, animated maps, music, and narration into hour-long presentations. Some of the tapes are available individually. Produced and distributed by Classic Images, P.O. Box 2399, Columbia, MD 21075.

A set of tapes with a similar creative mission is the limited collectors' edition of *Divided Union,* offered by Fusion Video, 17214 South Oak Park Ave., Tinley Park, IL 60477. The war is covered in five one-hour tapes: "Forward to Sumter," "Bloody Stalemate," "High Tide for the Confederacy," "Total War," and "Conclusion at Appomattox." The attractively packaged set comes with a bound index. The tapes also are available individually.

A three-volume series of thirty-minute videocassettes, *Civil War Generals,* profiles Robert E. Lee, Ulysses S. Grant, and Stonewall Jackson. Civil War historians, including Pulitzer Prize–winning author James McPherson and Ed Bearss, chief historian of the National Park Service, give their perspectives on the generals. Available in bookstores and larger video stores or direct from Atlas Video, phone (800) 999-0212.

As this book was being written, "The Civil War," the superb eleven-hour documentary that graced PBS in the fall of 1990, was being prepared for release on videotape by Time-Life.

"Gettysburg in Miniature" is an original production featuring more than ninety sets created especially for the film, and some 12,000 miniature military figures. Narration, music, sound effects, and maps enhance the forty-six-minute tape. Produced and distributed by Gettysburg in Miniature, P.O. Box 10541, Raleigh, NC 27605-0541.

"The Vicksburg Siege" is the subject of a videotape available through H&P Entertainment, P.O. Box 564, Molton, MS 39041, phone (601) 866-7004.

The 125th Anniversary Battle of Gettysburg was taped on and near the Gettysburg National Military Park, July 1 and 3, 1988. Three tapes, available individually or as a set, record the event: "The Soldier's Story," "Memorials and Ceremonies," and "Rededication of Peace Light." Bucher's Video, 1153 Biglerville Rd., Gettysburg, PA 17325, phone (717) 334-0038.

Video Vision, 37 East Washington St., Hagerstown, MD 21740, phone (301) 791-3494, distributes videotapes of two great Civil War battles: "Chickamauga—River of Death" and "Antietam—The Bloodiest Day." Both tapes are productions of the American Civil War Commemorative Committee.

"The Civil War Soldier: The Infantryman" is the first in a planned series of videotapes on the Civil War sol-

The USS Monitor, *an iron raft with a round gun turret, was the Union's response to the CSS* Virginia, *formerly the USS* Merrimac. *When the Confederate ironclad seemed to threaten Washington, the two warships clashed on March 9, 1862, in the harbor at Hampton Roads, Virginia, exchanging fire at close range for two hours. Little damage was done to either vessel, but injuries forced both commanders to withdraw. The battle was inconclusive, but naval warfare was forever changed.*

dier. This twenty-five-minute tape uses reenactors to demonstrate aspects of the soldiers' everyday life. Available through American Historical Productions, Inc., P.O Box 7444, Gaithersburg, MD 20898.

Edwin Newman narrates the videotape "Ironclads: The *Monitor* and the *Merrimac*," a documentary on the first and most famous ironclad vessels. The tape includes footage of the *Monitor* on the ocean floor off Cape Hatteras, North Carolina, where it sank in a storm in 1862. Mr. Newman also narrates "Civil War: The Fiery Trial," a thirty-five-minute recapitulation of the major battles of the war, using period art and photography and contemporary views of the battlefields. Both tapes are available through the producer, Atlas Video, Inc., 1418 Montague St., N.W., Washington, DC 20011.

Stan Cohen and Robert Hanson have produced two tapes on aspects of the war in West Virginia: the thirty-minute "Brother Against Brother—The Civil War in West Virginia," and the hour-long "Civil War Weekend," filmed at Carnifew Ferry, West Virginia, in June 1986. Both are available from Pictorial Histories Pub-

lishing Company, 713 South Third West, Missoula, MT 59801.

Artillery buffs will enjoy "Civil War Siege Artillery," a tape showing the step-by-step process of firing the thirty-pound Parrott siege rifle and the eight-inch siege mortar. Produced and distributed by Historical Ordnance Video Co., 21787 Ventura Blvd., Suite 202, Woodland Hills, CA 91364.

Available on audiocassettes are the Civil War seminars conducted periodically by the Civil War Society. The two currently available are *Antietam,* consisting of seven tapes, and *Second Manassas,* a program of six tapes. The sets, or the individual cassettes, are available from The Civil War Tapes, c/o Uptown Graphics, Ltd., 601 Manorbrook Dr., Silver Spring, MD 20904.

The music the soldiers marched to is on *Band Music 1861–65,* digitally recorded on stereo cassettes by the Regimental Band, 37th Georgia Volunteer Infantry, playing authentic vintage instruments. Available from Confederate Brass, Inc., 766 Riverhill Dr., Athens, GA 30606.

The First Brigade Band has recorded ten cassettes

In a Union camp somewhere in Virginia, members of the 4th Michigan Infantry band pose with their instruments. Soldiers traditionally marched into battle to the strains of martial music. In the Civil War era, the band was positioned at the head of the column and the bells of brass instruments were pointed to the rear so that the troops could hear the music more clearly. Band concerts helped relieve the routine of camp life.

of Union and Confederate band music, including "Rally 'Round the Flag," "Music for the President," and "Dusty Roads and Camps," which are available from Heritage Military Music Foundation, P.O. Box 1864, Milwaukee, WI 53201. Other music of the period can be found in *Homespun Songs of the CSA,* a series of four cassettes, and on three cassettes in the series *Homespun Songs of the Union Army,* available from Bobby Horton, 5245 Beacon Dr., Birmingham, AL 35210.

Both Union and Confederate selections are also included in "Echoes of Shiloh," by the Eighth Regiment Band, available from John Carruth, 22 Wellington Rd., S.E., Rome, GA 30161.

Music of the Civil War homefront is featured in "19th Century Grand Ball" by the Americus Brass Band. A booklet tells how to dance the favorites of the period: polka, waltz, galop, and mazurka. Available from P.O. Box 15888, Long Beach, CA 90815.

The 11th North Carolina Regiment band has three cassettes of Civil War music, including military, religious, sentimental, and minstrel numbers. C&R Pub-

lishing Co., P.O. Box 53513, Fayetteville, NC 28305.

"A Hard Road to Travel," by the Rose of El-A-Noy Minstrels, is a one-hour cassette offering authentic renditions of thirteen minstrel songs. Available from Dan Cheatum, R.R. 10, 289 Crab Orchard Estates, Carbondale, IL 62901. Also offered by Mr. Cheatum is "Campfire Companion," a ninety-minute cassette containing thirty songs, accompanied by guitar and harmonica.

Pianist Charles Davis performs Union and Confederate favorites on "Civil War Piano-Parlor Memories," some also accompanied by harp and wood flute. Available from Star Line Productions, P.O. Box 1571, Glendale, CA 92109.

Another singer of similar material is Glenna Belle Boyd. Two cassettes, "Four Years and Five Aprils," and "Civil War Songs," are available from Perkins Sound Productions, Gadsden, AL 35902.

" 'Dixie' and Other Songs of the Confederacy" features Dolan Wilson singing to the accompaniment of guitar, banjo, and harmonica. Available from Mars Records, P.O. Box 12772, Memphis, TN 38182.

Many motion pictures with Civil War themes are on videotape, and more are being released. The first great Hollywood motion picture was D. W. Griffith's 1915 epic *The Birth of a Nation,* which many critics consider the most significant film in screen history.

Most lists of the ten best films of all time include two other Civil War pictures: *The General,* the 1926 Buster Keaton comedy based on the capture of the Confederate locomotive *General* and the resulting chase. (The incident also inspired the 1956 Disney movie *The Great Locomotive Chase,* with Fess Parker, but Keaton's version is more fun.) The other, of course, is David O.

Selznick's 1939 *Gone With the Wind,* still breaking hearts after all these years. (While *GWTW* was being made, Warner Brothers released a movie with a similar theme, *Jezebel,* for which Bette Davis won an Oscar.)

A box-office flop but a personal favorite is John Huston's adaptation of Stephen Crane's classic novel of battle, *The Red Badge of Courage,* starring Audie Murphy, the most-decorated soldier of World War II.

In *Shenandoah,* James Stewart tries to keep his six sons from being drafted into the Confederate army. Gary Cooper is a Quaker trying to come to terms with the war in *Friendly Persuasion.*

Two Federal light artillery batteries, armed with three-inch ordnance rifles, begin to move out of a Virginia camp. Almost without exception, cannons in the war were muzzle-loaded smoothbore. Rifled guns, more accurate and longer ranged, were just coming into service. Smoothbores were well suited to the wooded, hilly country where many battles were fought; at close range they functioned like huge sawed-off shotguns.

The life of Abraham Lincoln inspired two excellent films: *Young Abe Lincoln,* with Henry Fonda, and *Abe Lincoln in Illinois,* with Raymond Massey. (Raymond Massey also played the abolitionist John Brown in the 1940 film *Santa Fe.*)

The assassination of Lincoln and its aftermath were featured in *Prince of Players,* with Richard Burton as the Shakespearean actor Edwin Booth and John Derek as his brother, John Wilkes Booth. In *The Prisoner of Shark Island,* Warner Baxter played Dr. Samuel A. Mudd, imprisoned because he set John Wilkes Booth's broken leg.

After *Gone With the Wind,* Civil War epics tended to be ponderous box-office failures, including *Tap Roots* with Susan Hayward and Van Heflin, and *Raintree County* with Elizabeth Taylor and Montgomery Clift. Offbeat Civil War movies were more successful: Shirley Temple shone in *The Littlest Rebel,* and an "Our Gang" one-reel comedy, *General Spanky,* was a delightful send-up Civil War spy movies.

A critical success came in 1989 with the motion picture *Glory,* the epic story of the 54th Massachusetts Infantry Regiment, one of the first black units to fight in the war. It depicts the struggle of black soldiers to gain recognition as fighting men, not as servants or laborers. The climax is the 54th's attack on Fort Wagner, South Carolina, and the heroism displayed by both the black troops and their white officers.

Many so-called Civil War movies are westerns in uniform, but a handful are excellent, including *The Horse Soldiers,* starring John Wayne, and *The Man from Colorado,* with Glenn Ford and William Holden.

Raiders and their exploits were made into movies: John Hunt Morgan *(Morgan's Last Raid),* John Singleton Mosby *(The Pride of the South),* and William Clarke Quantrill *(The Dark Command).*

✦ 11 ✦
CIVIL WAR LIBRARIES AND COLLECTIONS

Many American libraries have extensive Civil War collections, a few libraries are devoted exclusively to the war, and all welcome serious students seeking specialized information. Some loan material to other libraries; your local librarian can help you arrange such a loan. A letter listing the information you are looking for usually will bring a prompt reply. Here is a list of the major Civil War libraries and collections around the country:

ALABAMA

Birmingham Public Library, 2020 Seventh Ave. North, Birmingham 35203. Especially strong on the antebellum period, the collection includes 15,000 books, documents, etc.

Mobile Public Library, 701 Government St., Mobile 36602. Personal papers and documents of Daniel Geary, director of defenses of Mobile, 1861.

Museums of the City of Mobile Reference Library, 355 Government St., Mobile 36602. Confederate States of America collection.

Troy State University Library, Troy 36081. The collection includes the John Horry Dent papers, 1851–92, twenty-five volumes, manuscripts, etc., of a planter and plantation owner.

ARIZONA

Northern Arizona University Special Collection Library, P.O. Box 6022, Flagstaff 86011. Joe Strachan Collection; copies of letters written in German by Capt. Carl Kostmann, Third Iowa Infantry.

CALIFORNIA

Claremont College, Honnoid Library, Ninth and Dartmouth Sts., Claremont 91711. Much Civil War material in 70,000-volume library.

University of California, San Diego, Central Library, La Jolla 92093. Manuscript collection includes family correspondence from the war.

Occidental College Library, 1600 Campus Rd., Los Angeles 90041. Uncataloged manuscripts, maps, and pictures.

California Institute of Technology Memorial Library, 1201 East California Blvd., Pasadena 91125. Three thousand volumes: uncataloged manuscripts, maps, pictures; wartime family letters including the Morley and the Amos G. Throop papers.

Lincoln Memorial Shrine, A. K. Smiley Public Library, 125 West Vine St., Redlands 92373. One of the larger collections about Lincoln and his times. Includes broadsides, letters, prints, campaign badges, stamps, medals, etc., and more than 3,000 pamphlets.

San Diego Public Library, 820 East St., San Diego 92101. Three thousand volumes, maps, and pictures.

San Diego State University Malcolm A. Love Library, 5300 Campanile Dr., San Diego 92182. Includes original documents, letters, diaries, journals, maps, pictures, and other artifacts from the period.

University of California, Santa Barbara, Library, Santa Barbara 93106. 31,000 volumes including the William Wyles Collection of Americana.

Stanford University Libraries, Stanford 94305. Collection includes the papers of Generals Frederick Steele and William R. Schafter.

CONNECTICUT

Trinity College Library, 300 Summit St., Hartford 06106.

DELAWARE

Hagley Museum and Library, P.O. Box 3630, Greenville 19807. Collection includes papers of Adm. Samuel Francis du Pont (1803–1865) and Gen. Henry du Pont (1812–1889).

DISTRICT OF COLUMBIA

American National Red Cross, National Headquarters Library, 17th and D Sts., N.W., DC 20006. The Clara Barton Memorial Collection and material pertaining to the Sanitary Commission and to women in the war.

Georgetown University Library, 37th and O Sts. N.W., DC 20057. Correspondence of various war figures and politicians.

Library of Congress, DC 20540. Papers of William Tecumseh Sherman and photographs by Mathew Brady and staff, including Alexander and James Gardner, James F. Gibson, and Thomas C. Roche.

GEORGIA

Emory University, Robert W. Woodruff Library, Atlanta 30322. Sixteen thousand volumes and manuscripts, maps, and pictures.

Carnegie Library, 607 Broad St., Rome 30161. Collection of 450 volumes and maps.

Georgia Southern College Library, Statesboro 30458. The Spencer Wallace Cone papers.

ILLINOIS

McLean County Historical Society Library and Museum, 201 East Grove, Bloomington 61701. Three thousand volumes, maps, manuscripts, and photographs. A strong collection on the military heritage of Illinois, particularly the 33rd and 94th regiments (Third Volunteer Infantry).

Chicago Historical Society Library, Clark St. at North Ave., Chicago 60614. Manuscripts, maps, 150,000 volumes. Meserve Americana (27 volumes) with 8,000 war-era portraits.

Chicago Public Library, 78 East Washington St., Chicago 60602. Seven thousand volumes. Civil War sections span the prewar sectional crisis as well as Reconstruction. Rare antislavery pamphlets; large collection of regimental histories; manuscripts of Grant, Sherman, Breckinridge; letters and diaries of soldiers; original photographs; Confederate battle plan for the Battle of Shiloh; swords, rifles, uniforms, flags, etc. Includes Grand Army Hall and Memorial Association of Illinois Collection.

Newberry Library, 60 West Walton St., Chicago 60610. Extensive collection.

Galesburg Public Library, 40 East Simmons St., Galesburg 61401. Focus on Lincoln, works of Illinois authors, and Illinois regimental histories.

Knox College Library, Galesburg 61401. A collection of 4,870 volumes.

Illinois State University, Miller Library, Normal 61761. The Harold K. Sage Lincoln Collection of some 1,200 volumes, 1,500 pamphlets, newspaper clippings, and correspondence. Many of the books are limited editions, presentation copies, or autographed copies with correspondence from authors and editors inserted.

Illinois State Historical Society Library, Old State Capitol, Springfield 62706. Sixteen thousand volumes, manuscripts, maps, and pictures.

INDIANA

Indiana University, Lily Library, Seventh St., Bloomington 47405. Collection of 160,000 volumes, including manuscripts, maps, and pictures.

Willard Library, 21 First Ave., Evansville 47710. Five hundred volumes, including battle accounts, lives of generals, memoirs, letters, and diaries.

Butler University, Irwin Library, 4600 Sunset Ave., Indianapolis 46208. Charles W. Moore Lincoln Collection.

Morrisson-Reeves Library, 80 North Sixth St., Richmond 47374. Collection emphasizes the war and the life of Lincoln.

IOWA

State Historical Society of Iowa Library, 402 Iowa Ave., Iowa City 52240. Iowa regimental histories, diaries, records, etc.

LOUISIANA

Louisiana State University, Troy H. Middleton Library, Baton Rouge, 70803. Warren L. Jones Lincoln Collection.

Tulane University, Howard-Tilton Memorial Library, 7001 Freret St., New Orleans 70118. Extensive collection of letters and diaries of Louisiana soldiers and officers. Includes some correspondence of P. G. T. Beauregard, T. J. Jackson, A. S. Johnston, R. E. Lee, G. G. Shepley, J. H. Stubbs, R. Taylor, and M. J. Thompson.

MAINE

Bowdoin College Library, Brunswick 04011. The Chamberlain papers, the Fessenden Family papers, the Oliver Otis Howard papers, the Charles Henry Howard papers, the Hubbard Family papers, and the McArthur Family papers, all pertaining to the war.

Maine Historical Society Library, 485 Congress St., Portland 04101.

MARYLAND

Hood College, Joseph Henry Apple Library, Rosemont Ave., Frederick 21701. The Irving M. Landauer Civil War Collection.

Salisbury State College, Blackwell Library, Salisbury 21801.

Antietam National Battlefield Site Library, P.O. Box 158, Sharpsburg 21782. Copies of limited letters and diaries, monographs of regiments and soldiers.

MASSACHUSETTS

Memorial Hall Library, Elm St., Andover 01810. Collection includes original drawings of Lincoln by Charles Barry, made in Springfield, Illinois, in 1860.

Boston University, Mugar Memorial Library, 771 Commonwealth Ave., Boston 02215.

State Library of Massachusetts, 341 State House, Boston 02133. Especially strong on the New England contribution to war.

Harvard University, Widener Library, Cambridge 02138.

Concord Free Public Library, 129 Maine St., Concord 01741. Extensive collection including manuscripts, maps, and pictures.

Lynn Public Library, 5 North Common St., Lynn 01902.

MICHIGAN

University of Michigan, William L. Clements Library, Ann Arbor 48109. Extensive collection of original material relating to the war.

Andrews University, James White Library, Berrien Springs 49104. The Courville Civil War Collection of more than 350 items, including weapons and memorabilia.

Monroe County Library System, 3700 Custer Rd., Monroe 48161.

MISSISSIPPI

University of Southern Mississippi, William David McCain Graduate Library, P.O. Box 5148, Southern Station, Hattiesburg 39406. The Ernest A. Walen Collection on the history of the Confederate States of America, including more than 600 Confederate imprints. Various manuscript collections.

MISSOURI

Central Missouri State University, Ward Edward Library, Warrenburg 64093.

MONTANA

Eastern Montana College Library, 1500 North 30th St., Billings 59101. George Armstrong Custer's personal and military papers, and those of his widow relating to his career, also incomplete Seventh Cavalry records and many Civil War papers. (Collection formerly at the Custer Battlefield National Monument.)

NEW HAMPSHIRE

New Hampshire Historical Society Manuscripts Library, 30 Park St., Concord 03301. Military records of New Hampshire units throughout the Civil War.

NEW JERSEY

Princeton University Library, Nassau St., Princeton 08540. The James Perkins Walker manuscript collection features Civil War papers.

NEW YORK

Buffalo and Erie County Historical Society, 25 Nottingham Ct., Buffalo 14216. A collection specializing in Civil War military history.

Saint Lawrence University, Owen D. Young Library, Canton 13617. The collection features more than 100 letters written home by two soldiers in the Union Army between 1861 and 1864. Also the papers of Pryce Lewis, a spy for the Union army.

Fenton Historical Society Library, 67 South Washington, Jamestown 14701. Includes muster rolls and history of New York State regiments, letters, and diaries of soldiers.

Columbia University Libraries, 801 Butler Library, 535 West 114th St., New York 10027. Includes historian Allan Nevins's files (40,000 items), U.S. Civil War Collection (1,300 items), Peter Wellington Alexander papers (7,500 items), and Sydney Howard Gay papers (20,000 items).

New York Historical Society Library, 170 Central Park West, New York 10024.

New York Public Library, Fifth Ave. and 42nd St., New York 10018. Twenty-five thousand volumes.

Union League Club Library, 38 East 37th St., New York 10016. Thirty thousand volumes.

University Club Library, 1 West 54th St., New York 10016. Houses the Southern Society Collection of materials on the South, the Civil War, and Reconstruction.

Saint John Fisher College Library, Rochester 14618. One thousand items including papers, records, and Civil War records of the Grand Army of the Republic.

University of Rochester, Rush Rhees Library, Rochester 14627. The William Henry Seward papers, approximately 150,000 items relating to his career, 1825–72.

NORTH CAROLINA

Duke University, William R. Perkins Library, Durham 27706. Comprehensive collection including papers of R. E. Lee and P. G. T. Beauregard, Confederate government and leaders (Jefferson Davis, etc.), thousands of letters and diaries from Union and Confederate soldiers.

University of North Carolina, Chapel Hill, Wilson Library, Chapel Hill 28514. The Wilmer Collection of Civil War Novels, consisting of more than 825 novels

from 1861 to the present, and related bibliographical material.

OHIO

Ohio University, Vernon R. Alden Library, Athens 45701. The Brown Family papers focus on the war and the activities of the 36th Ohio Regiment, the Fourth West Virginia Regiment, and the Kentucky campaign.

Public Library of Cincinnati and Hamilton County, 800 Vine St., Cincinnati 45202. A collection of 1,033 Civil War unit histories.

Western Reserve Historical Society Library, 10825 East Blvd., Cleveland 44106. The William P. Palmer Civil War Collection.

Ohio Historical Society, Archives Library Division, 1982 Velma Ave., Columbus 43211. Good collection of regimental histories and Ohio narratives of the Civil War.

Wilmington College, Watson Library, P.O. Box 1227, Wilmington 45177. A collection relating to Ohio Quakers and their activities during the war.

PENNSYLVANIA

U.S. Army Military History Institute, Carlisle Barracks, Carlisle 17013. The Civil War collection consists of personal letters, diaries, and memoirs of Union and Confederate officers and enlisted men.

Adams County Historical Society, Gettysburg 17325. Strong collection of manuscripts, maps, and photographs.

Gettysburg College, Musselman Library, Gettysburg 17325.

Gettysburg National Military Park, Gettysburg 17325. A collection of materials on the campaign and battle of Gettysburg, including 18,000 pictures.

Military Order of the Loyal Legion of the United States, War Library and Museum, 1805 Pine St., Philadelphia 19103. Ten-thousand-volume Civil War collection.

Union League of Philadelphia Library, 140 South Broad St., Philadelphia 19102. Civil War collection, including Stanton's notes on Lincoln's assassination.

University of Pittsburgh, Hillman Library, Pittsburgh 15260. Ten thousand volumes, including the manuscript collections of Eli H. Canfield, William Corliss, Ephram Elmer Ellsworth, Rush Christopher Hawkins,

John Hay, Abraham Lincoln (part of the McLellan Lincoln Collection), and Augustus Woodbury.

Brown University, John Hay Library, 20 Prospect St., Providence 02912. The McLellan Lincoln Collection, considered one of the great Lincoln collections at the turn of the century, was acquired for Brown by John D. Rockefeller. It has increased in size and importance, and comprises 15,000 volumes and much related material.

Providence Public Library, 150 Empire St., Providence 02903. The Harris Collection on the Civil War and Slavery. Regimental histories, military and naval tactics, accounts of the war by women, writings of abolitionists.

SOUTH CAROLINA

College of Charleston Library, Charleston 29401. Wartime papers from the Bank of Charleston, and personal papers of families and individuals relating to their experiences during the war.

South Carolina Historical Society Library, 100 Meeting St., Charleston 29401. Fifty thousand volumes focusing on the state's role in the war.

University of South Carolina Library, Columbia 29208. Reputedly the best collection in the South. Particularly strong in regimental histories of the Union army.

TENNESSEE

University of Tennessee, Chattanooga, Library, Chattanooga 37401. The Civil War Collection (3,500 volumes) emphasizes the Southern viewpoint, and the Wilder Collection emphasizes the Union viewpoint.

Lincoln Memorial University, Carnegie Library, Harrogate 37752. The Abraham Lincoln Center for Lincoln studies was established to display one of the largest collections of Lincoln and Civil War materials in the country. Includes material from the National Civil War Council Center concerning military surgery and medicine during the war, and from the Center for the Study of Military Music. The Library has 7,000 pieces of sheet music dating from the War of 1812.

Memphis Pink Palace Museum Library, 3050 Central Ave., Memphis 38111. The library has a number of books on loan from Shiloh Military Trail, Inc.

Public Library of Nashville and Davidson County, Eighth Ave. North at Union St., Nashville 37203.

TEXAS

University of Texas Libraries, P.O. Box P, Austin 78713. The Littlefield Collection of research materials includes many rare items on the history of the antebellum South.

Rice University, Fondren Library, 6100 South Main St., P.O. Box 1892, Houston 77251. Several collections of letters, papers, diaries, and military records.

Sam Houston State University Library, P.O. Box 2179, Huntsville 77340. The Porter Confederate Collection is rich in rare materials relating to Texas in the Confederacy.

VIRGINIA

University of Virginia, Alderman Library, Charlottesville 22901. About 1,500 collections are gathered here containing materials pertaining to the Civil War, particularly the Army of Northern Virginia and campaigns and battles in the state. There are letters, diaries, reminiscences, maps, and pictorial material of Confederate soldiers and civilians, as well as papers of R. E. Lee, J. E. B. Stuart, Thomas L. Rosser, Jubal A. Early, John Daniel Imboden, William "Extra Billy" Smith, Henry Alexander Wise, Eppa Hunton, John S. Mosby, and Samuel Barron.

George C. Marshall Research Foundation and Library, Drawer 920, Lexington 24450. The William F. Friedman Collection features Civil War code items.

Petersburg National Battlefield Library, Box 549, Petersburg 23804. Detailed information on various engagements during the siege of Petersburg.

Portsmouth Public Library, 601 Court St., Portsmouth 23704. Specializes in Tidewater and Lower Tidewater history.

Washington and Lee University Library, Lexington 24450. The collection of 25,000 volumes and 10,000 manuscripts emphasizes the life of R. E. Lee, Virginia, and the Civil War; 8,000 glass-plate photographs by Miley.

Virginia State Library, 12th and Capital Sts., Richmond 23319. Includes a vast collection of pictorial materials.

WISCONSIN

State Historical Society of Wisconsin Archives, 816 State St., Madison 53706. Focuses on Wisconsin's involvement in the war.

University of Wisconsin Memorial Library, 728 State St., Madison 53706. Extremely rare collection of manuscripts of a military brass band that marched with General Sherman's army.

University of Wisconsin, Milwaukee, Library, 3203 North Denver St., 53201. The Allen M. Slichter Collection of war materials reflects the Confederate point of view.

◆ 12 ◆

DISCOVERING YOUR
CIVIL WAR ANCESTORS

Millions of Americans are descended from the men who fought in the Civil War, but only a small percentage know anything more about their ancestors' war records than which side they were on. It is fascinating to discover how someone in your own family was involved in one of the most important events in American history. The more you know, the more the past will come alive for you. Tracing your personal Civil War heritage requires some time and effort, but the rewards are worth it.

The National Archives in Washington, D.C., houses one million cubic feet of every conceivable sort of information, going back to the founding of the country. The National Archives is open to all, and the information is available to all. Better yet, the Archives staff will search the records for you.

For the Civil War, the National Archives has compiled service records for almost every soldier, Union or Confederate, regular or volunteer; the service records of most of the Union and Confederate navies and marine corps; pension records for all Union veterans; prisoner-of-war records; records of Union court-martial trials; medical records; draft records; and burial records.

To begin the search, you need to know the full name of your ancestor, and the military unit in which he served. If you don't know what unit your ancestor served in, of if you aren't certain whether he served, you need to do some primary research. First, check your family records. Perhaps there is a family Bible that lists your ancestors and where they were born. If not, you can work backward from your mother and

father. Write for copies of their birth certificates, which will give the names of your grandparents and where they were born. Write for their birth certificates, then write for the birth certificates of your great-grandparents, and go back another generation if necessary. When you find the names of male ancestors who would have been from eighteen to thirty-five years of age during the years 1861 to 1865, write or phone the information number for the state in which they lived, and ask what department has the records of men who served in the Civil War. Send the department the names, and it should be able to determine whether they served and, if so, in what unit. You may wish to work with a professional genealogist who knows how to gain access to the appropriate sources easily and quickly. Using a professional will cost between $100 and $150 to get the information you need.

When you have your ancestor's name and unit, the next step is to request the free NATF Form 26 (Military Service Records) in writing from Reference Branch (NNIR), National Archives (GSA), Washington, DC 20408. Mention in the letter whether your ancestor was a Confederate soldier because a special request form is required.

If your ancestor was a Union veteran, check the boxes on the form for both military service and pension record. In *red* ink, write after the veteran's name "Please send complete contents of file." Enclose a check for ten dollars made out to the National Archives Trust Fund, and mail the form to the Cashier (NJC), National Archives and Record Service, Washington, D.C 20408. If your ancestor served in more than one unit, you must submit a separate form and check for each unit.

Allow two to three months for a reply. You may be disappointed, particularly if your ancestor was an enlisted man. The records of officers are extensive, but records of enlisted men are sparse and occasionally nonexistent. If the records aren't found, your money will be refunded. You can resubmit your request. Chances are good that you will get a different researcher the second time around, who may have better luck.

After receiving the records, you may ask for additional information: complete medical records, for example, or a court-martial record. Each is requested on a separate NATF Form 26, with a check for five dollars, and a note in red ink saying "Please send complete

D. W. C. Arnold, a Union Army private.

records." Again, if nothing turns up, it's worthwhile to resubmit.

Did your ancestor enlist, or was he drafted? Find out by writing the Navy and Old Army Branch, National Archives (GSA), Washington, DC 20408. The records here are arranged by state and county. Give your ancestor's full name, state, county, city (including the ward, if you know it), or town. The more data you can supply, the better your chance of getting information.

The Navy and Old Army Branch also has the records of amnesty oaths taken by Confederate soldiers, and the amnesty papers for high Confederate officials and Southerners owning more than $20,000 in personal property. These are arranged by state, then alphabetically by surname, and show where and when the oath was taken, the signature, and sometimes the person's age, personal description, and military unit. Request these records in writing, as described above.

If your ancestor was a prisoner of war, information can be requested from the Reference Service Branch. File M347 contains the names of Confederate soldiers held in Union prisons and of Union men in Confederate prisons. These files also contain lists of Union soldiers buried in national cemeteries, arranged by state, then alphabetically by cemetery. Send the veteran's name and, if you know it, the name of the cemetery he is buried in. If this is unproductive, write to the Memorial Division, Quartermaster General's Office, Washington, DC 20025. Its files, called the Roll of Honor, are similar to those of the Reference Service Branch.

The graves of many Union veterans buried in nonmilitary cemeteries are marked by headstones provided by the government, under a law enacted in 1879. Applications for headstones for the years 1879 to 1903 are on file at the Reference Branch. Your request for information should include your ancestor's name, military unit, date of death, and, if possible, place of burial.

The National Archives also publishes the *List of National Archives Microfilm Publications*. It contains regimental histories as well as material on specific battles and ships. Some material can be duplicated for you, or the microfilm loaned to a local library, where you can view it. For a free copy of the list, write Publications Sales Branch (NEPS), General Services Administration, Washington, DC 20408.

When tracing a Confederate ancestor, the best source of information is usually the archives in his home state. His pension application may be on file, containing his age, place of birth, date and place of enlistment, branch of service, company, and command. If one was wounded, the application will tell when, where, and during which battle, as well as the nature of the wound, the name of the attending surgeon, and whether he suffered the loss of an eye or limb. If he was a prisoner of war, the application will note when and how he was paroled or discharged; whether he was at the final surrender, or took the oath of allegiance to the Union during the war; if he was married and had children; what his occupation was after the war; if he owned real estate; and the names and addresses of two of his comrades who witnessed his application.

State archives have the records of state militia units that served in the war. These units are similar to today's national guard units. Most state archives have available on microfilm the *Index to Civil War Military Service Records* for both Union and Confederate soldiers. State archives usually answer requests more promptly than the National Archives.

Some local sources worth exploring include city or county historical books, particularly those published from 1865 to 1900. Send a self-addressed, stamped envelope to the county clerk and ask if any Civil War enlistee records have been kept. Write—always enclosing a self-addressed, stamped envelope—to local historical and genealogical societies and public libraries, asking if they have records of wedding announcements of veterans, rosters of Civil War enlistees, newspaper obituaries, and memorial records of local branches of Civil War national organizations.

When you have accumulated the basic information on your Civil War ancestor, you can begin to learn the details of his war experience. If he served in a particular regiment, you may be able to find books about that regiment's history, and regimental archives may exist. To determine which battles he fought in, you should know when he joined the regiment and how long he served.

If that isn't possible, find a library that has the 128-volume *Official Records of the Union and Confederate Armies in the War of the Rebellion* (1880–91) and/or the thirty-volume *Official Records of the Union and Confederate Navies in the War of the Rebellion* (1890–1901). These records, also available on microfilm, contain all available Union and Confederate records, reports, or-

ders, and memorandums ever issued. The amount of information is vast, and the material is very reliable. Of special interest are firsthand reports written by regimental colonels, brigade commanders, and ships' captains who directed and took part in the great land battles and naval engagements of the war.

Other reference works may help you trace your ancestors' role in the Civil War. All are out of print but may be found in large public libraries and Civil War libraries. They include:

Official Atlas of the Civil War (1950), a companion publication to the *Official Records,* gives the locations of all battles, naval engagements, encampments, and railroads.

Civil War Books: A Critical Bibliography (1972), in two volumes, is the best available source for locating wartime diaries, regimental histories, biographies, and battle descriptions.

Military Bibliography of the Civil War (1961), in three volumes, is particularly strong on military units. It includes books and magazine articles, and a code listing of libraries that have the books, so that interlibrary loans can be arranged.

Personnel of the Civil War (1961), in two volumes, is helpful with the often-confusing task of identifying Union and Confederate units by nicknames and proper names. For example, "Pee Dee Wild Cats" was the sobriquet of Company K, 26th North Carolina Infantry. Other excellent sources for identifying units are *Confederate Military Land Units* (1905) and the *Bibliography of State Participation in the Civil War, 1861–1865* (1880).

American Civil War Navies (1976) contains a bibliography of books, articles, and papers published from the 1850s to 1972 about Union and Confederate naval forces.

A Compendium of the War of the Rebellion (1896), in three volumes, contains histories of more than 2,000 Union regiments.

Confederate Military History (1889), in twelve volumes, contains Southern regimental histories.

Photographic History of the Civil War (1957), in five volumes, is the definitive collection of Mathew B. Brady's photographs of battlefields, camps, and troops on the march.

Confederate Veteran Magazine Index (1974) lists the memoirs, photographs, anecdotes, incidents, and per-

In Richmond's Libby Prison, a converted tobacco warehouse, more than 1,000 Union soldiers were confined in eight large rooms. Early in the war, captured prisoners were released on parole because there was no place to put them. Later the prisoner exchange program collapsed over the problem of exchanging former slaves serving in the Union Army. Camps in the deep South, like Andersonville, helped relieve overcrowding in Virginia.

sonal stories published in the magazine through the 1930s.

Official Army Register of the Volunteer Force of the U.S. Army for the Years 1861–1865 (1905), in eight volumes, is the best source for biographies of volunteer officers.

Official Army Register for 1861–1865 (1878) is a similar collection of biographies of regular Army officers.

Historical Register and Dictionary of U.S. Army (1890) includes biographies of regular-army officers from the organization of the army, September 29, 1789, to March 2, 1903.

Officers in Confederate States Navy 1861–1865 (reprint, 1983), is an excellent collection of biographies.

List of Pensioners on the Rolls, January 1, 1883, in five volumes, lists pensioners by cause of death or disability, alphabetically by state and county, giving name and address, the reason the pension was issued,

its amount, and the date when payments were first issued.

An excellent aid for Civil War research is *A Guide to Archives and Manuscripts in the U.S.,* a state-by-state list of archival collections by title and subject, with a brief description of each. Larger libraries also have the multivolume *National Union Catalog of Manuscript Collections,* updated regularly by the U.S. government.

The Reference Branch of the U.S. Army Military History Institute has a vast amount of source material: more than 300,000 books, 30,000 bound volumes of periodicals, 9,300 boxes of manuscripts, thousands of photographs, and other documents—troop rosters, diaries, letters, regimental histories, etc., covering U.S. Army regular soldiers, volunteers, and militia. Given a soldier's military unit, the Reference Branch will research the soldier and supply information on his unit. Books are loaned to other libraries. Write to Reference

Branch, U.S. Army Military History Institute, Carlisle Barracks, PA 17013.

It is one thing to research your ancestor's Civil War experiences, but quite another to organize the material and write it up coherently. Take the time, make the effort. Have the documents and photographs photocopied, and have sets bound for each of your children. Wouldn't it be sad if, sometime in the future, one of your descendants had to do that work all over again?

After you have determined what your ancestor did in the war, you will be eligible to join one or more organizations that perpetuate the memory of various Union and Confederate units. Membership is a good way to learn more about your heritage and meet others whose ancestors share a common experience. The major organizations include the following:

Armies of Tennessee, CSA & USA, Mickey M. Walker, Commanding General, P.O. Box 91, Rosedale, IN 47874.

Association for the Preservation of Civil War Sites, Inc. (APCWS), Gary W. Gallagher, President, P.O. Box 1862, Fredericksburg, VA 22402.

Children of the Confederacy, P.O. Box 4868, Richmond, VA 23220.

Civil War Token Society, Cynthia Grellman, Secretary, P.O. Box 3412, Lake Mary, FL 32746.

Civil War Press Corps, Lt. Col. Joseph Malcolm, P.O. Box 856, Colonial Heights, VA 23834.

Civil War Round Table Association, Jerry L. Russell, National Chairman, P.O. Box 7388, Little Rock, AR 72217.

Confederate Memorial Literary Society, The Museum of the Confederacy, 1201 East Clay St., Richmond, VA 23221.

Confederate Historical Institute, Confederate Historical Institute, P.O. Box 7388, Little Rock, AR 72217.

Daughters of Union Veterans, Vivian Getz, Treasurer, 503 South Walnut St., Springfield, IL 62704.

Hood's Texas Brigade Association, Col. Harold B. Simpson, Director, Hill College History Complex, P.O. Box 619, Hillsboro, TX 76645.

Military Order of the Loyal Legion, William A. Hamann III, Recorder-in-Chief, 1805 Pine St., Philadelphia, PA 19103.

National Lincoln–Civil War Council, Edgar G. Archer, Director, P.O. Box 533, Harrogate, TN 37752.

Robert E. Lee Memorial Association, Lt. Gen. John F. Wall, Stratford Hall Plantation, Stratford, VA 22558.

Sam Davis Memorial Association, Katherine Walkup, Regent, P.O. Box 1, Smyrna, TN 37167.

Jefferson Davis Association, Frank E. Vandine, President, P.O. Box 1892, Rice University, Houston, TX 77251.

Ulysses S. Grant Association, Ralph G. Newman, President, Morris Library, Southern Illinois University, Carbondale, IL 62901.

Institute of Civil War Studies, International Institute for Advanced Studies, Suite 403, 8000 Bonhomme St., Clayton, MO 63105.

Ladies of the GAR, Elizabeth B. Koch, 204 East Sellers Ave., Ridley Park, PA 19078.

Military Order of the Stars and Bars, William D. McCain, Adjutant General, Box 5164, Southern Station, Hattiesburg, MS 39406.

Military Order of the Zouave Legion, B. F. Scalley, Acting Adjutant General, 513 Greynolds Circle, Lantana, FL 33462.

National Society of Andersonville, Helen H. Harden, Secretary, P.O. Box 65, Andersonville, GA 31711.

National Woman's Relief Corps, Florence Rodgers, Treasurer, 629 South Seventh St., Springfield, IL 62703.

Sons of Confederate Veterans, Adjutant-in-Chief, Southern Station, P.O. Box 5164, Hattiesburg, MS 39401.

Sons of Sherman's March, Stan Schirmacher, Director, 1725 Farmer Ave., Tempe, AZ 85281.

Sons of Union Veterans, Frank Miller Heacock, Suite 614, 200 Washington St., Wilmington, DE 19801.

United Daughters of the Confederacy, Mrs. Donald R. Perkey, P.O. Box 4868, Richmond, VA 23220.

✦ 13 ✦

COLLECTING CIVIL WAR ANTIQUES

B e warned: If you are genuinely interested in the Civil War, sooner or later you will be tempted to buy an artifact connected with the war. It may only be a minié ball, a tintype of a soldier, or a bayonet. Nothing expensive, just something from the war for your very own. But then you find that one isn't enough; you want more. Collecting Civil War artifacts and memorabilia is addictive, and there are enough addicts to make it a multimillion-dollar business.

The prices of Civil War antiques are going up, a reflection of increased demand. Yet Civil War antiques still are relatively inexpensive when compared with other collectibles—art, for example, or rare books, or Georgian silver. Some Civil War objects can be purchased for less than fifty dollars, good ones for under a thousand dollars, and only very fine and very rare items sell for many thousands of dollars. All but the least expensive are good investments, particularly if you choose wisely.

There are a number of factors that affect the price of any antique: rarity, appearance, and condition, of course, and its affiliation with a particular personality, unit, battle, or other event. Sometimes geography can affect price. An object connected with a Tennessee regiment usually commands a higher price in Nashville than in Boston. Confederate items always fetch more than comparable Union items because they are in shorter supply.

Several books provide an overview of the Civil War antiques market. *The Illustrated History of American Civil War Relics,* by Stephen W. Sylvia and Michael J.

O'Donnell, available by mail from Moss Publications, P.O. Box 729, Orange, VA 22960, traces the history of Civil War artifacts from the end of the war to the present, and has almost one thousand photographs of collectibles. Also helpful are *The Official Price Guide to Military Collectibles,* published by The House of Collectibles and available in bookstores, and North South Trader's *Civil War Price Guide,* available by mail from North South Trader, 918 Caroline St., Fredericksburg, VA 22401. If you decide to specialize in a particular type of antique, such as swords or medical equipment, there are books with comprehensive information and photographs of collectibles. Any book dealer specializing in the war should stock them.

Visiting museums also is a good way to develop an appreciation of the various collectibles. The danger is that seeing Robert E. Lee's dress coat or a presentation sword that once belonged to George Meade may give you a thirst for the unaffordable and the unattainable.

There are several ways to buy Civil War antiques. The best sources are reputable dealers, such as the ones suggested at the end of this chapter, though this is by no means a complete list. They are reputable, their prices are fair, and they stand behind their wares. Some dealers sell only in their shops, others sell only by mail order through lists and catalogs, and some do both. Another way of buying war memorabilia is through a mail auction. The auction list contains a price range for each item, the lower number usually being the lowest acceptable bid. As in a regular auction, the high bid takes the item; unlike a regular auction, you only get to bid once. The problem is that you don't see the item before you bid on it, but only the description on the list, and perhaps a photograph. Mail auctions often are advertised in Civil War publications, and if you buy antiques by mail order, your name will automatically be added to mailing lists for mail auctions.

Throughout the year, dozens of Civil War memorabilia shows are held around the country. Antique dealers, book dealers, and traders display their wares, usually over a three-day weekend. The shows are great fun for buyers and browsers alike, and provide an opportunity to meet other collectors. Civil War collectibles also turn up at flea markets, but beware, because a lot of Civil War objects have been replicated over the years, and too often are sold as the real thing. Two items to be wary of are the Union kepi, or forage cap, and the front page of the *New York Herald* that carried the story of Lincoln's assassination. Thousands were reprinted as a promotional stunt for the 1892 Columbian Exposition in Philadelphia, and have yellowed and aged sufficiently to pass for the real thing.

A U.S. Navy recruiting poster

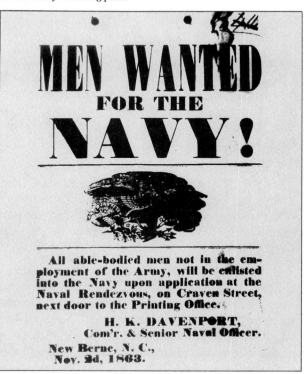

Several publications are useful for the beginning collector. They are *Civil War News,* the North South Trader's bimonthly *Civil War,* and *Civil War Book Exchange & Collector's Newsletter,* all described in detail in Chapter 8. They feature news of forthcoming events and carry advertisements from dealers and individual collectors.

Some collectors go directly to the source; they buy a metal detector and a shovel, and head for a battlefield. Digging and the use of metal detectors are illegal at national and state battlefields, but there are numerous places where small engagements were fought that are unprotected areas. A lot of relics are still found this way, particularly bullets, artillery shells, and accoutrements—the generic term for military buckles and plates. Lists and catalogs head many of their price lists D. and N.D. for "dug" and "non-dug" relics. Usually dug relics are less expensive.

For the novice collector, the major categories of collectibles are described below. As with all collectibles and antiques, prices can go up very quickly. The prices given are only guidelines.

Accoutrements. The most common items are the large oval U.S. belt and cartridge-box plates. In good condition, they fetch from $50 to $100. Plates with state identification are worth more. A large oval VMM (Maine) cartridge-box plate costs between $250 and $300; a cast brass NY sword belt plate commands $300 to $375. An eastern-style, egg-shaped CS oval fetches between $1,000 and $1,500; a rare solid-cast CS oval surrounded by eleven stars brings $4,000 to $5,000. A two-piece sword plate marked with the Virginia state seal commands $850 to $1,000.

Artillery Equipment and Shells. A water bucket used by a Union gun crew brings $250 to $300; a gunner's calipers, $125 to $250. A brass gunner's quadrant or gunner's level fetches about $500, as does either a valise saddle or a driver's saddle.

Literally hundreds of types and sizes of artillery shells were fired by the armies and navies. They range in price from $45 for the spherical six-pounder used by both sides, to more than $1,500 for a winged-shot CSA thirty-two-pounder. Most fall into the $300 to $600 range, and non-dug shells command a higher price than dug shells.

Related categories are fuses, hand grenades, rockets, and land mines. A Bormann time fuse brings from $15 to $25; many fuses are available under $100, with the most expensive rarely exceeding $500. Non-dug hand grenades range from $250 to $1,500. Rockets sell from $250 to $600; the Confederate Rains land mine from $500 to $600.

Bayonets. Many rifles of different calibers and manufacturers saw service and used bayonets of special sizes or fittings. The twelve most common angular-type Union bayonets, non-dug and in good condition without scabbard, range in price from $45 to $150; Confederate socket bayonets bring more than twice as much. Sword saber bayonets are rarer and more costly. Union bayonets of this type are $90 to $800; Confederate bayonets, $250 to $1,500 and up.

Bottles. An inexpensive way to begin to collect Civil War memorabilia is to search out vintage bottles. There are many at $25 or less. Those marked "US Hospital Dept." are among a handful that fetch more than $100.

Bullets and Bullet Molds. There were several hundred types of bullets fired in the war, and some can be purchased for as little as 75¢. Most are less than $25, and only a handful cost $100. Brass and iron molds for various types of bullets range in price from $15 to $25 for the .41-caliber round ball to $400–$500 for the brass mold for the cylindrical long Whitworth bullet.

Buttons. A Civil War soldier's coat sometimes had the name of his state and often his regiment embossed on the buttons. Thousands of buttons from this era are available, ranging in price from $15 to $20 for Union infantry to more than $1,000 for an obscure button bearing the inscription "CSA 2D ARK. RGT." encircling a five-pointed star. The majority of buttons, however, are in the $75–$350 range.

FIREARMS

Nine separate motions were required to fire a Civil War musket. Army regulations specified that a soldier should fire three aimed shots per minute, allowing twenty seconds per shot—less than two seconds per motion.

Camp Gear. The paraphernalia that the armies took into the field is not expensive, although difficult to display. A camp bed with identification markings fetches $350–$500, or less than half that price without identification markings. An officer's camp bed with a hand-wrought frame with markings is $600 to $800; a painted chest with markings is $500 and up; a field desk, $150–$350; and a folding camp lantern, $65–$100.

Cannons. If price and size aren't considerations, why not a cannon? A twenty-four pound Coehorn mortar can be purchased for as little as $3,500. At the top end of the scale, Confederate bronze guns in good condition could fetch $25,000. Note that this only purchases the gun tube. An original field carriage is unavailable, but a reproduction will add $6,000 to $8,000 to the price, depending on condition and delivery costs.

Canteens. A canteen of one of the more common Union or Confederate models recovered from a battlefield fetches less than $100, while a tin-drum canteen with "CS" embossed on the side may cost $5,000, and there are canteens at almost every price level between the two extremes.

Cap and Cartridge Boxes. A standard cap box costs $50–$60. A cap box marked "CS Arsenal, Baton Rouge, La." fetches as much as $2,500. A similar range of prices exists with cartridge boxes, although the most expensive is the Union Blakeslee quick-loader cartridge box with sling, at $1,500.

Cartridges. A bullet is what is fired from a gun. A Civil War cartridge is the paper, metal, rubber, or even skin container of powder that fires the bullet, sometimes available with the bullet attached. Many varieties and makes are available, most in the $15–$25 range, although some rare examples command $100 or more. Cartridges recovered from battlefields are usually less valuable.

Cavalry Equipment. A lively market exists in spurs, stirrups, bits, picket pins, and saddles used in the war. U.S. Cavalry-issue spurs range from $15 to $30 each; Union officers' spurs, with "US" stamped on both sides on the neck, cost $350 to $400 each. Stirrups range from $40 to $300. An officer's saddle with an eagle-head pommel, complete with stirrups, stirrup leathers, and girth, fetches $500 to $1,000. Confederate cavalry equipment commands considerably higher prices.

Corps Badges. Metal badges of the twenty-two Union corps without identification are consistent in price, about $200 to $250 dug, $125 to $175 non-dug. Individual identification radically increases price. Cloth corps badges not sewn on kepis or uniform blouses cannot be authenticated and are of questionable value.

Field Glasses and Telescopes. Most Union field glasses and telescopes, both army and navy, fall into the $200–$500 range, depending on condition and markings. Confederate equivalents are quite rare and command significantly higher prices.

Firearms. The longarms carried by the majority of Union soldiers are in good supply. If in very good condition, most are in the $500–$1,000 range. An exception is the M-1855, which ranges from $1,200 to $2,500, depending on the mounting. A number of special rifles were issued by the Union—carbines, revolving carbines, rifle muskets—and while many are in the $500–$1,000 range, a few rarities fetch hefty prices. A Symmes carbine, for example, probably would sell for whatever price was asked. Confederate rifles are scarcer and consequently costlier. No such rifle in very good condition sells for less than $2,000; the majority fetch from $3,500 to $5,000, and a good example of a Tallassee Carbine may reach $50,000.

The same price relationship exists in handguns. A number of Union revolvers fetch from $300 to $700. Notable exceptions are the Colt Army and Navy revolvers, which cost from $1,000 to $2,000 in better condition. Any Confederate revolver will command at least $2,000, most are in the $4,000 to $6,000 range, and such rarities as the Coffer, Columbus, and Schneider & Glassick revolvers are $10,000 and up, often way up.

Edmund Ruffin, the Confederate soldier who fired the first shot against Fort Sumter.

Some collectors buy dug weapons, although most have deteriorated badly, with the wooden stocks and handles gone. Prices range from about $100 for a Springfield rifle to $450 for a Colt .44-caliber pistol.

Flags. A U.S. flag of Civil War vintage, with thirty-three or thirty-four stars, will bring from $150 to $500. Artillery guidons and company flags fetch $1,000–$1,500. Brigade, division, and other distinctive flags are $1,000–$3,000; regimental colors, $3,500–$5,000. Confederate flags are more expensive. A swallowtail pennant is about $1,000; the Stars and Bars of any pattern fetches $1,000–$3,000; company flags, $3,500–$5,000; and regimental battle flags, $5,000–$15,000. Approach these with caution, for there are many imitations around.

Hard Rubber. Uniform buttons, flasks, cups, pipes, soap boxes, syringes, and other Civil War impedimenta were made of hard rubber, which also was called vulcanite and ebonite. Buttons range in price from a few dollars to $125 to $175 for a Confederate navy Manton's Patent button. Most other hard rubber objects fetch less than $100.

Knapsacks and Haversacks. The regulation Union knapsack of tarred canvas brings $75–$150, while less common knapsacks may go as high as $1,000. Union haversacks made of various materials range from $250 to $500. The standard Confederate haversack fetches $750 to $1,500.

Identification Discs. The dog tag, as identification discs are now called, were used first in the Civil War. Some were handmade by the individual soldier; others were stamped with such legends as "War of 1861" and "Against Slavery." The price range is small, $75–$300, with dug discs commanding higher prices. A dug hand-made Confederate disc fetches $200 to $300.

Insignia. This category includes stamped-brass headgear devices for enlisted men and officers, embroidered headgear for officers, and matched pairs of officers' shoulder straps. Prices range from $25 to $65 for an enlisted man's infantry hunting-horn device to $175 to $500 for an officer's mounted rifles wire-trumpet device. Rank determines the price for shoulder straps. A second lieutenant's straps are $50–$75, while a lieutenant general's bring $350–$450.

Knives. The bowie knife was used by soldiers of both sides. A Union bowie knife with a patriotic engraving such as "The Union Must & Shall Be Preserved" in good condition is $400–$500. A Confederate bowie knife engraved "Death to Abolition," for example, is $1,000 and up. Without engraving, Union bowie knives range from $100 to $500, depending on type and whether or not it comes with the original scabbard.

Medical. The rudimentary surgical instruments used in the war are avidly sought by many collectors. An identifiable Union army surgeon's operating kit is $1,000–$2,500; a comparable Confederate kit is double that figure. Individual instruments range from $25 to several hundred dollars. A U.S. surgeon's frock coat, sword, sash, and gauntlets will bring $1,600–$1,800. Even an identified artificial leg fetches around $600.

Mess Gear. Knife-fork-spoon combinations range from $75 to $175, depending on the manufacturer. An ordinary tin cup is $20–$40, or $125–$175 if it's marked "MIX." A standard-type tin mess plate is $35–$75.

Musical Instruments. Soldiers responded to calls from several types of bugles—single and double twist, made of copper or brass—and these range in price from $65 to $750, depending on type and condition. The most expensive is the standard brass government-issue bugle marked with the manufacturer's name. Bugles similar to some types used in the war were made in those years in Britain and France, and too often are offered for sale as the real thing. Fifes made of rosewood, boxwood, and granadilla were played in fife-and-drum corps. A good example of a Civil War fife, pitched in E or B-flat, is $25 to $65. A Civil War bass drum fetches $150 to $450, depending on condition, and $750

to $2,500 if emblazoned with a state seal and/or an American eagle. Unemblazoned snare drums are $125–$500; emblazoned, these sell for $1,000–$3,000.

Photographs. Soldiers going off to fight in the Civil War often had their photographs taken. Several photographic processes were in use: tintypes and ambrotypes, *carte de visite* photographs and albumen prints. The image was made directly on tin in tintypes, on glass in ambrotypes. *Carte de visite* photographs were positive images on paper, made from negatives and mounted on card stock. Albumen prints were similar to *carte de visite* photographs but larger. The value of these images varies with the subject, the quality of the image, and whether the subject is identified. A picture of, say, a Union cavalryman with his sword, belt, and large pistol would be $60–$80 as a tintype or ambrotype; $85–$150 if the soldier is identified; $75–$100 as a *carte de visite;* $100–$125 identified; $100–$150 as an albumen photograph; $200–$250 identified. Original photographs of well known Civil War figures are much more valuable. All the price ranges given above assume the picture is in excellent condition. Many Civil War photographs are copies, photographs of photographs, lacking in clarity and contrast, and worth about half as much. Once a dealer or a collector points out the difference, copies are relatively easy to detect.

Swords. Many types of swords, sabers, and cutlasses were issued to Union and Confederate officers. (Swords have straight blades, sabers have curved blades, and cutlasses are short sabers.) Different sabers, for example, were carried by the cavalry, dragoons, artillery, and topographical engineers. Different swords were carried by general and staff officers, infantry, foot artillery, noncommissioned officers, corps of engineers, medical corps, and the pay department. Officers in state militia units often carried distinctive

non-regulation swords and sabers. In addition, swords with elaborate engraving and special scabbards were presented to outstanding officers. The majority of Union swords and sabers available to collectors are in the $250–$1,000 range, and a few of the rarer blades reach three or four times that much. Confederate swords and sabers are much more. Only a few are available at $1,000. Most are in the $2,500–$5,000 range, and a number exceed $5,000.

Uniforms. No relic quite evokes the glory and romance of the war like an authentic uniform. Unfortunately, the prices asked reflect the appeal. At the low end of the price scale are state militia uniforms. A militia frock or coatee with state seal buttons is $150–$550; the matching trousers are $100–$350; the kepi is $75–$450. A regulation-issue infantry frock coat with blue piping on the collar and cuffs, complete with original buttons, fetches $1,700–$2,200. An enlisted man's kepi with a bound edge brings $350–$550. A Zouave jacket attributable to a specific regiment is $1,500–$3,500; the trousers are another $1,000–$2,500. Officers' single-breasted frock coats worn by lieutenants and captains are $400–$1,200; double-breasted frock coats worn by majors, colonels, and generals are $550–$1,200. An officer's fatigue blouse, lined with shoulder insignia, is $1,500–$3,700, and a Hardee (Jeff Davis) hat with silk edging, branch of service and eagle insignia, hat cord, and plume is $1,100–$2,500. A bargain by comparison is a naval officer undress double-breasted frock coat with shoulder and cuff insignia, at $550–$1,150. Only some 200 authentic Confederate uniforms are believed to be in private collections, and it is rare to see one for sale. A Confederate officer's

---

BATTLE FATIGUES

Though not by design, the Confederate army was the first in the world to go into battle wearing uniforms of a protective color. As the fortunes of the Confederacy dwindled and the Union blockade grew tighter, the South increasingly used a cheap homespun cloth for uniforms. It was butternut brown, and blended well with the colors of the field.

frock coat with insignia is estimated to be worth $4,000–$8,500, and an enlisted man's frock coat might fetch $15,000. Rarest of all are Confederate navy and marine corps uniforms; an officer's frock coat could bring as much as $25,000. Caution is urged in buying uniforms. Many items from the Indian Wars or from costumers are represented as authentic Civil War uniforms.

ANTIQUE DEALERS

Below is a list of some of the many established antique dealers who specialize in Civil War relics and memorabilia. Most of these sell by mail order; write for their catalogs.

R. E. Neville
3863 Old Shell Rd.
Mobile, AL 36608
(write for information)

The Ordnance Chest
P.O. Box 905
Madison, CT 06443
(three catalogs annually, $5)

Mike Brackin
P.O. Box 23
Manchester, CT 06040
(five catalogs annually, $6)

Bellinger's Military Antiques
P.O. Box 76371
Atlanta, GA 30328
(catalog $2)

Lawrence Christopher
4773 Tammey Dr., N.E.
Dalton, GA 30720
(404) 226-8894
(Confederate bullets; list $3)

Stone Mountain Relics, Inc.
968 Main St.
Stone Mountain, GA 30083
(404) 469-1425

Plainesman Gun Shop
22168 Hillview Dr.
Barrington, IL 60010
(list, send SASE)

Alex Peck
P.O. Box 710
Charleston, IL 61920
(217) 348-1009
(medical and surgical antiques)

Confederate States Metal
    Detectors
2905 Government St.
Baton Rouge, LA 70806
(504) 387-5044
(three lists annually, $4)

Maryland Line Trader
P.O. Box 190
Linthicum Heights, MD 21090
(write for information)

Sutlers Wagon
P.O. Box 5
Cambridge, MA 02139
(617) 864-1628

Henry Deeks
P.O. Box 1500
East Arlington, MA
(617) 488-1862

Paul Millikan
The Manual of Arms
P.O. Box 372
Mattawan, MI 49071
(616) 668-3570
(catalog $5.50 per year)

Walter Budd
3109 Eubanks Rd.
Durham, NC 27707
(four catalogs annually, $5)

Will Gorges
3822 Canterbury Rd.
New Bern, NC 28562
(catalog subscription, $6)

L&G Early Arms
P.O. Box 113
Amelia, OH 45102
(gun specialist; send SASE for free list)

Kenton's Trace
Box 778
Springfield, OH 45501
(catalog $2)

Civil War Antiques
David W. Taylor
P.O. Box 87
Sylvania, OH 43560
(list $1)

Dale C. Anderson Co.
4 West Confederate Ave.
Gettysburg, PA 17325
(six catalogs annually, $12)

Larry & Debbie Hicklen
Route 10, Old Nashville Hwy.
Murfreesboro, TN 37130
(615) 893-3470
(annual list subscription, $4)

Sword & Saber
P.O. Box 4417
Gettysburg, PA 17325
(717) 334-0205
(five catalogs annually, $5)

Dennis E. Lowe
RD #2, Box 2699AA
Hamburg, PA 19526
(write for information)

The Regimental
    Quartermaster
P.O. Box 553
Hatboro, PA 19040
(list $1)

John's Relics
227 Robertson Blvd.
Walterboro, SC 29488
(catalog $1)

Dr. Gerald Hovater
Rte. 1, P.O. Box 278
Henderson, TN 38340
(901) 989-2977
(six bimonthly lists, $3)

The Horse Soldier Shop
777 Baltimore St.
Gettysburg, PA 17325
Mail Order: P.O. Box 184
Cashtown, PA 17310
(two catalogs annually, $6)

Steve Johnson
343 53rd Ave. North
Nashville, TN 37209
(annual list subscription, $4)

Mike Miner
1046 Topside
Sevierville, TN 37862
(615) 453-0023
(Tennessee antiques only)

Lost Cause Relics
2237 Brookhollow Dr.
Abilene, TX 79605
(two lists, $2)

Catlett Brothers
Rte. 1, P.O. Box 170
Fredericksburg, VA 22401
(703) 786-7600
(annual list subscription, $6)

The Galvanized Yankee
918 Caroline St.
Fredericksburg, VA 22401
(703) 373-1886
(three catalogs a year, $6)

Peter C. George
P.O. Box 74
Mechanicsville, VA 23111
(804) 321-7272

✦ 14 ✦

CIVIL WAR COLLECTIBLES

A number of contemporary artists specialize in the Civil War, creating prints depicting battle scenes of the war and portraits of popular leaders. Among the best artists working in this field are Tom Lovell, Don Troiani, Michael Gnatek, Jr., Keith A. Rocco, Don Stivers, John Duillo, Peter W. Gaut, and Lisa S. Brown. Produced in limited editions, the prints qualify as works of art and should increase in value over time. Unframed prints range in price from $65 to $150, framed prints from $150 to $250.

Small sculptures of leaders and battle scenes are sold by mail and in a number of art galleries. James Muir and Francis Barnum are among the artists specializing in Civil War sculpture. The subjects available in limited editions include "Johnny Shiloh," Pickett's Charge, Lee at Antietam, and J. E. B. Stuart.

If you have a photograph of an ancestor who fought in the war, you can have an oil portrait painted of him, either full length or head-and-shoulders.

Toy soldiers, known formally as military miniatures, are available from a number of sources. Collectors can purchase miniatures painted and ready to display or unpainted, or one can buy molds and make them from scratch.

Over the years, a number of commemorative postage stamps have been issued that relate to the war; subjects have included Lee and Jackson, Ulysses S. Grant, the Stone Mountain Memorial, Gettysburg, and Fort Sumter. Stamps can be purchased individually or mounted and framed, grouped by subject: the Civil War, Confederates, Federals, Battlefields, and Abraham Lincoln. Most stamp dealers stock these commemoratives, and sets are advertised frequently in Civil War publications.

Among the most treasured and expensive war collectibles are autographs and documents. Many variables affect the price: the writer's fame, the number of autographs and documents he signed, the importance of a given document, and its condition. Autographs of minor generals, for example, are available in the $200–$300 price range. A "fine presidential document," signed by Ulysses S. Grant and dated January 27, 1877, framed with an engraved portrait, recently was advertised for $975. The same New York gallery offered a signed *carte de visite* of a uniformed Robert E. Lee for $3,850, and a Civil War military commission signed by Abraham Lincoln and dated July 15, 1864, framed with an engraved portrait, for $8,500.

ART GALLERIES AND PUBLISHERS

K & J Enterprises
P.O. Box 3778
Tucson, AZ 85722
(recreations of Civil War drawings; catalog $1)

Historical Art Prints, Ltd.
P.O. Box 660
Southbury, CT 06488
(203) 262-6680
(works of Don Troiani)

Collector Military Art, Inc.
3118 Barcelona St.
Tampa, FL 33629
(813) 831-9517

Americana House, Inc.
18 East Chestnut St.
Chicago, IL 60611
(312) 944-3085

American Print Gallery
P.O. Box 4477
Gettysburg, PA 17325
(800) 448-1863

General Longstreet's
   Gallery
3821 St. Elmo Ave.
Chattanooga, TN 37409

Breedlove Enterprises
1527 East Amherst Rd.
Massillon, OH 44648
(800) 426-4659
(pencil sketches of war leaders; catalog $1)

Martin's Gallery
219 Steinwehr Ave.
Gettysburg, PA 17325
(800) 448-1863

Heron Publishing
P.O. Box 14607
Odessa, TX 79768
(800) 999-0445
(works of Clyde Heron)

Virginia Fine Art Studio
3600 Sprucedale Dr.
Annandale, VA 22023
(703) 750-0025
(portraits of Confederate leaders; send SASE for list)

Fredericksburg Historical
   Prints
614 Caroline St.
Fredericksburg, VA 22401

ART SERVICES

Boone-CW
32-26 102nd St.
Flushing, NY 11369
(oil portraits from photographs)

Roberta Philips
P.O. Box 1073
Fritch, TX 79036
(806) 857-3075
(oil portraits from photographs)

AUTOGRAPHS AND DOCUMENTS

Antiques and Gifts
2226 Grove Way
Castro Valley, CA 94546
(documents and Confederate money; send SASE for free catalog)

Joseph Rubinfine
Suite 1301
505 South Flager Dr.
West Palm Beach, FL 33401
(305) 659-7077

Victor Marine
259 West 11th St.
Ship Bottom, NJ 08008
(609) 494-4781
(documents)

Kenneth W. Rendell Gallery
200 West 57th St.
New York, NY 10019
(212) 935-6767

Robert F. Batchelder
1 West Butler Pike
Ambler, PA 19002
(215) 643-1430
(documents and autographs)

Sword & Saber
P.O. Box 4417
Gettysburg, PA 17325
(five illustrated catalogs a year, $4)

Jim Hayes
P.O. Box 12557
James Island, SC 29412
(803) 795-0732
(six monthly lists, $6)

Gregory A. Ton
4200 Central La.
Memphis, TN 38117
(Confederate currency)

Deborah Lembert
1945 Lorraine Ave.
McLean, VA 22101
(list $1)

MISCELLANEOUS COLLECTIBLES

Der Dienst
P.O. Box 221
Lowell, MI 49331
(replicas of Civil War medals; catalog $1)

Collectors Antiquities
60 Manor Rd.
Staten Island, NY 10310
(arms and accoutrements; quarterly catalog, $8 a year)

Heath & Sons
827 South 57th St.
Springfield, OR 97478
(503) 747-8169
(battlefield medallions)

The Horse Soldier of
   Gettysburg
P.O. Box 184
Cashtown, PA 17310
(cavalry, general antiques, and replicas; annual catalog subscription, $4)

Dale C. Anderson Co.
4 West Confederate Ave.
Gettysburg, PA 17325
(arms, accoutrements, and collectibles; six catalogs a year, $12)

Heritage Rare Coin
   Galleries
311 Market St.
Dallas, TX 75202-9990
(Confederate war bonds; free list)

The American Historical
   Foundation
1142 West Grace St.
Richmond, Va 23220
(800) 368-8080
(replicas of Civil War pistols)

FLAGS AND GUIDONS

FLAG Company
4758 W. Caron St.
Glendale, AZ 85302-3666
*(flag, book, and gun
catalog, $2)*

Military Collectibles
Box 971
Minden, LA 71055
(illustrated list, $2)

The Flag Center, Inc.
9 South Harvie St.
Richmond, VA 23220
(catalog $2)

MINIATURES AND WAR GAMES

S. J. Games
P.O. Box 9210
Huntsville, AL 35812
*(battles programmed
for IBM computers;
brochure $1)*

Jack Scruby's Toy Soldiers
P.O Box 1658
Cambria, CA 93428
(805) 927-3805
*(painted miniatures; free
lists)*

Stone Mountain
Box 584
Broomfield, CO 80020
*(miniatures and war games;
catalog $3)*

Le Petit Soldier Shop
528 Rue Royale
New Orleans, LA 70130
(504) 523-7741
*(military miniatures,
helmets, swords, medals,
and decorations)*

Armchair General's
  Mercantile
1008 Adams
Bay City, MI 48708
(517) 892-6177
*(miniatures and games;
catalog $2)*

Warwick Miniatures, Ltd.
P.O. Box 1498
Portsmouth, NH 03801
(603) 431-7139
*(painted miniatures;
catalog $3)*

Dutkins' Collectibles
1019 Route 70
Cherry Hill, NJ 08002
*(molds for casting; send
SASE for flier)*

Pewter Graphics
Box 89
Burnt Hills, NY 12027
(unpainted miniatures)

Burlington Antique Toys
1082 Madison Ave.
New York, NY 10028
(212) 861-9708
(toy soldiers)

The Soldier Shop
1222 Madison Ave.
New York, NY 10028
*(miniature soldiers and
military books)*

Miniature Images
P.O. Box 308
Manassas, VA 22110
(free list)

~ 15 ~

REENACTING THE CIVIL WAR

During the one-hundred-twenty-fifth anniversary of the Civil War, April 12, 1986, to May 26, 1990, hundreds of thousands watched as volunteers in authentic uniforms participated in hundreds of reenactments and other commemorative events. Latter-day Billy Yanks and Johnny Rebs re-created battles and skirmishes, ran field hospitals, demonstrated artillery, made encampments, marched in parades, and presented living-history demonstrations in remembrance of the war that changed America.

The events weren't confined to the original battlefields. The Battle of Spotsylvania was reenacted in the New Jersey Pine Barrens. Shiloh's Hornet's Nest was re-created in Maine. In California, battles were reenacted every Sunday from April to October near Bakersfield. Nor were such events confined to the United States. The first day of Gettysburg was reenacted near Toronto, although the hosts were the 10th Louisiana and the 137th New York.

Reenactments of battles are frequently presented at most of the national battlefields, particularly during the summer. Park Service regulations, however, prohibit reenactors from "firing" at one another. For this reason the reenactment of the Battle of Gettysburg was held on private property ten miles south of the actual battlefield. To find out when reenactments are being presented, telephone the national battlefield you would like to visit. For other events, consult your local newspapers or the appropriate Civil War publications (see Chapter 8).

The reenactment of battles and skirmishes became popular during the war's centennial in the 1960s, and participants were more enthusiastic than authentic. Many reenactors wore work clothes, blue for Yankees, gray for Confederates, and carried modern rifles and shotguns. Today, that has all changed. "More than ninety percent of today's reenactors are authentic from cap to underwear," says William Keitz, editor of the *Camp Chase Gazette,* which prints news of reenactments and reenactor units.

Reenacting is growing rapidly in popularity, and some 40,000 people from all walks of life now participate. It no longer is an all-male avocation. Women serve as nurses, or dress in authentic period costumes to lend moral support to the troops. This may be partly defensive; wives of reenactors often refer to themselves as "Civil War widows."

Being a reenactor is expensive. A private needs an initial $1,000 worth of gear. An Italian-made replica of the 1853 Enfield rifle costs $495. A bayonet with scabbard is $32.50; the sling, $10.50. A uniform overcoat is $135; trousers, $50; a kepi, $21.50; a belt, $12.75, and its buckle, $3.50; a pair of Army Jefferson shoes (the first shoes issued in which one fit the left foot, the other the right), $74.50; authentic underwear, $13.75; linen suspenders, $7.95.

A private also needs badges and insignia, a canteen, and a poncho for rainy days. He probably will invest in a tent and in replicas of vintage mess gear. If he is in an artillery unit, he may have to pay part of the cost of

Reenactors in battle at Fredericksburg.

the cannon and gun carriage. A cavalry unit is the most expensive of all, as anyone who has kept a horse will attest. Reenactors who are officers need even deeper pockets. A Union officer's tailored frock coat is $375, and a sword is $300 and up. Reenactors also must shoulder the expenses for participating in reenactments.

The pages of Civil War magazines and newspapers are filled with advertisements from companies that cater exclusively to reenactors. Sutlers (civilian provisioners to the army) attend every reenactment, hawking firearms, uniforms, and supplies.

For those interested in becoming reenactors, a list at the end of this chapter has the names of many of the active units across the country, and tells where to write for additional information. Also listed are the mail-order companies that supply arms, equipment, and replicas of uniforms to reenactors.

Art Buker of Baltimore became a reenactor in 1975, and for the past ten years has commanded Company C of the 2nd Burdan's Sharpshooters. Buker is an engineer for a public utility, and his company of sharpshooters includes a NASA engineer, a medical technician, a building contractor, a draftsman, a personnel director, and a junior high school student who is the company bugler. The regiment is scattered around the country, and a newsletter helps them keep in touch.

"We're a distinctive unit," says Buker. "We wear green uniform blouses, the color traditionally used by sharpshooters, and carry the .52-caliber Sharps carbine, which fires bullets and doesn't have to be loaded with a ramrod like the standard Civil War rifle. In the

Cannon and reenactor at Petersburg.

war, Burdan's Sharpshooters were an elite regiment. Every man had to be an excellent shot."

Buker became a reenactor by going to a reenactment as a spectator, liking what he saw, and chatting with the participants. Most reenactors still are recruited that way. Often a man is invited to take part right then and there. He need only buy a canteen and the authentic Jefferson shoes from a sutler, and the unit will loan him the rest of the uniform and a rifle. Buker carries extra equipment to events just for that purpose.

"Sometimes a man will purchase a complete outfit and rifle from a sutler at his first event," Buker says. "And that's a healthy investment. Our rifle alone costs $750."

There are three basic types of reenactors, according to Buker. At one end are the men who are primarily interested in taking part in battle reenactments—

charging across fields and firing their guns. In the middle are those who find the hobby a fascinating extension of their interest in the history of the Civil War. At the other extreme are the serious marksmen. Their real interest are the meets where reproduction vintage weapons are fired in competition. "We like the living history aspect," says Buker. "Even our young bugler is invited to visit schools to talk about what it was like to go off to the Civil War as a lad. He has learned all the old bugle calls and enjoys playing them."

Burdan's Sharpshooters have appeared in the miniseries "North and South" and the major motion picture *Glory*, the story of a black Union regiment. In "North and South," actor Parker Stevenson played the commandant of Burdan's Sharpshooters and invited Buker to come to Hollywood (at Stevenson's expense) for the cast party. But while it may be exciting for a reenactor to perform before the cameras, it's not a way to get rich. Reenactors are paid a non-union $50 a day.

A reward of a different kind came to Burdan's Sharpshooters. A new recruit was the great-grandnephew of an original soldier in the regiment. Although the family had lost track of the veteran over the years, the reenactors were able to locate his grave in a small town in Wisconsin. Under a century-old law, the federal government is obligated to provide a special headstone for all Union veterans. The government was petitioned, and the new headstone was dedicated with an honor guard of Burdan's Sharpshooters in full regalia in attendance.

Mary Tippee, a sutler to a Union brigade.

ALABAMA

3rd Alabama Infantry
Lamar Fox
P.O. Box 35, Rte. 1
   River Rd.
Theodore, AL 36582
(205) 973-1485

3rd Alabama Cavalry
Preston Williams
342 Ogden Rd.
Montgomery, AL 36606
(205) 834-7062

15th Alabama Infantry
Stephen McKinney
4542 Wake Forest Dr.
Montgomery, AL 36109

*19th Alabama Infantry,
   Co. I*
Archie Barnett
P.O. Box 337, Rte. 6
Killen, AL 35645
(205) 757-3082

*28th Alabama Infantry,
   Co. H*
Craig Morris
108 Americana Dr.
Birmingham, AL 35749
(205) 856-2915

51st Alabama Cavalry
Kenneth Morrison
Box 161-AA, Rte. 14
Oxford, AL 36203
(205) 835-2915

51st Alabama Cavalry
Jimmy Shell
201 Pecan St.
Evergreen, AL
(205) 578-2216

ARIZONA

1st U.S. Cavalry
Gary Roberts
14024 North 180th Ave.
Waddell, AZ 85355
(602) 584-7083

2nd U.S. Artillery, Co. B
Joe Meeham
32 Columbine
Flagstaff, AZ 86004
(602) 774-6272

4th Virginia Infantry, Co. C
Edward Gouvier
1543 West Surrey
Phoenix, AZ 85029
(602) 993-2843

4th Virginia Cavalry
Bob Wright
P.O. Box 3616
Sedona, AZ 86340
(602) 282-7252

23rd New York Infantry
Larry Stewart
P.O. Box 5606
Mesa, AZ 85201
(602) 834-4004

CALIFORNIA

1st Texas Infantry
George Otott, Jr.
6013 Elkport St.
Lakewood, CA 90713

*2nd Massachusetts Cavalry,
   Co. A*
David Stevens
465 East K St.
Benicia, CA 94510
(707) 745-4312

1st Texas Infantry
Howard Ostrowsky
291 Salsbury Ave.
Goleta, CA 93117

4th U.S. Infantry, Co. C
Joe Alarid
45 East Cannon Green
Goleta, CA 93117

9th North Carolina Cavalry
Mike Danley
4732 Camino Del Rey
Santa Barbara, CA 93102

*34th North Carolina
    Infantry*
Barry Smith
4222 Brookside Pl.
Goleta, CA 93117

4th U.S. Infantry, Co. A
Norton Aronow
1572 Tuba St.
Mission Hills, CA 91345
(818) 891-7641

4th U.S. Infantry, Co. C
Dom Dalbello
16 Alemeda Padre Serra
Santa Barbara, CA 93103
(805) 968-8187

9th Virginia Cavalry
Pete Fischer
3934 East Sussex Way
Fresno, CA 93726
(209) 227-3563

5th New Hampshire Infantry
James Kidd
11039 South Lindesmith
Whittier, CA 90603
(213) 943-1529

3rd U.S. Artillery
David Partak
1581 Pepper La.
Saratoga, CA 90603
(213) 354-1529

CONNECTICUT

*5th Alabama Battalion,
    Co. A*
William J. Boudah, Jr.
45 Broad Brook Rd.
Enfield, CT 06082
(203) 749-6261

5th Connecticut Infantry
Guy M. Mazzarella
19 Browns La.
Old Lyme, CT 06371
(203) 414-9849

17th Connecticut Infantry
Lee H. Melcher
15 Beaumont St.
Fairfield, CT 06430

7th Virginia Cavalry, Co. A
Edward Friedrich
51 Elm St.
Rockville, CT 06066

DELAWARE

2nd U.S. Delaware Infantry
L. Michael Corbin
Box 110-K, Rte. 2
Dagsboro, DE 19706
(302) 539-2251

Pulaski (Georgia) Battery
Ed Kalinowski
P.O. Box 327
Delaware City, DE 19706
(302) 834-4807

1st Virginia Infantry, Co. D
Maurice Whitlock
135 Clinton St.
Delaware City, DE 19706
(302) 834-8730

FLORIDA

The Confederates, Inc.
Barry Domenget
P.O. Box 1536
Oneco, FL 34262-1536
(813) 794-5525

2nd Florida Cavalry, Inc.
Roger Ragland
3545 LaSalle Ave.
St. Cloud, FL 32769
(305) 957-3759

*1st Louisiana Wheat's
    Tigers, Co. B*
Glen R. Martz
4647-83 Ter.
Pinellas Park, FL 34665
(813) 544-3292

*1st New York Engineers,
    Co. A*
John Poe
704 Elisa Dr. East
Jacksonville, FL 32216

*Field Hospital Medical
    Service*
Patrick McHone
5527 Keystone Dr. South
Jacksonville, FL 32707

Boone's Louisiana Battery
Dave Hale
3106 East Baldwin Rd.
Panama City, FL 32405
(904) 785-3234

*Confederate Service Arms,
    Headquarters*
Edward O. Dennison
14500 S.W. 289th St., #62
Homestead, FL 33032
(305) 247-3537

*Hart's South Carolina
    Battery*
Joseph Perry
17101 S.W. 200th St.,
    #E-13
Miami, FL 33187
(305) 233-6766

Chapman's Virginia Battery
Robert Mooney
13660 S.W. 79th St.
Miami, FL 33183
(305) 385-4952

7th Florida Infantry, Co. C
Douglas Lambert
12225 S.W. 35th Ter.
Miami, FL 33176
(305) 723-2553

USS Ottawa Union Gunboat
James Sheets
704 Elisa Dr. East
Jacksonville, FL 32216

*Union Army, District of
    Florida, Inc.*
Tim Weinzen, Commander
20017 Wiygul Rd.
Umatilla, FL 32784
(904) 669-5514

17th Connecticut Infantry
Larry Dodd
111 Gulf Dr., Suite A
New Port Richey, FL 33552

U.S. Signal Corps
John Olbert
269 Ruth Ave.
Longwood, FL 32750
(407) 323-8569

47th Pennsylvania Infantry
Rocky Sawyer
665 Park Lake
Orlando, FL 32703
(407) 323-8569

115th New York Infantry
Mark Coolidge
2624 N.E. 28th St.
Ft. Lauderdale, FL 33306
(305) 564-2563

*1st Battalion, U.S.
    Engineers*
Gene Delzingaro
955 Slippery Rock Ave.
Orlando, FL 32826
(407) 281-3722

42nd Pennsylvania Infantry
Ashley Shankle
6010 Chipola Circle
Orlando, FL 32809
(407) 855-3300

97th Pennsylvania Infantry
Rick Moock
437 Boca Ciega Dr.
Madeira Beach, FL 33708
(813) 391-4565

1st U.S. Artillery
Kenneth Hill
10928 North 15th St.
Tampa, FL 33612
(813) 971-8491

47th New York Infantry
John Higgins
2340 Sun Valley Circle
Winter Park, FL 32792
(407) 657-7081

33rd Massachusetts Infantry
Don Kedina
810 Lianna Dr.
Orlando, FL 32817

Keystone Light Artillery
Ron Fornoff
P.O. Box 14OR3, Rte. 1
High Springs, FL 32643
(904) 454-1443

U.S. Naval Detachment
Art Frietag
7784 22nd Ave. North
St. Petersburg, FL 33170

*Pensacola Civil War
 Reenactors Assn.*
Robert Eckols, Chaplain
1909 Lansing Dr., Apt. 4
Pensacola, FL 32504
(904) 478-1587

3rd Maine Infantry
John Greene
361 Diane Court
Casselberry, FL 32707
(305) 699-1523

*6th New York Infantry,
 Co. G*
Lawrence Ellis
511 S. E. 13th Court
Pompano Beach, FL 33060
(305) 942-2411

GEORGIA

12th Georgia Light Artillery
Buck Hames, Commander
27 Chicopee Dr.
Marietta, GA 30064
(404) 391-5404

52nd Ohio Infantry, Co. B
C. Matthew Murdzak,
 Commander
70 Lake Harbin Rd.,
Apt. A-3
Morrow, GA 30260

40th Virginia Infantry
Bill Hazen
108 New Jessup Hwy.
Brunswick, GA 31520

*14th Georgia Cavalry,
 D Troop*
Lynwood Belcher
4004 Winfred Dr.
Albany, GA 31707
(912) 698-4915

30th Georgia Infantry
Tom L. Fusia
605 Welton Dr.
Riverdale, GA 30296
(404) 568-7863

*14th Georgia Cavalry,
 E Troop*
Ron Carlisle
4834 Josephine St.
Columbus, GA 31907
(404) 568-7863

A reenactor shaves during a quiet moment before battle.

Cavalry reenactors in formation.

24th Georgia Cavalry, Co. B
Danny McCook
Rte. 1
Culbert, GA 31740
(912) 732-3864

ILLINOIS

14th Corps Medical Service
John B. Kochera
909 Rosewood
Effingham, IL 62401
(217) 342-9310

15th U.S. Regulars
Ross Richardson
Rural Rte. 4
Effingham, IL 62401

Virginia Light Artillery,
  Co. C
R. H. Young, Jr.
301 Crestwood Dr.
Collinsville, IL 62234
(618) 344-4916

22nd North Carolina CSA
Don E. Brown, Commander
P.O. Box 254
Salem, IL 62881
(618) 548-4808

The Regimental Observer
John L. Satterlee
6 Lambert La.
Springfield, IL 62704
(217) 546-2423

13th Indiana Infantry,
  Co. A
Philip John Law
16750 Shea Ave.
Hazel Crest, IL 60429

2nd Illinois Light Infantry
Jack Whitlock, Commander
605 West Walnut St.
Carbondale, IL 62901
(618) 549-3763

7th Illinois Infantry
Robert L. Coons
P.O. Box 282, Rural Rte. 3
Lincoln, IL 62656
(217) 732-8844

102nd Illinois Infantry
Dale Larson
Rural Rte. 1
Berwick, IL 61417
(309) 462-3450

Camp Fuller Field Music
David Franz
609 Oak St.
Lena, IL 61048
(815) 369-2353

79th New York Infantry,
  Co. B
Ray Morrison
156506 South Cherry Hill
Tinley Park, IL 60477
(312) 429-2353

36th Illinois Infantry
Steven M. Snyder
439 Niagara
Park Forest, IL 60466
(312) 747-9192

16th Iowa Veteran Volunteer
  Infantry
John and Mary Allen
205-B Arlene Court
Wheeling, IL 60090

9th Indiana Infantry
William Schroter
7200 Heritage
Chicago, IL 60636
(312) 737-6564

INDIANA

1st South Carolina Infantry
Brendan Moore
20447 Darden Rd.
South Bend, IN 46637

44th Indiana Infantry
Michael Clay
14810 Amstutz Rd.
Leo, IN 46765

20th Indiana Infantry
Merv Wood
P.O. Box 245
Crown Point, IN 46307

1st Wisconsin Light Artillery
Charlie Mount, Commander
P.O. Box 20276
Indianapolis, IN 46220

5th Tennessee Infantry CSA
Tom Chandler
P.O. Box 403, Rte. 2
Winslow, IN 47598

9th Indiana Infantry
Wayne Tice
932 North 200 West
Valparaiso, IN 46383

49th Indiana Infantry
Dave Shackelford,
    Commander
P.O. Box 20276
Indianapolis, IN 46220

**19th Indiana Infantry (Iron
    Brigade Assn.)**
3610 43rd St.
Highland, IN 46322
(219) 924-8860

IOWA

*Inspector-General of Iowa
    Recreated Units*
Milan A. Vodic
2218 East 11th St.
Davenport, IA 52803
(319) 786-3504

Alvin Schroeder, Chaplain
1010 West Benton St.,
Apt. 110-F
Iowa City, IA 52240
(319) 351-3208

KENTUCKY

*3rd Missouri Cavalry
    (Dismounted) Co.*
Albert L. Page, Secretary
6045 Fernview Rd.
Louisville, KY 40291
(502) 239-0043

*5th Kentucky Infantry CSA,
    Co. D*
Doug Rigsby, Commander
15801 Trace Rd.
Rush, KY 41168
(606) 928-3694

5th Tennessee Infantry CSA
Dan Dudgeon, Commander
9021 Thelma La.
Louisville, KY 50220
(502) 491-5038

LOUISIANA

Shreveport Grays Artillery
Simon Ebarb, Jr.
607 Sugarleaf Ter.
Shreveport, LA 71106
(318) 686-9247

*28th Louisiana Infantry,
    Co. I*
Michael D. Jones
P.O. Box 1318
Iowa, LA 70647
(318) 582-6154

Washington Artillery
Chris Becker
5863 West End Blvd.
New Orleans, LA 70124
(504) 486-2998

Boone's Louisiana Battery
John R. Bangs
23 South Bernadotte
New Orleans, LA 70119
(504) 488-1658

MAINE

20th Maine Infantry, Co. B
Vance and Ben Brown
P.O. Box 53
Searsport, ME 04974
(207) 548-2508

20th Maine Infantry, Co. A
Corey D. Chase
P.O. Box 251, RFD 2
Bowdoinham, ME 04008
(207) 666-3056

*28th Massachusetts Infantry,
    Co. H, 2nd Irish
    Regiment*
Steven Eames
P.O. Box 713
North Berwick, ME 03906
(207) 676-5556

MARYLAND

2nd U.S. Infantry, Co. C
Douglas C. Elam
P.O. Box 119F
Bryans Road, MD 20616
(301) 375-8901

*13th Virginia Infantry CSA,
    Co. H*
Roy Smith, Commander
6737 Old Waterloo Rd.,
Apt. 114
Elkridge, MD 21227
(301) 799-8597

*42nd Pennsylvania Infantry,
    Co. F*
Ray Wetzel
295 Clear Ridge Rd.
Linwood, MD 21764
(301) 775-2048

*13th Alabama Infantry,
    Co. F*
Philip Oliver
P.O. Box 969
Bowie, MD 20715

4th Texas Infantry, Co. B
Walter I. Beall, Jr.
77 West 5th St.
Frederick, MD 21701
(301) 662-0502

*2nd Maryland Infantry,
    Co. G*
Donald Patrick
P.O. Box 740
Ridgely, MD 21660
(301) 926-9095

5th South Carolina
Hugh F. Clayton
21020 Brink Court
Gaithersburg, MD 21237
(301) 926-9095

20th Maine Infantry
Robert E. Crickenberger, Jr.
3617 7th St.
North Beach, MD 20714

19th Georgia Infantry CSA
Bruce R. White, Commander
18824 Bent Willow Circle,
Apt. 314
Germantown, MD 20874
(301) 540-8367

MASSACHUSETTS

10th Massachusetts Infantry
Thomas Hogan, Commander
P.O. Box 63
Florence, MA 01060
(413) 584-7147

12th Massachusetts Infantry
Warren E. Pitts
580 Center St.
Hanover, MA 02339
(617) 826-6641

*Union and Confederate
    Volunteers*
Richard Johns, Commander
P.O. Box 266
Lynn, MA 01060

*5th New Hampshire
    Volunteers*
Patrick McMahon
61 Old South St.
Northampton, MA 01060
(413) 586-1559

*5th Alabama Battalion,
    Co. A*
Philip R. Kirdulis
P.O. Box 1306
Warren, MA 01083
(413) 436-9324

*Massachusetts 9th Light
    Battery*
Russell J. Myette,
    Commander
86 Riverbank Rd.
Northampton, MA 01060
(413) 586-2984

MICHIGAN

*24th Michigan Infantry (Iron
    Brigade Assn.)*
P.O. Box 10013
Lansing, MI 48901
(517) 694-1851

8th Michigan Infantry
Thomas M. Hannenberg
329 Pearl St.
Chesaning, MI 48616-1285

*84th Regiment of Foot, Royal
    Highland Emigrants*
21047 Tiffany Dr.
Woodhaven, MI 48183
(313) 675-1770

*26th North Carolina
    Infantry*
3310 West Willow
Lansing, MI 48917
(517) 321-8162

10th Michigan Infantry
David S. Rowley
908 West McConnell
St. Johns, MI 48879
(517) 224-6381

27th Virginia Infantry
James B. Pahl
P.O. Box 214
Sunfield, MI 48890
(517) 566-8023

21st Michigan Infantry
Richard W. Reaume
21078 Eastwood
Warren, MI 48078
(616) 694-2014

13th Michigan Infantry
Howard Nunemaker
358 West River St.
Ostego, MI 49078
(616) 694-2014

Rutherford Rifles CSA
John A. Braden
5519 Taylor
Fremont, MI 48412
(616) 924-6544

7th Tennessee Cavalry CSA
Hank Kaminski, Jr.
4860 Rochester Rd.
Dryden, MI 48428
(313) 796-3528

7th Michigan Infantry
Robert McBrien
331 Reed St.
Lansing, MI 48428
(313) 796-3528

*3rd Michigan Infantry,
    Co. A*
Scott A. Cummings
1008 Adams St.
Bay City, MI 48708
(517) 895-8962

*5th Michigan Regimental
    Band*
Jerry Bauer, Commander
    Color Guard
661 Heatherwoode
Novi, MI 48050
(313) 349-9143

*2nd Tennessee Cavalry
    CSA, Co. C*
Walter Anschutz,
    Commander
2421 Eleven Mile Rd.
Breckenridge, MI 48615
(517) 842-3665

*4th Kentucky Infantry
    Jeff Davis Rifles*
Geoff Walden, Commander
No. 4 35197 23-Mile Rd.
New Baltimore, MI 48047
(313) 725-3842

MINNESOTA

1st Minnesota Infantry
Stephen E. Osman
Fort Snelling History Center
St. Paul, MN 55111
(612) 726-1171

MISSISSIPPI

27th Mississippi Infantry
Gary L. Pierce
4408 High St.
Greenwood, MS 38930
(601) 455-3440

15th U.S. Infantry
Marty C. Brazin
115 Holly Hills Dr.
Biloxi, MS 39532
(601) 388-1388

*9th Mississippi Infantry,
    Co. C*
Joseph W. Thomas
P.O. Box 49, Rte. 1
Tillatoba, MS 38961
(601) 623-5121

*7th Tennessee Cavalry,
    Co. D*
Bryan Locke
P.O. Box 495
Corinth, MS 38834
(601) 286-3304

MISSOURI

24th Missouri Infantry
Donald Strother
P.O. Box 341
Purdy, MO 65734
(417) 442-3241

4th Missouri Cavalry, Co. C
David C.Smith, Commander
P.O. Box 322, Rte. 2
Rolla, MO 65401
(314) 364-6491

*2nd Missouri Infantry CSA,
    Co. A*
Scott Brown
2009 N.E. 54th Ter.
Kansas City, MO 64118
(816) 454-7709

NEVADA

82nd Illinois Infantry, Co. D
James Hindes
406 Caslimesa
North Las Vegas, NV 89115
(702) 643-7433

*5th Michigan Cavalry,
    Co. E*
David Evans
311-D Brookside La.
Las Vegas, NV 89107
(702) 645-0719

*33rd Virginia Infantry CSA,
    Co. K*
Bruce Eubank
901 Brush
Las Vegas, NV 89108
(702) 645-0719

U.S. Medical Service
Joshua Landish
818 East Charleston
Las Vegas, NV 89104
(702) 873-1106

*5th Virginia Cavalry CSA,
    Co. C*
Eric Sautter
2735 Seabridge
Las Vegas, NV 89121
(702) 733-6308

NEW HAMPSHIRE

20th Maine Infantry, Co. B
Ben Hadley
56 North Main St.
Wolfeboro, NH 03894
(603) 569-3327

28th Massachusetts
Steven Eames
27 Mill St.
Dover, NH 03894

NEW JERSEY

1st U.S. Cavalry, Co. H
Frank Doyle
96 Ocean Blvd.
Cliffwood Beach, NJ 07735

7th New Jersey Infantry
Tony Daniels
501 Sunset Blvd.
Mantoloking, NJ 08738
(201) 793-6397

2nd U.S. Regulars
Rick Bilz
28 Hudson Ave.
Waldwick, NJ 07463
(201) 447-2221

7th Virginia Cavalry
Daniel C. Hatcher
33 Hagaman St.
Port Reading, NJ 07064
(201) 969-3317

7th Virginia Cavalry
Edward F. McGuinn
33 Hagaman St.
Port Reading, NJ 07064

12th Georgia Infantry, Co. B
Joe Majeski
2017 Greenwood Ave.
Trenton, NJ 08609
(609) 588-9241

NEW MEXICO

New Mexico Territorial Volunteers
Dean D. Fish
3010 Monroe St., N.E.
Albuquerque, NM 87110
(505) 881-1828

NEW YORK

148th New York Infantry
George Shadman
29 Carlton Rd.
Waterloo, NY 13165
(505) 881-1828

1st New York Light Artillery, Battery L
Frank Cutler, Commander
6343 Kelly Rd.
Sodus, NY 14551
(315) 483-9254

143rd New York Infantry
Charles Young, Commander
P.O. Box 75, Rte. 1
Ferndale, NY 12734
(914) 292-3067

94th New York Infantry
William Strong, Commander
146 Hailesboro St.
Gouverneur, NY 13642
(315) 287-3391

5th Alabama Battalion, Co. A
Robert J. Malinka
60 East Lake Dr.
Amityville, NY 11701
(516) 598-3361

119th New York Infantry, Co. H
Glenn F. Sitterly, President
306 Rockwood Ave.
Baldwin, NY 11510
(516) 868-4521

Mosby's Rangers CSA
Don Stumbo
3972 O'Neill Rd.
Lima, NY 14485
(716) 367-2843

124th New York Infantry, Co. A
Charles LaRocca
209 Goodwill Rd.
Montgomery, NY 12549
(914) 457-5564

NORTH CAROLINA

3rd North Carolina S.T.
Tony Bean
3020 Sell Rd.
Winston-Salem, NC 27105
(919) 595-3890

43rd North Carolina Infantry
Tom Teff
1210 Woodland Ave.
Monroe, NC 28110
(704) 289-4850

Charlotte Grays, 11th North Carolina
Paul K. Troutman
932 Poindexter Dr.
Charlotte, NC 28209

5th North Carolina Infantry, Co. F
Charles L. Bigham
P.O. Box 16123
Monroe, NC 28110
(704) 289-4749

6th North Carolina Infantry
Bob Peterson
2287 Winterberry Dr.
Winston-Salem, NC 27106
(919) 924-0511

OHIO

13th Ohio Infantry, Co. F
John Sarver
3241 Blue Rock Rd.
Cincinnati, OH 45239

Independent (Mounted) Cavalry
David Naliborski
5016 Stickney Ave.
Cleveland, OH 44144
(216) 351-5158

5th Kentucky, Thomas' Mudsills
Dave Slater
188 Collingwood Ave.
Whitehall, OH 43213
(614) 236-1060

Corps of Topographical Engineers
Robert Thomas
5640 Yermo Dr.
Toledo, OH 43613
(419) 472-9274

43rd North Carolina, Co. D
Daniel T. Wiley, Commander
6111 Foth
Toledo, OH 43613

8th Ohio Infantry
Thomas Downes
2910 Clinton Ave.
Cleveland, OH 44113
(216) 861-3638

11th Ohio Cavalry (Dismounted)
Al Martellotti
13395 Shitepoke Rd.
Sardinia, OH 45171
(513) 446-2101

1st Ohio Light Artillery
Thomas Baker
5113 Drivemere Rd.
Hilliard, OH 43026
(614) 876-9624

29th Ohio Infantry, Co. H
Stephen Burr
450 North Munroe Rd.
Tallmadge, OH 44278
(216) 633-3170

29th Ohio Infantry, Co. H
Dave Baglia
11463 Fraze Rd.
Doylestown, OH 44230
(216) 658-4481

Jeff Davis Rifles
Darrell Arnold
291 County Rd. 800
Polk, OH 44866
(419) 945-2475

PENNSYLVANIA

111th Pennsylvania Infantry, Co. H
Dan Ward
1422 Pittsburgh Ave.
Erie, PA 16506

3rd Pennsylvania Cavalry, Co. H
Nelson I. Petit
P.O. Box 240
Scotland, PA 17254
(717) 263-2506

Independent Battery E, Inc.
Lloyd Berkey, Jr.
P.O. Box 63, RD 3
Rockwood, PA 15557
(814) 926-2227

13th Virginia Infantry,
  Co. K
Gregory J. Finn
905 North 19th St.
Harrisburg, PA 17103
(717) 238-4323

11th U.S., Co. C
Frank Magerko, Jr.
377 RD 1
New Salem, PA 15468
(412) 438-8378

2nd Virginia Infantry
Chuck Mercer
P.O. Box 126-B, RD 5
Clarks Summit, PA 18411
(717) 587-5214

4th Virginia Infantry
Kenneth S. Mink
980 Highland Ave.
Gettysburg, PA 17325
(717) 337-1557

Adjutant General SVR
Charles H. Lilienthal
254 West Trenton Ave.,
  Apt. B-314
Morrisville, PA 19067

87th Pennsylvania Infantry
Timothy J. Pritchard
P.O. Box 11-A, RD 3
Red Lion, PA 17356

6th Vermont Infantry
Jeff Driscoll
The Shipley School
Bryn Mawr, PA 19440
(215) 525-2871

13th Virginia Cavalry
Robert Badders, Jr.
P.O. Box 185, RD 1
Thomasville, PA 17364
(717) 225-3118

53rd Pennsylvania Infantry
Todd Beckmeyer
3390 Cranmore La.
York, PA 17402

83rd Pennsylvania Infantry,
  Co. E
Russell W. McLaughlin
11846 Martin Rd.
Waterford, PA 16441
(814) 796-3594

RHODE ISLAND

2nd Rhode Island Infantry
Thomas Bookout
68 Kay St.
Newport, RI 02840
(401) 841-3056

SOUTH CAROLINA

Campbell's Battery CS
Bennie Campbell
704 West Gap Creek Rd.
Greer, SC 29651
(803) 895-1855

Cvenshaw's Battery CS
Charlie Cvenshaw
Charlie's Machine Shop
Washington Ave.
Greenville, SC 29611

Palmetto Brigade, 1st South
  Carolina Volunteers
David and Cathy Benton
30 Harvey Ave.
Goose Creek, SC 29445
(803) 572-7221

Palmetto Brigade, 2nd South
  Carolina Volunteers,
  Co. B
C. B. Miller
609 Perry Rd.
Greenville, SC 29609

20th South Carolina
  Volunteers
Chris Snelgrove
615 Old Barnwell Rd.
West Columbia, SC 29169

23rd South Carolina
  Volunteers
Ken McCracken
P.O. Box 12484
Florence, SC 29501
(803) 665-4779

26th South Carolina
  Volunteers
Tony Purvis
105 Dogwood Circle
Cheraw, SC 29520

TENNESSEE

63rd Tennessee
  Infantry CSA
Headquarters
P.O. Box 126
Cumberland Gap, TN 37724
Richard Beeler, Commander
P.O. Box 76
Cumberland Gap, TN 37724

63rd Tennessee Infantry,
  CSA, Co. A
Steve Adams
P.O. Box 249-A, Rte. 1
Ewing, VA 24248

63rd Tennessee Infantry
  CSAS, Co. D
Ken Smith
1150 Burnett Station Rd.
Seymour, TN 37865

7th Tennessee Cavalry
  (US/CS)
Kevin Duke
1696 Carruthers
Memphis, TN 38112
(901) 725-1455

59th Tennessee Infantry,
  Cos. C & F CSA
Headquarters
101 Skytrail Circle
Bristol, TN 37620
(615) 764-3234

19th Georgia Infantry CSA
Robert Bailey
2850 McCallie Ave.
Chattanooga, TN 37404
(615) 622-2163

VERMONT

The New England Artillery
James Dassatti, Commander
West Main St.
Wilmington, VT
(802) 464-5569

VIRGINIA

5th Virginia Infantry
James S. George II
200 North 31st St.
Purcellville, VA 22132
(703) 338-5998

4th Virginia Cavalry
Steve Taylor
9760 Windy Hill Dr.
Nokesville, VA 22123
(703) 791-6056

27th Virginia Infantry
William Todd
5912 Minuteman Rd.
Springfield, VA 22152
(703) 569-8343

33rd Virginia Infantry
Thomas R. Rodd,
  Commander
9509 4th Pl.
Lorton, VA 22079
(703) 690-6842

27th Virginia Cavalry,
  Co. E
Robert Fleet
P.O. Box 230-1A
Blacksburg, VA 24060
(703) 951-7257

12th Virginia Infantry,
  Co. G
Michael L. Vice
P.O. Box 55-V, Rte. 1
Fredericksburg, VA 22401

19th Virginia Infantry,
  Albemarle Rifles, Co. B
Mike Allen
1208 Blueridge Rd.
Charlottesville, VA 22901
(804) 295-1442

1st Delaware
Bruce Stocking
9899 Rickover Court
Manassas Station, VA 22110

A reenactor encamped before battle.

**2nd South Carolina
   Palmetto Shay Shooters**
Digger Swink
P.O. Box 945
Lexington, VA 24450
(703) 463-4960

18th Mississippi, Co. C
Frank James, Jr.
3625 Amherst St.
Norfolk, VA 23513
(804) 855-3036

<u>WEST VIRGINIA</u>

**36th Virginia Infantry,
   Co. A**
Mike Sheets
212 Clem St.
Huntington, WV 25705
(304) 525-5065

<u>WISCONSIN</u>

*33rd Wisconsin Infantry,
   Co. E*
Kent Bolyard
1599 North Port
   Washington Rd.
Grafton, WI 53024
(414) 377-3857

1st U.S. Cavalry, Co. H
Craig Berken
1127 Melody Dr.
Green Bay, WI 54303-6360
(414) 499-0904

<u>CANADA</u>

21st Mississippi, Co. F
Ray Henriksbo
22 Charing Dr.
Hamilton, Ont. L8W 2H5

20th Maine Infantry, Co. B
James Hamilton
52 Pheasant Run Dr.
Nepean, Ont. K2J 2R4
(613) 825-4904

<u>MAIL-ORDER SUTLERS</u>

Border States Leatherworks
Rte. 4, 13 Appleblossom La.
Springdale, AR 72764
(501) 361-2642
*(cavalry saddles and
equipment)*

Fall Creek Sutlery
P.O. Box 530
Freedom, CA 95019
(408) 728-1888
*(general merchandise;
catalog $2)*

Grand Illusions Clothing
   Company
90 East Main St.
Newark, DE 19771
(302) 366-0300
(men's vintage clothing)

Military Replica Arms
P.O. Box 360006
Tampa, FL 33673-0006
(813) 933-0902
(swords; catalog $2)

Cavalry Depot
2313 Springdale Rd., S.W.
Atlanta, GA 30315
(404) 762-9605
(rain covers and ponchos)

New Columbia
P.O. Box 524
Charleston, IL 61920
*(uniforms and vintage
clothing; catalog $3.75)*

The Post Sutler
Rte. 1, Box 197
Waterman, IL 60556
(815) 824-2829
*(uniforms, equipment, and
period goods, catalog $2)*

Crescent City Sutler
17810 Highway 57N
Evansville, IN 47711
*(uniforms, equipment, and
tents; catalog $2)*

Fall Creek Sutlery
P.O. Box 92
Whitestown, IN 46075
(317) 769-5355
*(general merchandise;
catalog $2)*

Mary Ellen & Co.
29400 Rankert Rd.
North Liberty, IN 46554
(219) 656-3000
*(Victorian clothing;
catalog $3)*

Upper Mississippi Valley
  Mercantile Co.
1505 West 17th St.
Davenport, IA 52804
(319) 322-0896
*(general merchandise;
catalog $2)*

Period Impressions
1320 Dale Dr.
Lexington, KY 40502
*(patterns for vintage clothing;
catalog $1)*

Dirty Billy's Sutlery
102 East Hammaker St.
Thurmont, MD 21788
(301) 271-2613
*(men's and women's hats;
send SASE for free brochure)*

The Yankee Sutler
P.O. Box 4416
Center Line, MI 48015
*(uniforms and equipment;
catalog $1)*

Lepierre Sutler
P.O. Box 377
Dryden, MI 48428
(317) 796-3207
*(leather goods and
accoutrements)*

Past Patterns
P.O. Box 7587
Grand Rapids, MI 49510
(616) 245-9456
*(patterns for vintage clothing;
catalog $5)*

Kentwood Sutlery
P.O. Box 88201
Kentwood, MI 49518
(616) 281-2835
*(camp goods; send SASE for
free brochure)*

Quartermaster Shop
3115 Nokomis
Port Huron, MI 48060
(313) 987-4127
*(uniforms and period
clothing)*

C & D Jarnagin Co.
Box 217, Rte. 3
Corinth, MS 38834
(general merchandise)

John A. Zaharias, Sutler
P.O. Box 31152
St. Louis, MO 63131
(314) 966-5160
*(insignia, buttons, buckles,
etc.; catalog $2)*

Tentsmiths
P.O. Box 496
North Conway, NH 03860
(603) 447-2344
(tents; catalog $2)

F. Burgess & Co.
200 Pine Pl.
Red Bank, NJ 07701
*(saddlery and horse
equipment; catalog $3)*

Old Sutler John
P.O. Box 174,
Westview Station
Binghamton, NY 13905
*(general merchandise;
catalog and list $1)*

C & C Canteen Works
P.O. Box 455
Indian Trail, NC 28079
*(uniforms and camp
equipment; send SASE for
free list)*

A Stitch in Time
832 Glengary
Toledo, OH 43617
(419) 865-4359
*(custom-made period
clothing; catalog $2)*

The Regimental
  Quartermaster
P.O. Box 553
Hatboro, PA 19040
(weapons; list $1)

Dixie Gun Works, Inc.
Gunpowder La.
Union City, TN 38621
(901) 885-0700
(firearms; catalog $4)

Rapidan River Canteen Co.
P.O. Box 5, Rte. 2
Beaverdam, VA 23015
(804) 449-6413
(canteens)

Virginia House
  Leatherworks
2930 Roanoke Rd.
Christiansburg, VA 24073
(703) 382-8992
(cavalry equipment)

The Fredericksburg Ladies'
  Emporium
5413 Jamie Ct.
Fredericksburg, VA 22401
(703) 898-1331
*(custom-made period
clothing)*

The Cavalry Shop
P.O. Box 12122
Richmond, VA 23241
(leather goods; catalog $1)

Fair Oaks Sutler
Rte. 2, Box 1100
Spotsylvania, VA 22553
(703) 972-7744
*(kepis, bummers, and
chevrons; send SASE for free
catalog)*

The Winchester Sutler
P.O. Box 1000
Winchester, VA 22601
(703) 888-3595
*(general merchandise;
list $2)*

Panther Lodges
P.O. Box 32
Normantown, WV 25267
(304) 462-7718
(tents)

PHOTOGRAPH CREDITS

Cover photos (clockwise from top): Ulysses S. Grant—National Archives; Canon at Antietam—Department of the Interior, National Park Service (photo by W. E. Dutton); Poster, "A Great Rush to join the 36th Regiment, New York volunteers, commanded by Col. W. H. Brown."—National Archives; 1st Virginia Regiment—Valentine Museum; Poster, "Union Nomination for President, Abraham Lincoln of Illinois. For Vice-President, Andrew Johnson of Tennessee." —National Archives

Danville (VA) Museum, 94

Casemate Museum, Ft. Monroe, VA, 97

Stonewall Jackson House, Lexington, VA, 98

Virginia Military Institute, Lexington, VA, 100

Photos by Allan Richardson used through Courtesy of Winchester-Frederick County Chamber of Commerce & Visitor Center, VA, 104 (both)

Tennessee Department of Tourist Development, 125

Carter House, Franklin, TN, 126, 127

Andrew Johnson Homestead, Greeneville, TN, 129

Montgomery (AL) Area Chamber of Commerce, 133, 134

Savannah (GA) Area Visitor Bureau, 155

Atlanta (GA) Convention and Visitors Bureau, 161, 162

Bowie Lanford, 170, 173

Vicksburg (MS) Visitors Bureau, 174

Courtesy of Beauvoir, The Jefferson Davis Shrine, Biloxi, MS, 177

Surratt House, Clinton, MD, courtesy of the Maryland National Capital Park and Planning Commission, 209

Tourism Council of Frederick County, MD, 225

New York Convention and Visitors Bureau, 228

Author's collection, 89, 140, 142, 146, 168, 222, 244

Courtesy of National Park Service: ii–iii (title pages; Richard Frear), 50, 54, 64, 67, 68, 70, 77, 113, 116, 120, 151, 160, 167, 171 (Jack E. Boucher), 181, 205 (bottom), 206, 207 (bottom), 208, 215, 216, 233, 236, 243, 248–249, 287, 291, 292, 297

All photographs not otherwise credited are courtesy of National Archives.

INDEX